"Dr. Tony Merida's *Exalting Jesus in Acts* is like having a master preacher, expositor sitting alongside you in the study. This is a commentary by a preacher for preachers. It's exegetically accurate, pastorally keen, and homiletically powerful. In perusing these pages, one not only learns about Acts, but better yet, one is apprenticed into the way of preaching the Scriptures where sermons faithfully and accurately testify about Christ (John 5:39). I can't recommend Merida's offering enough."

Dr. Yancey C. Arrington, teaching pastor, Clear Creek Community Church, Houston, Texas

"Effective pastoral preaching is consistently distinguished by three overarching qualities: (1) accuracy (fidelity to the sacred text, including its Christocentric implications); (2) clarity (pulpit obscurity undermines biblical potency); and (3) simplicity (an extraordinarily difficult task to which very few expositors give necessary attention). *Exalting Jesus in Acts* by Dr. Tony Merida meets these criteria and is a wonderful gift to those called to strengthen the church by the means of preaching and teaching. Without getting entangled in exegetical minutia, Tony wonderfully summarizes, illustrates, and applies what is arguably the most exciting book in the New Testament."

Arturo G. Azurdia III, senior teaching pastor, Trinity Church of Portland and associate professor of pastoral and church ministry, Western Seminary, Portland, Oregon

"Tony Merida has written a learned and eminently practical commentary on Acts for preachers. Tony leads readers through the text like a wise tour guide and then gives preachers tips on how to make the text sing and sting! This is a commentary on Acts by a preacher and for the preacher. Few books on Acts will be as helpful as this one."

Dr. Michael F. Bird, PhD, University of Queensland, lecturer in theology at Ridley College, Melbourne, Australia

"Dr. Tony Merida's commentary on Acts is a perfect mix of exegetical insight and practical application for preachers and laypersons alike. It can, therefore, serve as a valuable source for sermon preparation as well as personal enrichment."

Joseph R. Dodson, PhD, Aberdeen, associate professor of biblical studies, Ouachita Baptist University

"As we seek a church-planting movement in North America and around the world, the church's inspired story of gospel impact in Christianity's early days provides an essential model. Tony Merida's commentary on the book of Acts gives us impressive scholarship and boldly spotlights the text in a way that will help mobilize churches to complete God's mission both locally and around the world. This will be an outstanding resource for pastors as they prepare Jesus-centered sermons on the book of Acts."

Kevin Ezell, president, North American Mission Board, SBC

"The Christ-Centered Exposition series is my preferred commentary for careful exegesis, relevant illustrations, and faithful application. *Exalting Jesus in Acts* by Tony Merida typifies this approach. Merida has done the heavy lifting by subdividing the book into sections that capture the author's intended meaning. It is especially helpful how he spells out the main theme at the beginning of each chapter and then highlights preaching points throughout. I am certain this will be your go-to commentary for the book of Acts in the years to come."

Robby Gallaty, senior pastor, Long Hollow Baptist Church, Hendersonville, Tennessee

"Much has been written on the book of Acts, but this commentary makes its own valuable contribution for the pastor. Tony Merida carefully handles the text of Acts without missing the excitement of Acts. He faithfully expounds the truth of Scripture without forgetting the people to whom we preach. And as he traces the mission of the gospel in Acts, he never loses sight of the glory of the Savior that the gospel announces."

C.J. Mahaney, Senior Pastor, Sovereign Grace Church of Louisville

"One of the challenges people face when studying the book of Acts is trying to figure out what is prescriptive and what is descriptive, especially when it comes to application. What Tony does in this homiletical commentary is provide a healthy understanding of the two while remaining faithful to the author's intent. The book of Acts tells incredible stories of how the gospel moved from region to region as it transformed the hearts and lives of people. Tony brilliantly takes you through each adventure and at the same time shows you the how the golden thread, which is Jesus, runs through the entire book. This is a commentary you want by your side as you navigate through the book of Acts."

One Mokgatle, senior pastor of Rooted Fellowship, Pretoria, South Africa

"Combining vivid, memorable examples and illustrations with careful exegesis, Christ-exalting explanations, and practical application, Tony Merida gives us a sure guide to the book of Acts. If readers will read this commentary reflectively, devoting time in the study questions that follow each chapter to godly introspection and missional resolve, then they will find their lives reflecting their Lord and Savior more fully, and they will find themselves able not only to edify themselves but to edify others."

Philip Moore, European director of Acts 29

"Tony Merida is one of the best preachers of our generation. He knows God's Word, and he knows how to bring God's Word with authority. Merida speaks not just to the mind or the heart or the will, but to the soul. This commentary on Acts will equip you to understand how Jesus worked through his people in the earliest days of our church. This book will also show us how to carry the gospel in an age that looks more and more like the culture of the book of Acts. That means we need the power of the book of Acts. Read and prepare."

Russell Moore, president, Ethics & Religious Liberty Commission

"Tony Merida has given us a highly readable and engaging commentary that scores high marks on careful exegesis and Christocentric exposition along with accessible illustrations and relevant applications. These of course are the aims of The Christ Centered Exposition Commentary. He has been careful to respect both the genre of the book and its goal to inspire the church to be a marching missional infantry based on the historic truth of her foundations. I highly recommend it to pastors and studious lay Christians."

Femi Osunnuyi, lead pastor, City Church, Lagos, Nigeria

"An experienced preacher and a lucid thinker, Merida has given us a pastor's dream commentary. It is scholarly without being unwieldy, clear without being reductionistic, and practical without ignoring contextual nuance. In fact, it is because Merida does such a good reading of the text on its own terms that it comes alive in his hands, with Christ as its radiant center. The inclusion of reflection and discussion questions at the end of each section makes this a robust resource for Bible studies as well. This will be a gift not only to preachers but to the congregations they serve."

Glenn Packiam, associate senior pastor, New Life Church, Colorado Springs, Colorado

"As always, Tony delivers fresh biblical insight with compelling conviction and exegetical clarity. This commentary on Acts is a superlative work for all. The consistent application of the text to the local church will be a tremendous resource for God's people."

Kevin Peck, lead pastor, The Austin Stone Community Church, Austin, Texas

"Tony Merida is one of my favorite pastor-scholars. All of his academic work is in service of the church, and his pastoral preaching is plain spoken but undergirded by faithful scholarship. Merida understands the Christian life as spiritual warfare and the book of Acts as a God-inspired field manual for our continuing Great Commission gospel mission. Merida recognizes God as the ultimate author of both history and Scripture. Thus, he gives concentrated attention to the unique contribution of Luke as the author of Acts but never loses sight of the place of Acts in the Christ-centered canonical whole of Scripture."

David E. Prince, pastor of preaching and vision, Ashland Avenue Baptist Church, Lexington, Kentucky

"Luke closes out his Gospel to Theophilus with the believers in the temple praising God. Now he picks up the story and explains what happens next. So does Tony Merida. In a style Bible teachers, pastors, and scholars will want to read, this commentary has the mind of a scholar and the heart of a pastor. I love his outlines, which, in the words of Arthur Golding's translation of The Sermons of J. Calvin in 1583, are 'grist for the preacher's mill.' Read it, study it; but more importantly, let it study you. Tony has mined for gold and found it. You will be richer after you've read it as well."

Dr. Ken Whitten, senior pastor, Idlewild Baptist Church, Lutz, Florida

CHRIST-CENTERED

Exposition

NT / COMMENTARY FEATURING

AUTHOR **Tony Merida**

SERIES EDITORS **David Platt, Daniel L. Akin, and Tony Merida**

CHRIST-CENTERED
Exposition

EXALTING JESUS IN

ACTS

REFERENCE

NASHVILLE, TENNESSEE

Christ-Centered Exposition Commentary: Exalting Jesus in Acts
© Copyright 2017 by Tony Merida

B&H Publishing Group
Nashville, Tennessee
All rights reserved.

ISBN: 978-1-4336-4709-3

Dewey Decimal Classification: 220.7
Subject Heading: BIBLE. O.T. ACTS—
COMMENTARIES\JESUS CHRIST

Printed in the United States of America

2 3 4 5 6 7 8 9 10 • 22 21 20 19 18

SERIES DEDICATION

Dedicated to Adrian Rogers and John Piper. They have taught us to love the gospel of Jesus Christ, to preach the Bible as the inerrant Word of God, to pastor the church for which our Savior died, and to have a passion to see all nations gladly worship the Lamb.

—David Platt, Tony Merida, and Danny Akin
March 2013

CONTENTS

ACKNOWLEDGMENTS

This commentary is evidence of God's grace. I wouldn't have completed this book apart from the Spirit's strength and the help and encouragement of many people.

My "dear companion," Kimberly, thank you for being my wife! I can't imagine life without you. May the Lord grant us much grace as we seek to magnify him together.

My children—James, Joshua, Angela, Victoria, and Jana—thank you for making my life so adventurous and exciting! I pray you will grow up to make much of Jesus, like the believers in the book of Acts.

To the elders at Imago Dei Church, thank you for your encouragement. I treasure our friendships and partnership in sharing the gospel. May the Lord use us to shepherd the flock faithfully.

Members at Imago Dei, you're a joy to pastor! What an incredible blessing it was to work through the book of Acts with you! May the Lord help us take the gospel to the ends of the earth.

Cody Cunningham, thank you for your hard work in reading through this document and providing editorial improvements. May the Lord bless you as you continue your studies.

Catherine Ridley, thank you for your help with the bibliography. May the Lord make his face to shine upon you.

Ben Palka, thank you for your hard work on parts of this commentary. You're a wonderful brother, a dear friend, and a fine expositor. May the Lord use you mightily in the years ahead.

Joey Dodson, thank you for your encouragement. I thank God that you took your sabbatical in my neighborhood while I was expounding Acts! Your insights and support helped me and ministered to me. May the Lord continue to bless you as you minister the Word in your home, in the academy, and in the church.

To all those cited in this commentary, I also say thank you for your labor in the Word. I couldn't have written this book without standing on the shoulders of so many faithful expositors.

And finally, risen King, Jesus, I thank you. Apart from you, we have no life. Apart from you, we can do nothing. Please use this commentary to build up your blood-bought church and to advance your never-ending kingdom.

SERIES INTRODUCTION

Augustine said, "Where Scripture speaks, God speaks." The editors of the Christ-Centered Exposition Commentary series believe that where God speaks, the pastor must speak. God speaks through His written Word. We must speak from that Word. We believe the Bible is God breathed, authoritative, inerrant, sufficient, understandable, necessary, and timeless. We also affirm that the Bible is a Christ-centered book; that is, it contains a unified story of redemptive history of which Jesus is the hero. Because of this Christ-centered trajectory that runs from Genesis 1 through Revelation 22, we believe the Bible has a corresponding global-missions thrust. From beginning to end, we see God's mission as one of making worshipers of Christ from every tribe and tongue worked out through this redemptive drama in Scripture. To that end we must preach the Word.

In addition to these distinct convictions, the Christ-Centered Exposition Commentary series has some distinguishing characteristics. First, this series seeks to display exegetical accuracy. What the Bible says is what we want to say. While not every volume in the series will be a verse-by-verse commentary, we nevertheless desire to handle the text carefully and explain it rightly. Those who teach and preach bear the heavy responsibility of saying what God has said in His Word and declaring what God has done in Christ. We desire to handle God's Word faithfully, knowing that we must give an account for how we have fulfilled this holy calling (Jas 3:1).

Second, the Christ-Centered Exposition Commentary series has pastors in view. While we hope others will read this series, such as parents, teachers, small-group leaders, and student ministers, we desire to provide a commentary busy pastors will use for weekly preparation of biblically faithful and gospel-saturated sermons. This series is not academic in nature. Our aim is to present a readable and pastoral style of commentary. We believe this aim will serve the church of the Lord Jesus Christ.

Third, we want the Christ-Centered Exposition Commentary series to be known for the inclusion of helpful illustrations and theologically driven applications. Many commentaries offer no help in illustrations, and few offer any kind of help in application. Often those that do offer illustrative material and application unfortunately give little serious attention to the text. While giving ourselves primarily to explanation, we also hope to serve readers by providing inspiring and illuminating illustrations coupled with timely and timeless application.

Finally, as the name suggests, the editors seek to exalt Jesus from every book of the Bible. In saying this, we are not commending wild allegory or fanciful typology. We certainly believe we must be constrained to the meaning intended by the divine Author himself, the Holy Spirit of God. However, we also believe the Bible has a messianic focus, and our hope is that the individual authors will exalt Christ from particular texts. Luke 24:25-27,44-47 and John 5:39,46 inform both our hermeneutics and our homiletics. Not every author will do this the same way or have the same degree of Christ-centered emphasis. That is fine with us. We believe faithful exposition that is Christ centered is not monolithic. We do believe, however, that we must read the whole Bible as Christian Scripture. Therefore, our aim is both to honor the historical particularity of each biblical passage and to highlight its intrinsic connection to the Redeemer.

The editors are indebted to the contributors of each volume. The reader will detect a unique style from each writer, and we celebrate these unique gifts and traits. While distinctive in their approaches, the authors share a common characteristic in that they are pastoral theologians. They love the church, and they regularly preach and teach God's Word to God's people. Further, many of these contributors are younger voices. We think these new, fresh voices can serve the church well, especially among a rising generation that has the task of proclaiming the Word of Christ and the Christ of the Word to the lost world.

We hope and pray this series will serve the body of Christ well in these ways until our Savior returns in glory. If it does, we will have succeeded in our assignment.

David Platt
Daniel L. Akin
Tony Merida
Series Editors
February 2013

Acts

Spirit-Empowered Witnesses

ACTS 1:1-11

Main Idea: Luke begins his second volume by highlighting the ongoing ministry of the ascended Christ that continues through his Spirit-empowered witnesses.

I. **How Should We Study Acts?**
   A. Not like cold scholars
   B. Not like casual admirers
   C. Like committed soldiers
II. **Luke's Message Continues (1:1-2).**
III. **Jesus's Ministry Continues (1:1-11).**
IV. **The Church's Witness Continues (1:8).**
   A. The people who witness: all believers
   B. The path of a witness: suffering
   C. The power of a witness: the Holy Spirit
   D. The people in need of a witness: the nations
   E. The passion of a witness: Jesus

Multiple times I've been asked, "How old is your church?" Since our congregation is a church plant, people often raise this question, and I have to do the math in my head to answer them. To simplify matters, and to teach a bit of church history, I have started to respond by saying, "We are about two thousand years old!" You see, the account of the early church recorded in the book of Acts is *our* history. The people mentioned in that book are our brothers and sisters.

Of course, the people of God did not originate in the first century. God has always had a people for himself—a people to whom he displays his glory, and a people through whom he displays his glory (to paraphrase my friend, Steve Timmis). Nevertheless, the book of Acts marks a pivotal turning point in redemptive history. Acts describes the history of the mission of the early church, and because we are part of the church's history and mission, the book is of great importance to us.

My children are currently studying United States history, so we are going over the facts and details of the American Revolution, the early presidents, and our founding documents. Learning about these topics

3

is important because we are Americans. American history is our history. But as vital as learning about the founding of our nation is, it is even more important that my children understand church history. It is our spiritual history, a family history.

This history recorded in the book of Acts covers a relatively short period of time. Commentator Michael Green says,

> Three crucial decades in world history. That is all it took. In the years between AD 33 and 64 a new movement was born. In those thirty years it got sufficient growth and credibility to become the largest religion the world has ever seen and to change the lives of hundreds of millions of people. It has spread into every corner of the globe and has more than two billion putative adherents. It has had an indelible impact on civilization, on culture, on education, on medicine, on freedom and of course on the lives of countless people worldwide. And the seedbed for all this, the time when it took decisive root, was in these three decades. It all began with a dozen men and a handful of women: and then the Spirit came. (*Thirty Years That Changed the World,* 7)

So much happened in thirty short years! It makes me ask, What may God do through a modern local group of believers throughout the same period of time?

How Should We Study Acts?

Because Acts involves history, I should clarify what a proper approach to studying history entails. Generally speaking, three types of people study the past: scholars, admirers, and soldiers.

Not like Cold Scholars

While some scholars are no doubt also committed soldiers, anyone who wants to study Acts needs to reject the posture of what I'll call a *cold scholar.* Our purpose in launching into the book of Acts is not merely to analyze dates, places, and people as if we were cramming for a test. Instead, our goal is to allow the message of this book to transform our hearts and lead us to a mission. We must not study the Bible as people scrutinizing a book for insights into the distant past. Rather, we should approach it as people who are desperate to see the God about whom we read move mightily in the present.

Not like Casual Admirers

Some who study history are more hobbyists than scholars; they have a casual interest in historical events that may lead them to read a piece on the Civil War, World War II, or the New York Yankees purely for pleasure. Such people may visit museums and even collect antiques and memorabilia related to their interests, but casual admirers rarely dive deeply into the contents of history. Seldom do they allow the events they read about to change them in the present. We, however, must move beyond merely admiring things about the history of the early church. We must not read the Bible lightly or scan it as if gathering insights to add to a mental museum. We should not be casual admirers but committed soldiers.

Like Committed Soldiers

Good soldiers are known to study history, and they do so to become better soldiers. Good soldiers know there is much to be done. And they see themselves—and we must view ourselves—as continuing a mission. Acts is not merely the history of the early church; it's the history of *the mission* of the early church. And we are to continue that mission. So let us dive into the contents of the book that we may better serve our King.

We need to keep a few principles in mind. First, we should read Acts in light of the entire Bible, with the teachings of both the Old and New Testaments in mind. A failure to allow the whole Bible to help us rightly interpret the book could lead to some serious problems. Second, we should read Acts in light of Luke's Gospel in particular because Dr. Luke wrote both books. Third, we must read Acts in light of its genre. It is a historical book, which means that while in it Luke describes the events of the early church, he does not always commend its practices to us. For instance, I don't think we should read of Paul's "healing handkerchiefs" and assume we need to start a handkerchief ministry! Rather, we must allow the whole of the Bible to help us make interpretations and applications for the modern world. We've got to be sensible soldiers, honoring the dual authorship of this book: it was penned by Luke and inspired by the Holy Spirit.

Since Acts is the second volume by Luke, the book opens as a story already in progress. There is also an abrupt ending to Acts, leaving us with the correct impression that even today the church is living out the mission. As we look at the opening verses of this book, we'll see that three acts are continuing: the message, the ministry, and the witness of

Christ's church. We will look back on the opening section throughout our studies in Acts.

Luke's Message Continues
ACTS 1:1-2

Luke begins his second volume by dedicating it to Theophilus. Luke addresses the same recipient in the prologue to his Gospel. That Theophilus is called "most honorable" (Luke 1:3) implies that he was a Roman official (cf. Acts 24:2; 26:25). And based on Luke's intention of providing more "certainty" to Theophilus (Luke 1:4), he seems to have been a Christian seeker or perhaps a young believer. It is also possible that he gave financial assistance to Luke, allowing his author-friend the means to research and report on the astonishing work God was doing through followers of Jesus Christ.

What do we know about Luke? We know he was a doctor (Col 4:14). As such, he would have been educated and presumably wealthy. He made trips with Paul and was loyal to him, even while the apostle was in prison (Acts 28; 2 Tim 4:11). I can imagine that his medical skills came in handy; Paul regularly needed a doctor after all those beatings he took.

Luke was also a prolific writer. He recorded for us the stories of the prodigal son and the good Samaritan. And his work shows a remarkable depth of precise historical research. Luke traveled and carefully interviewed those with key roles in Christ's life. (In his quest to collect details, he was more like Indiana Jones than a history professor!) He investigated and reported on a vast amount of information. In fact, Luke-Acts is comprised of more material than all of Paul's letters combined, and since Luke was a companion of Paul, it's clear he was involved with writing the majority of the New Testament.

Yet Luke records virtually nothing about his own life. This is a sign of humility. He does not boast about his relationship with Paul, nor does he go into detail about his own story. Instead, in Luke-Acts we read about the man's passion for the life-changing gospel, his sensitivity to the disadvantaged, his heart for prayer, and his concern for the Gentiles. Each of these characteristics reflects the church in Antioch (11:19-30), Luke's hometown according to an ancient second-century document (*Anti-Maricon Prologue to Luke*).

All of this history reminds us that Christianity is not built on man's speculation or on someone's wild imaginings but on historical revelation.

Jesus Christ really did live. He died. He rose bodily. He appeared to hundreds of witnesses. He taught for forty days before ascending. Luke records details about the real life and ministry of Jesus as well as insights into the beginnings of the early church. This is supremely important. While the world wouldn't need a historical Buddha to have Buddhism, it must have a historical Christ to have genuine Christianity. And we do! Further, if Jesus is dead, then Christianity is dead. But he's alive! Historical facts like these serve as wonderful faith builders for Christians and as important apologetic arguments that are useful as we commend the faith to present-day Theophiluses.

Luke says in his Gospel that he wrote about all that Jesus "began to do and teach." In Acts, Luke writes about the same thing: the ministry of Jesus—which continued after his ascension and is still in progress today. The title of the book could be "The Acts of the Lord Jesus through the Apostles and the Church by the Power of the Spirit." After all, the church is continuing the ministry of Jesus. So Luke not only has a *historical* purpose behind his writing efforts but also *ministry* purposes.

Additionally, Luke's second volume appears to have a *political* purpose. He seems concerned about the Roman attitude toward Christianity. Luke, then, plays the peacemaker. He illustrates that Christianity is militarily harmless by showing that some of the Roman officials, such as Cornelius, became Christians; that Christians were legally innocent (the Romans could find no fault in Jesus or in the apostles); and that Christianity was lawful (it was not a new religion but a fulfillment of Judaism).

Finally, Luke clearly has an *evangelistic* emphasis. He not only writes about the good news and Christ's converting power, but he also includes some twenty sermons in Acts, which occupy around one-fourth of the book! Luke surely wanted to win his readers to Christ, and he also underscores the centrality of proclamation in world evangelization. The Christian faith, our faith, is a heraldic faith. Luke shows what led to the explosive growth of Christianity: gospel proclamation.

Jesus's Ministry Continues
ACTS 1:1-11

Luke refers to Jesus in each of the opening eleven verses. This is a fitting opening, for Luke is preparing us to see how Jesus's ministry continues through the church.

Teaching and Doing

Luke reminds us that Jesus's ministry involves both *words* and *deeds*. He refers to all that Jesus began to both "do" and "teach" (1:1). During his earthly lifetime Jesus taught the disciples, and then after his resurrection the risen Christ taught the disciples about the kingdom of God for forty days. What a magnificent forty-day Bible conference that must have been!

In verses 7-8 Jesus responds to a question about whether he will restore Israel. He essentially tells the disciples, "*That's* none of your business" (v. 7), and then proceeds to tell them, "*This* is your business," as he issues to them the mission of bearing witness to him throughout the world (v. 8).

Jesus was all about teaching and doing. Jesus's deeds illustrated his words, and his words explained his deeds. He left the church with the same ministry, intending that we let others see our good deeds that glorify the Father (Matt 5:16) and helping others understand the good news that leads to eternal life.

The words and works of Jesus go together. In the Gospels we see Jesus performing various merciful and miraculous deeds. We also see him teaching with astonishing authority. Similarly, in the book of Acts, we see the church caring for physical needs (e.g., 3:1-10) while also relentlessly preaching the good news (e.g., 3:20) with the Spirit's help. In Romans Paul reflected on his own ministry passion, the Christ-empowered ministry of word and deed among the nations (Rom 15:18-19).

Many things do not belong together. I recently drove by one of those strange places that has two fast-food chains in the same building; they have side-by-side kitchens but divergent menus. The scents wafting from the partnering kitchens combined to form one terrible stink. These two restaurants should never have been joined. The ministry of deeds and words, on the other hand, go together. And when done by the power of the Spirit for the good of others and the glory of the King, they produce a pleasing aroma of worship to God.

The ministry of Jesus is continuing in the book of Acts. But are we faithfully taking part in this mission?

Response to Christ's Resurrection

The ascension of Jesus is in some ways like Elijah passing off the mantle to Elisha. The disciples had been with the greater Elijah, and now Jesus was giving them the privilege and responsibility of doing his work and proclaiming his Word after his home going.

Importantly, this mighty ascension of Jesus was preceded by a transitional period of forty days. We know from the Gospels and from 1 Corinthians 15 that he appeared to more than five hundred people after he rose from the dead. They saw him, touched him, and learned from him; they *knew* he had truly been resurrected. The ministry of Jesus continues, in fact, because Jesus really is alive!

Christ's ascension also included an exaltation. In verses 2 and 11 we read that Jesus was "taken up." Verse 9 says, "A cloud took him out of their sight" (v. 9). This cloud reminds us of Daniel's vision of the Son of Man (Dan 7), of Jesus's transfiguration (Matt 17), and of the exodus cloud (Exod 13). The whole sight is one of magnificent glory. This glorious exaltation demonstrated Jesus's promotion from earth to heaven, and it prefigured the manner of his return—visible, glorious, and climactic.

Some of the early church fathers viewed Psalm 24 as being ultimately fulfilled in the ascension of the totally righteous Lord Jesus and his entrance into heaven. The psalmist says,

Lift up your heads, you gates!
Rise up, ancient doors!
Then the King of glory will come in.
Who is this King of glory?
The LORD, strong and mighty,
the LORD, mighty in battle.
Lift up your heads, you gates!
Rise up, ancient doors!
Then the King of glory will come in.
Who is he, this King of glory?
The LORD of Armies,
he is the King of glory. (Ps 24:7-10)

If this was the heavenly reaction to Jesus's ascension, how did the disciples react to it on earth? With *bewilderment*. Like children watching a floating balloon drifting skyward, the disciples were enamored with the sight. But soon just thinking about the glorious scene filled them with *worship* and *joy* (Luke 24:52), and they returned to Jerusalem in *obedience* to Jesus's words. Our response to the ascended King should mirror theirs: we should joyfully worship and obey him.

The risen King's ministry continues because the King is not dead. It continues because we have his Spirit and his Word. It continues because the kingdom of God is here, and it is still advancing through his Spirit-empowered witnesses.

Acts outlines how Jesus advances his Word among the nations, and the plan is summarized in 1:8. In chapters 1–7 the Lord's Word spreads throughout Jerusalem. In 8–12 the Lord's Word spreads in Judea and Samaria. In 13–20 the Lord's Word spreads to the ends of the earth (in Asia and Greece). And in chapters 21–28 the Lord's Word spreads throughout Rome.

The Church's Witness Continues
ACTS 1:8

In verse 7 the disciples demonstrated a particular interest in and misunderstanding about the restoration of Israel. Jesus directs them to the global nature of his kingdom and to their part in the mission as he calls them to be his witnesses. The disciples were too limited in their thinking. So Jesus rocks their world as he tells them that the plan is for them to cross not just geographical barriers but cultural barriers as well. Jesus blows up any triumphalistic ideas they have as he calls them his witnesses—or more literally, his martyrs. The way of the kingdom is one of suffering before glory.

These believers were to proclaim the person and work of the risen Christ (Luke 24:44-49) as taught by Jesus and foretold in the Old Testament. They were to proclaim how Christ accomplished the ancient prophecy of crushing the head of the serpent, Satan, providing a way for sinners to be reconciled with the Father. Importantly, we as modern disciples of Jesus participate in enjoying this message of life with the first disciples. But they were witnesses in another sense: they actually saw Jesus's death, resurrection, and ascension (Acts 2:32; 3:15; 10:39; 22:15). While we do not enjoy this privilege, we are the recipients of eyewitness testimony that comes to us in the form of the writings of the disciples. Now, like them, we have the privilege of bearing witness about the good news of the Messiah to everyone. Let us consider five aspects of a witness.

The People Who Witness: All Believers

One of the great gifts of Pentecost is that all believers can now speak for God (2:14-21). In a sense all believers are prophets. No believer is a mere fan but a player! The apostles certainly led the church, but the gospel advanced largely through the words and deeds of unordained and uneducated people—informal missionaries. The church today, in fact, desperately needs to recover this practice. The only difference in a believer sitting in his or her American home and a foreign missionary on the field is *location,* not *identity.* Every Christian is a missionary. And so each of us should ask, Where do I serve? To whom do I minister?

The Path of a Witness: Suffering

To follow the Lamb involves suffering. In several places in the Gospels, Jesus told the disciples they would suffer (e.g., Luke 21:10-19; John 15:18-27). In the book of Acts, we find that they indeed did suffer. Crossing cultural barriers and standing up in the face of opposition requires sacrifice. First we see that there was an escalation of persecution in Jerusalem; it moved from threats to floggings to martyrdom. A theme of suffering continues through the rest of the book, and it continues into our day as the evil one rages against the church (Rev 12). Even this, however, is part of God's ordained means of advancing the gospel—dedicated believers share his truth wherever they go, in spite of what they encounter. The gospel never triumphs apart from some measure of sacrifice. Someone has to sacrifice (and sometimes die) so that others may live.

The Power of a Witness: The Holy Spirit

Fortunately, we are not on our own in the mission Jesus assigned us, for Luke reminds us once again of the Spirit's power (cf. Luke 24:49). We must, in fact, be clothed with power to be faithful witnesses. Having received essential teaching, the disciples would eventually be given the essential power required in witnesses of Jesus. The ordinary people of God, equipped with the Word of God, empowered by the Spirit of God, dedicated to the Son of God, can accomplish the mission of God. Sharing the right message is only half the matter. We must also be personally reliant on the Spirit of God.

We see two marks of the Spirit's work in the disciples: *boldness* and *the magnification of Jesus.* References to Spirit-empowered boldness appear through the book (e.g., 4:29; 28:31). This is how Peter could stand at Pentecost and preach so courageously after cowering in the presence of a little girl just weeks earlier. Further, we are reminded that the Spirit purposes to glorify Christ (John 16:14). Peter has a spotlight ministry that always focuses attention on Jesus. This is a great reminder that when people are living a Spirit-empowered life, their thoughts and words will be centered on Christ, not self (see Acts 4:20).

The Peoples in Need of a Witness: The Nations

Christians have no tribal deity. We have a Savior who loves and died for the nations! That means that we must relinquish any prejudices that keep us from sharing him faithfully. We must repent of any ethnocentrism or unconcern for unreached peoples. Jesus sent ordinary people *to the nations*, just as he sends us.

The Passion of a Witness: Jesus

A zeal for the kingdom comes only when we have a passion for the King. As these disciples gazed into heaven in astonishment of Jesus's glory, and as they later received Jesus's promise of the Spirit's power, they were enamored with Jesus. And we should have a similar attitude toward him. Because to phrase things negatively, little love for the King produces little zeal for the King's mission.

May the Spirit deepen our love for this global Savior as we seek to understand and apply the message of Acts. Let us pray for Spirit-empowered boldness, for a love for all the diverse people groups around the world, and ultimately for hearts enthralled with the King of kings.

Reflect and Discuss

1. What are some ways people react to the idea of studying history? How should we study Acts?
2. What do you find most striking about the life of Luke?
3. Of what significance is Theophilus?
4. What were some of Luke's purposes for writing Acts?
5. Why do you think so many sermons/speeches appear in Acts?
6. How does Jesus's ministry continue in the church today?
7. How does the ascension of Jesus encourage believers?
8. Who should bear witness to Jesus? Why should they?
9. What does Acts 1:8 suggest about ethnic diversity and the value of people groups around the world?
10. What about Acts 1:8 encourages you most? Why?

How to Discern the Will of God

ACTS 1:12-26

Main Idea: The first major event after the ascension of Jesus, when the apostles and disciples convened to choose a replacement for Judas, teaches much about discerning God's will for our lives.

I. Choosing Judas's Replacement (1:12-26)
II. Make Decisions in View of God's Plan of Redemption.
    A. What are the immediate ramifications for the gospel?
    B. What are the eternal ramifications for the gospel?
III. Distinguish between God's Revealed Will and God's Concealed Will.
IV. Start with God's Revealed Will.
    A. Trust the Bible as your authority.
    B. Let the Bible interpret your life.
    C. Do what the Bible says.
V. Look for God's Concealed Will through the Lens of God's Revealed Will.
    A. Gather all the information.
    B. Seek God in prayer.
    C. As you trust in God's sovereignty, make a decision and go with it.

D o you have any important decisions to make? If so, do you want to know what God's will is regarding those decisions? Chances are you will answer both questions with an emphatic *yes!* You probably know other people who are faced with decisions as well. Some will consider adopting children. Some will consider changing jobs this year or relocating to another city, state, or country. Some will decide where to go to college or graduate school. Some will consider making major purchases like a home or a car or a business. Some face the prospect of getting married. Others will need to determine whether God wants them to pull up roots and go to a mission field overseas. And the list of possible decisions people face continues.[1]

---

[1] Jim Shaddix originally delivered this exposition at our local church.

Most of us make discovering God's will more complicated than it really is! The Father wants you to know his will about important decisions in your life, so he provides guidance in his Word. After Jesus ascended to heaven, his followers needed to know who was supposed to fill the apostolic office vacated by Judas, who committed suicide after he betrayed Jesus. The way they approached that decision is significant for two reasons: it had huge ramifications for the future of Christ's kingdom, and it provided a helpful model for the way his followers approach weighty decisions. Those two things must go together—finding God's will in decision making and doing so in view of advancing Christ's kingdom.

Choosing Judas's Replacement
ACTS 1:12-26

Luke has purposed in Luke and Acts to record details about the real life and ministry of Jesus as well as the beginnings of the early church. While Luke shows that Christianity is founded on the historical resurrection, he also demonstrates that those who proclaimed the resurrection were trustworthy. After his crucifixion and death, the Lord Jesus "presented himself alive to [his disciples] by many convincing proofs, appearing to them over a period of forty days and speaking about the kingdom of God" (v. 3). Jesus commanded them "not to leave Jerusalem, but to wait for the Father's promise" (v. 4). The disciples and apostles, along with Jesus's mother and half brothers, obediently returned to Jerusalem to wait and pray (vv. 12-14). The lives of these individuals had been changed by an encounter with Jesus, and they were committed to him and his mission.

Luke lists the eleven apostles by name (v. 13), helping readers understand Peter's imminent speech (vv. 16-22). Jesus previously appointed twelve apostles, corresponding to the twelve sons of Jacob, the tribal leaders of Israel. For Peter, the apostolic number of twelve had to be restored, as the true Israel needed to be complete. Israel was suddenly entering a new era in redemptive history. The eleven apostles thus went into the upper room and were in consensus with Mary and the brothers of Jesus as they "united in prayer" (v. 14). Luke will develop the importance of prayer throughout Acts.

Luke highlights a moment in which Peter stood up and spoke from the Psalms about God's providence over Judas's betrayal and God's command for Judas to be replaced (vv. 15-16). After the resurrection of Jesus, Peter realized that all of the Scriptures testify about Jesus. Here is another example of how the apostles were clearly Christ centered in their interpretation of the Scriptures. Citing Psalms 69:25 and 109:8, Peter applied the psalmist's judgment on a wicked man as being repeated in his own day—having happened even more literally regarding the fate of Judas than in the case of David's adversaries. As the treasonous men in Psalms 69 and 109 rejected the friendship and blessing of King David, even more so had Judas rejected the friendship and blessing of King Jesus.

Peter defines qualifications for the replacement apostle. The individual who would take Judas's place as the twelfth must be an eyewitness of Jesus's life and resurrection (vv. 21-22). Christianity is founded on the historical resurrection, and those who first proclaimed the resurrection had to be trustworthy and informed.

Two men, Joseph and Matthias, were put forward as meeting the criteria set forth by Peter. The apostles and disciples turned to the Lord in prayer to seek his will on the decision (vv. 24-25). Lots were cast and "the lot fell to Matthias," so he was numbered with the eleven apostles (v. 26).

Make Decisions in View of God's Plan of Redemption

The primary reason this story is in the Bible is not to help us learn how to find God's will. It informs us about how God sovereignly worked to advance his mission. However, that must reveal to us *something* about finding his will. And I think the obvious lesson is that we must make our decisions in view of God's unfolding plan of redemption. If the reason we're still on the planet is to advance his mission of redeeming people, then it just makes sense that every decision we face must be approached in view of that purpose. In filling Judas's spot, these early Christians were answering some questions that are important for us to ask any time we're trying to discern God's will.

What Are the Immediate Ramifications for the Gospel?

The word *apostle* means "one who is sent." Jesus had instituted the formal office in order to appoint some men who could be sent out to proclaim his gospel with supernatural power. Their role was crucial for the immediate advancement of the gospel after the Lord left the earth. The apostles were eyewitnesses who had observed Jesus's life and could confirm his resurrection (cf. 1:21-22). And they were firsthand learners—or disciples—who could accurately pass on his teaching. His words would thus become the solid foundation on which his church would be built (cf. Eph 2:19-22).

By filling Judas's office, the church was acknowledging and valuing the need for such eyewitness testimony to the gospel in the days following Jesus's departure. The formal apostolic office in view here obviously was a unique, irreplaceable role limited to these twelve men. They would have no formal successors since no further eyewitnesses could arise after they died. But these early Christians were rightly concerned about the immediate advancement of the gospel, and a similar concern should underlie every decision we make. We should approach every decision by weighing how each choice will either enhance or hinder gospel advancement.

What Are the Eternal Ramifications for the Gospel?

It was imperative to fill Judas's office also for a broader kingdom purpose. Jesus had told the twelve apostles they would have a unique role in the coming kingdom of God. They would judge the twelve tribes of Israel (Matt 19:28; Luke 22:28-30). By filling Judas's office, the church was acknowledging and valuing the special role of the apostles. These men had important work to do.

Every decision we make matters. Our choices can have eternal impact.

Distinguish between God's Revealed Will and God's Concealed Will
ACTS 1:12-26

Part of God's will is written in black-and-white. The believers about whom we read in chapter 1 knew part of God's will because they knew the Scriptures. They knew there was an apostolic office, and they knew they were to fill the office vacated by Judas because God said so.

The primary place we can find God's will is in the pages of the Bible. In his Word he has revealed everything necessary for our redemption. That means we don't have to wonder whether we should be making disciples, praying, living holy lives, bearing fruit, loving people who aren't lovable, being faithful in our marriages, or caring for orphans. Those things and more are part of his revealed will, the Bible. We can be confident that pursuing those things is always the right course of action.

Not all the specific outworkings of God's will for specific individuals, however, are recorded in the Bible. While the early Christians knew they were supposed to fill Judas's office, they didn't know the name of the guy who was supposed to step into the role. That detail was concealed, and they were responsible for uncovering it through prayer and wise action. God wasn't hiding the man's identity from them, and they knew he had chosen someone for the office (see v. 24), but they needed to work through the process of seeking God's will to find out who it was. And their experiences teach us an important principle.

We know marriage is sanctioned by God to reflect the gospel, but we have to discern who that specific spouse should be. We know we should work hard and not be lazy, but we don't always know which job God wants us to take or which degree we should pursue. We're responsible for discoving that stuff. We must do the work of making sound choices.

Start with God's Revealed Will

Many Christians spend inordinate amounts of time and energy trying to find out God's concealed will while ignoring so much of his revealed will. Doesn't it make sense that he would want us to give first priority and attention to the stuff he has revealed in the pages of Scripture? Why should he tell us where we should go to college or whom we're supposed to marry if we're not at all interested in making disciples or living holy lives? The believers in Acts 1:12-26 demonstrated a confidence in and allegiance to the Scriptures that ultimately made finding even his concealed will relatively simple. And it will work that way for us as well. Consider these principles.

Trust the Bible as Your Authority

The church submitted their lives, circumstances, and direction to God's Word. Peter gathers the small band of 120 believers and begins by telling them, "It was necessary that the Scripture be fulfilled" (v. 16). The Scriptures are totally *trustworthy*. The church operated on the resolve that the Scriptures would absolutely prove true.

Then Peter references Scripture as that which "the Holy Spirit through the mouth of David foretold about Judas" (v. 16). This statement highlights the *inspiration* of Scripture. God spoke it through a human author (cf. 2 Tim 3:16-17; 2 Pet 1:20-21).

You, like the first believers, can and should trust the Scriptures for directing your life! The Bible is objective while our senses of discernment and judgment can be subjective. That's why the Scriptures must be our guide.

Let the Bible Interpret Your Life

Luke adds a parenthesis for the reader concerning the fate of Judas (vv. 18-19)—the horrific nature of Judas's death. Matthew reports the type of death (Matt 27:5): suicide. Combining the data leads to the conclusion that he hanged himself and the rope broke, allowing his body to fall onto rocks that disemboweled him. The disciples were likely confused and shocked about the fate of Judas in the unfolding plan of God, so Peter cites Psalms 69:25 and 109:8 to help them make sense of it. These psalms have in view wicked and treasonous men who are enemies of God's king. Peter took the psalmist's judgment and applied it to Judas, who was wicked and treasonous toward God's ultimate King. Longman and Garland comment,

> We need not insist that the early Christians believed that the primary reference of these two psalms was to Judas, as if no one could have understood them prior to the betrayal. What they seem to be saying, however, is that just as the psalmist's portrayals of "The Servant of the Lord and the Righteous Sufferer" can on the basis of the Semitic concept of corporate solidarity be applied to God's Messiah, Jesus, the Servant and Righteous Sufferer, so the retribution spoken of as coming upon false companions and wicked men in general is especially applicable to Judas, who above all other men was false. So Peter quotes Psalm 69:25 in a Christian context and applies it to Judas's defection. In itself, of course, this verse gives no justification for replacing Judas—in fact, it even opposes it. Therefore Peter goes on to cite Psalm 109:8 on the Jewish exegetical principle of analogous subject in order to defend the legitimacy of replacing a member of the apostolic band. (*Luke–Acts*, 728)

For Peter and the other disciples, God's Word, responsibly applied, provided the proper interpretation and perspective on confusing and shocking events.

Like the disciples, we too at times will struggle to comprehend the plan and sovereignty of God in our world and in our lives. We will ponder the prosperity of the wicked and the suffering of the righteous. And we will wrestle with the setbacks of life and with affirming the sovereignty of God. Yet, like Peter, we should look to the Scriptures to make sense of our world and our lives. In the Scriptures we will continually rediscover perspective, truth, instruction, and the beauty of our Savior.

Do What the Bible Says

Jesus previously had appointed twelve apostles, corresponding to the leaders of the tribes of Israel. For Peter, the apostolic number of twelve had to be restored because the true Israel needed to be complete. Israel was now entering a new era in redemptive history. Longman and Garland are helpful again here:

> The twelvefold witness was required if early Jewish Christianity was to represent itself to the Jewish nation as the culmination of Israel's hope and the true people of Israel's Messiah. The "remnant theology" of Late Judaism made it mandatory that any group that presented itself as "the righteous remnant" of the nation, and had the responsibility of calling the nation to repentance and permeating it for God's glory, must represent itself as the true Israel, not only in its proclamation, but also in its symbolism. (*Luke–Acts*, 728)

God wants us to give first priority and attention to what he has revealed. He had made clear through his words that there were to be twelve apostles (Matt 19:28; Luke 22:30; Rev 21:10,12,14), and the apostles made choices and took action with that directive in mind. God has clarified many things for us in his Word. In the Bible he has instructed us to live holy lives, to participate in and contribute to the life of the church, and to love and serve our spouses and our families. These are clear instructions, and we should do what the Bible says.

Look for God's Concealed Will through the Lens of God's Revealed Will

God's concealed will should be discerned on the basis of his revealed will. God's words and our place in his unfolding mission should shape our decisions regarding what local churches we join, what homes we purchase, whom we marry, and the kinds of risks we take. Sometimes we may even discover that the question we are seeking to answer isn't even the right question! So consider these steps in discerning God's concealed will.

Gather All the Information

Peter supplied qualifications from God's Word for the replacement apostle (Acts 1:21-22). The eleven apostles then did their homework on potential candidates and put forward only two who met these qualifications: Joseph and Matthias (v. 23). Likewise, in discerning God's will on specifics, we should be doing our homework, gathering information in order to narrow our options.

Seek God in Prayer

The apostles prayed to the Lord regarding his choice of either Joseph or Matthias. Likewise, after we've done our homework, we should pray to the Lord for wisdom about which choice is best. While God has given us minds and the power of reason, his ways and methods are inscrutable. In other words, we should be reminded that the Lord doesn't see things the way we always see them. People judge by outward appearance, but the Lord looks at the heart (1 Sam 16:7). Seek him in prayer.

As You Trust in God's Sovereignty, Make a Decision, and Go with It

After determining qualifications and praying, "they cast lots for them, and the lot fell to Matthias" (v. 26). The practice of casting lots was common within Israel. For instance, God instructed the Israelites to divide land based on casting lots (Num 26:55; 33:54; 34:13; 36:2). This might seem odd at first, but the book of Proverbs says, "The lot is cast into the lap, but its every decision is from the LORD" (Prov 16:33). On this occasion the lot fell to Matthias, and the disciples understood this to be Matthias's appointment by Christ himself. This, however, is the last scriptural case of casting lots to make a decision. Shortly after the appointment of Matthias, the Holy Spirit came to indwell God's people. He is the Counselor who helps us make wise decisions.

When we as Christians understand our role in the unfolding drama of redemption, when we have a grasp on God's revealed will, when we've gathered the necessary information in order to narrow our options, when have prayed to the Lord, we should then simply trust God, make a decision, and go with it.

The Father knows if we truly desire to please him with a decision, and if things don't work out, that doesn't change his love for us! The cross has already demonstrated his loyal love (Rom 5:8). And he has given us the Holy Spirit to assure his sons and daughters of his love (Rom 8:9-17). Rest in this good news when faced with a stressful decision. Sometimes my kids try to please me with some honorable deed. In so doing they occasionally make an unwise decision, but that doesn't cancel out my love for them. I'm pleased by their desire to honor me.

If you're a perfectionist, you will struggle with making decisions. But don't let anxiety rule you. Learn to trust in the Father's love and learn to trust the Father's sovereignty. Do your homework, pray, seek guidance in Christian community, let the mission of God guide your decisions, and then act. Do it for the glory of your Father, through Jesus Christ, by the power of the Holy Spirit.

Reflect and Discuss

1. Why is the resurrection of Jesus Christ essential to our faith? How does this passage demonstrate the vital importance of the resurrection?
2. Why did the apostolic number of twelve need to be restored? What relevance does this have to our lives?
3. Why was it important that the candidate for apostle be an individual who had accompanied the other apostles "during the whole time the Lord Jesus went in and out among us—beginning from the baptism of John until the day he was taken up from us" (1:21-22)?
4. What action or saying in this upper room meeting sticks out in your mind the most, and why?
5. What does Judas's story teach about the pitfalls of spiritual leadership? How should we pray for and support our leaders?
6. What are some big life decisions you need to make? How will this passage help you make those decisions?
7. How does Peter use the Old Testament in this chapter? What might this tell us about reading and teaching the Old Testament?
8. Explain the difference between "God's revealed will" and "God's concealed will." How should God's revealed will help us discern his concealed will?
9. How does the Spirit help us to know God's will? Is it wrong to cast lots (or flip a coin) to determine God's will? Explain your answer.
10. Why is it important to make decisions as a member of the Christian community rather than in isolation?

The Promised Holy Spirit

ACTS 2:1-41

Main Idea: Luke describes the events that occurred on the day of Pentecost and includes Peter's clarifying, Christ-exalting, and converting sermon that followed.

I. **The Event of Pentecost (2:1-13)**
II. **The Explanation of Pentecost (2:14-36)**
   A. Pentecost means prophecy has been fulfilled (2:16).
   B. Pentecost means the last days have dawned (2:17a).
   C. Pentecost means everyone can know God intimately and should make him known faithfully (2:17b-21).
   D. Pentecost means Christ has ascended to the throne (2:22-36).
III. **The Evangelistic Harvest at Pentecost (2:37-41)**

When I was a kid, we used to play a mean little game called Psych. (It was really just a way to be a jerk to your friends.) The goal was to make up a story, and then when a friend got really excited about what was being promised, the storyteller would dash all of his hope in that idea by saying, "Psych!" That word meant, "No, not really. I'm just lying to you in a playful way." So, for example, I might set up a pal by saying, "Hey, this soda is really good. You can have the rest of it." But then, when he thanks me and reaches for the can, I grin wickedly and announce, "Psych!"

Of course this misdirection or lying hurts so badly because no one likes to be disappointed. No one likes to have someone overpromise yet underdeliver. But life is filled with such disappointments. Think about that time you made dinner reservations only to arrive at the restaurant to hear the greeter say, "I'm sorry, sir, but we don't have your name on the list." Or maybe your parent made a promise to you years ago and then failed to deliver. Or perhaps you had a girlfriend or boyfriend, or even a fiancé, whom you thought would be your spouse, but it didn't happen. Any such instance raises hopes only to dash expectations. Life sometimes yells, "Psych!"

But here's the good news: God never plays Psych! God always keeps his promises. He has *never* overpromised and underdelivered. His Word always proves true.

In Acts 2, on the day of Pentecost, a massive promise was fulfilled. God promised in the Old Testament to pour out his Spirit on all flesh (e.g., Joel 2:28-32). During his ministry Jesus taught about the coming Holy Spirit (e.g., John 14–16) and made the same promise in Acts 1:4-5,8. Later, Paul referred to "the promised Holy Spirit," a reminder that he was long anticipated (Gal 3:14; Eph 1:13). Acts 2 is a wonderful reminder of God's promise-keeping nature.

The Holy Spirit was present even in the Old Testament days, but his work took a wonderful turn under the new covenant. Paul tells us that after Jesus's ascension Christ "gave gifts to people" (Eph 4:8). Jesus has blessed his church by putting his Spirit in us—that is, by giving us gifts.

This means we currently live in the age of the Spirit, and we shouldn't see these events in Acts as something that came and went. Rather, what happened on the day of Pentecost has abiding significance. The Spirit came and *stayed.* The day of Pentecost was like a mayor installing a great water system in a city. From that point forward, every time a new home is built, households can connect to the water system. In other words, the day of Pentecost was the installation of God's new source of blessing and power for the benefit of his people. Now every person who turns to Christ in repentance and faith has access to this great source of power. The installation happens only one time, at the point of salvation, but the significance is ongoing.

This passage can be studied in three parts: (1) the events of Pentecost (2:1-13), the explanation of Pentecost (2:14-21), and (3) the evangelistic harvest at Pentecost (2:22-41).

The Events of Pentecost
ACTS 2:1-13

The day of Pentecost marked one of the three major feasts on Israel's annual calendar. The name comes from its occurrence on the fiftieth (*pentekoste*) day after Passover. Jesus positioned the disciples to wait in Jerusalem for this day (1:4-5). Thus, we see an important connection between the cross and the Spirit in this event. We should not separate the Spirit from the atoning work of the Passover Lamb, Jesus Christ.

Pentecost was a feast of harvest; in fact, that's another name for it. At the end of Peter's sermon, three thousand people converted to faith in Jesus; thus, this particular Pentecost marks a harvest of souls. As a result, the regenerate group of believers gathers and ministers in a beautiful way as the local church (vv. 42-47).

Throughout this Pentecost event, God gives the church some miraculous signs (vv. 2-4). **Sounds** like the wind were present (cf. John 3:6-8). Both the Hebrew and Greek words for Spirit can also mean "wind" or "breath," and the power of the Spirit is likened to breathing life into corpses (Ezek 37:9-10). Just as the Spirit consecrated the temple in the Old Testament, so here the Spirit is consecrating a new temple, God's new-covenant people. And he is doing so with the force of "a violent rushing wind."

The signs here of **sight** were also magnificent. The presence of fire in this passage should not surprise us. God's presence, in fact, is often associated with fire: at the burning bush, in the wilderness wandering, and in the tabernacle/temple (e.g., Exod 3:1-6; 13:17-22,25-27; 1 Kgs 6–8). Indeed, God is a "consuming fire" (Heb 12:29). Fire resting on each believer, therefore, may be a sign that believers are new temples. The Lord is residing in each believer like he resided in the sanctuary (cf. 1 Cor 6:19). That the fires look like tongues is significant, as the next sign indicates and as Peter later explains (Acts 2:14-21).

So, what about this gift of **speech**? Each believer was "filled with the Holy Spirit," and he is the source of their speaking. The quoted phrase has a range of meanings, leading to the debates associated with this passage. Usually in Luke-Acts this phrase is associated with some form of speaking. In this case it involves speaking in different languages. A person filled with the Spirit may do a variety of activities, but all of them will magnify Jesus.

While some argue that Acts 2 contains an example of speaking in a heavenly tongue (cf. 1 Cor 14), these empowered individuals were speaking in *known dialects*. In Jerusalem that day there were people from "every nation under heaven" (v. 5). And each of these travelers clearly heard the disciples speaking "in his own language" (v. 6). As a result, these pilgrims were "astounded and amazed" for many reasons, including the fact that those speaking were "Galileans" (v. 7)! The Galilean disciples had not been trained in foreign languages. They weren't known for having sophisticated educations. Imagine Uncle Si from *Duck Dynasty* standing up in front of a group of ambassadors from around the world—including China—and offering them the gospel in perfect Mandarin. That would leave people astonished! Yet that is just the sort of thing happening at Pentecost!

The crowd is puzzled (v. 8) by this unusual event. Indeed, the diversity of languages heard is amazing. People from the north, south, east, and west (vv. 9-11) were hearing the disciples telling about "the magnificent acts of God" in their own languages. Out of options for natural explanations for this strange phenomenon, some accused the gathered believers of being drunk.

So, what was God teaching the church with this marvelous sign? The obvious point is that *the gospel is for the nations.* Thus, the church must spread the gospel to every people, tribe, and to those of every *language,* for that is God's redemptive plan (Rev 5:9-10). God's ultimate community—the citizenry of heaven—consists of a transnational, transtribal, transracial, and translinguistic people.

We read of God's passion for the nations in the Old Testament, but the Israelites struggled to grasp the Gentile mission. Even in Acts 1, the Jews who had placed faith in Christ were still thinking about Jerusalem. Later, in 10:45, the people were amazed "because the gift of the Holy Spirit had been poured out *even on the Gentiles*" (emphasis added). Pentecost stands as a mighty demonstration of God's pursuit of worshipers from every tongue.

A missionary friend was trying to translate the Bible into the Kurdish tongue. His unbelieving Kurdish friend, who was helping him translate the book of Acts, marveled that the nations were present on the day in which God formed this new community, the church. The Kurdish man dropped his pencil after reading about the "Medes" and asked, "Do you mean that my people were there?" And then, because the Kurds trace their history back to the Medes, this man reconsidered his idea of Christianity. For him Acts 2 was proof that the gospel is for the world. What happened that day serves as hard evidence that we don't worship a tribal deity. Instead, we as followers of Jesus offer salvation to all the nations since our Savior died to win a people from all nations. Pentecost is a little foretaste of the global "multitude" (v. 6; Rev 7:9) that will one day unite in praise to the Lamb.

Some have called Pentecost a reversal of what happened at Babel. In Genesis 11, at the tower of Babel, God introduced diverse human languages that resulted in the dispersion of humanity; at Pentecost he united everyone in Jerusalem by allowing the gospel to cross language barriers. Pentecost, however, is not a total reversal of the Babel event. God didn't give everyone the same language at Pentecost. Instead, unique languages were preserved as everyone heard the same message. This is important. It tells us that God is glorified in Christ-exalting unity amid blessed diversity. Missionaries around the world today try to make the gospel known to people in their native tongues; each dialect has value. That's why Bible translators have been doing the laborious work of translating Bibles into diverse languages for centuries.

This topic brings up a good question: What language will we speak in heaven? When most Americans imagine heaven, they imagine everyone there speaking modern English! And Christians in France no doubt imagine heaven populated by people speaking perfect French! Some, however, assume the citizens of heaven will speak a common heavenly language—perhaps Hebrew. But I side with D. A. Carson, who envisions those present there as speaking *all* the languages—even those languages that have died out. After all, we will have all eternity to learn them (Carson, "Pentecost"). Likely Pentecost gives us a foretaste of heaven's culture of God-given unity amid beautiful diversity.

Luke's account of Pentecost is spotlighting the coming kingdom of God, and *the church is an outpost of the kingdom.* The church, much like an embassy providing a flavor of its represented country while existing in a foreign land, should give the world a picture of what the kingdom of God is like. And as we do, people are given the chance to marvel at the church's ministries of mercy, its message of hope, and the diversity within local pews. The people God gathered on the day of Pentecost showed the world what the King of the kingdom was like, and they showed the world what it meant to be a citizen of heaven while living on earth (Phil 3:20). Soon in the book of Acts we will read of other newly established kingdom outposts in places like Corinth, Ephesus, and Philippi, too.

May we also aspire to show the world what the coming kingdom is like as we submit to King Jesus and continue the mission of the church as presented in Acts and empowered by the promised Holy Spirit.

The Explanation of Pentecost
ACTS 2:14-36

In verse 12 Peter responds to the question, "What does this mean?" His answer is the first of many sermons in the book of Acts. We shouldn't imagine, however, that what follows is everything Peter said since Luke goes on to write, "With *many other words* he testified" (v. 40; emphasis added). We probably have the shorthand account of his reply, but what we possess is nevertheless glorious and sufficient.

Peter begins by offering a word of *clarification*. He assures the audience that the disciples haven't been drinking; after all, it was only 9:00 a.m. (vv. 14-15). He then says that, according to the prophet Joel, these Pentecostal signs teach four truths.

Pentecost Means Prophecy Has Been Fulfilled (2:16)

Peter tells the audience they are witnessing what Joel prophesied would happen. Importantly, the listening crowd would have been reading the prophet Joel during Pentecost. With this in mind Peter essentially says, "*This* (what you are witnessing) is *that* (what Joel predicted)." Joel foretold this mighty downpour of the Spirit on the Israelites and how the blessings would flow to people from every nation and tribe.

Pentecost Means the Last Days Have Dawned (2:17a)

Instead of quoting Joel exactly, Peter begins by saying, "In the last days." Joel 2:28 opens by saying, "After this . . ." So now that Christ has ascended and Pentecost has come, we are awaiting the final act of the redemptive drama—the return of the King of the nations. We are living in the last days (cf. 1 Cor 10:11; 2 Tim 3:1).

Pentecost Means Everyone Can Know God Intimately and Should Make Him Known Faithfully (2:17b-21)

Joel foretold the day in which every believer, from every tribe and tongue, would be a *prophet*. Peter quotes Joel as saying that all of God's servants will prophesy. While God appoints some servants to the office of a pastor, *every believer* is called to teach in some capacity.

In the book of Numbers, Moses was exhausted from leading, so elders were appointed, filled with the Spirit, and they prophesied. When some were disturbed by this change and complained to Moses, he responded, "If only all the LORD's people were prophets and the LORD would place his Spirit on them" (Num 11:29)! Amazingly, the very thing for which Moses longed and about which Joel prophesied has arrived with the pouring out of the Spirit. God has equipped his people for the work they are to do.

In pointing this out, Peter is not saying every believer has the gift of prophecy (1 Cor 12:10). Rather, he means that every believer shares the general privilege and responsibility of Old Testament prophets. Such people were able *to know God intimately* and were commissioned *to speak God's Word faithfully*. They came to know him mainly through "dreams and visions." Now we know him through Jesus Christ, and we can grow in our knowledge through the revealed Word of God. But still like the prophets, we must declare God's Word to the world. It's our mission.

Luke recounts the story of the Word of God increasing and multiplying across geographical and cultural barriers by the power of the

Holy Spirit (2:42; 6:7; 11:24; 12:24; 13:49; 16:5; 19:20; 28:30-31). In many cases it was proclaimed by Christians who were nonprofessionals. Acts 8:4 says that "those who were scattered [the nonapostles, v. 1] went on their way preaching the word."

Later Paul says, "Let the word of Christ dwell richly among you, in all wisdom *teaching and admonishing one another*" (Col 3:16; emphasis added). To the Romans he said, "You also are full of goodness, filled with all knowledge, and *able to instruct one another*" (Rom 15:14; emphasis added). Peter urged believers to be ready to teach unbelievers: "[Be] ready at any time to give a defense to anyone who asks you for a reason for the hope that is in you" (1 Pet 3:15; cf. Col 4:5). Pentecost means that *every* believer can know God truly and must make him known faithfully.

We have to love that everyone is included in God's worldwide, unstoppable mission—young and old, rich and poor get to participate. No one is stuck being an observer. If you are a believer in Christ, you are a participant in the King's mission. He has empowered you by his Spirit to tell of his glory for the world's benefit.

In verses 19-21 we see both humanity's universal need to know Christ and the inclusive offer he makes so that everyone can know him. Peter mentions some future cataclysmic events destined to unfold before the day of the Lord comes. While it seems to me that he is referring to Christ's return, some view his words in this passage as a reference to the cross and resurrection; others see in them a link to the events that would take place around AD 70 when the Roman general Titus destroyed Jerusalem. Whatever the prophet envisioned, his words show us the holiness of the Lord and remind us of the need for everyone to call on the Lord and be saved (v. 21). This Lord is Jesus (v. 36), whom Peter now exalts in his Christ-centered sermon.

Pentecost Means Christ Has Ascended to the Throne (2:22-36)

Moving away from Joel, Peter now describes the life and ministry of Jesus, and in verse 33 he ties Pentecost to Jesus's ascension. Notice the chronology. Jesus ascends, and then the Father gives Jesus the promised Holy Spirit to pour out on his people. This reminds us of John 14:16: "I will ask the Father, and he will give you another Counselor to be with you forever." The risen King poured out gifts on his people as a sign that he has truly ascended to the throne, is reigning over all, and is ruling in the midst of his enemies.

Before Peter gets to this point, he articulates some glorious truths about Jesus. As in the other recorded sermons in Acts, Peter centers on the focal message of the Bible: the death and resurrection of the King. *The Man (2:22).* Peter begins with the humanity of Christ. He says, "You guys saw him. You know what I'm talking about." Signs and wonders validated the claims of Jesus. These miracles weren't violations of the laws of nature as much as they were restorations of the laws of nature. At his first coming Jesus showed everyone what his second coming and his kingdom would be like: there will be no leprosy, no illness at all, no demon possession, no fear of storms, no death. King Jesus will reverse the curse—all things will be restored.

The person of Christ depicted in the Gospels is gloriously attractive. Don't underestimate the power of encouraging a nonbelieving friend to read through the Gospels. A clear understanding of Christ's love and power can draw a person to him.

The Plan (2:23). Next Peter describes the death of Christ from both a human and a divine perspective. (This wasn't the most politically correct sermon!) Peter emphasizes both the sovereignty of God and the responsibility of man. The death of Christ was part of God's foreordained plan. This reality is emphasized even more strongly in 4:24-28. So, why did Peter open with this theological truth? The Jewish people couldn't fathom a crucified Messiah. Messiahs *win!* Jesus, however, was crucified in shame and agony. How could he possibly be the Messiah? Peter shows his audience that Jesus didn't die as a pathetic victim. He laid down his life in fulfillment of the sovereign plan of God, who purposed to sum all things up in Christ (Eph 1:10).

At the same time, the Bible doesn't teach fatalism. Every man and woman is accountable for his or her actions. Peter reminds his audience that they were responsible for Christ's crucifixion. And so are we. Fallen people scheme to dethrone God. They plot to kill their Maker. When Peter reminds this group of their guilt, many are "pierced to the heart" (v. 37).

The Resurrection (2:24-32). Peter tells the audience about the amazing thing *God did: he raised Jesus up (v. 24).* Jesus was raised because death couldn't hold him!

Then Peter tells them *what Scripture predicted: the Holy One would not see decay (vv. 25-31).* Christ was the promised one of Psalm 16. You can visit David's tomb and find his remains, but Christ's tomb is empty. Who, then, was David speaking about in Psalm 16? We must remember that David is a prototype. The things that happened to David became models anticipating another King to come. As you read through Psalms, you'll find that some things are applicable to David; often other things are inadequately expounded or unfulfilled in David. This transcendent language in the Psalms continues to build until you have an entire messianic expectation. The mystery leads people to wonder, *Just who is this King?* Peter says, "Compare the tombs of David and Christ. Then you tell me!"

His resurrection exposition is then followed with *what the disciples saw: the risen Christ (v. 32).* Much of the Christian gospel turns on eyewitness accounts. Richard Bauckham has written *Jesus and the Eyewitnesses,* which explains that the Gospel writers used eyewitnesses as their sources of choice for maintaining historical integrity. Multiple witnesses appear in the Gospels for the resurrection accounts. Seeing Jesus *transformed* the disciples.

The Messiah (2:33-36). Peter ties the events of Pentecost to Jesus's ascension in verse 33, and then he quotes Psalm 110. The early church loved to quote Psalm 110. Like the other Davidic typology, this messianic psalm also awaited fulfillment. David foresaw the ascended Lord in some way. He looked forward to one greater than himself. Jesus also quoted this psalm in Luke 20:41-44, silencing his opponents as he pointed to himself as the One who would sit on the throne forever.

Peter concludes his sermon with the confession of the early church (v. 36). Peter didn't try to domesticate Jesus. He didn't soft-pedal the gospel. He says that Jesus is King; therefore, people should submit to him. He preached in the spirit of Psalm 2: "Pay homage to the Son or he will be angry and you will perish in your rebellion, for his anger may ignite at any moment. All those who take refuge in him are happy" (Ps 2:12).

We need to recover awe of the ascended Lord of glory, as Revelation 6:15-17 describes Jesus. His love has been spurned; his purity has been trampled; his truth has been buried. But one day this merciful Jesus will rule with a rod of iron, and the most powerful of men will hide in fear of him.

Perhaps no one has illustrated the meekness and majesty of Jesus better in recent history than C. S. Lewis. In *The Lion, the Witch, and the Wardrobe,* Lucy is posing questions to Mr. and Mrs. Beaver about Aslan, a character representative of Christ:

> "Is—is he a man?" asked Lucy.
> "Aslan a man!" said Mr. Beaver sternly. "Certainly not. I tell you he is the King of the wood and the son of the great

Emperor-beyond-the-Sea. Don't you know who is the King of Beasts? Aslan is a lion—the Lion, the great Lion."

"Ooh!" said Susan, "I'd thought he was a man. Is he— quite safe? I shall feel rather nervous about meeting a lion."

"That you will, dearie, and no mistake," said Mrs. Beaver; "if there's anyone who can appear before Aslan without their knees knocking, they're either braver than most or else just silly."

"Then he isn't safe?" said Lucy.

"Safe?" said Mr. Beaver; "don't you hear what Mrs. Beaver tells you? Who said anything about safe? 'Course he isn't safe. But he's good. He's the King, I tell you" (Lewis, *The Lion, The Witch, and the Wardrobe*, 75–76).

Yes. Christ is good. But he isn't safe. Jesus really is the true King. So stand in awe of him. Don't be silly. Confess him as Lord. That's Peter's message. He says, "Know with certainty!" Be assured of this. Jesus is the ascended King.

The Evangelistic Harvest at Pentecost
ACTS 2:37-41

Finally, we read of the amazing results of Peter's preaching (v. 37). The audience felt convicted because they were guilty. They were pierced because they realized they were objects of God's wrath. They longed to be free from condemnation. Notice that they don't wait for Peter to offer an invitation. They ask him how they should respond to his message.

Once again, Jesus's words about the work of the Spirit are on display. In John 16:8-11 Jesus said,

> *When he comes, he will convict the world about sin, righteousness, and judgment: About sin, because they do not believe in me; about righteousness, because I am going to the Father and you will no longer see me; and about judgment, because the ruler of this world has been judged.*

Peter's sermon shows us how the Spirit of God takes the gospel and works in people's hearts. As you exalt Jesus through your witness, pray for the Spirit to bring conviction and repentance to your hearers.

In verses 38-41 we see God's glorious work of conversion. Peter describes the human and divine sides of conversion. Humanly speaking, one must repent and believe in order to be saved. This faith is expressed through baptism, a public declaration of one's faith in Christ. All who turn from sin and trust in Jesus will be indwelt with the Holy Spirit.

Some have suggested that this passage teaches "baptismal regeneration," that is, that one is saved by baptism. While Peter is emphasizing baptism, we must not ignore the context. Baptism follows belief in the Word. And when one reads the rest of the conversion texts in Acts, it is clear that baptismal regeneration is not being taught. Salvation through repentance and faith is in view (see 2:21; 3:19; 10:43; 13:38-39; 15:9; 16:31; 20:20-21).

The divine side of conversion involves God's sovereign activity. Peter says that the Lord is calling people to himself (2:39). This same idea is conveyed in various places in Acts, like in 13:48: "All who had been appointed to eternal life believed." The Lord's active work in the hearts of rebellious people gives us hope in evangelism. Keep lifting up Christ and pray for the Spirit to convict people and lead them to repentance.

Don't miss that on one day, at one event, the Lord brought three thousand to himself! Peter urged the crowd to turn from their personal sins as well as from the sins of their generation, and many of them did. This great harvest on the day of Pentecost established a new community, which is described in Acts 2:42-47.

What a promise-keeping God we have! Peter says, "The promise is for you and for your children, and for all who are far off." God doesn't play Psych! He really does promise and deliver salvation to repentant rebels. So let us offer the promise of eternal life, the promise of forgiveness, and the promise of the indwelling Spirit to guilty people. May the Lord bless our faithfulness to proclaim his truth, giving us a harvest of souls as we lift up the person and work of the crucified, risen, and exalted Lord Jesus.

In our walk through Acts, we have already seen how the Spirit works to accomplish his primary purpose: exalting Jesus (John 16:14). We have also found much to encourage us. We have the necessary equipment to be faithful witnesses because we have the Word and the Spirit. Thus, we can speak with confidence, knowing that the Spirit convicts people of sin and leads them to repentance. We see how the Spirit is transforming individuals to create a living church.

The church is a new community of new creations in Christ, who live on mission as citizens of his kingdom. We can now turn our attention to this community of faith and see the importance of belonging to a biblical community.

Reflect and Discuss

1. In what ways have people disappointed you? How are the promises of God encouraging to you?
2. What signs at Pentecost most resonate with you? Explain why.
3. In what specific ways are you seeking to make disciples of all nations?
4. What is unique about the day of Pentecost?
5. What are the ongoing effects of the day of Pentecost?
6. Have you ever thought of yourself as a prophet? Why or why not? What impact should the notion that you are meant to share God's Word have on your Christian experience?
7. Describe your reaction to Peter's sermon (2:14-36).
8. How does Peter use the Old Testament in this chapter? What might this tell us about how we should read the Old Testament?
9. Why should this story of multiple conversions encourage us?
10. If you're a Christian, pause and thank God for his forgiveness of sins and the presence of the Holy Spirit in your life. If you aren't a Christian, explain what's holding you back. Consider talking to a pastor or a mature Christian about what it means to follow Jesus.

A Healthy Body of Christ

ACTS 2:42-47

Main Idea: In this summary of the early church, Dr. Luke gives several significant descriptions of a healthy body of Christ.

I. **Descriptions of a Healthy Body**
   A. Devotion to the Word (2:42a,43)
   B. Devotion to one another (2:42b,44)
   C. Devotion to the breaking of bread (2:42c,46)
   D. Devotion to prayer (2:42d)
   E. Radical generosity, especially within the church (2:45)
   F. Constant interaction with one another (2:46a)
   G. Gathering in both large and small groups (2:46b)
   H. A spirit of awe, gladness, and praise to God (2:43a,46-47a)
   I. Displaying an attractive faith (2:47b)
   J. Daily evangelism (2:47c)
II. **Checking Our Vital Signs**
   A. Vital sign 1: Biblical nourishment
   B. Vital sign 2: Loving fellowship
   C. Vital sign 3: Vibrant worship
   D. Vital sign 4: Word and deed outreach

As my friend Jim put on his robe in preparation to walk across the stage to receive his doctorate, his young son asked him where they were going. Jim said, "Your daddy is graduating today. I'm going to become a doctor."

His curious son asked, "Well, where's your little black bag?" So Jim tried to explain to him the difference between a doctor of ministry and a doctor who helps the physically ill. But after receiving such a clarifying explanation, the son replied, "So, where's your little black bag?"

Even without a bag, Jim was and still is a wonderful doctor—a spiritual doctor for the body of Christ.

Thinking about this story reminds me that there are many similarities between those who care for physical bodies and those who care for Christ's spiritual body. Don't miss this. Luke, the author of Acts, is actually a double doctor! He really was a physician who took care of fractures and colds and illnesses, but as a Christian on mission he also understood and strengthened the figurative body of Christ. In this passage Dr. Luke tells us what characterized the early Spirit-filled congregation—what made it healthy, dynamic, and alive. He basically records the diet and exercise regimen of a healthy body of Christ.

Before jumping into verse 42, let's pause to remember how this church was born. Peter preached a Christ-exalting sermon, and as a result of the Spirit and the Word at work, three thousand people were saved. (That's a pretty good day!) God builds his church by his Word. Just as God spoke creation into existence in Genesis, he speaks this new creation—this new community—into existence through his mighty Word.

The church is God's plan. That plan is bigger than the random conversion of a few individuals. Christianity is personal but not individualistic. It's corporate. Jesus is saving *a people* for himself (Titus 2:14). This fact is made plain here in Acts 2; it has also been emphasized in Acts 1, as the people gathered together (1:14; 2:1). The communal nature of the church is reiterated throughout the New Testament and is illustrated by the fact that the epistles, or letters, were written to churches or in reference to churches.

Based on the importance of the church, it is imperative that we understand what the church is supposed to be and do.

Descriptions of a Healthy Body of Christ

Devotion to the Word (2:42a,43)

Luke tells us that the church was devoted to certain activities. At the top of the list is the study of the apostles' teaching, perhaps noted for emphasis since the Word of God informs everything else. Here, then, is the diet of a healthy body of Christ. Based on Peter's sermon in Acts 2 and the rest of the messages and descriptions in the book of Acts, the apostles taught everyone about the Messiah from the Scriptures.

In this Spirit-filled congregation the people didn't abandon study of the Word because the Spirit was at work. If you're walking in the fullness of the Spirit, you will be drawn to the Bible. All true spiritual awakenings involve healthy teaching from it (e.g., Neh 8). Consider the apostle Paul. Was anyone more Spirit filled or Spirit led than this man? Yet we repeatedly find him teaching the gospel message from the Word of God (18:11; 19:10; 20:20,31); it is central to his life. He repeatedly urges

Titus and Timothy to teach sound doctrine to churches because there's no substitute for it (e.g., 1 Tim 4:16; Titus 2:1). Healthy congregations, Paul knows, consume a healthy diet of sound doctrine. They feast on the Word of God, which tells the message of the Savior.

This truth is a great reminder that pastors must lay down any desire to preach opinions and must avoid the temptation to entertain or to play with people's emotions. Each must instead see and embrace his role as God's spokesperson. Each must seek to please an audience of One. Pastors must believe Scripture is sufficient to build up and bless the church. Churches, in turn, must submit to God's Word when it is faithfully taught. The early church here in Acts is demonstrating such humility before the Word.

In verse 43 Luke mentions the apostles' awe-inspiring signs and wonders. These signs weren't merely power displays; they validated the apostles' teaching. While the Lord may choose at any moment to perform a miracle, we must recognize the apostles' uniqueness. And we should realize that the miracles about which we read were serving the message.

Devotion to One Another (2:42b,44)

Having noted the diet of the healthy church, we now move to its exercise regimen. Its first exercise is fellowship. The first-century Christ followers shared a common way of life. They were spiritually united as "believers," and this spiritual union worked itself out into practical acts of love and support.

Such fellowship with one another is tied to the Christian's fellowship with the Father (cf. 1 John 1:3). Out of our common fellowship with the Father through Jesus, we enjoy fellowship with our spiritual brothers and sisters. If people are out of fellowship with Christ, then they will be out of fellowship with the church. And if people are out of fellowship with Jesus's people, that is an indicator they may be out of fellowship with Jesus. That's how strong the Christ-church union is.

The "one another" passages in the New Testament underscore the significance of and the early spirit of real devotion to the community of faith. Each of these teachings should be considered and prayed both for the spiritual growth of our own hearts and for those of our congregations:

- *I give you a new command: Love one another. Just as I have loved you, you are also to love one another.* (John 13:34)

- *We who are many are one body in Christ and individually members of one another.* (Rom 12:5)
- *Love one another deeply as brothers and sisters.* (Rom 12:10)
- *Outdo one another in showing honor.* (Rom 12:10)
- *Instruct one another.* (Rom 15:14)
- *The members would have the same concern for each other.* (1 Cor 12:25)
- *Serve one another through love.* (Gal 5:13)
- *Carry one another's burdens.* (Gal 6:2)
- *With patience, bearing with one another in love.* (Eph 4:2)
- *Be kind and compassionate to one another.* (Eph 4:32)
- *Submitting to one another in the fear of Christ.* (Eph 5:21)
- *In humility consider others as more important than yourselves.* (Phil 2:3)
- *Do not lie to one another.* (Col 3:9)
- *Encourage one another.* (1 Thess 4:18)
- *Always pursue what is good for one another.* (1 Thess 5:15)
- *Let us watch out for one another to provoke love and good works.* (Heb 10:24)
- *Don't criticize one another, brothers and sisters.* (Jas 4:11)
- *Do not complain about one another.* (Jas 5:9)
- *Confess your sins to one another and pray for one another, so that you may be healed.* (Jas 5:16)
- *Be hospitable to one another without complaining.* (1 Pet 4:9)
- *All of you clothe yourselves with humility toward one another.* (1 Pet 5:5)
- *Dear friends, let us love one another, because love is from God, and everyone who loves has been born of God and knows God.* (1 John 4:7)
- *No one has ever seen God. If we love one another, God remains in us.* (1 John 4:12)

While it's a challenge to cultivate and maintain edifying fellowship, it's also an amazing blessing that we within the church enjoy. Consider the privilege you have. You get to spend time with brothers and sisters in the faith. Do you realize what a source of encouragement and blessing they can be to you and you can be to them? In his classic book, *Life Together*, Dietrich Bonhoeffer says, "It is grace, nothing but grace, that we are allowed to live in community with Christian brothers and sisters" (20). May we never forget that.

Devotion to the Breaking of Bread (2:42c,46)

"The breaking of bread" is probably a reference to the Lord's Supper. The sacramental memorial was likely enjoyed in the context of a meal. Here in Jerusalem the church daily reflected on the torn body and poured-out blood of Christ. After these earliest days the church grew, became more stable, and spread out geographically. Then it seems "the church began to take the Lord's Supper in conjunction with the meal they shared together in the evening *on the Lord's Day*" (Hamilton, "How Often Should We Take the Lord's Supper?"; emphasis added). The pattern of weekly communion is demonstrated in 20:7.

It's not my purpose to dive into all of the arguments about the Lord's Table. I simply want to point out the Christ-centered nature of this community. The apostles preached to the ear about Jesus, and the Table preached to the eye about Christ. Healthy church bodies are filled with affections for the crucified and risen Savior. Let's not miss the big E on the eye chart! Everything the church does should be all about Jesus.

Devotion to Prayer (2:42d)

Throughout the book of Acts we find illustrations of the church's vibrant prayer life (e.g., 4:31; 12:5; 13:1-3). The apostles too were seriously devoted to prayer (6:4). The church practiced both free and formal times of prayer. The believers prayed together corporately. They personally prayed without ceasing. They prayed in the temple, in homes, as they walked along the road, as they encountered the sick and afflicted, before they preached sermons, before they heard sermons, while they were being persecuted, in planned times of intense intercession over particular situations, as they offered thanks for their food, as they gave thanks to Jesus for the forgiveness of sins, as they praised God in song, and as they offered up petitions for the Father to meet daily needs.

All of this reminds us that a healthy church is a *praying* church. The early church had few earthly resources, but that didn't keep them from shaking the world for Christ because they had heavenly resources. These they experienced through dependent prayer.

Radical Generosity, Especially within the Church (2:45)

Luke stresses the practical outworking of fellowship in verse 45. Extraordinary sharing and mercy ministry, especially within the household of God, marked the early church community.

Some see this picture and that of 4:32-37 and shout, "Communism!" But that's an inaccurate charge. The church didn't abandon the idea of owning private property. The fact that stealing is a sin, for instance, demonstrates that some things belong to individuals. Luke points out that "no one *claimed* that any of his possessions was his own" (4:32; emphasis added). The Bible doesn't teach communism, but it does teach radical generosity! These early Christians basically said, "We don't need stuff. We need to love our brothers and sisters. If we can share our possessions to serve them, we're happy to do it."

This practice (which caught the attention of outsiders) happened because regenerate people should be generous people. The federal government can't enforce this kind of logic. Just imagine a news bulletin like this: "Hey, you guys, just pray about what you ought to give for this year's taxes! That'll cover our national needs!" Such an approach, of course, wouldn't work because the vast majority of citizens would suddenly turn into misers, their selfishness forcing the government to grind to a halt. But the church gives freely, voluntarily, sacrificially, and generously to the work of God's kingdom because Jesus changed their hearts and they want to invest in what he's doing in the world. This church knew their Savior gave them the pattern and the power for generosity (2 Cor 8:9). The best and most sustainable model for generous giving is a deep understanding and appreciation of grace (2 Cor 9:6-15).

Alongside his point about their generosity, Luke also highlights the extreme *sensitivity* of the church. The people were aware of the needs within the community; thus, no one was permitted to go to bed hungry. No one slept on the street. But while the church clearly displayed kindness and mercy to those outside the community, they gave particular attention to the needs of their brothers and sisters (cf. Gal 6:10).

Constant Interaction with One Another (2:46a)

The church lived out this shared life "every day." They were involved in one another's lives. While the church has to love those outside the family in order to fulfill its mission, a healthy church meets together as a family regularly. The author of Hebrews says,

> *Let us watch out for one another to provoke love and good works, not neglecting to gather together, as some are in the habit of doing, but encouraging each other, and all the more as you see the day approaching.* (Heb 10:24-25)

Half the job of a good church member is showing up! You can't build relationships if you aren't meeting with God's people.

Gathering in Both Large and Small Groups (2:46b)

The church met both at the "temple" and "house to house." One gathering was large, and one was small. The believers had to have a large space to meet in since three thousand people can't fit into someone's home. The temple area provided them a place for a large, formal, corporate gathering while their homes were wonderful places for more informal, intimate gatherings. Many Christians today emphasize one but not the other. The early church, though, devoted themselves to meeting in both.

A Spirit of Awe, Gladness, and Praise to God (2:43a,46-47a)

The early church's gatherings contained a wonderful spirit of praise that was both joyful and reverent. Luke mentions "awe" (v. 43) and "joyful . . . hearts" (v. 46). Both are linked to vibrant praise. There are times to rejoice with gladness, perhaps with lots of instrumentation and celebratory worship; there are also times to be still before the Lord in meditation, silence, and contemplation.

Some people find it difficult to praise God when things aren't working out according to plan. But I like to remind them gently that while life may be hard at the moment, they should imagine how much harder life would be without the Savior. How terrible it would be if this life was all there is! As people redeemed by Jesus, we should praise God constantly—not merely when we feel like it.

Pray for your local church that a spirit of awe and gladness would replace any boredom or gloom. Pray for God to renew a heart of praise in his people.

Displaying an Attractive Faith (2:47b)

Not everyone loved the early church. Just read the next few chapters to see what I mean. But some people were impacted greatly as they observed the believers' way of life. What attracted outsiders? Surely the Christ-exalting praise and the Christlike love of the early church influenced others. In John 13 Jesus told his disciples that love for one another would get people's attention (John 13:34-35). We have an example of this reality at work in Acts 2.

The Christians sacrificially cared for one another and also cared for outsiders. A few years after Acts was written, a man named Aristides commented on the reasons for the spread of Christianity. He wrote the following to Emperor Hadrian in AD 125:

> If one or other of them have bondmen and bondwomen or children, through love towards them they persuade them to become Christians, and when they have done so, they call them brethren without distinction. They do not worship strange gods, and they go their way in all modesty and cheerfulness. Falsehood is not found among them; and they love one another, and from widows they do not turn away their esteem; and they deliver the orphan from him who treats him harshly. And he, who has, gives to him who has not, without boasting. And when they see a stranger, they take him in to their homes and rejoice over him as a very brother; for they do not call them brethren after the flesh, but brethren after the spirit and in God. And whenever one of their poor passes from the world, each one of them according to his ability gives heed to him and carefully sees to his burial. And if they hear that one of their number is imprisoned or afflicted on account of the name of their Messiah, all of them anxiously minister to his necessity, and if it is possible to redeem him they set him free. And if there is among them any that is poor and needy, and if they have no spare food, they fast two or three days in order to supply to the needy their lack of food. (*The Apology of Aristides, XV*)

Another ancient document describing the compelling nature of Christianity comes from the mid-300s. Emperor Julian angrily tried to stop the spread of Christianity. He said that a reason for its growth was due to Christians' "charity to the poor": "The impious Galileans not only feed their own poor but ours as well," he complained, "welcoming them to their agape; they attract them, as children are attracted, with cakes" (*Epistle to Pagan High Priests*).

What amazing descriptions of the King's people! Our broken world needs compassion, and the watching world needs to see Christians demonstrating it. In turn, many will be attracted to the faith.

Daily Evangelism (2:47c)

How were people added to the number of believers? Ultimately, the Lord added them. He alone converts people. But the Lord uses means, and that means in Acts was faithful evangelism on the part of the people. People were converted daily because believers were evangelizing daily.

A healthy church will have a burden for outsiders. They will boldly and compassionately proclaim the gospel to their friends and neighbors and coworkers. The early church enthusiastically communicated the gospel within their own networks, and the Lord worked mightily through their steady witness.

Checking Our Vital Signs

We could group these ten marks of a healthy church into four categories: (1) biblical nourishment, (2) loving fellowship, (3) vibrant worship, and (4) word and deed outreach. Each expresses the various relationships we have as Christians: our relationship with God (categories 1 and 3), our relationships with one another (category 2), and our relationship to the world (category 4).

Virtually every church will be stronger in some areas of church life than others, but we shouldn't neglect any of them. The church that God is renewing by his Spirit does them all with increasing faithfulness and vitality.

As you think about your local church, consider these four areas. Mentally test both yourself and your congregation, and pray for the Spirit to renew you and the church.

Vital Sign 1: Biblical Nourishment

Do you understand the gospel? Are you sitting under the authority and teaching of the Word, regularly and humbly? Are other brothers and sisters admonishing you? Are you submitting to hard truth and repenting in light of it? Are you being renewed in the gospel daily? Are you teaching the Bible to others?

The early church clearly loved the Word of Christ and the Christ of the Word. We need the Word personally, and we need relationships centered on it. Dietrich Bonhoeffer talks about seasons when we as believers are in great need of brotherly admonishment:

> The Christian needs another Christian who speaks God's Word to him. He needs him again and again when he becomes uncertain and discouraged, for by himself he cannot help himself without belying the truth. . . . The Christ in his own heart is weaker than the Christ in the word of his brother; his own heart is uncertain, his brother's is sure. (*Life Together*, 23)

You may be in need right now, or you may need to be the brother or sister giving the Word to someone else. Whatever the case, act appropriately. We can't live by bread alone. We need every word that comes from the mouth of God (Matt 4:4).

Vital Sign 2: Loving Fellowship

Do you have fellowship with God through Jesus? Are you working at building deep relationships with others in the church? Could it be that you love the idea of community more than the actual people in your church? Are you complaining about a lack of community rather than asserting yourself to serve and love others in your congregation? Do you show up to events and meetings faithfully? Do you arrive early enough to interact with people on Sunday, or are you a ninja, slipping in late and excusing yourself before the service ends? Are you involved in others' lives throughout the week? Are you sensitive to the needs of your brothers and sisters? Are you grateful for them? Have you told them about what they mean to you?

"Devoted" implies work and accountability. Community involves two-way commitment. We have to work at it. It's particularly difficult for those who live in a transient area or in places where people are spread out. Still, God can work mightily to make community happen. See the need for it in this passage and work to do life with others. If God has already blessed you with Christian brothers and sisters who care for one another, pause to thank the Father. To quote Bonhoeffer again, "The physical presence of other Christians is a source of incomparable joy and strength to the believer" (*Life Together,* 19).

Vital Sign 3: Vibrant Worship

Are you praising God with other brothers and sisters in large and small gatherings? How do you approach the Lord's Table? Do you attend services repentantly and joyfully? Are you experiencing awe and joy in your Christian life? Are you praying with other brothers and sisters? Are you grateful for the privilege of gathering corporately?

Many Christ followers around the world lack the privilege of gathering regularly with a local body of believers because they're serving in unreached places or live under threat of punishment should they gather in groups. All of them comment on how much they wish to gather with the saints to worship the King. When you gather in your local church body, remember what a great and holy privilege it is to hear the Word, to sing songs of praise, and to enjoy the Lord's Supper in community.

Vital Sign 4: Word and Deed Outreach

Concerning *word* outreach, how are you doing at speaking the gospel to the unbelievers in your networks? Are you practicing "Philip evangelism," going out into the neighborhood sharing the gospel as Philip did? Are you practicing "Andrew evangelism," inviting people to come and experience a corporate worship service as Andrew did? If you truly love Christ, you will share him.

How are you doing at *deed* outreach? Are you involved in a ministry to the poor? Are you serving your brothers and sisters as they have need? Are you practicing gospel-driven generosity? Those who love Christ actively love others.

In my local church we challenged one another with our "555 Plan." We each identified at least five unbelievers in five of our networks (familial, vocational, commercial, geographical, and recreational). We then committed to do one of five activities: to pray for them, to serve them, to give gospel-centered literature to them, to invite them, and to speak the gospel to them. As we continue to grow in our outreach within the city, we need the Lord to help us be ever more effective in our witness to outsiders as we declare the gospel clearly and display it compassionately.

The picture of the early church Acts gives is remarkably and refreshingly simple. These believers did the basics well. And perhaps within that truth is a clue as to where many modern church problems begin. It's easy to get away from these primary activities. But as we, the body of Christ, return to this simple spiritual diet-and-exercise plan, we can partner with the Great Physician to see renewal in our local church bodies.

Reflect and Discuss

1. What's the most challenging aspect of this text for you? Why?
2. What's the most encouraging aspect of this text? Explain your answer.
3. What are some contemporary challenges we face in imitating this early Christian community?
4. Which of these ten descriptions most resonated with you? Why?
5. With regard to these four vital signs, which is your local church's greatest strength?
6. With regard to these four vital signs, which is your local church's greatest weakness?

7. What are some changes you can make and steps you can take to address some of these weaknesses personally?
8. What is the biggest obstacle standing between you and deep, genuine relationships with other believers?
9. Do you think outsiders observing your local church would be attracted to the faith because of it? Why or why not?
10. How might you more fully devote yourself to the study of the Scriptures and prayer?

The Wonder and the Word

ACTS 3:1-26

Main Idea: Luke describes how the apostles continued Jesus's ministry in word and deed as the healing of a lame man attracted a crowd to hear Peter's Christ-centered sermon.

I. **The Wonder (3:1-10)**
II. **The Word (3:11-26)**
   A. The explanation of the miracle
      1. Two denials
      2. Six affirmations
   B. The evangelistic appeal
      1. Jesus is the Servant of the Lord (3:13,26).
      2. Jesus was glorified by God (3:13).
      3. Jesus is the Holy and Righteous One (3:14).
      4. Jesus is the source of life (3:15).
      5. Jesus rose from the dead (3:15,26).
      6. Jesus is the fulfillment of Old Testament prophecy and promises (3:17-26).
      7. Repent (3:19-21)!

Every time I read this text, I think about a pastor friend who leads a church that has many college students. He says that when school is in session the attendance triples but giving only increases by about seventeen dollars a week. On one occasion a broke college student actually put a bacon, egg, and cheese biscuit into the offering bucket with a little note: "Silver and gold have I none, but such as I have, I give unto you!"

That's a funny story, but this next section of Scripture is no joke. The full passage occupies a lot of space, reaching from 3:1 to 4:31, with the events described covering a few days. It ends with threats and a powerful prayer meeting.

Here we see the apostles continuing Jesus's ministry in word and deed. The healing of a lame man is a deed that leads to a sermon, a word. After hearing that sermon, more people are converted to faith in Jesus, and the Jewish religious authorities are enraged.

The passage breaks down neatly into two parts. This text is about a miracle and a message: the wonder and the word.

The Wonder

ACTS 3:1-10

Three foundations of the Jewish faith included the Torah, worship, and showing kindness (giving alms). Since these activities were part of the rhythm of the religious community, the beggar chooses a visible location to ask for alms of people going up for prayer. As people worship, they will have to see him, and perhaps they will feel more compelled to give to him since they are en route to offer prayer and praise to God.

"Each day" the beggar was laid at the Beautiful Gate (v. 2). This was probably the most extravagant and prominently used entrance into the temple court.

The man in view here is not simply broke. He's broken. He's physically crippled. He's humiliated. He's hopeless. And to make things worse, he's more than forty years old (4:22). Presumably, he'd lived this way for decades.

As this broken man asks Peter and John for alms, something miraculous happens. The disciples direct their gazes to him, get his attention, and give him a renewed life (vv. 4-7). The people observe this man's transformation, and they are filled with wonder. One moment he's a lame beggar, and the next moment he's practicing for "Dancing with the Davidic Stars"! Seeing such a miracle should have caused people to marvel. And it did. But this chapter contains more than an account of wonder. Peter helps us understand the miracle and uses it to declare the gospel to the crowd it attracted. Not everyone liked that.

This story highlights the need to care for the hurting people all around us. It is a sobering reminder that it is possible to attend religious events while ignoring the needs right in front of us. Just read the prophets for more on the truth behind that statement (e.g., Isa 1:11-20; Amos 5:21-24; Mic 6:6-8). Another point of application here involves the apostles' care for just *one* guy. In the previous passage three thousand people were saved. And from this switch in focus comes a new principle: Those who reach the many care about reaching the one. May God give us compassionate hearts for meeting the physical and spiritual needs of every individual. To see those who might feel lost in the crowd.

The Word

ACTS 3:11-26

Let's break Peter's message into two main parts: (1) the explanation of the miracle and (2) the evangelistic appeal.

The Explanation of the Miracle

We can detect two denials and six affirmations concerning this wonder.

Two Denials. First, Peter denies that this act was the work of witchcraft, magic, sorcery, or any mind-over-matter technique (Piper, "Jesus' Name Made This Man Strong"). The lame man is still holding on to Peter and John when Peter essentially says, "Why are you looking at me? I'm not some kind of wizard!" (vv. 11-12). There are apparent healings of all sorts associated with witchcraft and works of darkness, but this miracle was the work of Christ, the source of life.

Second, Peter denies the intrinsic worthiness of either the healer or the healed man. This miracle couldn't be attributed to Peter's power or godliness. If God uses a person to heal, it's not the healer who should receive the glory. God alone gets the glory. The former lame man was not healed because of his piety either. He didn't even ask to be healed! He was begging for money when God generously healed him anyway.

Some people think the reason God has not yet healed them is because they aren't worthy of healing. Some think God doesn't answer their prayers for someone else to be healed because their prayers aren't perfect enough to merit his attention. But that kind of thinking is wrong. I'm not saying a person's moral life doesn't matter. I simply want to point out what Peter (a godly man!) said: This miracle came because the all-powerful Savior decided to intervene and perform a wonder! You see, Jesus is on the throne, ruling and reigning, and he can decide to intervene and perform a miracle whenever he pleases. On this day he was pleased to do so. Peter says, "It's not about me; it's about him!"

Six Affirmations. First, as mentioned, Jesus healed this man. In verses 13-16 Peter explains how faith in the crucified, glorified Christ literally healed. This point runs right through this chapter and into the next.

Second, God gave Peter and John the gift of faith and healing and miracle working in this moment. In verse 16, Peter was given faith to heal. John Piper explains,

> First, notice that the faith to heal (Peter's faith, not the man's; there is no reason in the text to think he was believing when Peter spoke) is "through Jesus"—that is Jesus gave it. It came

through the working of Jesus (cf. 5:31). This, it seems to me, is the key to what happened in verse 4 when Peter gazed at the lame man. Luke tells us in verse 2 that this man was laid daily at the gate. So Peter had passed this man many times before without healing him. But today, when he looked at him, something happened. What? The faith to heal him came THROUGH JESUS. The living Jesus did something in Peter, and Peter knew it was the day. When he said, "What I have I give to you," he probably meant, "Today I have been given something special for you. Jesus has just given me the faith to speak healing to you and I now share this gift with you. Rise." That's what the last part of verse 16 says, "The faith, which is through Jesus [not in Jesus!] has given this man perfect health." Jesus gave the faith to heal, and Peter acted on it. ("Jesus' Name Made This Man Strong")

Might God decide to do something like this among us today? Sure. I think apostolic miracles were unique in number and nature, but I know God still does miracles through his people in particular moments for his own purposes.

In 1 Corinthians 12:9-10 Paul lists these three gifts together—*faith, healing, and miracles*. Where do we most often see these gifts on display today? Certainly one place is within the prayer ministry of the church. James writes,

> *Is anyone among you sick? He should call for the elders of the church, and they are to pray over him, anointing him with oil in the name of the Lord. The prayer of faith will save the sick person, and the Lord will raise him up; if he has committed sins, he will be forgiven.*
> (Jas 5:14-15)

As we pray for healing, we need to remember that God always answers: either presently or at the resurrection. But God always invites us to pray, hears our prayers, and will ultimately heal his people.

It seems that God is also pleased to perform wondrous works on the mission field where there is little biblical revelation. Multiple missionaries attest to this. But whether it happens in prayer or on the mission field, healing happens as a gracious gift of God.

Third, we need to affirm that Christ should be praised as the source of life who provides through "ordinary means" as well as through what would be easily recognized as miracles. In 3:15 Peter refers to the Lord as the author or "source" of life. This covers both physical and spiritual life. As Creator of all life, God sometimes works through miracles, but more often he provides for the needs of the ailing human body through farmers, pharmacists, and surgeons. The doctrine of providence teaches that God cares for his creation, and he sustains it. Whether you eat because you raised chickens or because you drove through the Chick-fil-A line, the Lord of life is to be praised. And whether your condition cleared all at once in the midst of a prayer meeting or was alleviated over time through the use of antibiotics and a medical procedure, God deserves glory for your healing.

Fourth, we should affirm that this miracle involving the lame man was a sign of the messianic kingdom to come. Later, Peter refers to "the restoration of all things" (v. 21). In the new heaven and new earth there will be no lame legs! Jesus gave a sneak preview of that joyous day through his many healing miracles, and Isaiah foresaw such a day:

> *Then the lame will leap like a deer,*
> *and the tongue of the mute will sing for joy,*
> *for water will gush in the wilderness,*
> *and streams in the desert.* (Isa 35:6)

Isaiah pointed to this glorious future, inaugurated at Jesus's first coming (Luke 7:18-23) and fully consummated at his second. This particular lame man, then, became a living example of Isaiah 35. Jesus's miracles of healing were signs of his identity and glimpses of his kingship. The restoration of this lame man makes us, who groan with the aches and pains of living under the curse of sin, long for the "restoration of all things." Take heart! That day is coming soon!

Fifth, because Christ gave the faith and worked the miracle, his name alone is exalted. Just notice how often "the name" is mentioned in chapters 3 and 4. The name of Jesus means everything that is true about him. He is to be exalted as the source of life and as the forgiver of sinners. His is the only name by which people can be saved.

Finally, we must affirm that this miracle serves the gospel message. It was a launching pad into the sermon. Peter doesn't stop after the miracle, say, "My work is done here," and then move on. No, there's a purpose for the wonder. The physical miracle was a fact, but it was also a picture, a parable. Jesus's miracles too were often illustrations or validations of the message he shared. The miracle attracted a crowd, but the message offered to that crowd was more important than any wonder. Why? Simple. You can be healed miraculously today, but your heart and body will eventually wear out. You need the message of eternal life more than a miracle of temporary healing.

The lame man's healing is a powerful reminder that Jesus is the source of life. He gives life! Jesus heals the disabilities of the human heart! He causes redeemed sinners to dance in his presence with joy!

The Evangelistic Appeal

Not one to pass up an opportunity to preach the gospel, Peter uses this miracle to point everyone to the Messiah. He exalts Jesus in several ways and along the way sharply indicts the unbelieving crowd.

Jesus is the servant of the Lord (3:13,26). In verses 13 and 26 Peter refers to Jesus as God's "servant." This title refers to the promised Servant in the Old Testament (e.g., Isa 52:13–53:12). This promised Servant appeared in human history and said, "Even the Son of Man did not come to be served, but to serve, and to give his life as a ransom for many" (Mark 10:45). In a world all about climbing the social or career ladder and being served, Jesus pointed to another, better way to live. He served us all the way to the cross, and he continues to serve his church today. Once you begin to grasp how Christ has served you, you will gladly serve him and others.

Jesus was glorified by God (3:13-14). The God of our fathers glorified his Servant, Jesus. A happy sharing of glory exists within the Godhead. Prior to his cross work, Jesus prayed to the Father:

> *The hour has come. Glorify your Son so that the Son may glorify you. . . . I have glorified you on the earth by completing the work you gave me to do. Now, Father, glorify me in your presence with that glory I had with you before the world existed.* (John 17:1,4-5)

In this first part of the sermon, Peter also gave Jesus this messianic title of Servant (see Isa 53:11; Mark 1:24). But tell people that Jesus alone is the Holy and Righteous One, as Peter does in verse 14, and you will have a religious controversy with which to deal.

Many think Jesus is like other religious teachers. They thus think of him as a historical figure to be studied, like one of the many presidents whose contributions are summarized in a United States history textbook. While an understanding like that might lead a few to honor Jesus by chiseling his likeness on Mount Rushmore, it completely misses the truth that he's in a class by himself. Peter rightly says there's Jesus, and then there's everyone else—including all other religious leaders.

So, in light of this fact, how can we be holy and righteous? We need *Jesus's* holiness and righteousness. That, in fact, is the good news of the gospel. Jesus, the Righteous One, traded places with sinners like us. By repentance and placing faith in Christ, we receive his righteousness (2 Cor 5:21). Incredibly, his work gets credited to our accounts. While other religions teach that people work *for* righteousness, the gospel message so unique to Christianity is that people work *from* Christ-given righteousness. Only in Christianity—because of the work of Christ—does a verdict come *before* a performance. As a believer in Jesus, you are declared righteous. Out of that position you get to obey the Righteous One in his power for his glory, knowing that he has already dealt with your greatest problem.

Jesus is the source of life (3:15). Peter exalts Christ with this amazing "source of life" title. John writes, "In him was life, and that life was the light of men" (John 1:4). Paul says, "For everything was created by him. . . . all things have been created through him and for him. He is before all things, and by him all things hold together" (Col 1:16-17). In other words, apart from Jesus there's no life. Apart from him you don't even have a physical life. But let's say you do. Even so, you are dying even as you think about what I'm saying, and you will die a spiritual death as well as a physical one unless you are united to him by faith. When your computer, iPad, or smart phone is detached from a power source, it eventually dies. Similarly, people must be united with the source of life in order to live. Peter found that making such a statement about Jesus before Jewish people enraged many. But his words offer wonderful news about how we can overcome death.

Jesus rose from the dead (3:15,26). Christ's resurrection is the constant message of the apostles. God raised Jesus from the dead, and the apostles saw him alive. This validated all of Jesus's claims, displayed the Father's acceptance of the Son's atoning death, and proved that he indeed is the source of life. Peter's point is clear: we aren't saved by the quality of our faith but by the object of our faith! So put your faith in Jesus, the resurrected Lord, who came to rescue people like you.

Jesus is the fulfillment of Old Testament prophecy and promises (3:17-26). Peter alludes to several Old Testament texts as he points people to Jesus the Messiah. From Abraham onward, the flow of redemptive history culminates in this Jesus. Peter says "all the prophets" (vv. 18,24) predicted his coming—including Moses, who predicted someone greater and more glorious than he. Peter essentially says, "The Messiah came!" But this audience, like many people today, is still waiting for the fulfillment of all those prophecies. Doing this is as uninformed as saying, "I hope Mickey Mantle plays for the Yankees." He already played. If you don't know that, you missed it!

Jesus is the final prophet. There aren't any prophets after Jesus because he is what the prophets were speaking about! Further, unlike the other prophets Scripture mentions, Jesus doesn't simply *speak* the truth; he *is* the truth! He doesn't just *show* us the way; he *is* the way. He doesn't just *tell* us what meaning is; he *is* the meaning (John 1:1).

As the greater Moses, Jesus led a greater exodus. Jesus is the ultimate Redeemer. As the greater King, Jesus reigns forever. As the offspring of Abraham, in Jesus all the families of the earth are blessed. The Old Testament sustains this messianic hope throughout the narrative, and it gets fulfilled in Christ, our great Prophet, King, and Redeemer.

We should pause for a moment and consider all the *indictments* Peter makes against his audience:

- Verse 13: You handed over Jesus.
- Verse 13b: You're worse than Pilate.
- Verse 14: You traded the Holy and Righteous One for a murderer.
- Verse 15: You killed the one who gave you life.
- Verse 17: You're ignorant.
- Verses 18-25: You don't understand the Bible.
- Verse 26: You denied your privilege.
- Verse 26b: You're wicked.

Repent! (3:19-21). In light of these serious charges, we must ask whether there is any hope for such wicked people. The answer is yes! Look back at 3:19-21. In the center of this passage about the glory of Christ and the gravity of sin, Peter offers amazing gospel hope to everyone.

Notice the *necessity* of repentance in verse 19. He says there's hope if you turn from your sins. Down in verse 26 he tells his hearers that God wants "to bless you by turning each of you from your evil ways." In other words, our ability to repent is God's gracious gift.

Notice also the *blessings* of forgiveness. In verses 19-21 Peter mentions three benefits of genuine repentance: (1) total forgiveness, (2) spiritual refreshment, and (3) universal restoration.

Regarding the first, he says that through repentance, "your sins may be wiped out" (v. 19). This is a beautiful word picture. Parchment was expensive, so sometimes scribes used acid-free ink as they wrote on it.

The ink just lay on top of the parchment, so a person could take a wet sponge and wipe a message away, blotting it out. To put Peter's point in modern terms, imagine having all your sins listed on a dry-erase board. Now, imagine sitting there pondering the weight of your sin record and the certainty of coming judgment without having any hope of changing your sad reality. But then, when you feel eaten by shame and fear, someone marches in and forever wipes that record of your wrongs off the board. He declares you innocent. Would that not make you soar in worship to the one wiping away your sin? It should! That's what's happened! Jesus Christ has wiped out our wrongs. We have no guilt. We are under no condemnation. And as sure as Jesus wipes our sin away the moment we ask him to do so, he will wipe our tears away later (Rev 21:4).

But there's more. Through repentance you can enjoy spiritual refreshment (v. 20). The language Peter uses here speaks of respite, rest, refreshment, or relief. It's a word about the messianic age, when the Spirit will be poured out. It's a reminder that those who turn to Jesus find rest. What good news the gospel offers to people who have been trying to earn forgiveness of sins and to achieve eternal life: simply come to Jesus and find rest and refreshment for your weary soul. His actions on the cross set us free!

Finally, Peter says, if you will repent, then you will enjoy the hope of Christ restoring all things (vv. 20-21). Paul spoke of the day in which our sufferings will give way to glory (Rom 8:18-37). Christ gives us hope to endure the difficulties of this life because he has given us the promise of glory to come. How terrible would it be to have hope only in this life? The gospel, however, offers an unshakable hope that our best days are yet to come.

According to Acts 4:1-4, some people actually received Peter's message. The number of believers grew to include five thousand men! This is another reminder that God uses ordinary people to declare his extraordinary message. Lives are transformed as Christ is exalted from his Word. As the Spirit worked through Peter the fisherman, he can work through you.

As we minister in word and deed like these apostles, let's be confident in the name of the One who saved us. Acts 3–4 contains multiple references to "the name" (3:6,16; 4:7,10-12,17,29-30). Jesus issued the Great Commission by saying, "All authority has been given to me. . . . Go . . . and make disciples" (Matt 28:18-20). When you truly believe Jesus is in control of all things, and he is with you, the way you pray, live, serve, and evangelize will change. John Piper puts the authority of King Jesus in perspective:

> All authority. He has authority over Satan and all demons, over all angels—good and evil—over the natural universe, natural objects and laws and forces: stars, galaxies, planets, meteorites; authority over all weather systems: winds, rains, lightning, thunder, hurricanes, tornadoes, monsoons, typhoons, cyclones; authority over all their effects: tidal waves, floods, fires; authority over all molecular and atomic reality: atoms, electrons, protons, neutrons, undiscovered subatomic particles, quantum physics, genetic structures, DNA, chromosomes; authority over all plants and animals great and small: whales and redwoods, giant squid and giant oaks, all fish, all wild beasts, all invisible animals and plants: bacteria, viruses, parasites, germs; authority over all the parts and functions of the human body: every beat of the heart, every breath of the diaphragm, every electrical jump across a million synapses in our brains; authority over all nations and governments: congresses and legislatures and presidents and kings and premiers and courts; authority over all armies and weapons and bombs and terrorists; authority over all industry and business and finance and currency; authority over all entertainment and amusement and leisure and media; over all education and research and science and discovery; authority over all crime and violence; over all families and neighborhoods; and over the church, and over every soul and every moment of every life that has been or ever will be lived. ("The Lofty Claim")

Minister with this massive promise: Jesus Christ has all authority, and he is *with you!*

Reflect and Discuss

1. What is the most challenging aspect of this text for you?
2. What aspect of this text do you think your church needs to hear the most?
3. Why should Christians care for people in need?
4. What are you doing to care for the broken?

5. What does this text teach about caring for both physical *and* spiritual needs?
6. What about this miracle most resonates with you? Why?
7. Does God heal people today? Explain.
8. How do you think this sermon should influence how we read and teach the Bible?
9. Is there anyone in your life whom you are trying to lead to salvation in Christ? If so, how does this text inspire and instruct you?
10. How should the authority of Jesus impact the way you live this week?

With All Boldness

ACTS 4:1-31

Main Idea: Luke records a heated showdown between the religious establishment and Peter and John concerning their Christ-centered preaching.

I. Peter and John: Interrupted by the Religious Establishment (4:1-4)
II. Peter and John: Bold before the Religious Establishment (4:5-12)
III. The Religious Establishment: Paralyzed before Peter and John (4:13-18)
IV. Peter and John: Bold before Threats (4:19-22)
V. The Church: Bold in Response (4:23-30)
VI. Conclusion (4:31)

In 2015 a horrific video was circulated on the Internet, detailing the brutal executions of twenty-one Egyptian Christians by the Islamic State (ISIS) terrorist group. The video, which I do not recommend watching, showed ISIS soldiers marching the brave Christian martyrs to the seashore. Then, with swords in hand, the ISIS captors made the Christians kneel down and gave them a chance to recant their Christian faith. Remaining true to their convictions, however, the Christian men would not recant. In response, their captors systematically beheaded all twenty-one of our brothers as they quietly mouthed, "Jesus, help me!" Their crime? These men were "people of the cross."

So it is and has been for our brothers and sisters in the faith throughout history. We have been opposed, arrested, persecuted, and muzzled. And this section in Acts highlights an early situation in which opposition to the people of the cross was heightened.

As we consider the history of opposition to the Christian faith and as we approach this text, we must ask whether we are being opposed. If we cannot cite evidence of at least mild forms of persecution at work in our own lives, it is possible that we have a nimble faith—or perhaps a closet faith—that evades opposition. I heard a preacher once say that everywhere Paul went there were riots, and everywhere American Christians go there are conferences! While I do not think we should seek persecution or opposition, his point raises this question: Are we bold like Peter and John when it comes to telling others about Jesus? Peter knew what it was like to cower and fear. Not even a hundred days before this event he had cursed and even denied knowing Christ in front of a slave girl (John 18:17). What Judas did for profit, then, Peter did for free! Both men betrayed Jesus. But there is something different about Peter at this point in his story. Let's look at why this man is now fearless in front of the religious elites that just crucified his Master!

Peter and John: Interrupted by the Religious Establishment
ACTS 4:1-4

Following the spectacular healing of the lame man in Jerusalem, Peter made a bold evangelistic appeal that called his listeners to repent and believe in the risen Jesus (3:11-36). While Peter and John were finishing up their appeals, they were interrupted by various members of the religious establishment who were angered by their Christ-centered teaching on the resurrection of the dead (4:1-2). Peter and John were arrested. Yet the gospel message they shared remained powerfully alive and at work in those who heard, and many believed.

The priests, the temple commander, and the Sadducees "were annoyed" (v. 2). The Sadducees were the theological liberals of their day. They didn't believe in miracles like the resurrection or in angels. Bold peaching regarding the literal bodily resurrection inaugurated by Jesus must have annoyed all the groups but especially the Sadducees!

The apostles were not preaching *rules*; they were preaching *resurrection*. Likewise, in our preaching and teaching, we dare not commend a set of moral rules to make people more acceptable before God. Rather, we should commend the risen Lord Jesus Christ, who alone makes us acceptable. He is the hero of the whole Bible and is the One to whom the whole Bible testifies. He is our message. He is our theme. So may we say with Paul, "We proclaim him, warning and teaching everyone with all wisdom, so that we may present everyone mature in Christ" (Col 1:28).

Peter and John: Bold before the Religious Establishment
ACTS 4:5-12

The next day Peter and John are brought before the Sanhedrin, the Jewish leadership, to face questioning for their resurrection preaching. The "rulers, elders, and scribes" (v. 5) were the religious power players in Jerusalem. Even Annas and Caiaphas, who figured prominently in the trial and condemnation of Jesus, are in attendance. Why is such firepower aimed at two ordinary men? Most likely these religious bullies saw the disciples and their spreading message as a threat to their own social and political power.

They ask, "By what power or in what name have you done this?" (v. 7). Peter and John are standing there before the religious powers that had just tried, arrested, and murdered their Lord. Perhaps in these moments they are wondering, *Will we be crucified, too?* So how will Peter, who just days before was cowering in front a child, respond? Remarkably, *with all boldness.*

Peter shows no fear (vv. 10-12). Why? Before Jesus's crucifixion, when Peter faced that little girl, he was alone. At this point, however, he is indwelt by the Spirit of God!

You may be thinking, *Wasn't he already filled with the Spirit at Pentecost back in chapter 2?* Yes, he was! So does Luke's comment here regarding "filling" call into question the permanence of the Spirit's indwelling in a Christian's life? No! Instead, Luke is saying that the indwelling Spirit freshly empowered Peter, which enabled him to preach boldly. This is a wonderful reality for believers. God is with us forever. And God will often supernaturally fill us with his Spirit to enable us to do his will. This episode seems to be one fulfillment of Jesus's words in Luke 21:12-15:

> But before all these things, they will lay their hands on you and
> persecute you. They will hand you over to the synagogues and prisons,
> and you will be brought before kings and governors because of my
> name. This will give you an opportunity to bear witness. Therefore
> make up your minds not to prepare your defense ahead of time, for I
> will give you such words and a wisdom that none of your adversaries
> will be able to resist or contradict.

In his answer Peter declares the death and resurrection of Jesus to be fulfillment of Old Testament prophecy (v. 11; cf. Ps 118:22). The psalmist highlights how God's Servant was formerly rejected by the establishment but by divine decree was raised to honorable office. The Servant leader is the stone on which the temple would be built. Likewise, Jesus Christ was rejected by the establishment but was exalted to the right hand of God. He is the stone on which the new spiritual temple is built.

Peter is emphasizing God's sovereignty and providence in the life, death, and resurrection of Jesus. In response to the religious powers' question regarding the name or authority on which he acted, Peter essentially says, "The Messiah whom you beat, humiliated, rejected, and

killed—yet whom God has raised from the dead—is my authority." Peter
knew Jesus Christ as Lord. Jesus is the new foundation of a new temple:
the church.

Ultimately, Peter boldly tells them that their plan did not work. The
Jesus they thought they killed and discarded had just healed a man.
That fact should've been a pretty good indication that Jesus was no longer dead but alive. The religious establishment was on the wrong side
of God's work in the world, which meant they were in big trouble. They
were the ones on trial. The helpless, crippled man whom they considered to be a nothing was on the right side, and they needed what he had
just experienced. And what that man had experienced was the blessing
that resulted from the apostles' faith in the only name that is able to save.
And that name—Jesus—is the name the religious establishment did not
want Peter and John speaking. As it turned out, the apostles could not
help themselves!

Consider some takeaways from their response.

Be bold because the resurrection is true. In verse 10 Peter's boldness grows
as he denounces the religious establishment for their role in Jesus's
death. Peter is emboldened because, although Christ had been murdered, God raised him from the dead. Weeks later, through the Holy
Spirit and in the name of Jesus, the gospel was spreading and being
validated by signs and miracles. Therefore, the apostles would not be
silenced because they knew to anticipate the other resurrection Christ
promised. For Jesus, death clearly was not the last word. Likewise for us,
his followers, death will not have the last say. Most of us will never face
physical death because of our faith. However, some of us might. Take
courage no matter what you face because all who are united to Jesus will
be raised like Jesus. As Martin Luther said, "The body they may kill, His
truth abideth still!" ("A Mighty Fortress Is Our God").

Be bold out of love for neighbor. Peter's exclusive claim (v. 12) is an
implicit invitation to the religious powers to trust in the name of Jesus.
The lame man received physical deliverance through Jesus Christ. He
is also the only One who can grant a greater deliverance. The gospel
of Jesus Christ is the good news about how God loves us and gave himself for us. Those transformed by Jesus are known for their love (John
13:35; 1 John 3:14; 4:20). Love calls us to take risks and to seek the well-
being of others (even if it requires us to suffer). Love does not consider
the glory of self as the bottom line. It pursues God's glory and others'
good. As Christians, we ought to desire for people to know God and

be forgiven because that is their highest good and it results in praise to God.

Remember the exclusivity of the gospel. The pathway to salvation is narrow. We cannot create our own pathways to God based on our own efforts or ideas. God has provided a glorious way for sin to be atoned for and righteousness to be found in Jesus Christ. The gospel is incompatible with both universalism (in the end all will be saved) and inclusivism (in the end some who were ignorant of Jesus but who responded to "the light they've received" will be saved). This is an offensive aspect of the gospel to the modern mind. But no matter what we might hear from some Christian teachers today, the early church took the exclusive claims of Christ seriously. I think they did so for a couple of reasons.

First, to say there could be another way to God proves unloving because it is simply untrue. The Scriptures teach that God provided one way. Even if a person's faith in an idol or moral code is sincere, *sincerity* of faith does not save. Rather, the *object* of our faith saves, and that object is none other than the Lord Jesus. While it may seem accommodating and loving to tell someone there are other ways to God, it is actually wicked because it is a lie from the enemy. In suggesting such a thing, you are withholding from them the only source of life and leaving them clinging to something that will not save.

Second, implying there is another way is disrespectful to Jesus. It suggests he didn't really have to die on the cross. If there is another way to God, then trusting in what Jesus did at Calvary simply becomes another way among a plurality of options for salvation. This diminishes Christ's glory and devalues his work. Scripture reveals plainly that "there is one God and one mediator between God and humanity, the man Christ Jesus" (1 Tim 2:5). There is one door to God (John 10:9), yet he welcomes anyone in the world who would believe on him (John 3:16; Rom 10:13). We are loved by Jesus and should desire for him to be rightly esteemed by others. And this is our neighbor's highest good—to glorify Jesus.

Many who don't believe in Christ may consider the exclusivity of the gospel narrow-minded or even hateful. Yet we ought to speak the truth *in love,* even knowing that the truth may make some people think we are bigoted. That is a small risk to take when we sincerely desire that our unbelieving friends enjoy what we have in Christ. After all, what medical professional would keep the cure to cancer to himself? We work for the Great Physician who has shared with us the only cure to death itself, and he freely offers it to all who repent and call on his name. We, his colaborers, must not fail to tell about it.

In discussing witnessing and the exclusivity of the gospel, consider the early church. Their context was inclusive, relativistic, agnostic, and atheistic in similar ways to our modern culture. Consider Tim Keller's comments and counsel on the evangelistic edge of the early church,[2]

> They were both attractive and growing, yet hated and attacked.
> This description of the early church cuts us two ways. If on
> the one hand, we experience no attacks or persecution for
> our faith, it means we simply are being cowards. We are not
> taking risks in our witness, we are not being bold. On the
> other hand, if we experience attacks without a . . . fruitfulness
> and attractiveness (i.e., if we get lots of persecution and no
> affirmation), it may mean that we are being persecuted for
> being harsh or insensitive or strident. Jesus said we would only
> be blessed if we were persecuted "for righteousness' sake."
> It is quite possible (indeed, it is very normal) for Christians
> to be persecuted not for their faith, but for their discourtesy,
> insensitivity, and lack of warmth and respect in their dealings
> with others. Insensitive, harsh Christians will have persecution
> but not praise. Cowardly Christians will have praise but not
> persecution. Most Christians (whose walk with God is weak)
> actually get neither! But Christians who are closest to Jesus will
> get both, as he did. (*Evangelism*, 45)

May God give us a closeness to Jesus so that we might commend him lovingly like the early church did. And may we be bold risk takers in our witness to Christ while also being marked by sensitivity and warmth.

The Religious Establishment: Paralyzed before Peter and John
ACTS 4:13-18

It particularly confounds the religious leaders that these common fishermen are the ones speaking so boldly about Scripture (v. 13). Men with their lack of education and training were not expected to speak with either courage or confidence before the supreme powers of the

---

[2] Various references are made throughout this commentary to Tim Keller. Unless noted otherwise, I am quoting from *Evangelism: Studies in the Book of Acts, Leader Guide.*

land. The only explanation for the ability of Peter and John to do so is that they had received a tremendous education about Scripture from the Savior they claimed to follow! They were bold because they had the Holy Spirit, and they personally knew the One who had all authority in heaven and on earth (Matt 28:18). They "had been with Jesus"!

God can effectively use anyone—even the uneducated—who will listen and to follow his Son. You may never get the chance to receive formal training in Scripture, but be encouraged: God can use you. One day you may even speak to kings and people in high positions. Should that happen, there's no need to fear: You know the ruler over all creation (Col 1:15). God can use the PhDs (think Paul) and the GEDs (think Peter), the doctors (like Luke) and the tax collectors (like Matthew). Praise God for his wonderful grace!

When the religious leaders conclude that the boldness of Peter and John resulted from their being with Jesus, and they see that a crippled man has indeed been miraculously healed, they are dumbfounded (v. 14). They order the apostles to leave the Sanhedrin and have a little huddle to discuss the big mess. On the one hand, a notable miracle has taken place in a public way they cannot deny. On the other hand, they must stop the news about Jesus from spreading. Thus, they command Peter and John not to say the name of Jesus.

In taking this approach, these leaders act out of fear for their own futures rather than out of fear of God. They do not want to lose their power and influence. So instead of asking, "What must we do to be saved?" they ask, "What must we do to keep our power?" They love the praise that comes from people more than the praise that comes from God. That's why they are more concerned with doing damage control than they are with taking seriously the message of repenting and believing.

Peter and John: Bold before Threats
ACTS 4:19-22

Peter and John reply boldly to the demand of the Sanhedrin (vv. 19-20). The New American Standard Bible renders their response this way: "We *cannot stop* speaking about what we have seen and heard" (v. 20; emphasis added). They had seen with their own eyes and touched with their own hands the resurrected Lord Jesus. His glory was undeniable. They were acting in obedience to him.

Importantly, while Christians are called to obey rulers and authorities on earth (Rom 13:1-17), they aren't to do so in ways that contradict

God's Word or violate their consciences. If you are faced with an absolute decision in which you must obey God or the authorities, you can be certain that obeying the Lord is the right path. Doing so can be risky, but disobeying God's explicit Word is never an option. Like Peter and John, we must have the primary aim of pleasing God. May God make us both wise and bold in speaking about the gospel of his Son.

In view of the obvious healing miracle and now the rejoicing public, the leaders were still in a bind (vv. 21-22). The only action they could safely take against the men was to threaten the apostles further about speaking about Jesus. In the end the leaders could find no basis on which to punish them.

The Church: Bold in Response
ACTS 4:23-30

After their hearing, Peter and John return to their companions and tell them what transpired. In this scene we see the church sharing in the shake-up of Peter and John. Indeed, these Christians practiced good listening. But they also practiced empathy and were driven by the mission of God. Likewise, we should constantly remind ourselves that we are all participants in the Lord's mission. When one of our brothers or sisters suffers on behalf of the testimony of Jesus, we should not only aim to empathize with them but also to embolden them through prayer.

As we turn our attention to the church's prayer in this chapter, consider three observations.

This prayer is rooted in God's attributes (vv. 24-30). The gathered beleivers address God as "Master" (v. 24) or "Sovereign Lord" (ESV). This title ascribes absolute authority and rule to God. The church, at the outset, reminded themselves of God's control of all things (vv. 24-25).

Thinking about God's sovereignty should bring us great comfort and security. Our God is the One with unchallengeable power! Everything that was, and is, and ever will be answers to him.

This prayer is rooted in the Scriptures (vv. 25-28). In quoting Psalm 2:1-2 the church reminds itself of God's sovereignty and providence over all history. Psalm 2 in its entirety describes the victory of the Lord and his Anointed One against the conspiracy of the nations. Equipped with a Christ-centered understanding of Scripture, the church rightly understands Psalm 2 as foretelling gospel events (Acts 4:27-28). The descendant of David would suffer rejection but emerge victorious as ruler over all the nations. This is precisely what we see in Jesus's life, death, resurrection, and promise of return. It appears the early church kept that truth in view.

God told his people beforehand that the nations would conspire together against the Messiah, yet he would be triumphant and become ruler over all. The church realized they were in the final chapter of a great unfolding drama, and the next step is the return and reign of Christ. They trusted this promise and let that make them bold. We too should realize that we are in the final chapter of the true story of the world. No matter what you might face today, Jesus is indeed coming back soon. And then every knee will bow and confess he is Lord. Let this embolden you as you speak and live for the King.

This prayer is for mission above comfort (vv. 29-30). The church aligns itself with Christ and his sufferings. In this hostile first-century context, having more boldness meant more gospel preaching, but that preaching would inevitably put believers in difficult circumstances. In their mission, then, the church prayed for boldness and perseverance rather than comfort. They knew Jesus was worth more than their lives.

Suffering is unavoidable for the Christian. In every generation the gospel always cuts against cultural convictions and norms in some way. Paul would later write, "All who want to live a godly life in Christ Jesus will be persecuted" (2 Tim 3:12).

Thinking about all this in light of the freedoms we in the United States enjoy, I wonder how our prayers might differ from those offered by the early church in view of the "American dream" ideology that permeates our culture. Could it be that our prayers are more about our comfort being maintained or enhanced than they are about asking that God's greater glory be displayed? When we pray for a fellow citizen facing opposition, for instance, it's not usually sufficient to pray, "Father, alleviate this!" Rather, we might add, "But Lord, if you choose not to, may the gospel advance because of this struggle!"

Conclusion
ACTS 4:31

After the church prays, God awesomely answers (v. 31). Peter and John were shaken by the Sanhedrin, but Almighty God shook the church and gave them boldness as a result. They were again filled with the Spirit and continued to speak the gospel with boldness.

We live in a world where our brothers, who live only hours away from us by plane, are being killed for their faith in Jesus. Yet we so often worry ourselves with trivial things and become paralyzed by fear at the thought of sharing the gospel here in our land of freedoms. This should make us ask, Why are we not seeing a move of the Spirit like we see here in Acts? Could it be that we've grown more concerned about our social standing or reputations than about Christ and his mission? Are we more interested in accumulating new toys and gadgets than in seeing the mercy of Christ being powerfully proclaimed to and embraced by our neighbors?

Consider the power within us: "If the Spirit of him who raised Jesus from the dead lives in you, then he who raised Christ from the dead will also bring your mortal bodies to life through his Spirit who lives in you" (Rom 8:11). The same Spirit who empowered the early Christians dwells within us. No matter the trials and persecutions we may face today or in ten years, we have a glorious resurrection coming. Let this encourage you afresh toward sharing in the mission of redemption. May God grant us the boldness of Peter and John by the power of his Spirit.

Reflect and Discuss

1. Describe a time when you experienced timidity about your Christian faith. What do you think was causing your fear?
2. Why did the preaching of Peter and John upset the religious establishment?
3. How is the power of the Holy Spirit related to bold proclamation?
4. What did Peter mean by the phrase "the stone rejected by you builders, which has become the cornerstone" (v. 11)?
5. Consider the millions of unreached and lost people living today. Now consider what Peter says in Acts 4:12. How should we respond?
6. What characteristics did the religious establishment observe in Peter and John (v. 13)? What does this teach us about the importance of spending time with Jesus?
7. What does this story teach us about preaching Christ?
8. Why do you think the church addressed God as "Master" in its prayer (vv. 24-30)?
9. Why did the church quote Psalm 2:1-2 in its prayer?
10. Why should we pray for boldness? What does boldness look like in evangelism?

Inside the Huddle

ACTS 4:32–5:11

Main Idea: In these two contrasting stories, Luke shows us how Christian unity is established, experienced, and endangered.

I. **How Unity Is Established: The Gospel (4:32a)**
II. **How Unity Is Experienced: Generosity (4:32b-37)**
   A. Extensive sharing (4:32b)
   B. Empowered sharing (4:33)
   C. Extraordinary sharing among the affluent (4:34-35)
   D. Exemplified sharing in Barnabas (4:36-37)
III. **How Unity Is Endangered: Hypocrisy (5:1-11)**
   A. What they were: determined hypocrites (5:1-4)
   B. What happened to them: instantaneous judgment (5:5-11)
   C. What they needed (and what we need)

One of my favorite moments in a recent NBA All-Star game happened during the pregame huddle. Coach Steve Kerr looked at all of the incredible talent on his team and announced, "I've got a great play planned for the first play. So one of you guys get it, and, like, throw it to one of the other guys. And then you throw it to someone else, and then you shoot it." The entire huddle laughed at his intentionally vague words. Normally, however, such a playful attitude doesn't exist inside a huddle. A coach has issues to address and plays to call. He must work to get everyone ready to cooperate effectively.

In Acts 4:32–5:11 Luke takes us inside the interior life of the church—inside the huddle.

Acts regularly shows us the church *scattered* on mission. Its work happens at a fast pace, like the pacing of a basketball game: the gospel spreads throughout Jerusalem, Judea, Samaria, to ends of the earth; the apostles preach, heal, plant churches, head to Rome. As we read about the church scattered, however, Luke occasionally calls a time out and allows us glimpses into how things looked inside the church *gathered*. This passage is one of those time-outs.

One of the pictures Luke provides here is wonderfully positive and encouraging (4:32-37); the other is terrifying and sobering (5:1-11).

These two stories are intimately, and no doubt strategically, tied together. Historically, Luke describes the actions of certain members of the church who lived during the same time period. Their stories are tied together grammatically. After telling the first story, he begins the next story with the word *but* (5:1). Both accounts describe the selling of property and the giving of an offering from the sales. Both stories also use the adjective "great": in the first story we read of "great grace" (4:33); in the next we read of "great fear" (5:5,11). Luke uses the two scenarios to highlight the kindness and severity of God at work in the church. As a whole, the two stories cooperate to illustrate the nature and importance of *unity*. Verse 32 describes the unity of the church. The first story highlights how unity is experienced, and the next shows how unity is endangered.

The Bible is filled with examples of marvelous togetherness and awful division within Christ's body. The psalmist expresses the blessing of unity in Psalm 133:

> *How good and pleasant it is when brothers live together in harmony!*
> *It is like fine oil on the head, running down on the beard,*
> *running down Aaron's beard onto his robes.*
> *It is like the dew of Hermon falling on the mountains of Zion.*
> *For there the LORD has appointed the blessing—life forevermore.*
> (Ps 133:1-3)

In my experience, it seems that the older godly saints get, the more important unity becomes to them. They value it more and more. They hate seeing anything threaten the unity of the church. Why? Because they realize that God is conforming us to the image of Christ, and the more we Christians look like Jesus, the more we will value one another and remain committed to the mission he has called us to fulfill. Jesus wants his people unified (cf. John 17).

These two passages help us understand and pursue Christian unity. Maintaining unity is not easy, but it's not complicated either (Azurdia, "The Simplicity of Unity").

How Unity Is Established: The Gospel
ACTS 4:32A

How many people comprise "the entire group"? Probably more than ten thousand. In verse 4 Luke mentioned five thousand *men*. Surely most of them were married.

How is it possible for ten thousand people to be unified? It's simple. They "believed" the gospel. Faith in Jesus united them. In verse 33 we read that the apostles kept preaching this message, and the people were in harmony around this most powerful unifier.

They had the same mind in that they understood what mattered. They were utterly committed to the same gospel of the risen Christ. They were one in heart, meaning that a great spirit of love permeated the church.

Therefore, we don't create unity. God establishes it. We maintain it, but we don't create it. God is redeeming a people. God's gospel brings people together in mind and heart.

The presence of such unity in Acts 4 is astonishing when you consider the backgrounds of these people. In 2:1-13 people from "every nation under heaven" were present. People from diverse lands and cultures believed in the risen Christ, and they enjoyed this God-established unity. This scene is a great reminder that unity doesn't mean *uniformity*. Diverse individuals were united in gospel belief. Our strongest source of unity, then, isn't our common affinities; it's our gospel identity. And the further we drift away from this ultimate unifier, the further we get away from the kind of countercultural, world-impacting, Christ-exalting unity Luke highlights.

How Unity Is Experienced: The Gospel
ACTS 4:32B-37

So how does our *established* unity become an *experienced* unity (Azurdia, "The Simplicity of Unity")? It's not difficult to see how the church in Acts 4 experienced such remarkable oneness: they were generous. Theirs was a sharing congregation.

When every member shares consistently, the church is united powerfully. We often think that unity will be experienced through our agreement on every minuscule doctrinal matter, on childhood educational philosophy, or even should we all share a political party. But it's possible to agree on every point yet have division in the church. The type of unity Luke describes begins with a common gospel identity and a radical practice of sharing. Every member shares a common way of life. They share one another's burdens and joys. They share their time and possessions. Let's consider four aspects of their sharing.

Extensive Sharing (4:32b)

Consider the wide-reaching nature of the church's generosity. First, Luke tells us *who* shared: everyone. "No one claimed" that anything belonged to him.

Luke also tells us *when* they shared: all the time—whenever anyone had a need (vv. 34-35). This concept of caring for the "needy" is taken straight from Deuteronomy 15. God wanted his people to be a generous people. The old community failed to deliver, but God creates a new people, empowered by the Spirit, fueled by a vision of the generosity of their Savior (2 Cor 8:9). They care for the needy with great grace. This kind of sharing spilled over to unbelievers well.

Luke tells us *what* they shared: everything. No one claimed that "any of his possessions" was his own. They held all of their possessions loosely.

We shouldn't try to make this more complicated than it is. I teach my kids about sharing all the time. We sometimes play "Do the Opposite Game." In it I assign role-playing activities that encourage them to do the opposite of what they typically want to do—give up a seat, take someone's dishes to the sink, say a kind word, or get a refill for a brother or sister. Frankly, I can't say that my attempt to teach my kids sharing in this way is working well. My point, though, is that I want them to think about how they treat others and to feel how difficult it is to be truly kind and generous so that they will begin to ask the Father to change their hearts.

Generosity is easy to understand but difficult to apply. We don't need further explanation of the concept; we need to better apply it. We can easily become like the lawyer with whom Jesus shared the good Samaritan parable. He wanted to exegete the word *neighbor* (Luke 10:29). Jesus just wanted him to embrace his neighbor. Christ's message in the parable serves as a warning that we must avoid following the pharisaical pattern of talking philosophically about topics like kindness and giving and sharing without practically applying what we say we believe about them. Frankly, we sometimes like to make things more complicated than they are not because we lack understanding but because we don't want to obey. Our talk is often a smoke screen for our lack of willingness to do what we know we can and should do. So let's pause and ask God to make us a generous people.

The type of generosity he wants to see in us requires not only a relinquishing of possessions but also sensitivity toward others. We must be involved in people's lives if we are to know when they have a need. A generous person is a relationally involved person.

Empowered Sharing (4:33)

Here we see another great example of the need for word-and-deed ministry. The apostles are declaring the gospel in preaching, and the church is displaying the gospel in generosity.

As the apostles continued to teach the church about the resurrection, individuals within the church learned that the resurrection power of Jesus resided in them. They gained a proper perspective on possessions as they pondered the resurrection. They could speak and give fearlessly because they were secure in the Father's love (cf. Luke 12:32; Rom 8:14-7).

Additionally, they were recipients of the undeserved favor of God. He delighted in blessing them and loosening their grip on material possessions. When God's grace is at work, people get generous. This reality makes you wonder about professing Christians who never give. Do they truly understand the gospel?

Extraordinary Sharing among the Affluent (4:34-35)

Wealthy people existed in the early church. The Bible does not say there were no rich people among the first Christians; rather, we read that "there was not a needy person" among them. Luke isn't describing communism here. He is talking about a group of generous people who are sensitive to the needs of others. No one went to bed hungry because they could prevent it; no one slept on the street; no one went without clothes. The members took care of one another, and the wealthy even sold property in order to ensure this reality.

If you are wealthy, you need to see it as both blessing and responsibility. God has gifted you, but you're accountable for what you do with the resources entrusted to you. Scripture doesn't teach that you should necessarily sell it all (unless Jesus tells you to!), but you must take passages like 1 Timothy 6:17-19 to heart:

> *Instruct those who are rich in the present age not to be arrogant or to set their hope on the uncertainty of wealth, but on God, who richly provides us with all things to enjoy. Instruct them to do what is good, to be rich in good works, to be generous and willing to share, storing up treasure for themselves as a good foundation for the coming age, so that they may take hold of what is truly life.*

The wealthy people mentioned in Acts 4 provide a wonderful example of what it looks like to embrace and apply this text.

Exemplified Sharing in Barnabas (4:36-37)

At this point in the chapter, we're introduced to one of Luke's heroes: Joseph. He gets mentioned twenty-three times in Acts! Religiously speaking, the man was a Levite. Nationally, he was a foreigner from "Cyprus." And his nickname, Barnabas, means "son of encouragement" or "son of exhortation." This nickname embodied his life and ministry remarkably well. Azurdia says, "His ministry became his moniker" ("The Simplicity of Unity").

If mature believers were to look at your life and give you a nickname based on their impressions, what would it be? For what are you known?

Later in Acts we read more about Barnabas. He invested in the lives of younger believers (9:26-30). He had a good eye and a glad heart (11:19-23). He encouraged believers to remain faithful to the Lord (11:23). He was humble and trustworthy (11:25-30; 13:1–14:28). He was patient with the imperfections of others (15:36-41; cf. Col 4:10; 2 Tim 4). But here in this passage, Barnabas's generosity is emphasized.

Barnabas, like the others, didn't have to sell a field and bring the proceeds to the apostles, but he chose to do just that. This act of generosity demonstrated how he loved Jesus and people more than stuff. The fact that he "laid it at the apostles' feet" displays submission, humility, and trust. He trusted the apostles to distribute it. He didn't want credit for how it was used. He wasn't interested in self-glorification but in God's glory.

Luke introduces him here because he stands in stark contrast to Ananias and Sapphira. In doing this, Luke is saying, Be like Barnabas, not like Ananias and his wife.

Churches couldn't make it without generous heroes like Barnabas. The church has been sustained, enriched, and blessed by unsung heroes throughout her history, by those who have given generously to kingdom causes. We need to honor such servants. And we need to encourage people to see the extraordinary impact of a faithful personal giving ministry. Just as some Christians have a lifetime of teaching ministry ahead of them, others are positioned to spend their lifetimes blessing others through financial giving.

May we be a people who look for ways to give generously, sacrificially, and gladly. May the truth of the resurrection and a deeper grasp of Christ's grace make us Barnabas-like servants. May such generosity lead to a wonderful experience of unity.

How Unity Is Endangered: Hypocrisy
ACTS 5:1-11

We must respect Luke as a historian. He doesn't ignore the faults of the early church. He's not writing a fairy tale about the figurative body of Christ. In Acts 5 we find the sad story that follows the previous beautiful one. This is a reminder that even in the most Spirit-filled congregations, the evil one is at work. Every gospel-preaching church will face opposition from the outside (4:1-31), and this story teaches how sinful actions create opposition on the inside, too.

While I could point out many lessons in this passage, Azurdia expresses its overarching idea succinctly: "A dangerous holiness is God's response to a determined hypocrisy" ("The Simplicity of Unity"). Indeed, here we read about the duplicity of Ananias, the complicity of Sapphira, and God's resulting, terrifying holiness.

What They Were: Determined Hypocrites (5:1-4)

Jesus called out Pharisees for their hypocrisy. They wanted to be known and praised for their righteous acts. Ananias and Sapphira exemplified that same spirit.

They were spiritual posers (vv. 1-2). Theirs was a sham holiness, a fake piety. Ananias and Sapphira were forced neither to sell a field nor to give all of the proceeds once property was sold. Doing either was totally voluntary. So what was the problem? Ananias apparently pretended to give more than he actually gave. They kept some of the proceeds, claiming to give it all.

They were praise seekers (vv. 1-2). These two wanted a reputation like Barnabas without having the compassion of Barnabas. Perhaps Ananias wanted a nickname too, a phrase that would make him sound important and that just might increase his popularity. Unfortunately, this same quest for the praise of people still infects the church today. Many live for the applause of the powerful. Others want to be on the inside with the leaders. Still others want admiration from members.

They were liars (vv. 3-4). The couple lied about their charity! And they did it together! The ease with which one can lie without considering the damaging ramifications on self and others demonstrates the sinful nature of humanity. Paul says that a symptom of one's sin nature is lying (e.g., Rom 3:13). This contrasts with God's nature, for it is impossible for God to lie (Titus 1:2). And God calls his people to be a people of integrity. He despises lying (Prov 6:16-18).

The reason the judgment on these two people seems so outrageous to some is simple. Few understand how serious lying really is. Peter says the pair lied to God (implying the deity of the Holy Spirit). That concept is terrifying! It suggests that God takes the untruths we tell as personal offenses. When people don't value the holiness of God, they minimize sin. And when they do that, they devalue the cross, where Jesus traded places with liars.

They were greedy (v. 3). Peter says that Ananias and Sapphira "kept back" part of the proceeds. The verb used here means "to pilfer" or "to embezzle." The same rare verb occurs in the Greek version of Joshua 7:1-26, in the story of Achan, which Luke would have known. The stories of Achan and Ananias are similar in multiple ways, including in the fact that the progress of the mission central to each story gets interrupted because of sin inside the camp. The stories of Achan, Ananias, Judas, the rich young ruler, and millions more testify to the devastating nature of greed. *It must have no place within the church.*

*They were deceivers (v. 4).*These two planned what they did. How foolish to think that no one knows about sinful plotting. God always knows what is done and said in secret; we can't hide anything from him.

They were Satan's instruments (v. 3). Whatever we make of Peter's question about Satan filling Ananias's heart, we must affirm the real influence of Satan. The devil destroys through love of money, falsehood, and hypocrisy. He tempts people to act unwisely and godlessly. He tempts people to think that sin is no big deal. But make no mistake: his ultimate goal in all of this is to destroy people and the church. Jesus told Peter, "Simon, Simon, look out. Satan has asked to sift you like wheat" (Luke 22:31).

They were Spirit grievers (vv. 3-4). Ananias and his wife lied to the Holy Spirit. The Spirit is not a force but a person who can be grieved. One grieves the Spirit when he or she lies, deceives, steals, and participates in anything that is contrary to his holy nature.

What Happened to Them: Instantaneous Judgment (5:5-11)

As a consequence of this couple's massive offense, judgment fell. It came from God, not Peter. In this scene Peter simply does what brothers and sisters do: he holds these professing believers accountable. Some argue that they died of heart attacks or some other common cause, but in any case the resulting spirit of fear that came upon everyone as well as the unceremonious burial they were given indicate that the people recognized what happened to these two as divine judgment.

But wasn't this instantaneous judgment extreme? Only if you minimize the offense by minimizing the One against whom the sin was committed. God had been belittled by the actions of these two, and his church was facing a satanic assault made apparent by their deeds. God takes these things seriously. Paul spoke about God's terrifying judgment as people took the Lord's Supper impurely (1 Cor 11:28-30). That account wasn't as dramatic as this one, but what happened in that case was real and serious, too.

This story should make us repent and say, "God have mercy on us! Make us like Barnabas, not like Ananias." And, "Thank you Lord for your amazing patience with us. Grant us grace to avoid hypocrisy and to pursue integrity."

In verses 7-10 Peter approaches Sapphira about her own involvement in the matter. The results of that meeting were the same. She shared in her husband's conspiracy and would share in her husband's fate. Sometimes it's sinful for a wife to submit to her husband; her loyalty first belongs to God. She should not have gone along with Ananias's devilish plan.

What They Needed (and What We Need)

Obviously, Ananias and Sapphira needed *a healthy fear of the Lord*. The God of all the earth demands respect. So, as we consider this passage, we shouldn't think, *God would never do that to me*. Rather, we need to remember that "God is not mocked" (Gal 6:7). Just ask Uzzah, Nadab and Abihu, King Uzziah, the exodus generation, and the powerful people in Revelation who want the rocks to fall on them because their fear of the King's judgment is so extreme. Proverbs teaches us that the fear of God is the beginning of wisdom (Prov 1:7). If you don't stand in awe of God, you are unwise. Destruction will come eventually.

Sapphira and Ananias also needed *the application of the gospel*. They either didn't understand the gospel or had not allowed it to work down deep in their hearts. The gospel frees us from addictions to self and stuff. It frees us from pretending. It frees us from wanting praise from people. It frees us from wanting to lie, steal, and deceive. It makes us honest and generous. It sets our minds on the glory that is to be revealed. Let this story remind you of how badly you need to understand the gospel of grace and your identity in Christ.

Finally, this couple needed to live *in repentance*. We must learn from their mistake. When we are aware of personal sins, we must repent of them. In truth we are all guilty of hypocrisy, but as soon as we recognize it, we must repent. This couple had been living in known rebellion and sin. It appears they were OK with their hypocrisy.

This story calls the church to repent while there's time. God does extend grace. The next story, in fact, shows how the church continued to increase and multiply in spite of this scene. God purified his church for the good of others who would believe, offering even more grace along the way. This truth teaches believers to repent and go and sin no more by the grace of God. It's calling us to pursue the kind of existence outlined in 4:32-37 instead of 5:1-11.

May God make us a people known for gospel-saturated generosity, not evil hypocrisy.

Reflect and Discuss

1. What's the difference between Christian unity and other forms of unity?
2. In what ways have you seen others practice generosity in your congregation? Explain the impact of such giving.
3. What keeps people from being radically generous?
4. How is the concept of grace tied to generosity?
5. What does the resurrection have to do with generosity?
6. Identify a needy person who could use your help this week. Choose to act generously.
7. How does the story of Ananias and Sapphira challenge you?
8. What does the story of Ananias and Sapphira teach about hypocrisy?
9. What does the story of Ananias and Sapphira teach about the need for repentance?
10. Take a moment to pray for unity in your own local congregation in view of these passages.

Ministry and Hostility

ACTS 5:12-42

Main Idea: Faithful gospel ministry results in both opposition and blessing.

I.   Gospel Ministry Enriches the Poor in Spirit (5:12-16).
II. Gospel Ministry Enrages the Prideful (5:17-40).
III. Gospel Ministry Energizes the Minister(s) (5:41-42).

As we journey through the book of Acts, we must remember that we're learning about our ongoing history as a church. Even today we deal with the same types of issues our brothers and sisters faced in the first century AD. This week, in fact, I received an e-mail from one of our missionaries. It says,

> This past month I had the opportunity to teach and train
> a number of different groups, one of which was a group
> of Muslim-background believers (MBB). This is a group of
> brothers who are regularly leading others to faith in Christ,
> but have been beaten and persecuted because of it. Hearing
> their stories was both convicting and encouraging.

Experiences of suffering like those we read about in Acts 5 continue today. True accounts of faithfulness in spite of it are indeed both convicting and encouraging.

In the previous passage the church faced opposition from the inside. In this passage the church receives opposition from the outside. Satan enjoys using both tactics. He hates gospel-centered ministry because he knows gospel ministry brings phenomenal blessing and kingdom expansion.

If you've never experienced opposition to your ministry—whether you teach Sunday school or serve Jesus through your career—then it could be there is something wrong with your approach. I say this because opposition will inevitably come when we walk in the light in a dark world. We will encounter hostility when we follow Jesus wholeheartedly.

Impactful gospel ministry involves continuing the pattern of Jesus's ministry, which involved words and deeds. The apostles' actions follow this pattern in verses 12-42. And as they minister, persecution intensifies. At this point it impacts all of the apostles, and their opponents' tactics intensify from mere threats against the believers to flogging them (cf. Acts 3). The persecution continues to escalate until someone is actually martyred in Acts 7.

This text needs focused consideration because there is a growing hostility to gospel ministry around the world. According to D. A. Carson, more people have been martyred for following Christ in the last century than in all of the first nineteen hundred years of the church's history (*For the Love of God*, January 10). And it's a spreading problem. A growing hostility against the people of God is happening even right here in the States. At this point it often expresses itself in the forms of *intimidation, threats,* and an increased level of *negativity* toward anything Christian. Recently the following appeared in the "Ask Amy" column of the *Chicago Tribune*:

> DEAR AMY: I'm curious to know what you think of someone asking a semi-stranger, "What church do you go to?" or, even worse, "Do you go to church?" It seems as intrusive as asking "How much do you weigh?" or "How much money do you make?" or "Are your kids gay or straight?" Maybe churches today are trying to grow their memberships, but the way I was raised, someone's personal relationship with God was PERSONAL. I know people like to categorize, but to me the question is rude. Am I just out of step?—Offended ("Ask Amy: Reader finds faith queries offensive").

If you decide to live out your faith publicly, then prepare for similar responses to your attempts to share it.

Of course, the Christian faith is *not* a private faith. Remember, Jesus was crucified publicly—for all to see. His humiliation could not have been more complete were his execution carried out in the middle of a shopping mall during the holiday season. And after he rose, showing himself to many witnesses, he then commissioned the church to spread his fame publicly. And that is just what the early believers are doing in the first chapters of Acts.

This, we see, results in hostility. But don't miss the other side of the matter. Public faith blesses many. While gospel ministry will anger some, it also has power to bless others and to lift up those doing it. So let's take a look at these three effects of gospel ministry.

Gospel Ministry Enriches the Poor in Spirit
ACTS 5:12-16

Who receives the blessings of gospel ministry? Those who know they need it. For those who know they need a King come the benefits of embracing the good news. In this passage Luke tells us about such a group of people. Compare this text with the ministry of Jesus:

> *Now Jesus began to go all over Galilee, teaching in their synagogues, preaching the good news of the kingdom, and healing every disease and sickness among the people. Then the news about him spread throughout Syria. So they brought to him all those who were afflicted, those suffering from various diseases and intense pains, the demon-possessed, the epileptics, and the paralytics. And he healed them. Large crowds followed him from Galilee, the Decapolis, Jerusalem, Judea, and beyond the Jordan.* (Matt 4:23-25)

Immediately after this account in Matthew, Jesus begins the Sermon on the Mount, saying, "Blessed are the poor in spirit, for the kingdom of heaven is theirs" (Matt 5:3). So who received the benefits of Jesus's grace and power? Those who were humble, poor, and desperate.

The same sort of dynamic is happening here in Acts 5. The humble are being *saved* (v. 14). While many pulled back from the message, multitudes were drawn to Christ by the power and love of the church (v. 13). The humble are being *loved*. They were "all together" (vv. 12). They shared life together. They cared for people together.

Additionally, the humble are being *healed* (vv. 15-16). The poor in spirit desperately seek physical restoration and receive it. While we should recognize the unique nature of the apostles' ministry, we must still affirm that God heals people even today (cf. Jas 5:14-16), sometimes through medical assistance. But occasionally Jesus decides to intervene, giving the world a clear picture about what life will be like in his coming kingdom. Ultimately, we know that prayers for the healing of those who love Christ are always answered with a "yes, soon" or a "yes, later" (at the resurrection).

Finally, the humble are being delivered (v. 16). Those with unclean spirits receive spiritual freedom. What an awesome reminder of the power of the gospel: no evil power is a match for it.

Do you approach Christ as one poor in spirit? That's an important question because we must come to Jesus helpless and in need of grace.

We can't approach Jesus in a "middle class spirit," as if we could take care of ourselves without him but are nonetheless hoping to ensure his assistance as a backup plan. We come poor in spirit, or we don't come at all. Sadly, many won't turn to Jesus because they are "rich in spirit," that is, they're arrogant (see the next section). While a person can be rich in wealth and still become a Christian, Jesus says that's a hard thing to do (e.g., Matt 19:24). Why? Because the wealthy are rarely desperate. Christianity has frequently exploded among those living on the fringes of society because the marginalized generally admit great need and reach for the Savior. The gospel enriches the poor in spirit.

The apostles didn't develop a business plan or a military strategy that started with all the influential people, expecting the gospel movement to trickle down to everyone else. They followed a compassion strategy like Jesus modeled in his ministry (Matt 9:35-38). Thus, the church had a remarkable ministry to the marginalized. Its initial impact, in fact, was made on the social fringes. Jesus's first convert in Gentile territory was a man possessed by demons (Mark 5:1-20)!

As you have opportunities to minister to the poor, the hurting, the enslaved, or the sick in your community, take them. As you have opportunities to minister to such groups among the nations, step up. You will enrich the poor in spirit, you will reflect the love of Jesus, and you will glorify our merciful Father in heaven.

We must be committed to reaching everyone with the gospel message. Some people will respond to it in faith! So are you inviting people to make Jesus Lord of their lives? Are you moved to feed, clothe, and teach the multitudes who have no shepherd? Don't fear the small percentage of people who respond negatively to public proclamations and demonstrations of faith. While we shouldn't expect 100-percent acceptance of the message Jesus entrusted to us, we must act in the knowledge that some will respond in faith. Through remaining faithful to our mission, we give them the chance to do just that.

Gospel Ministry Enrages the Prideful
ACTS 5:17-40

What keeps people from the gospel? Pride. Some are handicapped by intellectual pride: the gospel is too foolish to believe. Others are hindered by social pride: they don't want to risk public alienation or a loss of power for believing. Others get tangled in family pride: they

recognize that following Jesus may damage relationships with unbelieving family members or bring shame to the family name. At this point
in Acts, we meet a group of prideful individuals exhibiting a mixture
of all three pride issues. As a result, the apostles' ministry "enraged"
them (v. 33).

The high priest and the Sadducees loved power. So as the apostles
gain popularity and influence, this group gets "filled with jealousy,"
arrests the apostles, and puts them in prison (vv. 17-18).

The Sadducees were the theological liberals of the first century.
They didn't believe in miracles like the resurrection or in the existence
of angels. That's why they were sad, you see? The Sadducees' disbelief
makes it a bit ironic that God sends an angel to miraculously free the
apostles in verse 19. The Sadducees were a large part of the ruling elite,
the Sanhedrin. They were wonderful at politics. They worked to keep
the Romans and the Jews happy.

Here this group is filled with jealous anger because their beliefs are
being challenged and they are losing power. They hated the relentless
testimony of the apostles, who kept telling them they were doubly guilty
of crucifying Jesus. But we shouldn't miss another obvious reason why
these men are so frustrated in this scene. Without even realizing it, they
are fighting against the very purpose for which the universe was created,
the exaltation of Jesus (Sandy Wilson, "Counted Worthy"). How foolish
it is to oppose the King!

Let's beware of jealousy. It leads to all sorts of other sins. And let's
not be surprised when others are filled with it and attack us as believers.

If you're wondering what the apostles did to create such outrage
among the religious leaders, here's the answer: they healed people!
They loved people! They shared the gospel with people. The religious
leaders want all of this to stop. Does that mean they wanted more people
to be sick or demon possessed? No. But they certainly didn't want their
own lack of power to grow more evident.

Even in our modern world, this type of reaction happens all the
time. Many hostile unbelievers attack mercy-minded Christian organizations like orphan-care ministries and crisis pregnancy centers. Why?
For many of the same reasons. Many hate the message and motives of
these organizations. And many have political agendas that clash with
our kingdom agenda. Some rail against these institutions because they
are fighting internally against the purpose of the universe, and that
inevitably leads people to say and do outrageous things. So be prepared.
Opposition often follows those who do good (1 Pet 4:12-19).

In verses 19-20 we see what happens to the apostles. An angel opens the door and tells the apostles to resume preaching in the temple (v. 20). This instruction is kind of funny because it was precisely that act that caused them to get put into prison in the first place. Yet, in obedience, the apostles offer people the words of life. God frees them physically in order to free others spiritually.

These rulers are using bully tactics, and we will encounter bullies too. But take comfort here. God may or may not send an angel to free you from prison should you find yourself incarcerated wrongly, but he is always with you. He does know the full truth. We don't enter the Christian mission alone. We have the power of God in us. The King of glory is for us.

So, what happened after the miraculous deliverance? In verses 21-23 the officers say something like this: "I've got good news and bad news. The doors were locked, the guards were in place, but the prisoners . . . weren't there!" The response of the council sounded like this: "We're totally baffled by what you're telling us" (v. 24, paraphrased). When someone reports the shocking news that the former prisoners are now teaching in public, the council changes tactics and brings them in "without force" so as not to upset the people.

They accuse the apostles of violating their command not to teach in the name of Jesus. They also say the apostles are making the council look bad (v. 28). You have to love the apostles' answer in verses 29-32. It involves civil disobedience and gospel opportunity.

God has set up authorities, and obeying authorities is part of the Christian walk. God's institutions include family, church, and state. In the case of the last, Peter himself would write, "Honor the emperor" (1 Pet 2:17; cf. Mark 12:13-17; Rom 13:1-2; Titus 3:1). The biblical writers consistently teach that we must *recognize* authorities as being established by God. We must respect them. (In Acts, the court manners of Peter and Paul are above reproach.) And we must *submit* to the authorities, providing they do not contradict God's Word. Ultimately, we *submit* to the state out of submission to Jesus (1 Pet 2:13). This act includes obeying things like speed limits and stop signs, wearing seat belts, paying income taxes, adhering to building codes, and renewing our fishing licenses out of reverence for Jesus, for we don't have two masters (Thomas, *Acts*, 134–35). But there are times when a Christian cannot obey the state, and should not.

I'm not suggesting we should rebel *when we simply dislike a law* that makes us uncomfortable or *because we don't like the leaders*. I'm talking about acting wisely on occasions in which the state forbids what God requires or sanctions what God forbids. Going against the state, of course, may lead to consequences. But many biblical examples of holy disobedience, as evidenced by the Hebrew midwives, Daniel, and Esther, remind us that the cost is worth the sacrifice (Thomas, *Acts*, 134–35).

Here in Acts 5 the apostles choose civil disobedience for an obvious reason: they can't stop preaching the gospel. Nevertheless, the apostles don't respond to the authorities with hate speech or violent demonstrations. They simply keep declaring the good news as people of the cross should.

Notice that Peter and the apostles also take advantage of every *gospel opportunity*. They see confrontation before the council as an occasion to proclaim a summary of the gospel (cf. Luke 21:12-19). They use it to remind the audience of Jesus's death, resurrection, exaltation, and trail-blazing work (vv. 30-31a). They remind them that Jesus came, and people need to repent to receive forgiveness. They point out that they saw Jesus and that now his Spirit testifies with them (vv. 31b-32).

The apostles are consumed with Jesus. They take every opportunity to make Christ known. So don't waste your own Sanhedrin moment! When you have someone's ear—even in the face of persecution—give the truth. That's all the apostles are doing. They didn't set out to create conflict; they set out to do ministry. When the Lord gives you opportunities to bear witness, take them (cf. Col 4:4-5). Remember that he is with you and that the gospel is the power of God unto salvation (cf. Matt 28:18-20; Rom 1:16).

In Acts 5:33-34 the enraged group finally receives some common sense wisdom from a leading Pharisee, Gamaliel (cf. 22:3). Gamaliel uses a pragmatic argument (vv. 35-39). While the men found Gamaliel's wisdom compelling, it didn't stop the religious leaders from assaulting the apostles (v. 40).

Christians have faced this type of hostility throughout church history. Evil leaders have beaten and tortured Christians. Illustrations of this sad fact abound from the days of Nero to the reign of ISIS. But no one can ultimately stop the mission of the King.

Gospel Ministry Energizes the Minister(s)
ACTS 5:41-42

How do the apostles respond to the threats and the flogging? Two things happen: (1) They rejoice because they're counted worthy to suffer dishonor for the name of Jesus; (2) they don't stop preaching the gospel. Remarkably, the persecution *energizes* the apostles!

Ministry done by the power of the Spirit and focused on the gospel brings a crazy sense of joy and energy to the person ministering. Why do Christians report feeling blessed by going to impoverished countries to love people? Why is it that after a gospel-centered conversation, a Christian's downcast spirit gets rejuvenated? It's because gospel ministry actually lifts us up. Passionate gospel-centered ministry energizes us on a personal level, and reports of it will often energize others in the church too.

This text is important in understanding a New Testament theology of suffering for the gospel. D. A. Carson reminds us of six related aspects of such suffering:

- Jesus himself connects his suffering with our suffering. He does this fundamentally by connecting his cross with our taking up of the cross (Matt 16:24-28; cf. John 15:18-25).
- This suffering for Jesus's sake presupposes that the world is evil.
- This suffering connects us with genuine believers across the ages (Matt 5:10-12).
- Paul teaches us that suffering for the gospel is part of our Christian calling. "For it has been granted to you on Christ's behalf not only to believe in him, but also to suffer for him," he tells the church in Philippi (Phil 1:29).
- Paul goes on to say that this suffering is tied to experiencing Christ's resurrection power (Phil 3:10-11).
- Christian suffering is tied to the dissemination of the gospel, and when suffering for gospel proclamation, the evangelists often experience great joy. ("Rejoice to Suffer for the Name")

Revelation 12:11-12 reminds me of Acts 5. It says,

> *They conquered him by the blood of the Lamb and by the word of their testimony; for they did not love their lives to the point of death. Therefore rejoice, you heavens, and you who dwell in them! Woe to the earth and the sea, because the devil has come down to you with great fury, because he knows his time is short.*

How did those in the passage overcome the rage of the evil one? By the blood of the Lamb and by the word of their testimony. The former involves throwing back to the accuser the fact that Christ, the Lamb, has taken our place. Christ's blood has cleansed us. The latter involves bearing witness—that is, talking about the gospel all the time. And John adds one more thing in this verse that I don't want us to miss: They didn't love their lives so much to shrink from death! All of this is found here in Acts 5, where we observe these relentless witnesses who follow the Calvary Road, loving Christ more than comfort, more than life.

Peter was present when Jesus taught about persecution in the Sermon on the Mount. He was there in Caesarea Philippi when Jesus taught about the calling to take up the cross. Peter listened to Jesus teach about the reality of people persecuting the servants of the Master (John 15:20). But now in Acts 5, Peter and his friends experience Jesus's teaching. Carson says,

> It is almost as if the apostles were, dare I say it, *relieved*. They had been given astonishing authority but instead of strutting around talking about their power, they were a little worried that they had not suffered yet. . . . Now they've been good and flogged, and they smile because they've been counted worthy to suffer for the name. ("Rejoice to Suffer for the Name")

What comfort Acts 5 must be to the suffering church in North Korea, in Somalia, in Iraq, in Syria, in Sudan, in China, and in so many other places that remain hostile to the gospel. And it should also be of great encouragement to those who continue to be mocked, shunned, intimidated, and shamed here in the West. If you find yourself suffering as a Christian, rejoice! You're in good company.

Do you want real Christian joy? Then follow the Acts model. Be compassionate toward the needy. Be bold in your Christian witness. Be filled with integrity, respect, and humility before people. You will face opposition, and you will be filled with joy—not just now but even billions of years from now. You will never regret having suffered for the Name.

Christians can take a beating with joy because Jesus took the ultimate beating for us, even rising from the dead for us. One day the mighty will cower at his terrifying justice. So align yourself with this King, and you too can rejoice.

Reflect and Discuss

1. What does it mean to come to Jesus as one "poor in spirit"?
2. How are you currently ministering to those in need?
3. What can we learn about gospel ministry from the apostles here in Acts 5?

4. Why should we expect opposition when we do faithful gospel ministry?
5. How do some people try to intimidate Christians today?
6. What does this passage teach about civil disobedience?
7. What does this text teach about being ready to present the gospel at all times?
8. Why does the act of doing gospel ministry bring joy?
9. What does this passage teach about God's sovereignty over persecution?
10. Take a moment to pray for the persecuted church around the world.

Growing Pains

ACTS 6:1-7

Main Idea: In this inside look at the early church, Luke describes the blessings and the challenges faced by the rapidly growing body of Christ in Jerusalem.

I. **We Should Celebrate Gospel-Centered Church Growth (6:1a,7).**
II. **We Should Expect Problems when the Church Grows (6:1-7).**
   A. Protecting the unity of the church (6:1)
   B. Keeping up with the number of legitimate needs (6:1,7)
   C. Overcoming overburdened leadership (6:2)
   D. Avoiding and handling criticism (6:3)
   E. Keeping ministerial priorities in order (6:4)
   F. Sharing the ministry (6:5-6)
   G. Advancing the mission while managing people (6:7)
III. **We Should Protect Biblical Priorities, Make Wise Adjustments, and Share the Ministry—All in a Spirit of Love (6:2-6).**
IV. **We Should See Growth Problems as Opportunities for More Gospel-Centered Growth (6:7).**

In the previous chapter we covered a lot of verses in a moving story of persecution. Here we will consider just seven verses in a story that reminds me of a middle school cafeteria drama! I titled this passage "Growing Pains" not because I have a particular attraction to Kirk Cameron, who played Mike Sever in the comedy of yesteryear, but because growth created the drama of Acts 6.

Perhaps a better illustration regarding growing pains involves Anthony Davis, the 6'11" All-Star power forward for the New Orleans Pelicans. When Davis was in high school, he grew from 6'2" to 6'10" between his sophomore and senior years—that's eight inches in eighteen months! When he was 6'2", he had one scholarship offer from Cleveland State University. By his senior year he was the number one high school player in the nation. His growth spurt was helpful, but it created challenges. Davis's parents had to buy him new clothes constantly. Davis had to learn how to play a different position. He had to learn how to rebound, block shots, and post up. His heroes shifted from small guards to big men.

In Acts 6 Luke describes the blessings and the challenges facing the rapidly growing body of Christ in Jerusalem. We see this practical truth illustrated: Gospel growth always brings blessing, problems, and opportunities. Just look at the first verse of Acts 6. The good news? The church is growing! The bad news? The people are complaining! Sound familiar? Luke goes on to describe how the early church handled growth problems and continued to advance the mission. Four lessons are related to these growing pains.

We Should Celebrate Gospel-Centered Church Growth
ACTS 6:1A,7

People react to church growth differently. Some find it easy to celebrate because their ministries are aiming for just this: more and more people. Others, however, have a negative opinion of growth because many are obsessed with it, and some feel many will sacrifice core principles in order to welcome growth. This passage helps us understand church growth sensibly.

The early church experienced a particular type of growth here, and it's this type of growth that must be sought: gospel-centered growth. It came as a result of passionate gospel preaching and compassionate ministry. There were no gimmicks behind it. The apostles weren't offering watered-down sermons. They weren't handing out gift bags. Yet the Lord blessed the church with a multitude of converts. This reminds us that while today's congregations can expand a *crowd* in a variety of ways, a *church is built only* through people embracing the gospel.

Let's make sure we keep the gospel primary. In 5:42 the church kept teaching and preaching Christ *every day*. If this is happening, and your congregation is growing, then rejoice.

Church-growth critics often complain, "You guys are all about the numbers." They are skeptical of growth because they associate a big church with an unfaithful church. But Luke doesn't have this aversion to seeing new faces joining the church. Luke, in fact, brackets the narrative with the subject of increasing numbers. In verse 1 he says, "Increasing in numbers"; in verse 7 he says, "Increased greatly in number."

So, is Luke all about the numbers? No. Dr. Luke counted people because people count. People matter to God, and they should matter to us. We should long to reach more and more people. And by the way, we have a book of the Bible called *Numbers*! Further, no good parent would dare say, "We're going on a weeklong trip, but we aren't going to count the kids before we get on the plane or in the car because I don't want to be all about the numbers!" People actually appreciate being counted (Driscoll, "Empowered by the Spirit to Fail")!

Not all growth, however, is good. One can be all about building a crowd or one's own kingdom. That's why we must reject church-growth idolatry. But when the gospel is front and center, we must rejoice when the church grows.

Luke has at least ten summary statements in which he mentions the growth of the church:

- *So those who accepted his message were baptized, and that day about three thousand people were added to them.* (2:41)
- *Every day the Lord added to their number those who were being saved.* (2:47)
- *But many of those who heard the message believed, and the number of the men came to about five thousand.* (4:4)
- *Believers were added to the Lord in increasing numbers—multitudes of both men and women.* (5:14)
- *So the church throughout all Judea, Galilee, and Samaria had peace and was strengthened. Living in the fear of the Lord and encouraged by the Holy Spirit, it increased in numbers.* (9:31)
- *The word of the Lord spread through the whole [Pisidian] region.* (13:49) (We should desire this type of multiplication also: planting new churches.)
- *So the churches were strengthened in the faith and grew daily in numbers [in the Galatian region].* (16:5)
- *In this way the word of the Lord flourished and prevailed [in Ephesus].* (19:20)
- *You see, brother, how many thousands of Jews there are who have believed.* (21:20)

Luke clearly sees this expansion as a good thing. By Acts 6 there could have been somewhere around twenty thousand people within the body of Christ! This harvest is the result of God's amazing grace, and this growth provides a foretaste of the great ingathering of the nations around the throne that is promised in Revelation 7:9. Jesus loves good growth. We should too.

We should desire to see thousands saved. What a blessing it would be to hear, "We don't have any more room in the second service because of all these Muslim converts who are joining us!"

We Should Expect Problems When the Church Grows
ACTS 6:1-7

Allow me to put Acts 6 in proper perspective for understanding our own problems in local churches. Remember Jesus's parable of the net (Matt 13:47-50)? It illustrates that debris and bad fish come when many fish are caught. This is a reminder that not all growth is *pure* growth (Piper, "Serving Widows, Preaching the Word, and Winning Priests"). In the book of Acts, both true converts and debris, or pretenders, are present within the gathered church—as in the case of Ananias and Sapphira (5:1-11) and Simon the magician (8:9-25). Thus, we should expect mess within a catch, knowing that the Lord will sort true believers from false at a later time (cf. Matt 13:24-30).

The early church dealt not only with debris but also with human limitations. It is a mistake to romanticize (or idealize) the church in Acts. Is it a model church? Yes. Is it a perfect church? Absolutely not! Did the early church have a lot of wins? Yes! Did it have any failures? Yes. In fact, we see one of them right here. The people were failing to attend to the needs of widows, which is a big deal according to the Bible. They were failing to live out James 1:27.

Though I do not excuse the church's failure on this point, I do find encouragement in the church's struggle here. It reminds me that even good churches fail at some things, at least temporarily. The Acts church was a good church. Typical complaints lodged against modern church leaders simply wouldn't work in its case. After all, the twelve apostles were leading based on their conversations with Jesus. The men were so in tune with the Spirit that Peter's shadow was able to convey Christ's healing power. And these guys could never be charged with not preaching enough Bible. Some of these guys actually wrote it (Driscoll, "Empowered")! Nonetheless, it wasn't a perfect church.

We must understand that failure isn't always the result of sin. Sometimes failure is simply due to human limitations. Did the apostles not care for widows? Of course they did—they did as much as they were able! But these men were human, and they were few.

Both of these reminders—that a catch of fish will bring a mess, and that even good churches fail—should make us adjust our expectations. We must kill our wishes about church, choosing to be realistic about human limitations and knowing we will face challenges. There will be messes to clean up as we serve Christ in a broken world. So let's face these realities with grace toward others and confidence that Jesus is building his church in spite of imperfections.

What were these apostles trying to deal with exactly? Seven problems.

Protecting the Unity of the Church (6:1)

The early church's unity was threatened for many reasons. For starters, its leaders were dealing with a mixture of injustice and sinful responses to it. The Greek-speaking widows were *complaining*, something Paul tells the churches to avoid (1 Cor 10:10; Phil 2:14). While they had a right to be bothered by being neglected in the distribution of food, they shouldn't have been complaining *against* the Hebrew widows. They should have taken the matter to the leaders. This is a good reminder that there will be times when people in the church will be justifiably offended, and they won't always respond appropriately.

Maintaining unity involved not only dealing with injustice and sin but also addressing cultural tensions. The Hebrew-speaking widows were the purists. The Greek-speaking widows previously lived outside Jerusalem, some of them for years. Their families could have been carried away in previous exiles. Over time, although they were Jews, they adopted the language of commerce. They had their own Greek-speaking synagogue (v. 9). The Pharisees despised the Greek-speaking Jews. They were looked on as dirty, as second-class citizens. So, as many of these widows moved back to Jerusalem in their twilight years and eventually lost their husbands, they needed care. When many of them converted, they were suddenly part of the same church that included many Hebrew widows. It's no wonder, then, that tension rose. Once one group felt neglected, bad feelings and division followed—that was, after all, the norm. The apostles had their hands full in maintaining unity amid such cultural drama.

Keeping Up with the Number of Legitimate Needs (6:1,7)

It would be a tremendous challenge simply to catalog the needs of twenty thousand people and numerous widows. In the early days the church may have had ten or twenty widows, which would have made it possible for Peter to say, "Hey, I'll swing by Esther's house and see if she needs anything." Or John could've said, "I have to get some groceries for my family anyway, so I'll go by Ruth's place and make sure she has supplies for the next week." While it's likely things in the church were more organized than that, taking care of people in the early days didn't require the same level of attention that it does by this point in Acts 6.

There was simply no way twelve apostles lacking access to Microsoft Excel could keep up with everything.

The number of Christ followers "was increasing" in verse 1, and the number expands "greatly" in verse 7. That means more administrating and readjusting were needed. Every leader of a growing organization or church knows how difficult it is simply to keep up with everything and to devise new ways to handle new problems.

Overcoming Overburdened Leadership (6:2)

In 6:2 the apostles admit, "We can't do it all." They don't have the time, and they can't give up prayer and preaching, though they know the work needs to get done. Their situation sounds like that of Moses, who was given sound advice on the importance of sharing the leadership burden:

> "What you're doing is not good," Moses's father-in-law said to him.
> "You will certainly wear out both yourself and these people who are
> with you, because the task is too heavy for you. You can't do it alone.
> Now listen to me; I will give you some advice, and God be with you.
> You be the one to represent the people before God and bring their cases
> to him. Instruct them about the statutes and laws, and teach them
> the way to live and what they must do. But you should select from all
> the people able men, God-fearing, trustworthy, and hating dishonest
> profit. Place them over the people as commanders of thousands,
> hundreds, fifties, and tens. They should judge the people at all times.
> Then they can bring you every major case but judge every minor case
> themselves. In this way you will lighten your load, and they will bear
> it with you. If you do this, and God so directs you, you will be able
> to endure, and also all these people will be able to go home satisfied."
> (Exod 18:17-23)

Moses listened to this advice, and shared ministry proved successful. That sounds a lot like Acts 6.

Avoiding and Handling Criticism (6:3)

Do you think everyone liked it when the apostles said they weren't going to personally distribute resources to the widows any longer, instead delegating the task to seven others? I doubt it! You can imagine a widow asking, "Who are you? Niconor? Where's Peter? I want his shadow to fall on me! I'm not feeling well." I'm sure the temptation to be critical of the new plan was present. Yet the people needed to avoid such complaining.

And the apostles needed to handle people's various reactions to this hard decision wisely and graciously. That started with having the people choose the men, which "pleased" them (v. 5).

Keeping Ministerial Priorities in Order (6:4)

The apostles declare that they will remain *devoted* to prayer and the ministry of the Word. They don't want to be distracted. In their concerns is a challenge for everyone in ministry—prioritizing the most important things. It's easy to busily run through an entire week doing good deeds while failing to pray one time.

Sharing the Ministry (6:5-6)

The apostles realize they are one body with many parts, so they propose a solution. The congregation selects the group, the apostles lay hands on them, and they share in the work of taking over this important task. This is a reminder that even modern leaders must wisely delegate tasks and deploy people to meet needs.

Advancing the Mission While Managing People (6:7)

Both management and mission are important. Some ministers don't like management or administration, but this can lead to problems since Paul says in 1 Timothy 3 that a pastor must *manage* the household of God. Pastoring involves management, but leaders within the church must be concerned about mission also. Some ministers are no good at this priority. They just rearrange the chairs on a sinking *Titanic.* While they are good at management, they aren't leading the church to reach unbelievers.

Here in verse 7 we see that after a management plan was created to care for widows, the church continued to grow in mission outreach. This should be our goal: to do compassionate and efficient management while aggressively advancing the gospel in our city and among the nations.

We Should Protect Biblical Priorities, Make Wise Adjustments, and Share the Ministry—All in a Spirit of Love
ACTS 6:2-6

When Christians face conflict, we can't just go with our gut instincts or follow traditions. We have to go to the Bible first. We must understand biblical priorities. The apostles' actions teach us this truth. After surveying the widows' problem, they rule two things out immediately: "We can't stop *praying* and *preaching.*"

Prayer is at the heart of pastoral ministry. Everything begins and ends with prayer. Yet it's the easiest thing to sacrifice. That's why many want to multitask their prayer lives. But we need to remember that Jesus got alone on multiple occasions to spend focused time with the Father. And if anyone could multitask his prayer life, it was Jesus. Surely he could do the "pray as you go" approach to ministry better than anyone, yet he sought solitude. Luke records three specific examples of Jesus withdrawing from the crowds in order to commune with the Father (Luke 5:16; 6:12; 9:18). The apostles followed the pattern of Jesus. They understood that ministry flows from one's communion with God. They wouldn't neglect that which gives life to ministry.

Spurgeon had this to say about prayerlessness in ministry:

> Of course the preacher is above all others distinguished as a man of prayer. . . . The minister who does not earnestly pray over his work must be a vain and conceited man. He acts as if he thought himself sufficient of himself, and therefore needed not to appeal to God. . . . He limps in his life like a lame man in Proverbs, whose legs are not equal, for his praying is shorter than his preaching. (*Lectures to My Students*, 42, 48)

Be honest. Would you be distinguished as a person of prayer? Or is your praying leg shorter than your ministry leg?

Recently, in the Dominican Republic, I was talking with my friend, Pastor Otto. We were discussing a mutual hero in ministry, John Stott. Otto told me two interesting insights about Stott regarding prayer that were shared with him via a source close to Stott. Reportedly, Stott kept a prayer diary with a thousand names in it, and he prayed for those individuals regularly. By praying in this way, he was able also to remember their names. Further, Stott wrote his sermons while on his knees. I can just see Stott praying in his prayer closet now, over his people and over the Word, and it convicts me. What a wonderful example he gives every pastor-leader.

Personal prayerlessness, by contrast, indicates self-sufficiency. It's a sign of pride. It's a sign that we don't believe God acts when we pray. It's a sign we don't love people as we ought. So let's repent of such arrogance and stupidity, saturating our lives and ministries with times of intercession, thanksgiving, lament, petition, adoration, and confession. Let's work to cultivate vibrant prayer lives like the apostles did.

The apostles also say, literally, "It would not be pleasing in the eyes of God" (Polhill, *Acts,* 180) to stop "preaching the word of God to wait on tables" (v. 2). Because they sought to please the One who saved them and appointed them to preach, they declare their devotion to a fundamental pastoral task (v. 4; cf. Acts 20:18-21; 1 Tim 5:17; 2 Tim 2:15; 4:1-4).

The apostles realize that if they don't preach the gospel, then there will soon be *no church.* Giving people food is a great idea, and it's a biblical idea, but without the preaching of the gospel, the church will quickly dwindle down to no one. Homeless shelters and food pantries are great things the body of Christ should support, but what gives the church its identity—what keeps it on mission—is the preaching of the gospel.

These apostles weren't arrogantly saying, "We're too good and important to care for widows." They were simply demonstrating a commitment to biblical priorities. The apostles weren't sipping lattes while the seven delegates did all the work. Look back at 5:42. They were teaching and preaching every day, all day—in the marketplace, in the synagogues, in homes. They were on the front lines, weary from battle and scarred by persecution. The easier option would have been to give up preaching to take care of benevolence ministry, not to give more attention to speaking the Word.

After prioritizing prayer and preaching, the apostles then make some wise adjustments. They appoint some guys to take care of the widows.

The biblical writers emphasize the importance of caring for widows, along with other groups of disadvantaged people—orphans, strangers, and the poor (cf. Ruth; Job 29:13; Pss 68:4-6; 146:9; Isa 1:17; Luke 7:11-15; 12:41-42; 18:1-8; Jas 1:27). While some structures are described regarding how to care for widows (e.g., 1 Tim 5:3-16), one should be flexible in implementing ministries based on the needs and the workers in a given situation. That's what the church displays here: an ability to make adjustments.

Because the church is both an *organization* and an *organism,* it requires constant reassessment and the development of new plans. That's why Christians making strategic changes must first ask, Is this approach biblical? And then, Is it wise and best?

In this case the apostles specify for the task faithful men filled with wisdom. This is a reminder that leaders need to exercise discernment in choosing what's best: the Bible doesn't always provide a clear answer to every dilemma. The problems and difficulties of ministry, therefore, require that leaders exhibit the ability to handle situations in a way that expresses love for God and neighbor. Christian wisdom flows from one's union with Christ, the source of wisdom (Col 2:3). By knowing Christ and walking with him, one learns to live wisely. The selected men enjoyed this sort of dynamic relationship with Christ.

The apostles weren't the only ones making adjustments. The people also had to make changes. They had to welcome the new leadership born out of the apostles' decision. Doing so demonstrated flexibility and understanding. The proposal for seven delegates to do widow-work "pleased the whole company" (v. 5). This is remarkable! People were actually pleased with *change*. Let's learn from this group. At times, in certain seasons, changes are required for the good of others and for the advancement of the kingdom.

The apostles protected biblical priorities, and they led the church to make wise adjustments—adjustments that involved *shared ministry*. This little story in Acts 6 provides a wonderful model of leadership and cooperation, a division of labor among equals.

The apostles instruct the people to choose qualified leaders with good reputations and who are full of the Spirit and wisdom (v. 3). The apostles didn't pull this checklist from the latest business book. They wanted men respected by others. They wanted men who bear the fruit of the Spirit. They wanted men filled with godly wisdom. Each of these qualities would be of great importance as the seven recruited others for the work of helping them care for so many widows.

Interestingly, the people select seven guys with Greek names (v. 5). It is likely that these men would have had a connection to the Greek-speaking widows. Thus, wisdom is displayed in the selection. The group is godly and culturally suited for their task. We know a bit about two of these delegates—Stephen and Philip—from the rest of the book of Acts. Their ministries weren't confined to widow care.

Is this the origin of the deacon ministry? The text doesn't call them deacons. The office of deacon isn't even mentioned in the book of Acts, though elders are mentioned multiple times. These men, then, aren't ordained to an office; they are commissioned, with a verb, to "deacon" tables.

Having said this, I think this passage does provide a pattern for sharing the ministry, and that's what deacons do: they assist the pastors and elders in ministry work. How did these men go about their tasks in Acts 6? They *helped* and they *harmonized*.

In this text they help the apostles by freeing them up to focus on prayer and ministry of the Word. They also help by showing everyone an example of what it looks like to serve. That's what church membership is all about: serving. Membership says, "This is where I serve," not, "This is where I listen to sermons." Deacons should provide an example of what it looks like to be a faithful church member, serving and also encouraging others to serve with them.

These seven servants helped maintain harmony in the church by addressing the drama associated with neglected widows. Deacons (and other exemplary servants) are shock absorbers. They are peacemakers. Unfortunately, deacons don't always have a reputation for bringing unity! But they should.

Don't miss the overall spirit of love that permeates this text. To make changes and to show grace to one another requires a spirit of love. We don't see a big church fight in Acts 6. Instead, we see a gathering in which the truth of God's Word leads the group and the love of God soothes the disagreement. Spirit-filled unity is encouraging to see.

We Should See Growth Problems as Opportunities for More Gospel-Centered Growth

ACTS 6:7

Luke describes the evangelistic consequences of the church's solution to the problem. The church solves the problem, keeps preaching the gospel, and as a result more people are converted. The lesson here is well summarized by Art Azurdia: "Impediments to growth caused by growth can become occasions for growth when priorities are protected and ministry is shared" ("Ensuring Evangelistic Expansion").

We should probably consider this the normal church pattern: preach, pray, grow, anticipate drama, manage the drama, pray, keep preaching, and then get ready for more drama. When it hits, keep praying.

Times of crises provide the church unique opportunities. Throughout the history of the church, controversy has served to purify and strengthen the church. So let's choose to see challenges as opportunities.

In the midst of the Acts drama, a number of Jewish priests converted to faith in Jesus as Messiah. This is amazing! John Polhill says as many as eight thousand priests could have been living in Jerusalem (*Acts*, 183). We read about the priests in 4:1. They didn't seem ripe for the harvest—they hated the apostles' message, just as they hated Jesus—yet here many accepted him.

This final note should encourage us. The fiercest enemies of the gospel can be saved. The conversion of these priests illustrates the dynamic power of the gospel! Surely some of these priests had said things we often hear—things like, "Believers are dumb sheep" and "No rational person believes in the resurrection." Yet suddenly we see them becoming members of the church. The Spirit of God worked powerfully through a small band of disciples to nudge even Christ's most heated enemies to accept him. May he do it again through our own local churches!

In summary, let's seek the salvation of everyone—the gospel can penetrate the hardest hearts. Let's celebrate gospel-centered growth. Let's have realistic expectations of one another and leaders. Let's show grace to one another. Let's remember that there's a difference between sin and human limitation. Let's play as a team; if you're a Christian, you are a player, not a fan, so participate in the mission. Let's say thanks to people who serve. Let's pray that each local church will effectively care for the needs of people and also faithfully proclaim the good news. And through it all, let's remember that Jesus is building his church and we are wonderfully privileged to be part of it!

Reflect and Discuss

1. What does this passage teach about church growth? How should we view it?
2. Why did the apostles consider caring for widows important?
3. Why was the unity of the church threatened?
4. Why must prayer and proclamation be central in pastoral ministry?
5. How did these seven men assist the apostles? How was their role similar to that of deacons today?
6. What does it mean to have shared ministry in a local church?
7. On which do you prefer your local church to focus: management or mission? Explain.
8. What is your reaction to the conversion of these priests? How should it impact your church's outreach to unbelievers?
9. What does this passage teach about appointing leaders in the local church?
10. Pause and pray for the unity of your local church, asking God to advance the gospel through it.

Christlike

ACTS 6:8–8:3

Main Idea: Luke describes the remarkable Christlike life and ministry of Stephen, whose martyrdom advanced God's mission.

I. He Was Empowered like Jesus (6:8).
II. He Spoke with Unanswerable Wisdom like Jesus (6:9-10).
III. He Endured a Trial like Jesus (6:11-15).
IV. He Preached the Old Testament like Jesus (7:1-53).
    A. A historical clarification (7:2-50)
    B. The Christological culmination (7:51-54)
V. He Suffered and Died like Jesus (7:54-60).
VI. Two Words of Encouragement (8:1-3)
    A. God is sovereign over persecution.
    B. Jesus can save the worst of sinners.

A popular jingle rang in the heads of young basketball fans around the country in the 1990s as kids sought to imitate NBA superstar Michael Jordan: "Like Mike! If I could be like Mike!" Gatorade even resurrected the tune to celebrate its own fiftieth anniversary, reminding me that I was among those kids who sought Mike-likeness. I had the shoes and wore the sweatband on my left forearm. I had a room decorated with Jordan posters. And there I practiced flying through the air with my tongue hanging out as I dunked my Nerf basketball.

Whom did you want to be when you were a kid? Many young children grow up wanting to be like their moms and dads. One of my pastor-friends recently observed his little daughter baptizing Cinderella in the bathtub, clearly imitating the actions of her Baptist father!

Regardless of who your model was as a child, every adult Christian should seek to imitate the same model: Jesus. The goal of the Christian is to be like the Savior. Paul wrote about this pursuit in Philippians 3:10-14. Growing more and more like Jesus was his life's aim.

In Acts 6:8–8:3 we meet a man who was as much like Jesus as anyone in Scripture up to this point: Stephen. Luke describes Stephen's Christlike character, ministry, and death. His death, in fact, is the first martyrdom we read about in the book of Acts. Persecution began with threats. It grew to include floggings. In this passage it involves a stoning.

My focus here, however, is not on martyrdom. Rather, I hope what we are about to discuss will make each of us wrestle with this question: Do I really want to be like Jesus?

To be like Jesus does not mean simply gathering facts about Jesus's life and then copying him, like children idolizing their favorite basketball players tend to do. We must not try to be like Jesus in our own power or imagine that we can earn salvation by copying Jesus's words or behaviors. Rather, as Christians we must realize that we can pursue likeness to Jesus because we have been united to Jesus. Through that union with Christ we can live out Christlike lives (Gal 2:20). Through Jesus we are able to bear the fruit of righteousness. Stephen was not sinless; like the rest of us, he needed the Savior. Once he accepted Jesus, he was empowered to live a life that reflected his Savior.

As we seek to follow Stephen as he followed Christ, we must first be united to Jesus and be willing to suffer. But Stephen's story shows us that suffering connected to honoring the Lord is worth it! As we walk in this martyr's steps, we will note five ways Stephen points to Jesus.

He Was Empowered like Jesus
ACTS 6:8

Luke begins by telling us the source of Stephen's ministry. He previously noted that Stephen had a good reputation and was "full of the Spirit and wisdom." He was "a man full of faith" (vv. 3,5). Here he adds that Stephen was filled with "grace and power" (v. 8). Stephen was a man filled with gifts from God.

God had poured out his grace on this man. The Spirit empowered Stephen to do ministry, which involved caring for widows, speaking and acting with wisdom, and performing signs and wonders. In this way Stephen followed the Master. Jesus was also a man "full of the Spirit" (e.g., Luke 4:1) and wisdom (Luke 2:52) and is himself wisdom (Col 2:3-4). This reminds us that wisdom is more than a set of principles; wisdom is a Person. When you are united to Jesus, he makes you wise. He enables you to make sense of this life.

Are you asking God to fill you with faith, power, and wisdom? Remember: you are controlled by whatever fills you. If you are filled with jealousy, the success of others will infuriate you. If you are filled with lust, your sexual appetites will lead you into great darkness. If you are filled with anger, you will quarrel and even murder with your thoughts. But if you are filled with God's power and wisdom, you will live a life like Stephen demonstrated—an others-oriented, Christ-exalting life.

He Spoke with Unanswerable Wisdom like Jesus
ACTS 6:9-10

The "Freedmen's Synagogue" was apparently a Greek-speaking gathering comprising former slaves from various locations. The most interesting location mentioned is "Cilicia," Paul's home region. The Cilicia mention means the apostle probably attended this synagogue. And judging by the surrounding context, he may have been the ringleader there. At this point Saul hated the gospel. He and others disputed, perhaps for days, with Stephen. But, as in the case of Jesus's teaching, no one could withstand Stephen's wisdom (cf. Luke 20:40).

The power of the gospel is illustrated throughout this narrative. Consider Saul. Eventually, after his conversion and name change, he will write a New Testament theology that reflects Stephen's sermon! In fact, it's likely that Paul personally shared this account with Luke so that it could be recorded for the church. Moreover, in 9:29 Saul disputes with the Hellenists after his conversion, declaring that Jesus is the Christ—most likely in this same synagogue!

So, what gave Stephen such confidence? How could he stand up against this group of religious bullies? He hadn't attended Bible college; he didn't have a seminary degree. He didn't even have a gospel tract to memorize. Stephen, then, could be filled with confidence for only one reason: he believed a particular promise made by Jesus. He trusted in Christ's words, which are recorded in Luke 21:12-18:

> *They will lay their hands on you and persecute you. They will hand you over to the synagogues and prisons, and you will be brought before kings and governors because of my name. This will give you an opportunity to bear witness. Therefore make up your minds not to prepare your defense ahead of time, for I will give you such words and a wisdom that none of your adversaries will be able to resist or contradict. You will even be betrayed by parents, brothers, relatives, and friends. They will kill some of you. You will be hated by everyone because of my name, but not a hair of your head will be lost.*

In Acts 6–7 Stephen, Christ's faithful disciple, is brought before religious leaders and is killed, just as Jesus predicted. But before that happens, he also experiences the other part of this passage: he is given an opportunity to share an unprepared message loaded with unanswerable wisdom.

Stephen is not the only one to whom this biblical text applies. We have already seen this reality unfold in the apostles' witness. And we too can speak up about Christ with confidence, knowing that God will be with us when we stand before the wolves.

We should not use this text as an excuse not to study God's Word. Stephen obviously was studied up on what it says; that's how he was able to retell the story of the Old Testament that appears in the next chapter. At issue here is the idea that we followers of Jesus are never alone when we live on mission. So, as you seek to advance the gospel among the nations, especially when sharing with hostile individuals, remind yourself of Stephen's witness. Pray for God to give you an ability to speak his Word with power and clarity, knowing that the sovereign Lord is with you and for you.

He Endured a Trial like Jesus
ACTS 6:11-15

These religious bullies decide to use the "If you can't beat them, bruise them" philosophy in their dealings with Stephen. They can't stand up to the man's wisdom, so they invent lies about him and haul him before a kangaroo court. What started with "opposition" in verse 9 then degenerates in verses 11-15. The men opposed to Stephen conspire against him (v. 11), create a smear campaign, cause his arrest, cause him to be hauled before the council (v. 12), and then make him face the charges of false witnesses (vv. 13-14). A read of Matthew 26:57-68 shows how Jesus endured a similar bogus trial.

Stephen was accused of speaking blasphemous words about Moses and God, demeaning the temple and the law. But in fact, in verse 15 Stephen's face is Moses-like (Exod 34:29); moreover, his speech clearly shows honor for Moses. And at no point did Stephen use God's name frivolously.

Stephen simply taught that Jesus was the fulfillment of the law and the temple. Jesus is the substance, and those things were shadows. Jesus said the same thing about himself (Matt 12:6; John 2:19). Thus, Stephen is a victim of the same accusation his Lord endured.

This passage is a great reminder that we must tell everyone that if they want to meet God, they don't need to go to a temple or a building; they must go to a person, Jesus. If someone wants forgiveness, he or she doesn't need to practice self-atonement or offer God a sacrifice of bulls and goats; all must go to Jesus, trusting in his work at the cross for salvation. As we tell the good news that Christ is the Savior of sinners and stand on this truth, we must be prepared to face opposition. We must be ready to be excluded, mocked, misrepresented, shamed, and even killed for believing it. It has always been this way, and it always will be this way until the King returns. So don't give in to the temptation to try to make Christianity cool.

When we as Christ followers are opposed, we are facing opposition against Jesus. In putting Stephen through an inquisition, the men in this account are essentially putting Jesus on trial all over again. They want to flog and kill him all over again. Remember, Jesus promised that many will hate us as they hated him (John 15:18-26). So let us be ready for such moments, remembering that we share a powerful intimacy with God as we identify with the suffering Savior in moments like these (Phil 3:10-11; 1 Pet 4:12-19).

Verse 15 transitions to the next scene. While Stephen is being unjustly treated, "his face [is] like the face of an angel"—radiant (cf. Ps 34:4-7). It could be that his changed countenance reflected the fact that God was standing on the side of Stephen, but it could also indicate Stephen's intimacy with God and his faithful representation of Moses. The leaders accused him of demeaning Moses, yet Stephen is reflecting the likeness of Moses—who had to cover his own face with a veil because it shone so brightly after he spent time in the presence of God. In chapter 7 Stephen teaches them how they should understand Moses.

He Preached the Old Testament like Jesus
ACTS 7:1-53

This is the longest sermon in Acts, a book filled with sermons. It is also the last sermon Stephen preaches. His Christ-centered, Christ-exalting sermon got him killed.

Stephen's sermon was a response to a question. The man didn't get to stand behind a podium after some inspirational music, looking out onto an eager audience ready to receive the Word. Instead, he had to respond to an angry Sanhedrin asking him whether it was true that he had been debasing the law and the temple.

How would you respond in this situation? I love Stephen's response. This guy knows his mission. He doesn't try to weasel out of the predicament. He decides to answer their question in a careful, subtle retelling of Israel's history, which climaxes with the work of Christ. Everything about his approach reflects his understanding that he is to be a "witness" (1:8), not a slick lawyer.

Some critical scholars claim this sermon has no real purpose. A few go so far as to suggest Stephen got stoned because his sermon was so bad and boring! But such criticisms miss the brilliance of Stephen's approach.

Here's his overall point: "I am not the one demeaning the law and the temple . . . you are!" Of course, he doesn't lead with this statement. He gets around to it gradually by first retelling biblical history. He then tells the religious leaders that they are actually demeaning the law and the temple because they have misunderstood the nature of the temple and because they have rejected the righteous One to whom the temple points. And he adds that such rejection of a Savior is what one should expect of Israel's leaders based on her past. The nation repeatedly rejected God's appointed saviors.

In Stephen's sermon the accused actually puts the accusers on trial. He tells them, "You guys don't understand Scripture!" Of course they know some facts about it, he admits, but they don't grasp its focal message.

Jesus often corrected the religious leaders' interpretation of the Old Testament. In John 5 he says,

> You pore over the Scriptures because you think you have eternal life in them, and yet they testify about me. But you are not willing to come to me so that you may have life. (5:39-40)

He adds, "For if you believed Moses, you would believe me, because he wrote about me" (5:46).

Stephen's approach for making this point involves telling some microstories in view of the macrostory of the Bible. That's good preaching! Scripture includes many narratives, but its main plotline is about God's salvation made available through Christ.

Let's break Stephen's sermon into two parts: (1) a historical clarification and (2) the Christological culmination. The first part is the longest, due in part to Stephen's getting mobbed before he could develop the second part. That section is the most indicting and is really the major point: Israel's religious leaders have rejected God's ultimate Savior.

A Historical Clarification (7:2-50)

In this long section Stephen essentially tells the Sanhedrin that God's presence is not confined to a building. God's presence has always been with his people, and that presence predates the law, the temple, and the land. He reminds them that God, by his nature, is not imprisoned in a place. Unfortunately, though, Israel often associated the presence of a temple with God's unconditional protection of them (e.g., Jer 7:4). Stephen reminds his hearers that the great heroes of the Old Testament never imagined God was confined to a temple or felt God was obligated to bless them because of its existence. The temple was a good thing, but the people often turned this building into something it was never intended to be or to communicate.

Stephen points to Abraham, Joseph, Moses, and the monarchy (David and Solomon). The whole story line shows God being with his people in various locations, and when the temple is built, he reminds them that "the Most High does not dwell in sanctuaries made with hands" (v. 48), as the prophet Isaiah said (vv. 49-50; cf. Isa 66:1-2). Solomon himself said this at the dedication of the first temple (1 Kgs 8:27).

After opening with a respectful, heartfelt tone (v. 2), Stephen starts with Abraham and describes how God was present alongside him even *in Mesopotamia* (vv. 2-8). God made a covenant with this pagan and, by amazing grace, made the man the father of many nations before the law, the temple, or the nation of Israel even existed.

Concerning Joseph, Stephen reminds them of how his jealous brothers sold him, but "God was with him." God used Joseph as a savior. All of this happened while Joseph was in pagan *Egypt.* In fact, Egypt is mentioned six times in verses 9-15. Was there a temple for God in Egypt? No.

Stephen describes three stages of Moses's life, showing how God was with Moses in each spot. In stage one (vv. 20-22) Moses was "beautiful in God's sight" and was "powerful in his speech and actions." In stage two (vv. 23-29) Moses understood his role as a savior to the people, but the people rejected him. In stage three (vv. 30-38) God appeared to Moses *in the wilderness.* God spoke to Moses and declared that place was "holy ground." Moses led the people out of Egypt and *into the wilderness* for forty years. Stephen draws the Sanhedrin's attention to Moses's teaching, with verse 37 being a prophecy about Jesus. So then, Stephen traced Moses's career through the Egyptian, Midianite, and wilderness periods, pointing out that God was with Moses in every case.

Jesus was like Moses in many of the ways in which Stephen describes Moses. Jesus was mighty in word and deed; Jesus was the rejected Savior; Jesus gave living oracles. And Israel had a history of not only rejecting God's appointed saviors but also of replacing God's glory with worthless idols (vv. 39-43).

Stephen finally brings up the Israelites' settlement into the land as well as the tabernacle and the temple. Both were constructed according to God's will. Both were good gifts. So Stephen is not saying that the people were wrong in constructing either site, but they were wrong to think that these buildings were God's home (v. 48; Stott, *The Message of Acts*, 139). Quoting Isaiah, he tells the crowd that God is the Creator, and he can't be confined to a building.

John Stott summarizes this lengthy section well:

> A single thread runs right through the first part of his defense. It is that the God of Israel is a pilgrim God, who is not restricted to any one place. . . . He has pledged himself by a solemn covenant to be their God. Therefore, according to his covenant promises, wherever they are, there he is also. (Ibid.)

This reality is highlighted by the divine initiative emphasized in the passage. God appeared. God spoke. God sent. God promised. God punished. God rescued. God is working out his sovereign will all over the earth. He most certainly is not confined to a building.

The Christological Culmination (7:51-54)

In this climactic part of the message Stephen tells his audience that they are actually the lawbreakers, and they have rejected the righteous law fulfiller.

Using the language of the prophets and Moses, Stephen tells the religious leaders that they are just like their stubborn, hard-hearted fathers who rejected God's Word. Like them, they are rejecting God's gracious appeals. Stephen then rebukes them for persecuting the prophets and ultimately for killing the One about whom the prophets ultimately spoke: Jesus, the righteous One. He calls the crowd "murderers." And in his last sentence he reminds them of the privilege of having God's Word while rebuking them for failing to respond to it appropriately.

Stephen's point is that the religious leaders and authorities are the lawbreakers, and they have rejected the Savior, who is himself the law fulfiller. Instead of speaking further about the temple and the law, Stephen points them to Jesus, who is the fulfillment or culmination of them both. True, someone was guilty of demeaning the law and the temple, but it wasn't Stephen.

He Suffered and Died like Jesus
ACTS 7:54-60

One can't help but see the relationship between Stephen's death and Jesus's. The two executions are not exactly the same, to be sure, but they bear many similarities.

The angry mob gets "enraged" by Stephen's message and, like animals, "gnashe[s] their teeth at him" (7:54; cf. Job 16:9; Ps 35:16). Instead of responding to the man's message in humble repentance, the self-righteous are outraged by it. But, like Jesus, Stephen has a heavenly perspective prior to his death. Stephen can view death positively because of heavenly realities. As the wolves prepare to attack, Stephen catches a glimpse of heaven (vv. 55-56).

Many have attempted to explain the idea of Jesus's "standing" instead of "sitting" at the right hand of God here; "sitting" is the most frequent expression used to describe his exalted position. So was this a sign of Jesus's honoring Stephen, as when the faculty stands at a graduation for PhD students? That scene is always a moving display of honor considering all the hardworking student has endured. Was it a sign of Jesus's welcoming and receiving Stephen, like a host who welcomes a beloved family member into his home? After all, when someone you love but haven't seen for a while comes to your place, you do tend to get up and greet him with joy. And if that person is a soldier who has been fighting in a war, your welcome will be even more dramatic! I, for one, want to believe that both of these are true. Clearly Jesus is acknowledging Stephen before the Father in heaven, just as Stephen acknowledged Jesus before men on earth. Jesus is thus advocating for Stephen. And this vision of glory empowers Stephen and enrages the wolves even more.

A riot ensues at this point in the narrative. No formal verdict is given against Stephen. No further questions are asked of him. Instead, this group that includes religious elites transforms into a lynch mob. The only semblance of justice in what happens is that he gets stoned in the presence of witnesses and is removed from the city beforehand. There the attackers lay down their garments, like baseball pitchers removing their jackets to throw the ball more effectively. These they lay at the feet of a young man named Saul (7:58).

In this whole narrative the only opponent mentioned by name is Saul (also in 8:1). He is at the head of the whole ugly scene. And according to 22:20, Saul never forgot this moment.

Our brother Stephen endured a horrible death. People were hurling rocks at him, and he eventually died from the many blows they landed to his head. But before Stephen passed away, he offered prayers to the Lord Jesus, his words reflecting the prayers Jesus prayed to the Father while suffering on the cross (vv. 59-60). This beautiful truth helps us see how one filled with the Spirit lives and dies. Stephen asks Jesus to welcome him home, and then Stephen prays for his murderers! Only people who know the forgiveness of Jesus at a deep level can offer such grace.

Now don't miss this. Saul himself would become the answer to Stephen's prayer! Saul would soon find forgiveness through Jesus. He would become an undeserving recipient of the martyr's request that this sin not be held against those responsible. Saul, further, would go on in Romans 12 to argue for leaving vengeance to God.

Following his Christlike prayer, Stephen "fell asleep." Did you know that for the Christian death is like sleeping? The use of this metaphorical description here reflects a sense of peace we shouldn't miss. And it reminds us that while Stephen fell asleep in this life, he awoke in glory. For as sure as he suffered and died like Christ, he was guaranteed to be resurrected like Christ. So when you go to sleep tonight, think about this text. Greet tomorrow morning with your resurrection future in mind.

Two Words of Encouragement
ACTS 8:1-3

God Is Sovereign over Persecution

While the church rightly grieved over Stephen's death (v. 2), God used it to advance his redemptive purposes. Because of persecution, in fact, the church scatters outside of Jerusalem (v. 1) and evangelizes in the regions mentioned in 1:8. The enemy could not thwart the purposes of God. So take heart, Christian witness. While suffering may be inevitable, God's mission is unstoppable.

Jesus Can Save the Worst of Sinners

Saul approved of Stephen's death (v. 1), and his rage escalated to the point that he went through "house after house," "ravaging" the church, dragging away men and putting them in prison (v. 3). He "was still breathing threats and murder against the disciples" in chapter 9. Consider his anger and hostility, but then remember the amazing way Jesus would transform him. In some translations, in fact, chapter 9 has this heading: "The Conversion of Saul." Only a miraculous change could take the guy that's the terrorist in one chapter and turn him into the evangelist of the next.

Marvel at this good news. And pray persistently for those outside of Christ. Speak this good news faithfully. Because having experienced the transforming grace of the same Jesus we serve, Paul the former persecutor wrote, "This saying is trustworthy and deserving of full acceptance: 'Christ Jesus came into the world to save sinners'—and I am the worst of them" (1 Tim 1:15).

Conclusion

After a remarkable season of emphasis on missions, the Austin Stone Community Church eventually sent more than one hundred people overseas with the goal of evangelizing unreached people groups. One of the travelers was a young man named Ronnie Smith. Ronnie looked like many young leaders in a local church: he was young, bright, funny, and passionate about following Jesus. He was also gifted. But though he received offers to take leadership positions at other churches, Ronnie and his bride determined to go all the way to dangerous Bengazi, Libya, to make the gospel known.

Later, in a conversation between Ronnie and a pastor friend, Ronnie was asked whether he thought things had escalated in that country to the point that it was too dangerous for him to remain in Libya. To this Ronnie replied, "It feels to be home . . . there is literally no other place on Earth that we would rather be. Nowhere" (Shaw, *All Authority*, 7).

That pastor soon described what happened after that discussion:

> [A] black Jeep circled Ronnie several times as he was on his daily jog in his neighborhood in Benghazi, Libya. The two Libyans in the Jeep pulled up to a car stopped nearby. "Is that the American?" they asked. The man smoking and waiting in the car said, "Yes. He lives here and he's a good man." Ronnie had lived in Benghazi for nearly a year teaching science to Libyan high school students. He loved working in education as it gave him the opportunity to pour into the lives and aspirations of Libya's next generation. The black Jeep circled

back to Ronnie. A quick word was exchanged and then the
Libyan men emptied six bullets into Ronnie's chest, killing
him instantly. Ronnie's wife and two year old son had returned
two weeks before to the USA for their Christmas holiday.
Ronnie died on Dec. 5, 2013, one week before he was to join
them. (Ibid.)

Many in the media wondered why a guy like Ronnie would move to
hostile Libya in the first place. But all of heaven knew exactly why he did
it: Ronnie Smith was following Jesus. Like Stephen, Ronnie didn't set
out to be a martyr. He set out to be like Jesus, but sometimes Christlike
living leads to Christlike dying.

Suffering will sometimes be inevitable as we determine to follow
Jesus in the work he desires that we do, but the great news is that the
King's mission is unstoppable. Jesus is building his church, and neither
bullets nor rocks can prevail against it! May God grant us grace to follow Jesus faithfully until we, like Stephen and Ronnie, fall asleep. In the
moment we open our eyes to see the glorified Savior, we will *know* that
living for Jesus is worth more than any sacrifice.

Reflect and Discuss

1. From where did Stephen receive power?
2. How are the Spirit and wisdom related?
3. How is Jesus "greater than the temple"?
4. What impresses you most about Stephen's sermon?
5. Could you narrate the Old Testament story that culminates in Christ
   if someone asked you to do so? If not, begin a reading plan that
   includes Genesis, Exodus, Judges, 1 and 2 Samuel, and Matthew.
6. How does the vision of Christ's standing at the right hand of the
   Father encourage you?
7. What about Saul's involvement in these matters most resonates with
   you?
8. What is your reaction to Stephen's willingness to forgive his murderers? Do you need to forgive some people in your life? What advice
   would Stephen give you?
9. How does Stephen's story inspire you?
10. How does God display his sovereignty in persecution?

The Gospel to Samaria

ACTS 8:4-25

Main Idea: Luke describes some of the remarkable events that happened when the gospel advanced into Samaria through the faithful witness of Philip and the apostles Peter and John.

I. The Samaritans: Transformed by the Gospel (8:4-8)
II. Simon and Philip: Magic versus the Gospel (8:9-13)
III. The Apostles: Sent for the Gospel (8:14-17)
IV. Simon and Peter: A Confrontation Related to the Gospel (8:18-24)
V. The Apostles: More Preaching of the Gospel (8:25)
VI. Gospel Applications

Following Stephen's death, great persecution arises against the early church, and the believers must scatter beyond Jerusalem (v. 1). But persecution and threat of death don't stop the church's growth. Luke next describes how the gospel begins to advance in Samaria. This means that despite the brutal murder of Stephen, God continued his mission of redeeming a people for himself—a people from every tribe and tongue. In fact, God uses persecution to launch his people into Samaria of all places! (See John 4:4,20-21.) Let's look at what happened as the gospel spread in mighty power to the glory of our unstoppable King.

The Samaritans: Transformed by the Gospel

ACTS 8:4-8

The persecution caused many in the church to scatter, preaching the good news wherever they went (v. 4). In the Old Testament, to be a scattered people was a sign of judgment (Gen 11:9; Deut 28:64); in this instance the church's scattering was actually a sign of judgment on the enemies of the gospel. The message the persecutors were attempting to contain and muzzle was spreading like wildfire on a windy day. How wonderful is God's providence and sovereignty? The enemies of the church tried to kill the message and messengers of Jesus, but God used their evil for good, for the salvation of many (cf. Gen 50:20).

Before his ascension, the Lord Jesus said to his disciples,

You will receive power when the Holy Spirit has come on you, and you will be my witnesses in Jerusalem, in all Judea and Samaria, *and to the end of the earth.* (1:8; emphasis added)

This command is fulfilled as the persecuted Christians head out from Jerusalem and carry the gospel to everyone they meet! And notice that "ordinary" Christians are spreading the gospel. It wasn't the apostles who preached the gospel first in Samaria; "those who were scattered" (8:4) did. Remember, every Christian is a missionary!

The early church went about preaching the Word wherever believing men and women went. Have you considered that even in your promotions, your demotions, and your setbacks, God has sovereignly ordained and allowed twists and turns in your life to give you opportunity to preach the gospel to your neighbors and acquaintances? The Lord has arranged opportunities for *you* to share Jesus in word and exemplify that message in deed to your new friends and colleagues. So, if you are wrestling with a job loss or have even had to flee a location because of real physical persecution, it's time to reflect on how God in his mysterious sovereignty has permitted your pain. Consider how he might use it as a way for you to teach and testify about Jesus's grace. God is on a big mission, and we're part of it! He's redeeming the world through his Son by the power of the Holy Spirit at work through ordinary people like you and me. This is how the gospel spread so effectively in the first century, and it's why the gospel continues to spread so effectively in the twenty-first. Consider Michael Green's words:

> As early as Acts 8 we find that it is not the apostles but the "amateur" missionaries, the men evicted from Jerusalem as a result of the persecution which followed Stephen's martyrdom, who took the gospel with them wherever they went. It was they who traveled along the coastal plain to Phoenicia, over the sea to Cyprus, or struck up north to Antioch. They were evangelists, just as much as any apostle was. Indeed, it was they who took the two revolutionary steps of preaching to Greeks who had no connection with Judaism, and then with launching the Gentile mission from Antioch. It was an unselfconscious effort. They were scattered from their base in Jerusalem and they went everywhere spreading the good news which had brought joy, release and a new life to themselves. This must often have been not formal preaching, but informal chattering to friends and chance acquaintances,

in homes and wine shops, on walks, and around market
stalls. They went everywhere gossiping the gospel; they did
it naturally, enthusiastically, and with the conviction of those
who are not paid to say that sort of thing. Consequently, they
were taken seriously, and the movement spread, notably
among the lower classes. (*Evangelism in the Early Church*, 243)

The early church "gossiped the gospel" wherever believers went.
What a wise and effective plan for multiplication God created! Neither
persecution nor relocation could stop the gospel from spreading. In
fact, these things only helped. The good news of Jesus was in the heart
of the widow and on the lips of the common man. And this message was
"the power of God for salvation to everyone who believes" (Rom 1:16).

Luke focuses on Philip as an example of an individual on mission.
Luke introduced us to Philip in Acts 6:5 as one of the seven selected
men of "good reputation, full of the Spirit and wisdom" (6:3) chosen
to serve widows. Later this gospel-preaching servant of the Lord would
appropriately be called "Philip the evangelist" (21:8).

The Samaritans who populated the region of Samaria were a mixed
people of partly Jewish and partly Gentile origin. Most Jews considered
them unclean and outside the covenant community of Israel. To make
matters worse, many Gentiles looked on them with contempt. The
Samaritans maintained significant aspects of Israelite religion but read
their own version of the Pentateuch, had their own temple, and held
differing views on the exact role and identity of the Messiah. There
was deep hatred and prejudice between the Jews and Samaritans at the
dawn of the first century. Recall, however, that Jesus engaged in a life-
changing conversation with a Samaritan woman at a well, offering her
salvation through himself (John 4:7-26). He also healed a Samaritan
leper while on the way to Jerusalem (Luke 17:11-19), and he made a
Samaritan the unlikely hero of a parable (Luke 10:25-37). These wonderful accounts remind us that God's saving mission in Christ was not
limited to the Jews but was meant for the entire world. What a great God
we have!

Philip follows the pattern set forth by his Master in extending the
gospel of Christ to his Samaritan neighbors (8:5). Jesus had so transformed Philip's life that any prejudice against the Samaritans was put to
death. This is a great reminder that we too should reject categorizing
people groups as being without hope in the gospel. In any situation in
which you notice a group being oppressed or considered outcasts, find

ways to reach out to them with the good news of Christ. What a wonderful testimony this can give to your culture!

The Lord was powerfully with Philip as "the crowds were all paying attention" (v. 6) to what he had to say. The Samaritans were presumably ready to hear the gospel, as they had their own longings and ideas about a coming Messiah. It could be that their hearts were prepared to receive it because both John the Baptist and Jesus had previously ministered there (John 3:23; 4:4-42).

Moreover, the Samaritans were attentive because of the exorcisms and healings being done by Philip through the power of the Holy Spirit. Like the apostles and Stephen, Philip had also received power to cast out demons and do miraculous healings to confirm the gospel message. The result was that both the spiritually tormented and the physically broken were being healed by the presence of the Spirit as Jesus was being proclaimed (8:7). Christ Jesus being brought near to the people was cause for "great joy." The Samaritans realized that God had visited them, and they were filled with gladness.

Some of us may feel curious about a passage like this. We might ask, What's up with the exorcisms and healings? Does what happened here mean we should expect present-day gospel preaching to be accompanied by the casting out of demons and the healing of the paralyzed and lame? Or does what we read here suggest it is appropriate to expect that some modern-day Christians will have power to cast out demons and heal others at will due to some supernatural gifting?

Remember, we must read Acts in light of its genre. This is a historical book, which means Luke penned it to describe the events of the early church without necessarily commending to us its same practices. I don't think we should read of Philip's exorcisms and healings and assume the passage's primary application to our lives is that each of our local churches needs to start an exorcism and healing ministry! To be sure, we should read and apply much of Acts directly, but we must also take care in making one-to-one correlations at every turn. We've got to allow the rest of the Bible to help us make interpretations and applications for the modern world.

There was something exceptional about the way God did signs and miracles through the apostles, Stephen, Philip, and the others mentioned in the book of Acts. There was a unique nature to the early church's ministry. Nevertheless, God can and does heal people today (cf. Jas 5:14-16). So, if Jesus decides to intervene, signs and wonders like those we read about in Acts may be manifested in our day. If so, they will happen in order to give the world even more powerful pictures of what life will be like in Christ's coming kingdom.

Simon and Philip: Magic versus the Gospel
ACTS 8:9-13

Luke turns our attention from Philip's gospel ministry to Simon the Sorcerer's magic craft.

Before Philip arrived, this Simon "practiced sorcery in that city and amazed the Samaritan people, while claiming to be somebody great" (v. 9). All the Samaritans therefore revered Simon. Their beliefs about him are summed up in their recorded statement about him: "This man is called the Great Power of God" (v. 10). In truth, however, Simon was a deceiver and a liar; still, his magic had so deceived the Samaritan people that they trusted him (v. 11).

Simon was a false prophet. While true prophets will direct praise toward God, false prophets receive praise as fuel for their own selfish egos. And in order to keep the accolades coming, they will set people's hope in the wrong place. True prophets, by contrast, faithfully exalt the cross so that people's "faith might not be based on human wisdom but on God's power" (1 Cor 2:5). Simon, as a false prophet, was flashy and "amazed" the people (v. 11). But true prophets come in humble dependence on God (cf. 1 Cor 2:3), faithfully expounding his oracles (cf. 1 Pet 4:11). Though false prophets like Simon will be exposed, true prophets will be rewarded (cf. 2 Tim 4:8).

Into a culture in which Simon enjoyed a cult following, Philip spread the message that Jesus alone was great and praiseworthy. In fact, Christ's kingly reign was breaking into the world through the powerful name of Jesus. So rather than giving their attention to Simon and his magic, the Samaritans believed Philip's message and gave themselves to King Jesus.

Surprisingly, "Simon himself believed" (v. 13). But while at first this seems to be an amazing victory for the kingdom of God, it soon seems that Simon did not *genuinely* believe. After Simon was baptized, he was noticeably amazed at the signs and miracles being performed by Philip (v. 13). And based on Peter's later rebuke to Simon (vv. 20-21) and his statement about Simon's wicked heart and need for repentance and forgiveness (vv. 22-23), it's safe to assume Simon had an *insincere* faith.

The gospel did triumph, however. Many in Samaria who were involved in magic and witchcraft bowed their knees to Jesus. Their response to the good news message reminds us that the gospel can impact anyone. There's much discussion today about how the gospel of Christ can change the hearts of the secular elites, transform blue-collar hedonists, and save the poor. But it proves just as powerful in setting free the spiritually oppressed and the demonically possessed. The good news of Jesus can liberate even those involved in black magic, mysticism, and witchcraft.

Our Lord Jesus can save those blinded by Satan (2 Cor 4:4). Through Philip's selfless preaching of Christ, God was pleased to give light to the blind. May we aim to be messengers of light, who with Paul say, "We are not proclaiming ourselves but Jesus Christ as Lord, and ourselves as your servants for Jesus's sake. For God who said, 'Let light shine out of darkness,' has shone in our hearts to give the light of the knowledge of God's glory in the face of Jesus Christ" (2 Cor 4:5-6).

The Apostles: Sent for the Gospel
ACTS 8:14-17

The joyous news about the gospel's power at work in Samaria reached the apostles in Jerusalem. This was a breakthrough moment in church history as the Samaritan "outsiders" were now clearly being incorporated into the church of God. The apostles still in Jerusalem sent Peter and John to join the work there. They went and "prayed . . . so the Samaritans might receive the Holy Spirit because he had not yet come down on any of them. (They had only been baptized in the name of the Lord Jesus)" (vv. 15-17).

Historically, these verses have been difficult for many to understand. Some contend this text teaches that not all believers receive the Holy Spirit at salvation and must, therefore, seek a later spiritual experience, which is often supplemented by speaking in tongues. Advocates of this view usually teach that a person can be genuinely saved and regenerate yet devoid of the Holy Spirit. Some slightly modify this view, teaching that the Samaritans mentioned in this passage were genuinely saved, regenerate, and possessed a measure of the Spirit but did not yet have the spiritual gifts. Still others have understood these verses to teach that the initial faith of the Samaritans was defective; therefore, the Spirit did not come until they had a genuine faith. Most who advocate this view believe this text emphasizes the dangers of insincere faith. I think, however, that each of these views is misguided. We must remember the unique place of this story in redemptive history.

The Spirit was withheld until the apostles could verify the gospel work. In this unique case of the gospel's first moving beyond Jerusalem, the Lord sovereignly waited to give any manifestation of the Spirit until the apostles could be there to witness it. That way they would *see* and could testify that the Samaritans received the same Holy Spirit given to the Christians in Jerusalem. In this way there could be no question that the gospel was for the nations and that the Jews and Samaritans, once bitter enemies, were now brothers and sisters and members of the same household of God because of their shared faith. The Jerusalem believers had received the Spirit at Pentecost (2:1-13), and now, at the proper time, apostles from the mother church were there to witness and welcome the incorporation of the Samaritan believers into God's church. We see a similar action in the case of Cornelius (11:14-17).

Simon and Peter: A Confrontation Related to the Gospel
ACTS 8:18-24

After the apostles laid their hands on the Samaritans, they received the Holy Spirit. Simon saw this event, and he audaciously offered the apostles *money* (v. 19) to impart the Spirit's power to him. Luke records Peter's fierce reply (vv. 20-23) and Simon's response (v. 24).

Perhaps Simon theorized that if he could possess the power he witnessed, he could make quite a profit for himself. He is clearly ignorant about the nature of the Spirit in this passage, perhaps thinking the Spirit an impersonal force that can be manipulated rather than as a divine person to whom he is to yield and by whom he should live.

Peter sharply rebukes him, essentially saying, "To hell with you and your money!" He sees in Simon a complete misunderstanding of God and his grace. Simon's misunderstanding was so serious, in fact, that Peter adds, "You have no part or share in this matter, because your heart is not right before God" (v. 21).

In Acts Luke uses the word *share* to mean either "ministry" (1:17) or "participation in salvation" (26:18). The latter option seems the best application here. Peter condemns Simon as one who does not have Christ's salvation. But then Peter, who has just consigned him and his money to hell, calls Simon to repentance (vv. 23-24), which is a command typically delivered to the unregenerate (2:38; 3:19; 17:30; 26:20).

Peter knew Simon was in extreme danger because his heart was so corrupt before God. Rather than possessing a humble faith that receives God's good gifts, Simon thought he could manipulate, control, and pay God off. Such wickedness, which was exposed in his question, was met with Peter's gracious and stern exhortation (see vv. 23-24). Peter perceives that Simon is poisoned in hostility ("bitterness," see Deut 29:18) and enslaved to sin ("bound by wickedness"). He tells him to pray, without presuming on God's grace ("if possible"), and to ask the Lord for forgiveness. Simon then responds in what seems to be sincerity (v. 24).

This event teaches us two important lessons.

1. *The Holy Spirit isn't for sale.* The prerogative to give the Holy Spirit belongs to God. We can't purchase salvation or the gifts of God. He isn't our personal genie; he's our omnipotent Lord. That means our money, social status, and talents cannot save us or cause God to appoint us to positions in his kingdom. Salvation is a gift from God by faith in Jesus Christ (15:11), and our spiritual gifts, which should be used to serve the church, are gifts from God that are distributed according to his perfect will (1 Cor 12:11). True influence in the kingdom should be sought, but we should do it Jesus's way for Jesus's glory. This involves humble faith, courageous hope, hard work, sacrificial love, and hearts continually enthralled with the grace of God.

2. *We really should marvel at God's amazing grace.* I feel a degree of sympathy for Simon, since he was rooted deeply in paganism and trying—at least at some level—to understand Christianity. It saddens me that he didn't realize that the gospel frees a person from addiction to self and possessions. It makes one honest and generous. But where I can't feel sorry for Simon is when I realize that his lack of understanding happened in part just because he was so interested in his own glory and power.

What a gift he received in Peter's rebuke! He was offered a chance to *repent* and be *forgiven*. This is grace.

Simon's case is different from the Ananias and Sapphira situation (5:1-11), in which the hypocritical couple was immediately judged. Perhaps the couple's sin was dealt with more harshly because it was premeditated while Simon's sin was committed at least in part by ignorance. Whatever the differentiation may be, Simon was graciously given a second chance. That's why his story should make us repent and say,

"God have mercy on us. Thank you, Lord, for your patience with us."
What a marvelous Savior we have in Jesus!

The Apostles: More Preaching of the Gospel
ACTS 8:25

After the episode with Simon, the apostles went back to Jerusalem.
En route, they did more gospel preaching "in many villages of the
Samaritans." Their focus reminds us that we should imitate their unceas-
ing efforts at proclamation.

Gospel Applications

Allow me to draw some big ideas from this text.

Proclaim the gospel. Philip, Peter, and John preached the gospel of
Jesus Christ. The gospel is "the power of God for salvation to everyone who believes" (Rom 1:16). It's not enough simply to "live out the
gospel." We must proclaim and explain it. In the pulpit, at our work-
places, around our dinner tables, wherever we are, we must tell about
the goodness of God, explain the truth about sin, and draw attention to
the glorious redemption we have in Jesus Christ. Recall what Paul told
the Corinthians:

> *For since, in God's wisdom, the world did not know God through
> wisdom, God was pleased to save those who believe through the
> foolishness of what is preached.* (1 Cor 1:21)

So preach Christ! Consider how to communicate the gospel com-
prehensibly to your culture.

Proclaim the gospel in various situations. Philip and the persecuted
Jerusalem Christians leveraged their scattering for the progress of the
gospel. On the way back to Jerusalem, Peter and John stopped to preach
the gospel to "many villages." This is a reminder of our need to live with
gospel intentionality. The church is made up of mothers, servers, bank-
ers, salespeople, cooks, students, athletes, police officers, and many
others—each of whom should adopt the posture of a missionary. In all
that you do, no matter your role, ask, How can I proclaim and teach
Christ in this situation?

God desires that you be deliberate about sharing the gospel with
your children, coworkers, customers, teammates, and colleagues. In

some situations this may mean you gradually bear witness to Christ in
how you live with the aim of sharing the good news when someone asks
what's different about you. Or—and in many cases—it may mean you
need to look for and take advantage of direct opportunities to describe
to others the good news and Christ's impact in your life. Evangelism
should be a thread woven throughout our daily lives. We must be deliberate about leveraging our lives for the progress of the gospel.

Praise God for his work of salvation among the nations. Thank God for
this wonderful narrative about the power and progress of the gospel at
work among the Samaritans. It subtly reminds us to repent of any prejudices toward those some think are less worthy of salvation than others.
May we pray for the faith to believe that no one is beyond the reach of
God's saving grace. And may we willingly share that good news with the
people whose lives intersect with our own.

Reflect and Discuss

1. Describe a time when you experienced persecution for your
   Christian faith. In what ways was God's mission advanced or hindered by persecution in the first century?
2. How is Acts 8:4-25 related to 1:8? Why is this significant?
3. Why did God delay pouring out his Spirit on the Samaritan believers? Why was this important? What lessons might we learn from this
   unique event?
4. What does this story teach about preaching Christ?
5. What disappoints you about the character of Simon? Why?
6. Do you think Simon had genuine faith in Christ? Why or why not?
7. Recall how Peter sharply called Simon to repentance. Why is repentance important?
8. Compare Luke 9:52-54 with Acts 8:14-25 and consider the change in
   the apostle John. How was his opinion of the Samaritans changed?
   How can you cultivate love for the unlovable?
9. Why is Acts 8:4-25 a good illustration of Matthew 28:18-20?
10. Pause to pray for opportunities to share the gospel this week. List
    three specific actions you can take to convey the good news of salva-
    tion through Christ to others.

How Ordinary People Live on Mission

ACTS 8:26-40

Main Idea: In this passage we see an illustration of God's saving grace among the nations as Philip helps an Ethiopian man understand the good news about Jesus from the Bible.

I. Love People with God-Centered, Christlike Love (8:26-40).
II. Yield Daily to the Spirit's Guidance (8:26-31).
III. Understand and Explain the Good News to People (8:32-40).
    A. Be prepared to explain the good news.
    B. Consider using questions as you explain the good news.
    C. Expect God to work as you explain the good news.

In an effort to improve our evangelistic impact in the city, my local church went through a sermon series called "Mission 555." Its goal was to help people identify five unbelievers in five of their normal networks (familial, vocational, geographical, commercial, and recreational). With that step done, each of us was to do one of five things for the individuals named. (1) We could pray for them; (2) we could invite them to church; (3) we could serve them in some meaningful way; (4) we could give gospel-centered literature to them; or (5) we could speak the gospel to them. The plan was designed to help the congregation see the power of living with evangelistic intentionality.

Halfway through the series, one of our aspiring church planters, Skylar, had an extraordinary encounter in an otherwise ordinary day. He was sitting at a coffee shop working when a guy asked whether he could share his table. As Skylar made room for the man and the two began to work alongside each other, they began talking. It wasn't long before the man shared about some stresses he faced. So Skylar, who could've just offered sympathy, started talking to the man about how God had provided for him in a similar situation. When he was done, Skylar asked, "What do you think about Jesus?"

"Well, I'm not against him," the man said. "I just don't know much about him. I grew up Catholic, but I never really read the Bible."

"And what do you think based on what you know?" Skylar asked.

"Well, the last time I remember opening a Bible, it opened to Psalm 18," he replied.

"Let's check that psalm out," Skylar said, opening up his Bible. He quickly scanned the psalm's themes of judgment and salvation before asking, "Do you know the story of the Bible?" When the man said no, Skylar began describing to him about how Jesus was judged in the place of sinful humanity to give us salvation.

And praise God, only a few minutes after hearing the gospel message, the man said, "Wow. I believe it." That day, in that coffee shop, he chose to surrender his life to Jesus and follow him.

The two parted with the man's promise to go home and read the whole Bible. And in the months ahead, Skylar continued to meet with the new convert and to study the book of Mark alongside him.

The Lord providentially arranged this meeting—something he can do in each Christian's life. Even today Skylar fondly says of the encounter, "It was the easiest gospel conversation I have ever had with anybody!" And it serves as a great reminder that divine appointments like this one may well await each of us. We must look for them.

Whether you are visiting a coffee shop in your town, shopping in Walmart, coaching third base, talking to a person on an airplane, dialoging with internationals in your town, or conversing with the trick-or-treaters, you should prepare for evangelistic opportunities. The Lord of all the earth is offering salvation, and he often uses ordinary conversations to display the glory of his grace to unbelievers. We, in fact, are Christians today because someone shared the good news with us, so let's live with sensitivity among those we encounter. God may use each of us to lead many others to him.

In this passage we see an illustration of God's saving grace at work among the nations, as Philip helps an Ethiopian man understand the good news about Jesus from the Scriptures. John Stott comments on the double goodness of God in this story:

> The fact is that God has given us two gifts, first the Scriptures and secondly teachers to open up, explain, expound and apply the Scriptures. It is wonderful to note God's providence in the Ethiopian's life, first enabling him to obtain a copy of the Isaiah scroll and then sending Philip to teach him out of it. (*The Message of Acts*, 161)

Indeed, the kindness of God leads us to repentance. God in his grace provides a copy of the Scriptures to this man, and then he orchestrates the arrival of a teacher who can to explain it to him. The whole story reminds us of other passages, like Luke 24, in which Jesus—appearing as a stranger in that account—meets up with some travelers and explains the Old Testament to them, using it to point to the reality that he is the Messiah.

There are a few other aspects of this story that we can't miss. In chapters 8–10 we read of an increasing degree of the Spirit's involvement. We already observed the Spirit's work in the "Samaritan Pentecost" (8:17). In this conversion story the Spirit's work is even more pronounced.

Important too is the global nature of God's offer of salvation. Acts 8 is an illustration of the Great Commission and of Jesus's commission to the disciples in 1:8. Already the church is advancing across ethnic and social lines when Philip, having established the mission to the Samaritans, becomes involved in an even more far-reaching missionary breakthrough. His witness to this Ethiopian in many ways parallels the story of Cornelius in chapter 10. Ethiopia was considered "the end of the earth" by the Greeks and Romans, and Philip's witness to the Samaritans and the Ethiopian is no doubt a foretaste of the completion of Christ's completed mission (Rev 7:9).

Finally, we shouldn't miss the gift of seeing a servant at work. We first met Philip in Acts 6 among the seven godly men assigned the humble task of caring for widows. After watching him willingly *serve in that case,* now we see him effectively *speak the gospel, too.* God continues to use humble men and women who walk and share by the Spirit's power as Philip did to accomplish extraordinary things.

In 8:26-40 we see Philip living out God's mission. Remember that Philip was among other Christians scattered due to persecution that helped fulfill God's plan of making disciples outside Jerusalem (vv. 1-4; cf. 1:8). Luke then records the account of Philip's preaching among the hated Samaritans (vv. 5-25). And here we find Philip in the desert, obeying the Spirit's calling yet again. He's given a divine mandate to rise and go south (v. 26), followed by a divinely planned meeting in a chariot (vv. 27-31). In obedience to the Spirit's guidance, Philip takes advantage of another occasion for sharing the divine message, the gospel (vv. 32-35). This results in a miracle of conversion (vv. 36-38). It's followed by Philip's gospel work in Azotus and Caesarea (vv. 39-40; cf. 21:8).

So what can ordinary Christians glean from this story about living out God's mission? Consider three big applications.

Love People with God-Centered, Christlike Love
ACTS 8:26-40

Philip's heart is open wide to all types of people, and he reflects the heart of God. In Acts 6 we see him caring for widows just as God cares for them (cf. Ps 146:9). Then in Acts 8 he displays a Christlike love for the despised Samaritans even though people considered them ethnically impure heretics (cf. John 4). Then, in our text, he displays Christ's love for the nations by caring for this Ethiopian man with respect. Philip displays love not just for the crowds (vv. 6-8) but also for individuals (vv. 26-40)—those of different ethnicities, different ranks, and even those who have different religious views.

What makes a good missionary? Loving people. Reaching beyond barriers.

Contrast Philip with Jonah. Jonah's arrogant ethnocentrism made him a reluctant missionary. Unfortunately, the spirit of Jonah is present today. Many find it difficult to love Muslims, Buddhists, those of particular skin tones, or those from certain social classes. Let's determine to follow Philip's model rather than Jonah's.

How can we grow in our love for others? We need to ponder the cross and to walk by the Spirit. Regarding the former, let's remember that Christ loved us when we were unlovable. Not one of us *deserves* Jesus's salvation, and the more we contemplate who Christ is and what he has done for us, the more we will love people as Philip did. Then we can love the least, the last, the lost, and even our enemies. Regarding the Spirit, remember that love is a fruit of the Spirit (cf. 1 Cor 13; Gal 5:22-23). In Acts 6 one of the marks of the "Magnificent Seven" is that the men were full of the Spirit. A result of this reality is a Christlike love for people. Therefore, every day, let's ponder the cross, and let's ask God to fill us afresh with his Spirit so that we may love people with a God-centered, Christlike love.

Yield Daily to the Spirit's Guidance
ACTS 8:26-31

Those walking by the Spirit are sensitive to God's leading. God's initiative in this story is unquestionable. An angel of the Lord visited Philip in a vision and called him to witness in a most unlikely place (v. 26). He directed him toward the wilderness in the south. He told him to leave the revival happening in Samaria to head for the desert.

What was called Ethiopia in those days corresponds to what we call the Upper Nile region. It reaches approximately from Aswan to Khartoum (Stott, *Message of Acts,* 160). John Polhill points out that in the Old Testament the same area is called the kingdom of Cush (*Acts,* 223; cf. Ps 68:31; Isa 18:7; Zeph 3:10). We're talking about Africa here. And the fact that Philip would minister to an African man is striking indeed. It's evidence of the spread of God's global mission.

We are told that this particular Ethiopian man was a "eunuch," and he was an important "official" in charge of all the treasury of Candace, queen of the Ethiopians. That means he was something like the minister of finance (Polhill, *Acts,* 224).

The Ethiopian was probably a God fearer who believed in the God of Israel, like Cornelius, but he couldn't experience full membership in the community of Israel because he was a eunuch, as proscribed in Deuteronomy 23:1 (Polhill, *Acts,* 224). While he could visit the temple in Jerusalem, he couldn't enter it.

Notice that he was reading aloud from Isaiah (v. 28), contemplating the promises of the prophet. Isaiah was particularly important for eunuchs because in his work the prophet describes the future, which promises eunuchs "a name better than sons and daughters" and "an everlasting name that will never be cut off" (Isa 56:3-8). Little did this eunuch know when he began his morning that he would soon personally experience the fulfillment of such promises! And Philip had the privilege of displaying the gospel of grace to him.

What happens here is a God-ordained meeting. Philip asks a man if he understands what he's reading (v. 30). The Ethiopian responds, "How can . . . I unless someone guides me?" (v. 31). He doesn't know he's just provided Philip with a great softball question; he has practically given him an invitation to share the gospel! The scene reminds me of the story of Ian Thomas, who was traveling on a plane, tired and hoping to sleep, when he heard someone say, "Psssst." When he looked to see where the sound had come from, his eyes met those of a stranger. The man said, "I am reading in the Bible about Nicodemus in John 3, and I do not understand it. Do you know anything about the Bible?" (Hughes, *Acts,* 120). Both of these stories remind us that the Lord does divinely arrange conversations. He continues to guide his people by the Word and the Holy Spirit (see 10:19; 11:12; 13:2,4; 16:6-7). So we must always make the most of every opportunity.

Pastor Bill Hybels describes another modern-day story of divine appointment. One cold January evening in Chicago, he hurried to take out the garbage. In his rush he hadn't even bothered to put on shoes. His plan was to drag the can out as quickly as possible and then run back in before his feet froze. As he started tiptoeing quickly down the driveway, however, he noticed that his new neighbor was taking the garbage out as well. Hybels didn't think much of it. He parked his own can at the curb and started to sprint back up the driveway as planned, but then he sensed the Spirit compelling him: "Go walk across the cul-de-sac and introduce yourself to that guy," he said. "But it's cold, God," Hybels replied, "my toes are freezing off. I'm sure he's cold too. I'll do it another time!" Nonetheless, Hybels couldn't get any peace about his plan to rush back into his warm house. So, somewhat reluctantly, the pastor walked across the cul-de-sac and said something like, "Hi, I'm Bill Hybels, your neighbor across the street. Welcome to the neighborhood."

"Nice to meet you, I'm so and so," the neighbor replied. "I own the new car dealership." And after that, both men pivoted and returned to their respective homes. But here's where it gets interesting. On every Tuesday night for the next year, Hybels and that neighbor took out the garbage at the same time. And every night, through the prompting of the Spirit, Hybels stopped to chat with him. Over time, through their conversations around the garbage cans, the men became close friends. And eventually Bill Hybels led this man and his family to faith in Christ (Mark Adams, "Attitudes Essential to Evangelism").

Do you have a neighbor you've been meaning to visit or a new co-worker you've intended to engage in conversation? Do you have a gift you've been thinking about giving to the struggling family down the street? Is there someone in your school who continues to be on your mind and heart? If so, it could be that God is up to something. You, like Philip, may have a chariot waiting for you.

A missional church is composed of individuals who are led by the Spirit like Philip. The Lord will direct us, but we must be willing to obey. Understand, Philip could have used the common excuse, "Not now!" to release himself from following God's prompting in his heart. After all, Christian ministry was exploding in Samaria. Why would he want to leave that to head down a desert road? Conventional wisdom, in fact, would lead him to think he was already doing what he was supposed to do. Yet Philip went as directed.

This whole chapter in Acts is a lesson about how God's ways are not our ways. This story makes no sense from a purely human perspective; in fact, much of Acts doesn't. But this conversion story didn't happen because of conventional wisdom or human planning. The Ethiopian was led to Jesus by Philip as a result of divine leading.

Some dislike the idea of "Spirit-leading talk," calling it superstitious or wildly charismatic. And certainly many people exaggerate and even abuse the "God spoke to me" notion to justify all kinds of wild actions and claims. But I'm not advocating that sort of thing. Instead, I am advocating for a vibrant belief in the Spirit's involvement in our everyday lives. If we don't joyfully welcome his guidance, then something is wrong (Rom 8:9-14). Martyn Lloyd-Jones, who was not a flaming charismatic, had this to say on the matter:

> Here again is a most extraordinary subject, and indeed a very fascinating one, and, from many angles, a most glorious one. There is no question but that God's people can look for and expect "leadings," "guidance," "indications of what they are meant to do." There are many examples of this in the Scriptures and I take one at random. You remember the story in Acts 8:26ff of how Philip the Evangelist was told by the angel of the Lord, "Arise, and go toward the south unto the way that goes down from Jerusalem unto Gaza, which is desert." . . . *Now there are leadings such as that.* . . . If you read the history of the saints, God's people throughout the centuries and especially the history of revivals, you will find that this is something which is perfectly clear and definite—men have been told by the Holy Spirit to do something; they knew it was the Holy Spirit speaking to them, and it transpired that it obviously was his leading. It seems clear to me that if we deny such a possibility we are again guilty of quenching the Spirit. (Cited in Etter, "The Leading and the Quenching of the Spirit"; emphasis added)

Importantly, I don't think you need to "feel led" to share the gospel with people before you actually do so. The Lord has given us a Great Commission to obey. It gives us all the license we need to go out every day and make the gospel known. Nevertheless, we should pray for divine opportunities and remain open and sensitive to the Spirit's promptings. And when he speaks, we must act.

Understand and Explain the Good News to People
ACTS 8:32-40

I love to picture Philip and the Ethiopian in a chariot rolling along under the desert sun. A scroll is unfurled between them as the Ethiopian shares that he has been reading Isaiah 53:7-8, from the famous Suffering Servant song.

For centuries Jews have debated about this passage. Is the prophet speaking of his own suffering, that of the nation as a whole, or that of the Messiah? Philip, who rightly viewed Jesus as the fulfillment of Old Testament prophecies like this one, was prepared to provide the answer. He explained that some 750 years before the crucifixion, Isaiah had described the suffering and exaltation of Jesus. At the heart of Jesus's mission, he shared, is Christ's substitutionary work for sinners. Philip used the Isaiah passage to explain the good news to his eager student. He knew that Christ is the key to Isaiah 53 and said so. He knew and could explain that is also the star of Scripture. Jesus is the Lamb of God, who has borne our sins in his body on the tree. He's the One to whom the redeemed from all nations cry, "Worthy!" (John 1:35; 1 Pet 2:25; Rev 5:8-14).

Though the Ethiopian man probably felt rejected because of his condition, Philip was able to tell him that he was loved and welcomed by the Messiah!

Throughout Luke-Acts we see a recurring need for people to explain the Messiah from the Scriptures. The disciples themselves had needed such guidance (e.g., Luke 24). And after receiving this instruction from Jesus, they in turn explained the Scriptures in light of Christ's work to the Jews in Jerusalem, as illustrated in Acts 2–7. Here this pilgrim from a distant land needed to understand the meaning of Isaiah, and the Lord sent him a wonderful guide in Philip. All of this magnifies the need for Jesus's witnesses to understand the story line of the Bible.

Be Prepared to Explain the Good News

We need to be prepared spiritually and theologically to do the work God intends us to do. The Ethiopian man needed more than a friend in his chariot. He needed an encounter with someone who could explain the truth of the gospel with the Spirit's help. To be faithful witnesses we need the Spirit, and we need a good grasp on the Word. Philip was not only prayed up; he was also studied up.

Recently my local church assembled a group of lay evangelists from our congregation to participate in an outreach experiment that we're calling the Philip Group. These forty people meet with me online every other week for prayer and sharing. Their first task was to identify multiple unbelievers they wanted to reach with the good news. After that, each person was to look for and take opportunities to share truth with those individuals, reporting back via e-mail and text about any gospel conversations they had and giving prayer requests related to their evangelistic efforts. It has been an extremely encouraging initiative!

Since the Philip Group began, I have heard several stories of people ministering to Muslims, Hindus, Buddhists, and atheists. The evangelists are excited to report about how God's Spirit is at work, and they often express a deepening realization of the need to teach the gospel accurately and clearly. As we talk about what questions unbelievers are asking and how they can be prepared to answer them well, I am reminded that the ministry of Philip continues to inspire and instruct.

When was the last time you opened the Bible and explained the good news to someone? Will you pause and pray for such an opportunity this week? If you don't feel capable of explaining the gospel from the Scriptures, it's time for a more rigorous plan of study. Consider opening a copy of Sally Lloyd-Jones's *Jesus Story Book Bible* first; technically it's a kids' book, but it's a great overview of the metanarrative of Scripture. Then progress to a good study Bible or a book on biblical theology. You may even want to look for podcasts you can listen to during your daily commute that focus on teaching Christ as the hero of the whole Bible. No matter what steps you take, pray and remember that such study will help you faithfully and more confidently explain the good news to others.

Consider Using Questions as You Explain the Good News

This whole passage in Acts turns on questions. Philip asks one question, and then the Ethiopian asks three. Asking questions, in fact, provides a wonderful way to start gospel conversations.

Philip began with, "Do you understand what you're reading?" (v. 30). You can do something like this on an airplane, in a coffee shop, at a library, or wherever books are being read because references to books will often get a conversation started. My wife recently started a book club in our community. She and several ladies meet for tea once a month to discuss a novel. It has been a wonderful way for her to meet neighbors and to open dialogues. One of our church members gave out a book on the gospel to all of his coworkers. Then, a few days later, he asked those who'd received it whether they had any questions or wanted to talk about what they read in it.

The Ethiopian asked a great question in reply to Philip's: "How can I . . . unless someone guides me?" (v. 31). The first time I read the Bible, I needed help. Many people feel that way, and it's common to hear people with whom you're attempting to share Christ admit, "I don't know the first thing about the Bible." Don't miss that Philip doesn't use a canned evangelism presentation. He's able to dialogue with the Ethiopian because he knows the Bible well. He knows the story line of Scripture, and he is ready to explain it. You need to see that your personal study of Scripture is *evangelism training*. It prepares you to meet people where they are, sharing Christ with them in ways that will resonate.

The eunuch's next question is, "Who is the prophet saying this about—himself or another person?" (v. 34). In this is a great reminder that even people who are interested in Christianity and have opened their Bibles may still fail to see how it all goes together and points to Jesus (John 5:39,46). Some approach the topic of Christ's identity like they're playing with a jigsaw puzzle but never bother to look at the picture on the box. That means there are even people coming to Sunday gatherings who have little pieces of the puzzle and yet don't really know how the pieces fit into the big picture. Philip types are able to show seekers this glorious picture (e.g., Acts 17:2-3). They understand that the whole Bible is a book about Jesus; it's a book about salvation in him (cf. 2 Tim 3:15).

Finally the Ethiopian asks, "What would keep me from being baptized?" (v. 36). As the chariot passes by a pool of water, the Ethiopian expresses his desire to identify with Jesus though baptism. He believes the gospel as explained to him by Philip. And Philip has the great privilege of baptizing a new believer, a new Christian brother, as a result of his faithfulness to the mission.

Expect God to Work as You Explain the Good News

Some people *will* repent and believe when they hear the gospel.

In this story a double barrier gets broken—physical and racial barriers fall (Polhill, *Acts*, 226). A eunuch, who was also a black man, was received into full membership in the people of Jesus Christ. Though he never would've been able to become a full Jew, he could become a Christian! And so can everyone who calls on the name of the Lord (2:21,37-41).

We don't know much about what happened to this new convert after this scene, only that he journeyed on "rejoicing" (v. 39). Church fathers, however, claim that he became a missionary to Ethiopia. And while their accounts can't be proven, he surely went home and told the good news to others (cf. Ps 68:31).

After disappearing (v. 40; cf. Jesus in Luke 24:31), Philip continues preaching the gospel, working his way north, until he finally lands at Caesarea, where we read about him later in 21:8. Philip had a home and four daughters. Luke simply calls him "the evangelist, who was one of the Seven." We have much to learn from this evangelist about loving people, being led by the Spirit, and explaining the good news from all the Scriptures to everyone. May God grant us grace to "do the work of an evangelist" (2 Tim 4:5).

Reflect and Discuss

1. How does this story highlight God's passion for the nations?
2. What does this passage teach about being led by the Spirit?
3. What does this story teach about the need to explain the Bible to others?
4. What impresses you about the character of Philip?
5. Read Isaiah 52:13–53:12. What does this text teach about Jesus?
6. Why is baptism important?
7. How does Acts 8:26-40 reflect some of the same themes as Luke 24:13-35?
8. Why is Acts 8:26-40 a good illustration of Matthew 28:18-20?
9. How does the conversion of the Ethiopian advance the message of the book of Acts?
10. How might you share the gospel this week?

From Terrorist to Evangelist

ACTS 9:1-31

Main Idea: In a dramatic display of God's saving grace, Luke records the most famous conversion in church history: that of Saul of Tarsus.

I. **Saul's Epic Transformation (9:1-19a)**
    A. The risen Jesus confronts Saul (9:1-9).
    B. The risen Jesus commissions Saul (9:10-19a).
II. **Saul's Early Trials (9:19b-31)**
    A. In Damascus: Astonishment, conspiracy, and escape (9:19b-25)
    B. In Jerusalem: Suspicion, conspiracy, and escape (9:26-30)
    C. Peace in the midst of trials (9:31)

For the past ten years I have had the privilege of teaching annually in Kiev, Ukraine, for a one- to two-week church-planting class. One of the joys of this experience has been taking other guys with me to meet the students. Recently I took my friend, Ben, from Buffalo. As I was showing Ben a map dotted with the locations of church planters from across the former Soviet Union who have come through Kiev Theological Seminary, I said, "Half of these guys are former drug dealers."

While that may have been an exaggeration, it's true that many of these pastors came from rough backgrounds. One brother named Emmanuel used to be in prison. The only time he touched a Bible in those days was to use its pages as rolling paper for his tobacco habit. He's a huge guy with tattoos on each finger, and his handshake hurts. But because of Christ's work in his heart, Emmanuel is now one of the most humble and gentle pastors you could ever meet. Instead of smoking the Bible, he's proclaiming it!

Major before-and-after-meeting-Christ stories like this brother's remind us that no one is so bad that he's beyond the reach of God's saving grace. God can change the most hardened sinners, the vilest men and women, and turn them into great ambassadors of the kingdom. Such transformation is called conversion.

In Acts 9 we read of perhaps the most famous conversion in the history of Christianity. The conversion of Saul of Tarsus is actually one of the most important events—aside from Jesus's resurrection—in the history of the world. Saul's conversion plays a monumental role in the advancement of the kingdom across nations and centuries.

This passage elevates our view of God's converting power, and it also reminds us of the various trials that accompany believers as they seek to obey the God who redeemed them.

Saul's Epic Transformation
ACTS 9:1-19A

Luke narrates Saul's conversion here in Acts 9. Later, in Acts 22, Paul retells it to a mob in the temple and then again to King Agrippa in Acts 26. He also reflects on God's transforming grace in other places, including Romans 1:1-5; 1 Corinthians 15:8-10; Galatians 1:11-24; Philippians 3:4-11; and 1 Timothy 1:12-17. This event changed everything for this man.

The Risen Jesus Confronts Saul (9:1-9)

This passage begins with Saul's persecuting the church intensely. He isn't content with merely persecuting believers in Jerusalem (8:3); his campaign extends to Damascus (9:1-2; see 26:11). Only the spilling of more blood will satisfy his obsessive hatred of Christians. He wants to liquidate every vestige of Christianity. The arrest warrants he receives from the high priest, authorizing him to arrest believers, fill him with the hope that others will soon face a fate similar to Stephen's.

The earliest Christ followers probably took on the title "the Way" based on the words of Jesus, who referred to himself as "the way, the truth, and the life" (John 14:6; see Acts 19:9,23; 22:4; 24:14,22). Saul, the text says, hoped to eradicate men and women belonging to "the Way" as he headed north toward Damascus.

But something happens along his journey. The risen Christ arrests Saul. A light representing the blinding glory of God (cf. Luke 2:9) flashes around the persecutor. Like the prophets who were called through the vision of God's glorious light, so this man is now confronted with the Holy One. The encounter happens around noon (see Acts 22:6), yet the midday sunshine is swallowed up by the greater light. Traumatized, Saul falls to the ground.

Like many Old Testament individuals, Saul is summoned by name. Then, as he wonders whose voice he hears, Jesus stuns him by identifying himself as the speaker (v. 5). Saul had thought he was on a righteous mission to eradicate followers of this very Person, but now he's quivering on the ground before the blinding glory of Christ, and he's made aware that he's on the wrong team. Saul learns that to persecute the church is to persecute Jesus. The Lord identifies with his bride. Theirs is an amazing union.

The risen Lord then directs Saul to go to the city in order to receive further instructions (vv. 5-6). Saul did not see, eat, or drink for three days (v. 9).

Saul's worldview got demolished. A new one was about to take its place. Jesus humbled this arrogant and violent man, turning the terrorist into a soon-to-be evangelist. The self-righteous persecutor is about to become the Christ-centered apostle.

The Risen Jesus Commissions Saul (9:10-19a)

In contrast with the Ananias mentioned in Acts 5, this Ananias in verse 10 is a faithful Christian who is set to welcome Saul into the company of disciples (cf. 22:12). When first the Lord tells him to go meet Saul, Ananias objects. Saul was well known for his violent acts in Jerusalem, and Ananias knew Saul's intentions in Damascus. The Lord, however, calms Ananias's fears; he describes Saul's entirely new identity and purpose. God's word would prove true. In the following chapters Saul—who would soon be known as Paul—addresses "Gentiles, kings, and Israelites." He suffers much for the sake of Christ; he will be shipwrecked, slandered, imprisoned, and worse.

Ananias goes, lays his hand on the waiting Saul, and says, "Brother Saul . . ." (v. 17). This means that the first word Saul hears from this man, this follower of the Way, is "brother." What a comfort! Surely in that moment Saul not only received his new identity but recognized that in Christ he also received a new family. Becoming a follower of Jesus involves coming into a family of brothers and sisters in the faith.

Ananias then reported why he came: Saul was to regain his sight and be filled with the Spirit. And just like that, boom! Everything changed. Saul can suddenly see again and gets baptized (vv. 18-19). Imagine it! Saul of Tarsus, who once despised Christ and his church, is now being buried with Christ in baptism and raised to walk in newness of life. From this point forward, he is identified with Christ and with Christ's people. The adversary thus becomes the apostle. He is no longer corrupt but cleansed, no longer a church foe but part of the family. What grace!

Paul says that his conversion is an "example" of Jesus's saving grace and mercy (1 Tim 1:16). While his conversion and commissioning are

unique, we still can learn several lessons about all conversions by studying this one.

Salvation is by God's amazing grace (cf. 1 Cor 15:10). Instead of execut-
ing Saul on that Damascus road, Jesus shows him unspeakable grace
(1 Tim 1:16). Later Saul would become a theologian of grace, writing
breathtaking passages about the nature of salvation (cf. Eph 2:1-10).
The good news of the gospel is that God pursues sinners. Saul was not
on a quest to find salvation; he was on a quest to persecute Christians!
Yet God arrested Saul by his sovereign grace (cf. Gal 1:13-16).

All conversions involve a life-changing encounter with Jesus Christ.
Conversion happens dramatically for some, but for others it happens
quietly. In Acts 16 we find the dramatic conversion of a jailor. God sends
in an earthquake, and then the man asks, "What must I do to be saved?"
(16:30). In a previous story, however, a lady named Lydia converted
more quietly. She simply heard the gospel, God opened her heart to
it, and she repented and believed (16:14-15). Both individuals were
changed after an encounter with Jesus.

All conversions involve a surrender to Jesus Christ. Saul can only humbly
surrender to the sovereign Lord. Jesus humbles Saul by showing him
the truth, namely that the resurrection is true. This Jesus, whom Saul
once thought a phony, showed himself in power. Jesus also humbles
Saul by blinding him, forcing the tough guy to be led by the hand. And
Jesus further humbles him by sending him to Damascus to await instructions. All of this helps Saul realize that he isn't in charge. The King is.
Saul can only surrender.

*While one may not have the same blinding experience as Saul, the metaphor
of blindness to sight, darkness to light, applies to every Christian theologically.*
Saul's blindness pictured the spiritual darkness and ignorance in which
he had been living, but God showed him the glory of the truth about
Christ. Paul writes about this to the Corinthians:

> *The god of this age has blinded the minds of the unbelievers to keep
> them from seeing the light of the gospel of the glory of Christ, who is the
> image of God. For we are not proclaiming ourselves but Jesus Christ
> as Lord, and ourselves as your servants for Jesus's sake. For God who
> said, "Let light shine out of darkness," has shone in our hearts to give
> the light of the knowledge of God's glory in the face of Jesus Christ.*
> (2 Cor 4:4-6)

Though Paul thought he was righteous (Phil 3:6), he was actually walking in spiritual darkness until Jesus arrested and transformed him. If

God has transferred you out of darkness and into the kingdom of his beloved Son, then your heart should soar in praise to him (Col 1:13-14).

Sincerity alone doesn't save. Saul truly believed he was righteous, yet he couldn't have been more wrong. All of his good deeds, all of his careful rule keeping amounted to nothing. To our culture's expression, "It doesn't matter what you believe, just be sincere," we must object. Saul was sincerely wrong about Jesus and the way of salvation, like many today (Rom 10:1-4). One must put faith in Christ alone for salvation (Acts 4:12).

Conversion involves the receiving of the Spirit. As Saul received the Spirit, so does every Christian who truly repents and turns to Christ for salvation. Saul would later go on to write much about the Spirit's involvement in Christians' lives (e.g., Rom 8:9-17).

God can save the worst of sinners. Some people think the least likely person to be converted to faith in Jesus is a terrorist, yet this story disproves the theory. Imagine a leader of the terrorist group ISIS being converted and then preaching Christ to his former jihadists. Would that not be remarkable? Yet here we have Saul, ravaging the church, "terribly enraged," persecuting them "even to foreign cities" (26:11), who suddenly begins preaching about Jesus because Jesus captured his heart. Don't doubt God's power to convert the worst of sinners. Pray even for the salvation of terrorists.

When you become a new person, you also receive a new purpose. All Christians are sent on a mission to preach the good news to the spiritually blind and to tell sinners how to find forgiveness (26:16-18). Saul was elected not just to salvation, but also for *mission.* Too many Christians walk around pontificating about theological topics like predestination without ever sharing the good news with lost people. This doesn't square with the Bible's idea of election. With the privilege of receiving salvation comes the responsibility of making much of Jesus in word and deed in this broken world. And when we share the good news, we can be confident that some people will say yes. If you're a Christian, you're a chosen instrument in the hands of God to be used for mission (cf. Eph 3:7-10).

Conversion involves receiving a new family. As Christians we participate in Christ's mission of making him known by partnering *together.* Saul will soon write some wonderful pieces about the body of Christ serving Christ and one another faithfully (cf. 1 Cor 12).

The ultimate question this passage invites us to ask is this: have I truly experienced conversion? John Stott emphasizes this need as he summarizes how we should apply Saul's conversion narrative:

We too can (and must) experience a personal encounter with Jesus Christ, surrender to him in penitence and faith, and receive his summons to service. Provided that we distinguish between the historically particular and the universal, between the dramatic outward accompaniments and the essential inward experience, what happened to Saul remains an instructive case study in Christian conversion. Moreover, Christ's display of "unlimited patience" towards him was meant to be an encouraging "example" to others. (*Message of Acts,* 166)

Have you surrendered to Christ in repentance and faith, receiving his summons to service? If so, then allow the grace of God to encourage you as you live on mission. God saves sinners, and he wants to reach others through you. Rejoice! If you haven't surrendered to him, then do so now. You can't use the excuse that you're too bad or even count on all of your religious efforts to buy your salvation. Look at Saul! You are just the right candidate for grace.

Saul's Early Trials
ACTS 9:19B-31

Jesus never promised Saul that his ministry would be easy, so it shouldn't have surprised Saul when he faced trials right after conversion. His life soon followed this pattern: Saul preached Christ boldly; Saul became the object of a murderous plot; Saul escaped. Welcome to the ministry, Saul!

In Damascus: Astonishment, Conspiracy, and Escape (9:19b-25)

At this point in Acts, Saul has a new family and a new message (vv. 19-20). He's undergone a total transformation! Saul is telling everyone about the One who changed him—Jesus, the Son of God (v. 22). This guy became an entirely new person through the work of Christ. Saul's whole ministry would be Christ exalting from beginning to end.

Everyone was "astounded" by Saul's transformation. He had raised havoc in Jerusalem, persecuting everyone who called on Jesus's name (v. 21; cf. 1 Cor 15:9; Gal 1:13,23; 1 Tim 1:13). Here the very name *Saul* once despised is the name he powerfully and unceasingly declares.

Over time Saul "grew stronger" (v. 22). This seems to reference spiritual strength. God continued to empower Saul to testify to the good news of the gospel. Soon the man's ministry began to frustrate the Jews in Damascus because they couldn't counter his claims about Jesus as the Christ. How I love that Scripture includes that detail because this same thing happened in Stephen's case: no one could withstand the wisdom with which he spoke either (6:10). Saul, in effect then, has taken Stephen's place (vv. 22-23), and it's not long before he too faces the threat of death. The Lord, however, doesn't allow a murderous scheme against him to succeed; he has much more work for the apostle to do. Verses 24-25 detail Saul's Indiana Jones-like escape.

Following Jesus isn't easy, but he is with us. Jesus's grace is sufficient. In 2 Corinthians Paul rattles off a host of trials he endured as he followed Christ. Chapter 11 of that book culminates in the escape from Damascus. He said,

> [I have faced] far more labors, many more imprisonments, far worse beatings, [and have been] many times near death.
>   Five times I received the forty lashes minus one from the Jews. Three times I was beaten with rods. Once I received a stoning. Three times I was shipwrecked. I have spent a night and a day in the open sea. On frequent journeys, I faced dangers from rivers, dangers from robbers, dangers from my own people, dangers from Gentiles, dangers in the city, dangers in the wilderness, dangers at sea, and dangers among false brothers; toil and hardship, many sleepless nights, hunger and thirst, often without food, cold, and without clothing. Not to mention other things, there is the daily pressure on me: my concern for all the churches. Who is weak, and I am not weak? Who is made to stumble, and I do not burn with indignation?
>   If boasting is necessary, I will boast about my weaknesses. The God and Father of the Lord Jesus, who is blessed forever, knows I am not lying. In Damascus, a ruler under King Aretas guarded the city of Damascus in order to arrest me. So I was let down in a basket through a window in the wall and escaped from his hands. (2 Cor 11:23-33)

Paul's words give us a needed dose of realism. Living in a fallen world is difficult, and following Jesus in a fallen world involves even more suffering (2 Tim 3:12). So don't be surprised when you face trials and opposition for proclaiming Christ.

Paul's words also remind us that in the midst of trials we still can rely on and rejoice in the all-sufficient grace of Jesus. In the next chapter of 2 Corinthians, Paul expresses this very fact—that Christ's power is made perfect in weaknesses (2 Cor 12:9). So go to Jesus to be strengthened by grace (2 Tim 2:1).

Finally, this testimony of Paul reminds us that no one can thwart the sovereign Lord's plans. Neither the city's governor nor a host of other people could capture Paul because Jesus was in charge and wouldn't allow them to succeed. In the midst of your trials, remember that there's only one sovereign Lord. Live with confident trust in him.

In Jerusalem: Suspicion, Conspiracy, and Escape (9:26-30)

In Jerusalem the Christians who'd received reports about Saul's conversion were full of suspicion. When he tried to join the disciples, they were afraid of him and did not even believe that he was a Christ follower (v. 26).

Enter Barnabas. Thankfully, the "Son of Encouragement" gave Saul a hearing and trusted his story. Barnabas then advocated for Saul, describing all of the previous transforming events in Saul's life to the apostles (v. 27) and vouching for him. Because of Barnabas's intervention, the disciples received Saul as a brother.

Twice Luke says that Saul preached "boldly in the name of the Lord/Jesus" (vv. 27-28). Based on some of Paul's writings, we shouldn't attribute that courage to a brash personality. True, he was a zealous man. But the former persecutor told the Corinthians that his preaching involved feeling "weakness," "fear," and enduring "much trembling" (1 Cor 2:3). Paul asked the churches in Ephesus and Colossae to pray for him so he might preach the gospel fearlessly (Eph 6:19-20; Col 4:3-4). This is a reminder that boldness, for all believers, is a gift of God, who gives it to those who humbly ask him (Acts 4:29,31). Let's ask God to grant us this boldness as we make Christ known.

In Acts 9:29 Saul is disputing with the Hellenists—a group that showed up in 6:9 at Stephen's trial. Saul was likely a leader in the Greek-speaking synagogue. Now he's disputing about Jesus with the men who once trusted his leadership!

As a result of Saul's bold preaching, he faces the same problem he faced in Damascus: he becomes the target of a murderous plot (v. 29). His Christian brothers send him away to Tarsus (v. 30), leading the narrative to close with Saul en route to his hometown (21:39; 22:3). Saul will reenter the Acts account when Barnabas retrieves him so that together they may visit the church in Antioch (11:25-26; cf. Gal 1:21).

This passage underscores the nature of being a witness and is a reminder of the importance of being an encourager to other believers. Regarding the former, Saul gives us a pattern for a faithful witness.

Faithful witnesses are first *Christ centered*. Saul goes about preaching Christ, not talking about himself or giving some how-to-live-a-better-life sermon. Second, a faithful witness is *empowered*. Saul was strengthened through his personal relationship with Christ (v. 22). Third, a faithful witness is *bold* (vv. 27-28). Fourth, a faithful witness will *suffer*. Let's pray for the Lord to empower us to proclaim Christ boldly even in the face of suffering.

Regarding the need to encourage other brothers and sisters, Barnabas, once again, provides a wonderful model for us. I love how Luke says, "Barnabas took him" (v. 27). It tells us Barnabas spent time with Saul. He listened. He encouraged. He advocated for him. He befriended him. Later he retrieved Saul and ministered alongside him. The investments this man made involved time, risk, and humility. He truly was filled with grace. Be on the lookout for ways you can be a Barnabas to other believers this week.

Peace in the Midst of Trials (9:31)

Luke moves the whole Acts narrative along with this summary:

> *So the church throughout all Judea, Galilee, and Samaria had peace and was strengthened. Living in fear of the Lord and encouraged by the Holy Spirit, it increased in numbers.* (9:31)

This tells us that though the church faced many threats and trials externally, it experienced great peace inwardly. We experience peace through a right relationship with God through Christ. This relationship involves walking by the Spirit and walking humbly before the God who is to be feared. When we walk humbly, prayerfully, and dependently, we find peace—even though we may be in a time of crisis.

In addition to enjoying these spiritual blessings, the church multiplied numerically. Jesus continued to build his church despite murderous plots and heated opposition. Both the conversion of Saul and the growth of the church showcase God's amazing grace. Both give us reason to give God praise.

Not long ago I took our family to watch the remake of the movie *Annie*. The film touched on many important themes and gave me many talking points for dinner-table discussion. One of the songs in particular gave me opportunity to talk with my family about the gospel.

Toward the end of the movie, Will Stacks (a wealthy cell-phone tycoon who runs for mayor) and Hannigan (a horrible foster mom) sing, "Who Am I?" The lyrics of their song are antigospel, revealing that both characters live for money. Self-centered and greedy, each realizes that change is in order. It's time to start thinking about other people.

But becoming less self-centered or even wildly dedicated to humanitarian causes doesn't really fix anything. The chorus, "I want to start again, so I'll look within," rings hollow—though it's based on a popular twenty-first-century notion. People can change their diets, their habits, even their passions, but self-effort alone can't completely change a life, alter a person's eternal destiny. People need the Life-Changer to do that.

Saul's life wasn't changed as a result of karma or looking within or because he followed a self-help plan. His following lists of religious rules fell short. Jesus is what changed Saul into Paul. Jesus changed him forever. So if you want to start again, look to him, the Life-Changer, Jesus Christ. In him there is hope for both the self-righteous moralist and the unrighteous hedonist. He can make all things new.

Reflect and Discuss

1. Read some of the other passages related to Saul's conversion and note the similarities and differences: Acts 22:1-21; 26:12-23; Romans 1:1-5; 1 Corinthians 15:8-10; Galatians 1:11-24; Philippians 3:4-11; and 1 Timothy 1:12-17.
2. What are some of the similarities between Saul's conversion experience and other conversion experiences? What are some differences?
3. What does this passage teach about God's grace in salvation?
4. What does this passage teach about Jesus?
5. What practical lessons might be learned from Ananias's inclusion in this story?
6. What about Jesus's commission of Saul most resonates with you?
7. What can we learn from Saul's trials?
8. Why is Barnabas an example worth following?
9. How can you speak with greater boldness?
10. How can Christians have peace even in times of crisis?

Grace for Every Race

ACTS 9:32–11:18

Main Idea: In order to convert the Gentile Cornelius and to show the Jewish Christians the gospel was for everyone without distinction, God had to first "convert" Peter.

I.   Scene 1: Introduction (9:32–10:8)
II. Scene 2: Vision (10:3-16)
III. Scene 3: Application (10:17-33)
IV. Scene 4: Declaration (10:34-43)
V. Scene 5: Confirmation (10:44-48)
VI. Scene 6: Resolution (11:1-18)
VII. Concluding Exhortations
    A. Jesus overcomes disease and death—rely on him!
    B. Jesus shows hospitality to all—imitate him!
    C. Jesus commands us to preach to everyone—proclaim him!
    D. Jesus saves irreligious and religious people—worship him!

After describing the conversion of Saul, Luke provided a summary of the church flourishing and growing "throughout all Judea, Galilee, and Samaria" (9:31). In this narrative on the ministry of Peter, we see the church's mission extending into greater Judea and, most importantly, "to the end of the earth" through the conversion of the Gentile Cornelius in Caesarea. Thus, the Acts 1:8 commission sees fulfillment.

Three big game changers in the book of Acts are Pentecost, the conversion of Saul, and the conversion of Cornelius. The Pentecost event described in chapter 2 was one of the most important in the history of the world. On that day the promised Holy Spirit was poured out on the Christians in Jerusalem, granting them gifts and power to fulfill Jesus's mission. Then in Acts 9, Saul (Paul) converted. Much of the rest of Acts (after these chapters) has to do with ministry among the Gentiles. And that's where Cornelius fits. Through Peter's ministry to Cornelius, God pours out his Spirit on the Gentiles and confirms to Peter and other disciples that the gospel is for the nations. God gave glimpses of his heart for the nations with the conversion of the Samaritans and the Ethiopian eunuch, but with this conversion his love for the nations is on full display for the church and for the world to witness and accept.

In order to convert Cornelius, and to show the Jewish Christians the gospel was for everyone without distinction, God had to "convert" Peter—not to Christianity but to the implications of Christianity (Azurdia, "The Conversion of Peter"). Peter had to be convinced that the gospel is for everyone, including those completely outside the Jewish nation.

God's saving grace extends to those of every people group who cry out to the Savior for salvation. Yet this basic truth is difficult for some Christians to apply because of deeply embedded prejudice that can lurk within even a redeemed heart. Consider the following example of an all-too-common attitude Christians display toward outsiders:

> Mahatma Gandhi shares in his autobiography that in his student days in England he was deeply touched by reading the Gospels and seriously considered becoming a convert to Christianity, which seemed to offer a real solution to the caste system that divided the people of India. One Sunday he attended church services and decided to ask the minster for enlightenment on salvation and other doctrines. But when Gandhi entered the sanctuary, the ushers refused to give him a seat and suggested that he go elsewhere to worship with his own people. He left and never came back. "If Christians have caste differences also," he said to himself, "I might as well remain a Hindu!" (Hughes, *Acts*, 149).

The sad fact is we have all heard other stories just as heartbreaking as this one. I have known church members, even pastors, to express a similar attitude toward particular people groups.

The propensity to discriminate is a result of humanity's sinful fallen nature. People discriminate against others based on age, appearance, ancestry, affluence, and achievements. The results of this bad habit are featured in the news regularly: senseless shootings abound and people spew hateful rhetoric against certain groups. But we must understand that prejudice in its many forms is evil, and we must repent of it. Further, we must *keep repenting* of the tendency to discriminate because it is deeply ingrained in many of us—even without our realizing it. Even the apostle Peter had to struggle to overcome the sin of showing partiality (Gal 2:11-14).

Remember the reluctant prophet Jonah? He didn't want to go to Nineveh. Why? Because he despised the Assyrian people who lived there. There are many similarities between Jonah and the reluctant apostle Peter. In fact, Peter's real name is Simon Bar-Jonah (Simon, son of Jonah; Matt 16:17). The Lord commissioned both Jonah and Simon Bar-Jonah to carry his message to their enemies. Both protested. Peter was no more willing to mingle with the Gentiles than Jonah was with the Ninevites. Nevertheless, both eventually withdrew their protests—Jonah after spending three days and nights in the belly of a great fish and Peter after receiving an instructive vision repeated three times. After preaching God's message as instructed, both men witnessed God's granting repentance to the outsiders. This provokes a hostile response from Jonah, representative of traditional Israel, and God corrects him. The positive response of Cornelius's household evokes an antagonistic response from others within traditional Israel, which God also corrects. Jonah and Simon Bar-Jonah are both sent to display God's heart for the nations, and both needed a missional conversion.

There are many impediments to the advancement of the gospel, as we've observed in our study of Acts. We've seen outside persecution. We've seen internal drama. And here we see another impediment: our own hearts. We must overcome discrimination in order to be good missionaries.

What is your disposition when you encounter a person with tattoos and multiple piercings? When you are introduced to a same-sex couple or encounter a cross-dresser when paying for your groceries? How do you speak and act when introduced to those whose politics are the opposite of yours? What about when you meet a Muslim family new to your neighborhood? Are you and your friends unaffected by the elitism, exclusivism, and discrimination that pervade our society? This text teaches that no wall should keep Christians from offering the gospel of Jesus freely and lovingly to everyone.

The Cornelius story is the longest of all the narratives in Acts. Its ripple effects were felt for years afterward. Allow me to note six scenes.

Scene 1: Introduction
ACTS 9:32–10:8

Peter (9:32-42). This section opens with a (re)introduction to Peter and then to Cornelius. Peter was last mentioned in Acts 8, with the Samaritan mission.

Having already witnessed God's working of miracles through Peter, we may wonder why these two miracles are included here. First, they reinforce the *authenticity* of Peter's apostleship. They remind us of who Peter is and that he is running in the footsteps of Jesus. Second, they demonstrate the *power* of Jesus. Peter's mission to the nations (and ours) is propelled by the resurrection power of Jesus. Third, these miracles provide *signs* of the coming kingdom of Jesus, who will heal the sick and raise the dead. Finally, these miracles aren't ends in themselves; in both stories people turn to the Lord for *salvation as a result of them* (9:35,42).

The first miracle, involving Aeneas, highlights *Christ's power over disease.* Peter is traveling about, preaching the gospel and visiting the believers in Lydda (9:32). Since these believers were living in a transitional period, they surely had lots of questions about how to apply the law and live out their faith. While in Lydda, some twenty-five miles northwest of Jerusalem and about twelve miles southeast of Joppa, Peter met Aeneas. The man had been paralyzed and bedridden for eight years.

I can only imagine the longings of this guy's heart. Maybe he desperately wished to feel his wife's feet snuggled beside him under their blankets, to be able to feed himself, to experience the satisfaction of a hard day's work, to feel the Mediterranean splash against his ankles on a summer day. Whatever dreams he cherished, he was about to see them come true.

When Peter sees Aeneas, he simply says, "Aeneas, Jesus Christ heals you. Get up and make your bed" (9:34). In doing this Peter points to the power, Jesus, who had a history of healing paralytics (cf. Luke 5:24-25). And Aeneas just got up and walked in response to Peter's words. Just imagine the joy in this man's heart!

Assuming this story follows the pattern of Acts 3, the miracle attracted a crowd, and Peter preached the gospel to them. Thus, many people were converted (9:35).

Next we see *Christ's power over death displayed* in the story of *Dorcas.* This saint fell ill and died, and Luke tells us what had made her so special: verse 36 says, "She was always doing good works and acts of charity." (What a great epitaph!) The widows for whom she had made clothes mourned for her deeply (v. 39). The disciples in Joppa promptly sent for Peter, hoping he might raise her up. They didn't even bury her; they placed the woman's body in a room, hoping for a miracle. And they weren't disappointed: God used Peter to display Christ's power over death.

Peter stands in the tradition of Elijah and Elisha, and especially of Jesus. Like Jesus and Elisha, Peter sends everyone out of the room when he shows up to call the dead back to life; he's left alone with the corpse (cf. 2 Kgs 4:33; Mark 5:40). Like Elisha, Peter falls to his knees in prayer, looking to the One with resurrection power as his help. (Jesus didn't have to pray in Mark 5 because he *is* the resurrection and the life!) Peter then calls Dorcas by her Aramaic name: "Tabitha," he says, "get up!" This is almost an echo of Jesus's Aramaic command to Jarius's daughter, "*Talitha koum*" (Mark 5:41). In response Dorcas opens her eyes like the Shumammite woman's son did in 2 Kings 4:35 as he awakened. Dorcas then sits up, as did the widow's son at Nain (Luke 7:15). Then, as Elijah and Jesus gave sons back to the widowed mothers (1 Kgs 17:23; Luke 7:15), so Peter gives the widow back to the saints.

Both of these miracles set the stage for the next one. Having shown us Christ's power over disease and death, Dr. Luke has prepared us to see Christ's power over discrimination.

Luke concludes the chapter by noting that Peter is in Joppa, staying with Simon, a tanner (9:43). This is significant. Clearly God was already overcoming some of Peter's cultural biases. A tanner was rendered perpetually unclean by the Jews because he dealt with dead animals in order to convert their skins into leather.

Cornelius (10:1-8). Caesarea was the capital of the Roman occupation of Israel. It was a military town. It's right on the coast, thirty-one miles north of Joppa. It's important to know that the Jews hated Caesarea. They called it the daughter of Edom, a place of ungodliness, that is a symbolic name for Rome.

Cornelius is a captain of the occupying Roman army. As a centurion, he would have commanded about a hundred Roman soldiers posted in Caesarea, and he would have been paid as much as five times more than an ordinary soldier. So he's a wealthy and influential man. Jews, however, surely resented him.

In this intensely Gentile place Peter comes to terms with his own prejudices. The gospel is about to shatter an antigospel tradition lurking in the apostle's heart.

What is the most despised location in the world to you? Which nation, city, or part of town could you do without? Take a moment to consider why you feel that way. Now, imagine traveling to that location, working to befriend those you meet there, and offering them the good news. That's Peter's assignment.

Luke doesn't want us to miss Cornelius's religious devotion (10:2). The man "feared God." The term "God fearer" was applied to Gentiles who adhered to Judaism's faith in one God as they obeyed the Ten Commandments while balking at the idea of submitting to circumcision or to following the kosher dietary restrictions of Leviticus (Johnson, *Let's Study Acts*, 124). Jews tended to respect such people, though they kept them at arm's length because of their practices. Luke also notes that the man's piety involved the giving of alms and prayer. Such generosity explains why he was well spoken of by the whole Jewish nation (v. 22). In some ways he is like the centurion at Capernaum, who had a respectable relationship with the Jewish people, supporting their work (Luke 7:4-5).

Importantly, though Cornelius was a religious man, he wasn't a regenerate one. Cornelius was like Nicodemus—the man to whom Jesus spoke the words of John 3:16—in that he was pious and respected. Jesus told the latter, "You must be born again." That is, even a "good" man must be radically converted. The gospel isn't just for irreligious people; it's for religious people too.

Scene 2: Vision
ACTS 10:3-16

Just as complementary visions between Saul and Ananias confirmed God's call to Saul, so here we have complementary visions confirming the import of what would happen between Cornelius and Peter.

Cornelius first receives a vision to meet with Peter (vv. 3-8). The former's sundial was set to the temple's time, to the time of the evening sacrifice, and during his time of prayer, he gets instruction from an angel. Cornelius isn't a Christian when this happens, and it's important that God doesn't save him in this vision. In Acts 11 we receive a bit more detail about what happened:

> [Cornelius] reported to us how he had seen the angel standing in his house and saying, "Send to Joppa, and call for Simon, who is also named Peter. He will speak a message to you by which you and all your household will be saved." (Acts 11:13-14; emphasis added)

In the vision God directs Cornelius to the evangelist. Cornelius becomes a Christian when he hears the message and believes it (cf. 4:12; Rom 10:14-17). While God began working in the heart of Cornelius by his initiating grace, Cornelius needed to know the gospel and embrace it.

I recently heard about a missionary in a dangerous part of the Middle East who started an underground church. Locals tried to discover the location of that assembly in order to persecute the believers there, but they could never find it. Late one night, however, the missionary heard a knock on the door of the secret church. He cautiously opened it to see a tribesman standing there. The man explained that he had walked for days in order to find the missionary. He said, "I had a vision three days ago that there would be a man standing at this address who would tell me how to get to heaven. Sir, are you this man?" That tribesman, like Cornelius, was given a vision leading him to an evangelist who would teach him how to cross from spiritual death to abundant life.

An old classmate was recently ministering to Muslims in Washington, DC. One day a Muslim man approached him and asked, "Who is 'I Am'? I keep seeing 'I Am' in my dreams." After giving a summary explanation, he gave the seeker a Bible and encouraged him to read the Gospel of John. It wasn't long until he led the man to faith in Jesus, and at that point the convert confessed, "Many of the 'I am' statements I read in John I heard first in my dreams!" This story, too, reminds us that even when God uses visions to nudge people toward faith in Christ, evangelists must still do the exciting work of explaining the gospel to them that they might understand and embrace it with confidence.

God doesn't always speak to nonbelievers—or even to Christians—through dramatic dreams. Sometimes he draws people through a deep-down hunger of sorts. Sometimes he begins to nudge people toward faith in Christ by making them curious about the gospel or about spiritual questions involving what happens after death or why people follow moral codes. If you are hungering to know more about Jesus or find yourself drawn into a conversation with someone who expresses such desire, realize that God does actually seek us. C. S. Lewis once remarked, "Amiable agnostics will talk cheerfully about 'man's search for God.' . . . They might as well have talked about the mouse's search for the cat" (C. S. Lewis, *Surprised by Joy*).

In 10:9-16 Peter receives a vision in which he is told to eat all kinds of meat without concerning himself with whether such foods are clean or unclean according to the Jewish dietary laws. Notice that Peter, like Cornelius, was praying when he received his vision. I'm not suggesting that something dramatic like this will happen every time we pray, but I do think it indicates that those who humbly seek the Lord in unhindered and unhurried prayer experience great blessing.

Peter is commanded to kill and consume diverse creatures, even those forbidden in Leviticus 11 (cf. Mark 7:19). While Peter doesn't understand the symbolism at work in this vision yet, these unclean animals symbolize God's cleansing of the unclean Gentiles. But Peter refuses to obey the command three times; he has a history of three-time rejection followed by affirmation! Food restrictions had long isolated the Jews from the Gentiles, but God was breaking down the wall.

To share food and drink at a table with others is a big deal. It's a declaration of friendship, and in that way it's like declaring a covenant. As Christians we should be willing to eat with anyone. And we should receive hospitality from anyone. Currently, many in my church have been reaching out to West Africans and other Muslims in our city. It has been so encouraging to hear stories about how these believers have shared meals with these neighbors. Doing so has broken down many walls and allowed for several fruitful discussions, and some of these Muslim friends have attended our worship services.

Scene 3: Application
ACTS 10:17-33

Next, Peter and Cornelius apply their visions. Peter is pondering the things he's seen when the visitors arrive at the gate. They won't enter it because they're Gentiles. Peter is told he must not hesitate to go with them (v. 20). After all, a Roman official didn't ultimately send them; God did. So Peter goes out to meet them. The men tell him a bit about Cornelius, the angel, and their purpose (v. 22). Then Luke says, "Peter then invited them in and gave them lodging" (v. 23). This hospitality offer may not seem like a big deal to us, but for Peter and other Jewish Christians it signaled a huge gospel moment! Peter and others are being "converted" out of the thinking that the good news is for the Jews alone.

Not only did Peter give the men lodging, but the next day he made a two-day journey to Caesarea, taking some of the brothers from Joppa with him (v. 23). These men would serve not only as companions but also as witnesses.

When they finally arrive in Caesarea, both Cornelius and Peter display deep humility. Cornelius, a Roman official, bows before this Jewish fisherman! Then the Jewish fisherman reminds Cornelius that both are simply men, created by God. There's no need to bow to one another. They are together only because they have submitted to God's Word and are acting in humility toward God and one another.

In verses 30-32 Cornelius replays the events for Peter, telling the apostle why he sent for him. Then Cornelius displays even more humility, expressing eagerness to hear Peter's word from God (v. 33). I can't imagine receiving a better invitation to preach the gospel!

Consider three ways we can display a love for all our neighbors, regardless of their ethnicity or background.

1. We can show no *hesitation* in befriending people unlike us (v. 20).
2. We can show *hospitality* toward everyone, opening our homes and lives to them (v. 23).
3. We can show *humility* before all people, regardless of their skin color or annual income, living with the understanding that we're all made in God's image (v. 26).

Would displaying love in these ways come easily for you, or might you first need to be "converted" like Peter? If you hesitate at the idea of befriending and associating with people unlike you or have never opened your home to those outside your usual circle, it's possible that you do have an air of elitism. If so, ask the Lord to change your heart, to give you his perspective.

Scene 4: Declaration
ACTS 10:34-43

I love that Peter responds appropriately to the spiritual softball Cornelius throws. He doesn't strike out but hits a home run as he preaches the gospel.

What exactly does he proclaim? First, he denies that God shows partiality across ethnic lines (v. 34; cf. Deut 10:17-19). Second, he affirms that God welcomes from every nation people who fear him (v. 35). In making this statement Peter isn't saying that God's welcome is based on works (see the necessity of faith and forgiveness in 10:43). Instead, he's simply saying that God shows mercy to those who humble themselves before him. Third, Peter stresses that Jesus, the sent One who preached peace, is Lord of all (v. 36). Fourth, Peter assumes the crowd is aware of Jesus's controversial earthly ministry (vv. 37-38), which included several elements. Peter mentions the descent of the Spirit at Jesus's baptism, Jesus's good deeds, Jesus's healings and power over the devil, and God's presence with Jesus. Fifth, Peter centers his message on the cross, the resurrection, and the return of Jesus (vv. 39-42). Then, finally, Peter mentions the prophets—but the sermon gets cut off before passages are quoted (v. 43; cf. 11:15) as the Spirit of God falls on the Gentiles in the middle of the sermon (10:44).

This passage provides essentials we should ponder and incorporate into our own gospel presentations:

1. Jesus, the Messiah, is Lord of all.
2. Jesus was empowered by the Spirit to liberate the devil's captives.
3. Jesus died under the curse deserved by others.
4. Jesus was raised up to reign forever.
5. Jesus will judge everyone.
6. All of this is in accordance with the Scriptures, which promise forgiveness for everyone—from every people—who trust in Jesus's name.

This message of salvation opened the door of the kingdom to the Gentiles, and it will continue to open the door to heaven for all who will embrace it. John Stott comments on Peter's door-opening ministry:

> We have already watched him [Peter] use these keys effectively, opening the kingdom to Jews on the Day of Pentecost and then to Samaritans soon afterwards. Now he is to use them again to open the kingdom to Gentiles; by evangelizing and baptizing Cornelius, the first Gentile convert (cf. Acts 15:7). (*Message of Acts*, 19)

And it's to this baptism we now turn.

Scene 5: Confirmation
ACTS 10:44-48

Luke records the Gentiles' amazing response to Peter's sermon. What happens here is essentially a Gentile Pentecost, verifying that salvation has come to them also. The verse 44 phrase "came down" appeared in 8:15 when the Spirit fell on the Samaritans during what some call the Samaritan Pentecost. The phrase "poured out" (v. 45) makes us think of the same expression used for the Pentecost that happened in Jerusalem in 2:17-18.

The Spirit is opening a new chapter in the spread of salvation to the ends of the earth! The Gentiles too are children of Abraham—not through circumcision, but by grace alone, through faith in Christ alone.

There are other parallels to the Jerusalem Pentecost. The Gentile believers were speaking in tongues, extolling God (cf. 2:4-11). Further, the onlookers were amazed (10:45; cf. 2:6-12). Finally, new believers were baptized (10:47-48; cf. 2:41).

While some of the Jewish brothers would struggle to welcome Gentiles, God welcomed them. He confirmed his welcome through these signs that demonstrated Jew and Gentile are on equal ground once they accept Christ (cf. Gal 3:28-29). The Spirit confirmed it, and seven Jewish believers witnessed these things. The massive gulf between Jew and Gentile was suddenly bridged.

Scene 6: Resolution
ACTS 11:1-18

Not everyone rejoiced at this change. When Peter returned to Jerusalem, he encountered great criticism because of his association with the Gentiles (11:1-3). Peter's response was simple: he retold the events. Then he mentioned how he remembered the Lord's words, which contrasted water baptism with Spirit baptism (1:5; 11:16). This showed him how God had given Gentiles the same gift, the same Spirit, and the same cleansing as the Jewish believers.

Then Peter asks the critical brothers, "How could I possibly hinder God?" (v. 17). In this we see that Peter was thoroughly convinced God was working to save the Gentiles; to stand in God's way was neither wise nor safe. (Just ask Jonah.)

The critics were awestruck (v. 18). This doesn't necessarily mean, however, that every single person was convinced of the Gentile mission. But Dennis Johnson notes, "Although there were some silent detractors, the church joined Peter in praising God for his gift to the Gentiles" (*Let's Study Acts*, 142). And they were right to glorify God. No one deserves salvation. Those who experience it—Jew and Gentile alike—should give the Savior ceaseless praise.

The point of this narrative is this: the gospel is for the nations. God's conversion of Peter's attitude and the spiritual conversion God brought about in Cornelius paved the way for the Gentile mission. Of course, God had already converted the Ethiopian eunuch prior to this work through Peter, but this story in Acts 10–11 has special significance:

> Like Cornelius, the eunuch seems to have been both a "God-fearer" and a Gentile. The significant new development in chap. 10 is that Peter became committed to the Gentile mission. His testimony would be instrumental in leading the

mother church in Jerusalem to endorse the Gentile mission and thus lend it legitimacy and continuity with the ministry of the apostles (11:1-18; 15:7-11). (Polhill, *Acts*, 249)

This new commitment to get the gospel to the nations will now unfold throughout the rest of the book of Acts.

Concluding Exhortations

Jesus Overcomes Disease and Death—Rely on Him!

Our source of power today comes through our union and communion with Jesus Christ. Do you need his strength in the midst of sickness, grief, or pain? Look to him. Do you need power to testify boldly about his grace? Rely on the One who raises the dead!

Jesus Shows Hospitality to All People Groups—Imitate Him!

This text provides a wonderful picture of gospel hospitality, of extending welcome to outsiders. Will you ask God to use you in reaching a Cornelius? To do so, you may need to pray for God to cleanse you of sinful attitudes toward others. John Piper says,

> Let us wash our minds and our mouths of all racial slurs and ethnic put-downs and be done with all alienating behaviors. And let's be the good Samaritan for some ethnic outcast, and let's be the Christ for some untouchable leper, and let's be the Peter for some waiting Cornelius. ("What God Has Cleansed Do Not Call Common")

Jesus Commands Us to Preach to Everyone—Proclaim Him!

Peter gives us a good model of what we're to do: we must preach the gospel. It's the power of God for salvation "to everyone who believes, first to the Jew, and also to the Greek" (Rom 1:16). Don't doubt the gospel's power. Have full confidence in it as you present it to everyone on the planet.

Jesus Saves Irreligious and Religious People—Worship Him!

God in his grace reaches down to convert vicious men like Saul, immoral people like the Samaritan woman at the well, and religious men like Cornelius who might appear to have everything together. Regardless of your preconversion state, if you're a Christian today, you should stand amazed at his grace to you. To him be the glory forever.

Reflect and Discuss

1. Why do you think Luke recorded these two miracle stories in Acts 9:32-42?
2. What do these two miracle stories teach about Christ and the kingdom?
3. Why is the story of Cornelius's conversion so important?
4. If Cornelius was so pious, then why did he need the gospel?
5. How does the story of Cornelius's conversion speak to the sin of partiality?
6. Why is table fellowship important in the Bible? How should we apply the principle?
7. How does this passage highlight the nature and importance of gospel hospitality?
8. How did God "convert" Peter to the implications of Christianity?
9. How does the story in Acts 10:1–11:18 advance the message of the book of Acts?
10. Pray for opportunities to welcome outsiders into your home, into your life, and into the kingdom this week.

The Antioch Model

ACTS 11:19-30; 12:25; 13:1-3

Main Idea: In these verses we see some of the reasons the church in Antioch—a model missionary church—changed the world.

I. **Effective Evangelism (11:19-21)**
   A. Cultural-engagement mentality (11:19-20)
   B. Gospel intelligibility (11:20)
   C. Personal anonymity (11:20)
   D. The Lord's sovereignty (11:21)
II. **Dynamic Discipleship (11:22-26)**
   A. Accountability (11:22)
   B. Encouragement (11:22-24)
   C. Instruction (11:25-26)
   D. Fruit (11:26)
III. **Mercy Ministry (11:27-30; 12:25)**
   A. It was selfless.
   B. It was generous.
   C. It was corporate.
IV. **Multicultural Leadership and Membership (13:1)**
V. **Spirit-Directed, Church-Sent/Supported Missionaries (13:2-3)**
   A. Worship and expectant prayer fueled the mission.
   B. The Spirit and the congregation together affirmed this mission.
   C. The church sent their best on mission.

In these verses we will look at my favorite church in the whole Bible. It's the one I want each local church to resemble the most. In fact, way back when my local congregation was thinking about what to call our church plant, I toyed with the idea of calling it Antioch.

Luke shows us how the church in Antioch was a launching pad for worldwide missions. It became a base of operation for Paul's missionary journey with Barnabas (13:1-3; 14:26-27) and subsequently a base for his journey with Silas (15:35-41; 18:22-23).

Antioch was the third largest city in the Greco-Roman world, behind Rome and Alexandria. It boasted some five hundred thousand people. It bore the nickname "the queen of the East." It was cosmo-politan and commercial. It was the capitol city of Syria, and it was also a base for the Roman military. Antioch was located three hundred miles north of Jerusalem and thirty miles east of the Mediterranean Sea, on the Orontes River, in what is now southeast Turkey. The city served as a crossroads, having major highways going to the north, south, and east. Greeks, Romans, Syrians, Phoenicians, Jews, Arabs, Egyptians, Africans, Indians, and Asians all populated Antioch, making it remarkably diverse.

Religiously, Antioch was pluralistic and idolatrous. Some called Antioch the "abode of the gods" since several Greek deities were wor-shiped there, including Zeus, Apollos, Poseidon, Adonis, and Tyche. Within five miles of Antioch was the city of Daphne, which was known for its worship of Artemis, Apollos, and Astarte. Cult prostitution was present in Astarte worship (Bock, *Acts*, 413).

All of this made Antioch a great place for a church. John Stott notes,

No more appropriate place could be imagined, either as the venue for the first international church, or as the springboard for the worldwide Christian mission. (*The Message of Acts*, 203)

The church in Antioch—not the mother church in Jerusalem—changed the world. The Jerusalem church was wonderful, and it should be appreciated for its uniqueness and power, but it had its challenges when it came to evangelizing non-Jews. Antioch, by contrast, was an international church.

What made the church in Antioch so powerful? What are the ingre-dients of a missional church? Luke describes at least five marks of a missional church. They are simple to understand but difficult to apply. We need to pray for "the grace of God" (11:23) as we seek to imitate the Antioch Christians.

Effective Evangelism
ACTS 11:19-21

The first thing to catch attention in this passage is this church's remark-able outreach to unbelievers. In fact, the Antioch church itself was birthed by evangelism—an important point. The gospel was planted in Antioch, and then a church was established there. While the theme of mass conversion and gospel advancement isn't new to Acts, and some of the same evangelism themes appear here as elsewhere, there are four distinct qualities about the church that we don't want to miss.

Cultural-Engagement Mentality (11:19-20)

Believers were scattered from Jerusalem during the persecutions there, and some of them traveled up to Phoenicia (in the area of present-day Lebanon). Some went to Cyprus (an island nation about a hundred miles off the coast). Others settled in Antioch. As they were scattered, these Christians went about preaching the Word—just as we observed previously in 8:1-4. Most of these believers, however, spoke the gospel *only* to the Jews. This would, to a certain extent, have been the natural approach since many of the refugees probably set out to start again in places where they had natural connections to family or existing business contacts.

But in verse 20 we see something new developing. Some men of Cyprus and Cyrene (northern Africa) arrive in Antioch and courageously preach the good news also to the *Hellenists* ("Greeks" or "Gentiles," NLT). Timothy Keller calls these evangelists "mavericks" (*Evangelism*, 98), and F. F. Bruce and John Stott refer to them as "daring spirits" (Bruce, *Book of Acts*, 238; Stott, *The Message of Acts*, 201). The men who had traveled from Africa are spreading the gospel among the Gentile unbelievers. To be clear, Peter had preached to Cornelius, a Gentile, but no one—as far as we can tell from the history Scripture records—had acted strategically and intentionally to preach to the Gentiles up to this point. The Samaritan awakening was not exactly like this one either, since the Samaritans were close cousins to the Jews (Keller, *Evangelism*, 98). These mavericks are doing something new.

It seems best to understand the *Hellenists* as Greek-speaking Gentiles (Witherington III, *Acts of the Apostles*, 369). I concur with Darrell Bock, who says,

> Following the work of Peter, it would seem that the term "Hellenist," if original, does not mean Hellenist Christians but possesses a largely racial, cultural sense, equal to "Gentiles." (*Acts*, 414)

Therefore, these men from Cyprus and Cyrene broke through a major cultural barrier.

So the first reason for their evangelistic effectiveness was their *cultural-engagement mentality*. We don't see in them an anti-Gentile bias. Rather, it appears that they knew how to be "all things to all people, so that [they] may by every possible means save some" (1 Cor 9:22) to quote their soon-to-be teacher, Paul (Acts 11:25-25). Consequently, they evangelized pagans remarkably well.

Often people who have been restricted by a deeply religious culture find themselves handicapped in evangelistic efforts. Many, though often well intentioned, care more about protecting their own way of life than they do about sharing the gospel with pagans who may bring all kinds of new challenges into the Christian community should they accept the Lord. They might, for example, want to introduce new styles of music or new ways of doing things. But the "hide safely in a bomb shelter and let those outside the family fend for themselves" mentality will never result in effective evangelism. We can't be salt and light if we are never involved with those who live in and know only a corrupt and dark world. The Antioch Christians didn't withdraw contact from people who did not yet understand the gospel. They shone in the midst of them. It is no surprise that this was the congregation God used to launch the Gentile mission.

To be an Antiochean church, we must be involved with people. We have to learn how to live faithfully, sensibly, soberly, wisely, graciously, and winsomely among those who are far from God. We're in a war, and war is never fought by escapism. It requires engagement—for the good of those we're engaging.

Gospel Intelligibility (11:20)

The men from Cyprus and Cyrene went about "proclaiming the good news about the Lord Jesus." They didn't preach about Jesus as the Christ but about Jesus as the Lord. Thiers wasn't a Jewish audience. Though we know the church eventually taught the community about the Christ—otherwise the citizenry couldn't label believers as "Christians"—those who first tried to reach the Gentiles of Antioch knew their listeners wouldn't have much interest in "the hope of Israel." The title, *Kurios*, "Lord," was commonly spoken, however. In the mystery religions the term was used in reference to a divine god who could give salvation to people. These evangelists were able to tell everyone about the Kurios who is the only Savior. Their message was understandable and displayed an awareness of their audience.

To be a good evangelist, you need to know the gospel well. You also need to consider the interests and knowledge levels of your audience.

Personal Anonymity (11:20)

Did you notice that we don't know the names of these men? Their outreach efforts in Antioch would have ripple effects for years to come, yet we know almost nothing about the people who initiated this worldwide mission.

If you've ever wondered whether unnamed Christians really make a difference for the kingdom, the answer is yes. These men were just being faithful to Jesus. They had no plan. No program. No budget. Just a zeal for the Lord! And he worked through them in a mighty way.

In our day of celebrity Christianity, we desperately need to rediscover the work of the men of Cyprus and Cyrene. These unsung heroes give us a model to follow. The most important people in the church aren't always the most famous, and we mustn't confuse popularity with significance. The church in Antioch got started because so-called nobodies witnessed to their neighbors.

Today many think that inviting a Christian sports star to come share his testimony in order to gain a crowd that can then be told the gospel is the surest formula for winning people to Christ. Well, I'm not discouraging that tactic because it undoubtedly will reach some, but I don't think it's the most effective route to evangelism. While it's a nice thing to have Tim Tebow speak at a church gathering, it's better to have our entire congregations daily spreading the good news within their many relationships.

The Lord's Sovereignty (11:21)

These evangelists were ordinary guys, so how did they see such results? The Lord's sovereign hand was on them. He blessed their witness. The Lord Jesus is the hero of the message ("the good news about the Lord Jesus," v. 20); he is the goal of the message ("turned to the Lord," v. 21); and he is the source of power ("the Lord's hand was with them," v. 21). Jesus was building his church right in hedonistic Antioch.

While we can't manipulate the hand of the Lord into doing amazing things in our own communities, we can take from chapter 13 a cue from the disposition of those believers in Antioch. They were a praying people. They were desperate for the Lord to work, just as those in Jerusalem were when they prayed, "Master, . . ." (4:24). Let's ask for God's hand of blessing as we speak about him to others.

The church in Antioch was birthed by effective evangelism, and as a result, "in Antioch we have the first church that is made up of Jewish and Gentile believers together" (Peterson, *Acts of the Apostles,* 351).

Dynamic Discipleship
ACTS 11:22-26

Now these diverse, newly converted believers need to be discipled. Two dynamic leaders, Barnabas and Saul, arrive to strengthen them. They disciple the Antioch Christians in three ways—through accountability, encouragement, and instruction.

Accountability (11:22)

Much as when the Jerusalem church sent Peter and John to endorse the evangelistic work in Samaria (8:14), this time the church sends Barnabas to check out things in Antioch. This was basically an effort at "quality control" (Keller, *Evangelism*, 99). The church wanted to evaluate what was going on in Antioch. Some may have been critical and suspicious about the great things being reported about God's work in that region, but others were probably hopeful and wanted to help. Barnabas was among the latter.

While many frown on using accountability methods, this church in Antioch certainly needed accountability. They had no apostolic leadership. The church was filled with new believers from all around the world. The work was brand-new. So Barnabas arrives, evaluates, and endorses the work.

Encouragement (11:22-24)

Barnabas was a Hellenist from Cyprus. He could relate to the Gentiles better than a Jewish Palestinian could. Further, he loved people. His gifts gave rise to his nickname, "Son of Encouragement." Barnabas was the right man for the job at Antioch. He wouldn't quench the fire of what the Spirit was doing there. He wouldn't be suspicious of the enthusiasm of the believers in Antioch; he would applaud it.

Had an inflexible person from the Jerusalem church visited this congregation, he might have made the mistake of past American missionaries. Rather than keeping to the work of helping people to get to know the Lord better through his Word, such a person might have tried to get the natives to wear the same clothes, sing the same kinds of songs, and do the same kinds of programs as he preferred. But the goal of missions isn't to impress one culture upon another. Missionaries must help people apply the gospel within their own cultures.

The music, dress, customs, and language of Antioch would have been different from those of Jerusalem. But because Barnabas knows the big picture, he can rejoice in spite of the differences, not feeling the need to impress a particular form of church life on the saints at Antioch. Grace-loving Barnabas knows this: God is at work. He encourages these believers to remain faithful to the Lord, which implies that they were already being faithful (v. 23).

What made Barnabas such an encourager? The Bible says, "He was a good man." Good men encourage other saints. Barnabas's goodness was a fruit of the fullness of the Spirit and faith at work in him (v. 24). His acts of encouragement flowed from his intimate relationship with God.

Don't think lightly of encouragement. The saints needed it back then, and we also need it today. Encouragement is empowered by the Spirit. Paul tells the Thessalonians, "Therefore encourage one another and build each other up as you are already doing" (1 Thess 5:11).

What does a good disciple maker need? Sound theology? Yes, but he or she also needs to be an encourager. Disciple makers should be known for stirring up others to faith and good works (Heb 10:24). They need to care for the hearts of people as well as helping them know the facts. Consider how other believers see you. Is it more likely that an encounter with you makes them think, *Yes! I need that guy or gal to speak to me right now* or, *Oh no, here comes the cold-water committee?* Make it your daily aim to encourage others to persevere in the faith.

Verse 24 says more people were "added to the Lord." This shows that Barnabas's discipleship efforts apparently involved helping to equip and encourage lay evangelists to share the gospel with their friends. And while Barnabas must have been thrilled with God's grace in Antioch, he needed help to keep up the work of discipling all the new believers. This, in fact, is a common problem leaders face when their churches grow. They are concerned about how best to disciple everyone, and it's not a job that can be done without help. In the case of Barnabas and his work among the Antioch believers, another disciple maker is needed. Wisely, Barnabas enlists Saul's help.

Instruction (11:25-26)

Barnabas goes to find Saul, with whom he had spent time previously (9:27). He knew of Saul's calling to be an apostle to the Gentiles (9:15-16). He knows of Saul's bridge-building capacity; the man could communicate to diverse groups and was well informed about Scripture. Barnabas knows Saul is just the man to instruct this world-reaching congregation.

I find it interesting that when Barnabas could have made a name for himself by becoming the leader of the new church, he humbly shared the load with a man whose teaching gifts were superior. He strategically recruited someone who could help him in the work at Antioch. Soon the Acts narrative will shine more on Saul/Paul than Barnabas, as we will read not of "Barnabas and Saul" but of "Paul and Barnabas" in chapter 13.

Later we read about more teachers in this church (13:1). Paul and Barnabas together provided more instruction to them (15:35). Here Luke makes a point to say Barnabas and Saul "taught large numbers" (11:26).

Teaching is a critical component of disciple making. Listening to music alone won't mature new believers. Neither will merely attending church services. Christians need to know and learn how to apply the Scriptures (Matt 28:18-20; 2 Tim 2:2). Each of us needs faithful instruction in God's Word.

So how long did Barnabas and Saul encourage and instruct in Antioch? They dedicated a year of their lives there. And the believers they taught patiently and persistently learned, being prepared for future missions to other cities.

Fruit (11:26)

The believers in Antioch didn't call themselves Christians. Rather, they were "called Christians." This title only occurs here, in 26:28, and in 1 Peter 4:16. In each case it's a term outsiders use. The saints in Antioch so identified with Jesus that fellow Gentile observers called them "little Christs."

This, then, is another turning point in the history of Christianity. The followers of Jesus were so different from the culture around them that citizens had to develop a third classification of people—something new beyond the Jew or Gentile distinction. Where once the world saw Christians as Jewish followers of Jesus the Nazarene and assumed they followed some divergent form of Judaism, something changed. Clearly the followers of the Way, comprised of people of all cultural backgrounds, weren't Jews. But because some of them had converted from Judaism, they weren't exactly Gentiles either. People from all sorts of nations were worshiping together. This unified group represented a third "race" of people (Peterson, *Acts of the Apostles*, 356). The Christians were a new humanity.

Even today some assume that one's religion is based on one's ethnicity, social class, or family, but the Antioch followers of Jesus showed the world something beautifully different about Christianity. The church in Antioch was like an embassy of the kingdom of God. Its people gave the world a picture of what Jesus's kingdom, when fully consummated, will look like one day. These individuals of different backgrounds displayed unique values, showed a unique way of life, and preached a unique message. They didn't just blend into the culture. They were different, and modern Christians should be described similarly.

What made the teaching of Barnabas and Saul so different from the teachings of other religions of the day? How could it break through social barriers to establish such unity amid such diversity? It comes down to their single-minded focus. They preached and taught the gospel as Jesus instructed. They saw themselves and the other believers as sinners saved by grace alone through faith in Christ alone. There is no ground for superiority and elitism in the Christian faith. Christ's followers are all about him.

Mercy Ministry
ACTS 11:27-30; 12:25

This section closes with a glimpse into the hearts of the Christians in Antioch. They display sacrificial mercy and generosity to those in need. They displayed the fruit of salvation in doing good works—especially to those of the household of faith (Gal 6:10). They committed to both word and deed ministry, as they were no doubt instructed to do by Barnabas and Saul.

In an event recorded in chapter 21, Agabus prophesies that a famine will impact the entire empire. This famine would be the result of the flooding of the Nile River in AD 45. The harvest of Egypt, breadbasket of the region, was damaged greatly by the flood. This sent grain prices skyrocketing throughout the Roman world for years, including in Judea (Witherington III, *Acts of the Apostles*, 368). The prophetic word spoken by Agabus gave the Christians an opportunity to show support for those in Jerusalem. In Acts 11 the Antioch Christians give, according to each person's ability, and they send the gift with Barnabas and Saul. We read about the completion of the mission in chapter 12:

After they had completed their relief mission, Barnabas and Saul returned to Jerusalem, taking along John who was called Mark. (v. 25)

Consider a few notable characteristics of this mercy ministry.

It Was Selfless

The famine hasn't taken place yet when the disciples determine to send relief. Yet, embracing Agabus's prophecy by faith, the Christians seem more concerned with preparing aid for others than they are with hoarding personal supplies in preparation for the hardship to come. They put others before self.

This is a great reminder that we must not only do mercy ministry when we think we're financially stable and secure. We need to begin now—even if that means starting small. It's important that we show mercy to this broken world as we can, "according to [our] own ability."

It Was Generous

The church doesn't ask, How much will it cost? They simply give as much as they can. This kind of generosity shows that the gospel has transformed them (cf. 2 Cor 8:9).

It Was Corporate

The church determines to care for another group of believers—one that's different from them in culture and ethnicity and one that's located a good distance away from them. Such partnership among churches is rare today. The Antioch church delivers the offering to the "elders" of the Jerusalem church; this is the first mention of the term *elders* in Acts (11:30). Both churches belonged to Jesus, so the people were brothers and sisters. The Antioch church gave a tangible expression of this solidarity through their gift.

We must remain mindful of the needs of other congregations around the world. We need to assist them in word and deed as we hear about their struggles. Despite the geographical or cultural distances that sometimes separate us from them, we are brothers and sisters with all who are in Christ. We're fellow *Christians.*

Darrell Bock says of this Acts passage, "This summary could hardly do a better job of showing a vibrant church at work" (*Acts*, 419). May the Lord grant us grace to experience such vibrancy!

Multicultural Leadership and Membership
ACTS 13:1

I would like to point out two more ingredients of this missional church.

First, we must reflect on the example of diversity in the leadership of the church in Antioch. There was a group of "prophets and teachers" who apparently served like a group of elders; I'll call them the Antioch Five. Luke doesn't provide definitions and distinctions for their roles, but he does give us a sense of their diversity.

Barnabas was a Cyprian Jewish believer (4:36). Simeon was called Niger; his name means "black" or "dark." Most believe he was from Africa (Stott, *Message of Acts,* 216). Lucian came from "Cyrene," that is, North Africa. Manaen, who was brought up in Herod's court, related to the royal upper class; he was either a foster brother or relative of Herod Antipas. And then there was Saul, who was a Jewish believer. He would have brought an academic, professorial dynamic to the group.

This leadership reflected the membership of the church. The congregation's diversity would no doubt shock some, but it would have attracted many to the Savior. Diversity within the church, in fact, has an *attractional dimension* to it. Outsiders from everywhere could have imagined themselves joining the Antioch congregation, knowing that it welcomed all sorts of people and could communicate the Scriptures to those of many nationalities and backgrounds.

This leadership would have also had an important *missional dimension.* These leaders surely saw things differently at times, but their diversity likely enabled them to be more creative and effective in reaching their city and in ministering to their people than if only one rank or class of men was leading the church.

The concept of worldwide missions was born in this diverse group. It shouldn't surprise us (Keller, *Evangelism,* 106).

Spirit-Directed, Church-Sent/Supported Missionaries
ACTS 13:2-3

We should follow the Antioch model of sending missionaries to the nations. John Stott reminds us of the uniqueness of the upcoming mission trips of Paul and his companions: "All the time the action has been limited to the Palestinian and Syrian mainland. Nobody has yet caught the vision of taking the good news to the nations overseas" (*The Message of Acts*, 215). But that changes as Luke tells us how world missions began. The whole church was involved in worship and fasting when the Spirit directed Barnabas and Saul to this new work. The church then blessed and affirmed these men as they sent them off. Three transferable lessons emerge regarding this episode.

Worship and Expectant Prayer Fueled the Mission

You don't get the sense that the setting of verses 2 and 3 was some special prayer meeting; it was the normal routine. The believers in Antioch were a worshiping and praying community. The fact that they were fasting indicates they were praying with expectancy and deep dependence on God.

True spiritual leaders don't run with their own ideas; they seek God in dependent prayer. These men are remarkably gifted, yet they're fasting! Churches that impact the world exalt Jesus passionately and seek him in prayer dependently and expectantly. The story begins in prayer, and then after Barnabas and Saul are selected, the believers pray again. This church's actions were drenched in prayer.

The Spirit and the Congregation Together Affirmed This Mission

Churches need to avoid both *individualism* and *institutionalism* (Stott, *The Message of Acts*, 217–18). This story doesn't suggest Paul had a "God told me to go to Spain" idea totally detached from any reference to the church (individualism), but neither does it show us that the church followed a mechanical decision-making process devoid of prayer and the Spirit, which often exists in bureaucratic systems (institutionalism). The Spirit gave the word (we aren't told how), and then the congregation affirmed this mission. Missionaries are directed by the Spirit and are sent and supported by the church. Ultimately, churches—not boards, organizations, or seminaries—send missionaries. We don't see the mighty apostle ever operating apart from community. Saul was a man directed by the Spirit, united with the church.

The Church Sent Their Best on Mission

Notice who is set apart for this missionary journey: Barnabas and Saul. This means the Antioch church is stepping out in an act of faith and making a sacrifice. They are willing to give away key leaders in obedience to God and for the good of others. Jesus loves churches that think beyond themselves.

These two high-capacity leaders are set aside for this work, even though the nature of the "work" isn't described here. Theirs was somewhat like Abraham's calling in that what they were commissioned to do was vague (Gen 12:1). While the calling itself is clear, the work and its location aren't (Stott, *The Message of Acts,* 217).

This chapter reminds us that we must continue to send high-capacity leaders and to support their work. That's what missionary churches do. And as we follow this pattern, we will reflect—albeit dimly—the missionary heart of the Father, who sent heaven's best, Jesus Christ, for the good of the nations (Azurdia, "The Antioch Paradigm")! "God had only one Son, and He was a missionary," said David Livingstone. The Father sent that Son that we may be saved, and now he sends us that others may be saved (John 20:21). Let's imitate our missionary Father and his missionary Son by sending out others for the advancement of the gospel.

Reflect and Discuss

1. Why is the church in Antioch so significant?
2. What made the evangelists in Antioch so effective?
3. How did the leaders disciple the converts in Antioch? What can we learn from this model?
4. What is mercy ministry? What motivates it?
5. What can we learn from this story about mercy ministry?
6. Why should Christians value diversity in the church?
7. How can diversity in leadership help attract and reach unbelievers?
8. What does this passage teach about worship and prayer?
9. What can we learn from Antioch about sending out people for evangelism and church planting?
10. Take a few moments to pray for the Lord to show you how best to support your local church in evangelism and church planting.

Opposition and Advancement

ACTS 12:1-24

Main Idea: King Herod launches a public assault on the leaders of the church in Jerusalem, killing James and imprisoning Peter, but he ultimately cannot stop the advancement of Christ's kingdom.

I. **Scene 1: The Evil Attack (12:1-5)**
   A. Opposition is inevitable.
   B. God's sovereignty is inscrutable.
   C. Prayer is effectual.
II. **Scene 2: The Lord's Rescue (12:6-19)**
   A. The Lord's peace is phenomenal.
   B. The Lord's grace is astonishing.
   C. The Lord's power is immeasurable.
III. **Scene 3: The Final Word (12:20-24)**
   A. Herod's idolatry
   B. Herod's obituary
   C. A word of warning and a word of hope

Rivalries exist everywhere. In politics it's Democrats versus Republicans. In computers it's Mac versus PC. In sports it's Auburn versus Alabama. In superhero movies it's Superman versus Lex Luthor. In the home it's kids versus vegetables! And in the kingdom of God, it's the kingdom of darkness opposing the kingdom of God's beloved Son (Col 1:11-12). Importantly, in this last example in particular, the rivals aren't equal. Not even close.

In this narrative Luke provides a vivid example of the folly of opposing the King of kings. I agree with John Polhill, who says it's "one of the most delightful and engaging narratives in all of Acts" (*Acts*, 276). It's told with brilliant artistry.

Here we see the church's mission taking significant steps forward. Before Luke tells about the major advancement of the gospel with the first missionary journey in chapter 13, he provides us with a story about opposition in the Jerusalem church. It reminds us that kingdom advancement doesn't come without a significant cost.

The tyrant leading the assault on the church is Herod Agrippa I, who killed the apostle James then imprisoned the apostle Peter. Such conflict isn't unusual. John Stott notes the following pattern, providing great hope for believers in the midst of conflict:

> Indeed, throughout church history the pendulum has swung between expansion and opposition, growth and shrinkage, advance and retreat, although with the assurance that even the powers of death and hell will never prevail against Christ's church, since it is built securely on the rock. (*Message of Acts*, 207)

In other words, we can relate to this story. Christians from every age will face conflict if seeking to advance the gospel. But we can face such conflict with *unshakable assurance* that Christ will win!

Scene 1: The Evil Attack
ACTS 12:1-5

"About that time" (when the Antioch church prepared the relief offering, 11:27-30) King Herod (Agrippa I) launched a violent assault on the church (v. 1). If you're familiar with the Bible, then you're familiar with the name *Herod*, but it's easy to get the Herods confused. This Herodian dynasty was notorious for attacking the people of God. They ruled Palestine with the delegated power of Rome. Herod Agrippa I's grandfather was Herod the Great, who was responsible for slaughtering the babies after the magi's visit (Matt 1:16-18). Herod Antipas, a younger son of Herod the Great, and uncle of Herod Agrippa I, beheaded John the Baptist in a moment of arousal (Matt 14:1-12). Here in Acts 12 we read of Herod Agrippa I. His son, Agrippa II, appears in Acts 25–26.

Herod Agrippa I bears many of the characteristics of his evil family. As a child he was sent to Rome and was reared among Roman aristocracy. He developed childhood friendships that eventually led to his ruling of the Jewish kingdom—nearly to the same extent as his grandfather (Polhill, *Acts*, 278). One of his classmates was the emperor Claudius, who extended Herod's rule. Herod was a political chameleon. When with the Romans, he lived in a Roman fashion. When around the Jews, he lived for their favor. He was a people pleaser, a glory seeker, and a Christ hater.

Herod Agrippa uses an approach different from Saul's house-to-house, one-by-one method of eliminating followers of Christ. Herod instead opts to put to death the leaders of the church, consequently destroying the morale of the church. He starts with James (son of Zebedee and brother of John, not to be confused with James, half brother of Jesus and author of the book of James, who became a leader in the Jerusalem church). This James, along with Peter and John, was a member of the innermost circle of Jesus. Herod kills this important leader "with the sword" (v. 2), which may imply beheading. So following the violent martyrdom of Stephen, the church grieved over the first martyred apostle, James.

This decision "pleased the Jews," and because it did, Herod proceeded to arrest Peter also (v. 3). There was no reason to execute James or to arrest Peter—the two weren't political revolutionaries—but Herod wants to play to the Romans and the Jews. In taking such drastic actions, he can assure the Romans that this little sect called Christianity isn't violating the ways of Rome, and he can also appeal to the Jews by showing that he is standing up for their traditions (i.e., the temple, the law, and separation from Gentiles). Herod loves power. He loves glory. He loves to please people.

We don't have to look far to find modern examples of the beheadings of those who claim the name of Christ. The images of ISIS beheading professing believers on the coast of Libya will never leave my mind. But Christians can die with confidence because our King can put heads back on.

Herod may have started with James and not Peter, who seems the more outspoken of the two, in order to gauge the crowd's reaction to his cruelty. When they were pleased with the death of James, Herod decided to go all the way to the top of the Christian movement's human leadership in making an attack on Peter. (The evil one always loves to attack those in leadership.)

One thing stood in the way of his beheading this second disciple: it was Passover season (v. 3). It was time for the Jews' annual celebration of the exodus, when God freed his people from Egyptian tyranny. During this time neither trials nor the carrying out of sentences was permitted. So Herod sends Peter to prison guarded by "four squads of four soldiers" (v. 4). That's a lot of soldiers for one guy, suggesting that perhaps the Sanhedrin informed Agrippa of the previous jailbreak (5:19). Herod intends to bring Peter out to the people for a show trial following

Passover. No doubt Herod thought this would curry great favor with the Jews and bring him much public glory.

Don't miss that when Herod attacks with the sword, the church counters with prayer (v. 5). This should always be the church's response during times of great trial and agony. We've seen the earliest Christians model it previously in the book of Acts (cf. 4:29-31).

Allow me to point out three applications.

Opposition Is Inevitable

The Bible gives accounts of battles within the broader context of one great battle. Various people lead assaults on God's people, using various means of warfare. Pick your tyrant: Pharaoh, Jezebel, Nebuchadnezzar, Herod. God's people have always faced persecution. Already, in eleven chapters of Acts, we have observed opposition in the form of threats, intimidation, physical beatings, and stoning. Now the sword turns against God's people. We shouldn't be surprised when we face opposition while living on mission; we should be surprised when we don't.

Jesus told his disciples, "You will have suffering in this world. Be courageous! I have conquered the world" (John 16:33). While Jesus told us the honest news, he also reminded us of the great news! Christ crushed the head of the serpent at the cross. He triumphed over death as he vacated the tomb. He ascended into heaven where he rules and reigns over all. And soon Jesus Christ will return to judge the living and the dead. In light of this bigger story, we can live out our little stories with faith, knowing that the King will always win. He's in control.

The King was in charge when James died and in charge when Peter went free. He could have saved James, but he didn't—for his own sovereign purposes. (And let's remember, the moment James died, Jesus was there to meet him in heaven.) The King can use miraculous deliverance or martyrdom for gospel advancement.

We see examples of the power of persecution throughout church history, and yet neither persecution nor death can ultimately stop the mission. Jesus just replaces martyrs with other missionaries. When Paul was in prison, he rejoiced in the ways the sovereign One was working in the midst of his imprisonment (cf. Phil 1:14). Jerome said,

> The church of Christ has been founded by shedding its
> own blood, not that of others; by enduring outrage, not by
> inflicting it. Persecutions have made it grow; martyrdoms have

crowned it. (Letter 82, in Piper, "Execution, Escape, and Eaten by Worms")

Opposition is inevitable, yet we don't engage in this war as victims but as victors. Our King rules and reigns.

God's Sovereignty Is Inscrutable

God's ways are fathomless. We can't ultimately comprehend the works of God (cf. Rom 11:33-36). Hymn writer William Cowper said, "God works in mysterious ways, His wonders to perform." Why does James die and Peter live? We aren't told all the reasons. We know that Jesus promised James's death in Mark 10:39, but we're not told why. Surely the church was praying for James, like Peter, yet he was put to death. John, James's brother, lived to be an old man. Sometimes believers suffer terribly, and sometimes God delivers miraculously (Schreiner, "God's Inscrutable Sovereignty"). We can't predict the ways of God.

Sometimes those who would be great parents can't have biological children. Sometimes those who are terrible parents keep having babies. Sometimes God answers prayers for healings, and sometimes he doesn't. Sometimes the wicked prosper while the righteous suffer—at least for a season (Ps 73).

While such trials bring much grief and pain, we must not be angry with God. Trials are not necessarily a sign that he's displeased with us. God calls us to trust him, even when life hurts. His ways are wise, good, and just. And we must remember this: God has given us his Son. God doesn't promise to give us an explanation for everything, but he has given us the promise that changes everything: he will raise us from the dead. We will dwell with him in the new heaven and new earth, where sin and suffering can't touch us. God doesn't explain everything, but through Christ, God has entered into our suffering, has taken the ultimate injustice at the cross, and has risen triumphantly so that all who call out to him may have eternal life. Latch on to this reality in suffering. Glory is coming. It's not here yet, but keep looking to God in faith. He gave his Son for sinners like us, and soon all suffering will end.

Prayer Is Effectual

One might wonder about the church's response here. Why not take up arms? Why not protest? While force and outcry are appropriate at times, prayer is always the first and best response. Prayer is the church's weapon, and using it isn't passive. The believers in this passage essentially go to war through prayer. Prayer is "an act of defiance to opposition" (Azurdia, "The Pendulum of Gospel Ministry"). The band Rend Collective sings a catchy victory song in "More than Conquerors," declaring, "We are more than conquerors, through Christ; You have overcome this world, this life; We will not bow to sin or to shame; We are defiant in Your name." In that hope-filled spirit the church prays. Prayer isn't retreat. It's an act of holy defiance. It's an act of placing dependent confidence in the sovereign God who hears the prayers of his people and rules over all. In the words of John Piper, prayer is a "wartime walkie-talkie" (*Let the Nations Be Glad*, 45). The church is at war, so they call up the Commander, who shuts lions' mouths, humiliates pharaohs, breaks chains, and opens prison doors, knowing he will act in whatever way he knows is best.

How do you regard prayer? Is your initial response to conflict one of planning or petitioning? Learn from the church in Jerusalem. The kingdom of darkness uses physical weapons; the church uses the weapon of prayer. Wield your weapon!

Scene 2: The Lord's Rescue
ACTS 12:6-19

The longest part of the narrative involves a great escape. Just as the Lord delivered his people from Pharaoh during Passover, he delivered Peter from the hands of this political tyrant. This passage gives us an elevated concept of the Lord's presence, power, and grace.

This story is wondrous, miraculous, and humorous. It displays the power of God and the human touch of a master writer. It's easy to read the Bible and miss humor, especially in the midst of a serious story, but John Polhill says that Luke includes a "comic touch" at various places in the narrative (*Acts*, 276). Thomas Schreiner says, "Luke was surely touched by the humor in the story. . . . You sense the humanity of Luke" ("God's Inscrutable Sovereignty").

While Herod prepared to bring Peter out of prison, Peter was "sleeping between two soldiers" (v. 6). He isn't biting his nails, pacing the floor, or trying to negotiate a deal. He's sleeping! The passage provides no hint of any anxiety at work in him, a fact that reminds me of a later story in which Paul and Silas sang hymns in prison. Paul sings; Peter sleeps (Stott, *Message of Acts*, 209). Here we find a wonderful application.

The Lord's Peace Is Phenomenal

The apostle Paul reminded the Philippian church of this wonderful truth:

> *Don't worry about anything, but in everything, through prayer and petition with thanksgiving, present your requests to God. And the peace of God, which surpasses all understanding, will guard your hearts and minds in Christ Jesus.* (Phil 4:6-7)

Peter was guarded by soldiers, but his heart was guarded by God. Know this peace. Live in this peace through the Prince of peace, who himself could go to sleep in the middle of a storm.

In verse 7 an angel comes in and stands next to Peter, and light shines in the cell, but that doesn't wake Peter up! The angel has to strike Peter on the side to move him. I've got to believe Luke loved to tell this story. He had to get some details from several sources to write it, but I think Peter's confession made him smile. Can't you imagine Peter reporting, "An angel was kicking me in the ribs, saying, Get up!"?

When Peter wakes, the chains fall off. Our Lord specializes in breaking chains (see Ps 146:7). Peter follows the angel, thinking he's dreaming. This detail is important because it tells us that Peter knew he couldn't claim that the rescue was owing to anything he did or could do. He wasn't freed because he was strong or fast. All he contributed to the event was walking dazedly through the prison area as told.

The "iron gate" opens the same way the stone was rolled away: by God's mighty power. It opened "by itself" (*automatē* in Greek). Upon exiting, Peter enters the street, the angel leaves, and Peter finally comes to and becomes aware of the Lord's great rescue.

The Lord's Grace Is Astonishing

Just as Moses told Israel, "Stand firm and see the LORD's salvation that he will accomplish for you today" just prior to the parting of the seas (Exod 14:13), Peter would receive grace as the angel led him out of prison. This story isn't about Peter's escape on his own; it's about Peter's deliverance by God. The Lord delivered Peter by sheer grace. He is the great Rescuer (2 Tim 4:17-18). Likewise, we're saved by simply receiving God's grace by faith (Eph 2:8-9). Consequently, all glory belongs to God (Rom 3:28). God's grace here was so astonishing that even a praying church had a difficult time believing it!

As Peter makes his way down the darkened streets, the church is gathered in prayer at the home of a generous woman of means named Mary. "Confusion and joyful humor" abound in what happens next (Hughes, *Acts*, 169).

First, there's Rhoda. She is the servant on guard duty. Peter arrives and knocks outside the gate that leads into the courtyard. Rhoda recognizes Peter's voice, and in her astonishment she goes back to tell the church about his arrival, but she neglects to open the door to let Peter enter! The last place Peter needs to be at this time is in the middle of the street, exposed to possible recapture (Polhill, *Acts*, 282).

Then the church enters into the poor decision making. They don't believe Rhoda. They tell her she's crazy! Here's a picture of a people who are praying but are struggling with believing that God actually works miracles! I don't think Luke included this insight as an indictment on the church. These men and women were ordinary humans who knew God doesn't promise a miracle every moment. Maybe they were praying conservatively: "Lord, just help Peter be strong in suffering. Cause Herod to give a lighter sentence." In any case, you can imagine them saying to the flustered servant girl, "Oh, be quiet. We're all stressed here. You're going to lose your mind if you aren't careful. We need to get back to prayer." Nevertheless, Rhoda insists Peter is truly outside. And here, surprisingly, some of the Christ followers take the time to theorize about whether the man at the gate could possibly be Peter's angel. In other words, they stand around discussing theology while the answer to their prayer is waiting outside!

And there, out in the darkness and exposed to danger, stands Peter. He just keeps knocking, perhaps pausing to whisper with more intensity: "Rhoda! Let me in!"

Thankfully, the church eventually opens the door, and Peter enters. Apparently the group then erupts with such astonishment and joy that Peter has to tell them to be quiet. He is a wanted man, after all, in the middle of a city. Once they calm, he goes on to tell the church "how the Lord had brought him out of the prison" (v. 17). He tells them about the Lord's grace.

The church's reaction to Peter reminds us of an important lesson.

The Lord's Power Is Immeasurable

God "is able to do above and beyond all that we ask or think" (Eph 3:20), yet the church here is surprised by God's ability. Let's elevate our concept of what God can do. "Thou art coming to a King, large petitions with thee bring for his grace and power are such; none can never ask too much," said John Netwon ("Come, My Soul, Thy Suit Prepare"). Trust in his power as you pour out your heart to him.

Two other pieces of information are relayed in the last part of verse 17. Peter instructs the church to "tell these things to James and the brothers." This is a small detail, but it speaks to the leadership of James in the Jerusalem church (Acts 15). Then Peter "left and went to another place" (v. 17). Peter uses practical wisdom here. He doesn't rely on a miracle for everything. He flees from Agrippa's wrath. He doesn't run back to the guards singing MC Hammer's, "Can't Touch This." He uses wisdom.

Herod, of course, wasn't happy with the turn of events. He proceeds to cross-examine the soldiers, probably torturing them. Convinced that only an inside job could free Peter, he eventually puts the soldiers to death (v. 19) in accordance with Roman law, which specified that a guard who allowed a prisoner to escape must receive the same penalty that the escapee would have received (Polhill, *Acts,* 283). After these executions, Herod went to Caesarea.

Such violence aside, I am struck by the tenderness and childlike wonder this story elicits. Should this passage not remind us of the need to live with joyful confidence in our King, under the care of our great Father? We need to believe like trusting children. To pray like children. To go to sleep like children. We need to laugh like children, trusting that our Abba is the sovereign Father over all things. He breaks chains. He frees prisoners. He humiliates bullies. We can trust him. We should petition him. We must rest with the peace that comes from him. He is amazing.

Scene 3: The Final Word
ACTS 12:20-24

What happened to Herod, this earthly king that opposed Christ's kingdom? He was eaten by worms and died. Or to say it another way, the Lord judged him. The lesson here is clear: those who oppose the Lord will lose. When they oppose his kingdom, they lose. When they oppose the truth, they will eventually lose. Though the Lord doesn't always settle accounts immediately, he will.

Herod's Idolatry

The coastal towns of Tyre and Sidon were on the inland areas that Agrippa ruled, and he controlled their food supply (v. 20). A guy named

Blastus served as a mediator between Herod and representatives from these areas; he apparently helped negotiate an agreement suitable to everyone. On an appointed day, on which the agreement would be formally announced, Herod prepared to make a glorious entrance. He put on his royal robes, took his seat on the throne, and delivered an oration (v. 21).

The historian Josephus recounts this event in great detail. Herod presented himself in the famous arena in Caesarea and wore a glistening silver robe. He was hailed as a god. Of course the crowd's words were empty flattery, but Herod still received the praise gladly. The event reminds me of the scene in the first Avengers movie. Natasha, the Black Widow, makes a comment about the battle between Loki and Thor right before Captain America leaps out of the Quinjet: "I'd sit this one out, Cap. . . . They're basically gods," she says. To this he replies, "There's only one God, ma'am, and I'm pretty sure he doesn't dress like that." And he doesn't dress like Herod either!

Herod loves the crowd's worship. When Cornelius bowed before Peter, Peter lifted him up, saying, "Stand up! I myself am also a man" (10:26). When the people of Lystra lauded Paul and Barnabas as gods, the pair replied with garment-tearing passion: "We are people also, just like you, . . . turn from these worthless things to the living God" (14:15). Peter and Paul point everyone to the glory of God, never to themselves. Herod's approach to life is quite the opposite. He's a self-exalting glory hog.

Herod's Obituary

Previously an angel "struck" Peter to wake him (v. 7); here, an angel "struck" Herod to kill him. Josephus provides a natural, human explanation of what happened: "A severe pain . . . arose in his belly, which became so violent that he was carried into his palace, where five days later he died" (Stott, *Message of Acts*, 213). No matter the precise diagnosis of Herod's condition, Dr. Luke tells us the ultimate reason for it: God judged him.

In contrast to Herod's demise, Luke summarizes events connected with the church of that day: "But the word of God flourished and multiplied" (v. 24). A great opponent to the work of Christ died, but the word goes marching on! Jesus continues to build his church. This reminds us that there's only one sovereign, and I'm reminded of Luther's triumphant hymn, "A Mighty Fortress," in which he says, "The body they may kill: God's truth abideth still, his kingdom is forever."

According to the opening verse of chapter 13, one of the leaders of the church in Antioch was "Manaen, a close friend of Herod the tetrarch." This is a reference to Herod Antipas, not Agrippa, but the men belonged to the same family. Even in the middle of this godless, Christ-hating household, the kingdom of Christ was advancing. It's remarkable!

A Word of Warning and a Word of Hope

John Piper summarizes this chapter of Acts well: "If we stay with Jesus, we win, and if we oppose him, we lose" ("Execution, Escape").

Indeed, there's both warning and hope here. The warning is this: Don't be a self-exalter. You may oppose Christ for a season, but God will have the last laugh. Daniel said, "He changes the times and seasons; [God] removes kings and establishes kings" (Dan 2:21). When Nebuchadnezzar boasted like Herod Agrippa, "Is this not Babylon the Great that I have built to be a royal residence by my vast power and for my majestic glory?" (Dan 4:30), a voice from heaven said, "You will feed on grass like cattle" (Dan 4:32), and God humiliated the self-exalter. The wicked may prosper for a season, but judgment is certain. The axiom of the kingdom holds truth: "For everyone who exalts himself will be humbled, and the one who humbles himself will be exalted" (Luke 14:11). All who oppose the King will face his wrath. Herod's death anticipates the great and final day of the Lord's judgment.

Self-exaltation fills the hearts of all kinds of people, not just leaders. In our fallen nature we want to be God. And we certainly don't want God to tell us what to do. But this text serves as a warning: we must humble ourselves before God; we must not try to be God.

This text also provides us with this great hope: the King's mission is unstoppable. While we will inevitably encounter opposition as we seek to advance the gospel through prayer and proclamation, we can engage in the war with boldness and courage. Our King is triumphant. He has paid the price for our sins, and he is the exalted Lord of glory. Unlike King Herod's, our King's body wasn't eaten by worms because he didn't stay in the ground for them to do their decomposing work! No one can overcome our King, and nothing can separate the believer from his love—not tribulation, distress, persecution, famine, nakedness, danger, or sword (Rom 8:31-39).

Reflect and Discuss

1. Why should Christians expect opposition when seeking to advance the gospel?
2. How does God use martyrdom to advance the kingdom?
3. How does this passage illustrate God's inscrutable sovereignty?
4. How does this passage illustrate the importance of prayer?
5. What does this passage teach about God's peace?
6. How does this passage encourage us to bring large requests to the King?
7. What does it mean to be a self-exalter? How can we fight against the temptation to be one?
8. How does Herod's death highlight the centrality of the glory of God?
9. How does this passage provide believers with hope?
10. Read Romans 8:31-39 in light of this passage. Spend a few moments in worship and prayer.

The Holy Spirit, a Bible, a Passport, and a First-Aid Kit, Part 1

ACTS 13:4-52

Main Idea: In these initial stops on the first missionary journey of Barnabas and Paul, we find several important applications for Word-driven, Spirit-empowered missionaries.

I. **Stop 1: Paul and Barnabas in Cyprus (13:4-12)**
   A. Some people will be open to God's Word (13:4-7).
   B. Some people will oppose God's Word (13:8-11).
   C. Some people will embrace God's Word (13:12).

II. **Stop 2: Paul and Barnabas in Perga (13:13-14a)**
   A. Be ready for relational conflicts within your ministry team (13:13).
   B. Be ready for physical challenges as you make the gospel known (13:14a).

III. **Stop 3: Paul and Barnabas in Pisidian Antioch: Proclamation Suitable for Their Audience (13:14b-52)**
   A. Introduction: Preparation for the coming of Christ (13:16-25)
   B. Proclamation: The death and resurrection of Christ (13:26-37)
   C. Application: The promise of forgiveness and justification for all who trust in Christ (13:38-41)
   D. A mixed reaction (13:42-52)

Someone once advised, "When traveling, you should lay out all your clothes and all your money. Then take half your clothes and twice the money!" That sounds pretty wise because traveling usually costs more than anticipated—and not just in terms of dollars spent. Murphy's Law often holds true on the road: Nothing is as easy as it looks; everything takes longer than you think; and if anything can go wrong, it will! (Especially if you're traveling with five kids in a minivan!)

In Acts 13–14 we will journey with Paul and Barnabas on the first missionary journey and will consider several important applications for Word-driven, Spirit-empowered missionaries. Though their journey involved numerous tribulations, many gospel victories were won because of the faithfulness of Barnabas and Paul. The passage teaches an important missions law: "We won't reach the nations apart from personal sacrifice" (Azurdia, "Progression by Intention, Part 2").

Previously, we considered the significance of the Antioch church's sending of missionaries. We noted five significant characteristics of this world-changing church: (1) effective evangelism (11:19-21); (2) dynamic discipleship (11:22-26); (3) mercy ministry (11:27-30; 12:25); (4) multicultural membership/leadership (13:1); and (5) Spirit-directed, church-sent/supported missionaries (13:2-3). Now in Acts 13–14 we see the two commissioned missionaries, Paul and Barnabas, going out to make disciples in several unreached places.

The intentional sending out of missionaries to overseas locations was unique to the church in Antioch. So far in Acts the gospel has advanced outside of Jerusalem mainly because of persecution and a few special cases of divine intervention—as when Peter was called to visit Cornelius and Philip encountered the Ethiopian. In other words, to this point people have been *forced out* of Jerusalem and taken up missions efforts as a result. As Christians were scattered, they carried the gospel with them and by God's grace made many new disciples. But in this particular passage we witness a planned attempt to take the gospel to the world. Here the missionaries are intentionally *sent out*, which is evidence of the church's beginning to grasp a bit of God's heart to make the gospel known to the ends of the earth (1:8).

While these missionary journeys throughout Acts have particular relevance for international missionaries, people who cross the street to bear witness to Jesus can also find much instruction and inspiration in these moving narratives.

Here we will look at the stops Paul and Barnabas made in Cyprus, Perga, and Pisidian Antioch.

Stop 1: Paul and Barnabas in Cyprus
ACTS 13:4-12

Before telling us where the missionaries travel, Luke reminds us that these two men were "sent out by the Holy Spirit" (v. 4; cf. v. 2). We must recognize the absolute necessity of living by the Spirit when living out Jesus's mission (1:8).

From Seleucia, the port for Antioch, Paul and Barnabas sailed west to the island of Cyprus, stopping first at the eastern port of the island, Salamis (13:4-5). Barnabas was a native of Cyprus (4:36), and the Hellenists had already begun some work there (11:19). Also, there were other Christians from Cyprus who belonged to the Antioch church (11:20).

The missionary team employed a strategy that would characterize Paul's evangelism efforts elsewhere: they started by proclaiming the Word in the local Jewish synagogues (v. 5). Pragmatically, this made sense because the Jews believed the Scriptures, though they failed to see Christ as the fulfillment of them. Nevertheless, the motivation for starting in the synagogues may have been driven more by this conviction: God's promise to Israel's patriarchs demanded that the gospel be preached to the Jew first and then to the Greek (see Rom 1:16; 2:9-10; Johnson, *Let's Study Acts*, 157).

As Paul and Barnabas labor, they work the ninety-mile width of the island until they arrive in Paphos. The missionaries there encounter "a sorcerer, a Jewish false prophet named Bar-Jesus" (v. 6), and a Gentile, Sergius Paulus (v. 7). The latter was the proconsul, the Roman governor of Cyprus, and "an intelligent man" (v. 7). Here we learn three important truths for Word-driven, Spirit-empowered missionaries.

Some People Will Be Open to God's Word (13:4-7)

Sergius Paulus "summoned Barnabas and Saul and wanted to hear the word of God" (11:7). He was hungry for more than the idolatry of his day and the counsel of his personal prophet, Bar-Jesus ("Son of the Savior"). While Bar-Jesus may have promised to know the way of salvation, Paul's message was radically different from anything he taught. And Paul's teaching apparently attracted Sergius Paulus, an intelligent man of high standing.

When we engage neighborhoods and nations with the gospel, we should expect that some people will be open to our message. We may find an audience with "the least of these," those who are poor, uneducated, and marginalized or with "the greatest of these," those who are powerful, wealthy, and influential. In this case the missionaries found an audience with an influential leader. Their experience reminds us that you never know to whom the Lord will direct you—who will listen to the gospel. Understand that these apostles were nobodies compared to the Roman proconsul, yet here they find themselves in front of him, speaking the good news to his heart. Paul told the Corinthians that the conversion of the powerful was rare (1 Cor 1:26), but here in Paphos a powerful man found himself attracted to the Word.

Some People Will Oppose God's Word (13:8-11)

The opponent in this passage is Bar-Jesus, also known as *Elymas*, meaning "sorcerer" (v. 8). Romans placed value on omens and divination. They also thought the Jews had inside information on spiritual matters, a fact helping to establish Bar-Jesus as a popular sage. He, however, was a false prophet in touch with dark powers. He was not a "magician" (v. 6 ESV) who pulls rabbits out of hats but a superstitious occult leader.

Bar-Jesus proved to be a false prophet opposing the Word of God that Paul and Barnabas taught. Bar-Jesus tried to turn the proconsul away from the faith, seeing the missionaries as a threat to his prestige and livelihood (Stott, *Message of Acts*, 219).

Two reasons people oppose the gospel are *pride* and *materialism*. Many people arrogantly refuse to admit they're wrong. They refuse to humbly repent and say the gospel is true and salvation is in Christ alone. And many others refuse to give up their materialistic lifestyles to follow the path of discipleship. The gospel confronts idols. And when collisions happen, heated opposition sometimes ensues.

In verse 9 Luke alerts us to the shift of Saul's name to Paul. *Paul* was probably his Roman name, and since his missionary ventures would be in Greco-Roman territory, it makes sense for him to be addressed primarily as Paul from this point forward. Further, from here on he will be mentioned first or alone, indicating that he became the team leader (13:13,42,46,50; 14:1,3).

The confrontation between the missionaries and Bar-Jesus was intense (vv. 9-11). Perhaps you think Paul's resulting curse on the man isn't very nice. Know that the fate of Sergius Paulus's soul was at stake in this situation, and Paul—out of deep compassion—wanted him to believe. Remember how firmly Jesus spoke about those who hinder children from coming to him? He said it would be better for them to tie millstones around their necks and jump into the sea than to cause someone to stumble away from faith (Matt 18:6). Eternal life is serious business.

Paul is "filled with the Holy Spirit." Bar-Jesus is filled with "deceit and trickery." Paul is a child of God. Bar-Jesus, far from representing his name, is a "son of the devil" (cf. John 8:44). Paul is telling everyone about the righteous One who makes sinners righteous. Bar-Jesus is an "enemy of all that is right." Paul is announcing the way of salvation (cf. Luke 3:4). Bar-Jesus is "perverting" the way of salvation. Instead of advocating real conversion, Bar-Jesus advocates spiritual perversion.

As a consequence, the Lord judges Bar-Jesus. He strikes him blind, perhaps representing his spiritual blindness (John 3:19-20; 9:39). This move was particularly fitting since the man was a proponent of darkness (Isa 5:20). His judgment was a foretaste of what will happen to all who fail to bow the knee to Jesus: they will be thrown into utter darkness (Matt 8:12; 25:30).

Consider three personal exhortations tied to this encounter between Paul and Bar-Jesus.

View opposition from a Christian perspective. Expect spiritual warfare when doing gospel ministry. Christians today will be opposed not only by Islamic terrorists but also by secularists in the media, professors at the universities, and by those who like to argue. Opposition, as we have seen, is inevitable.

A joy, however, comes from standing firm in the face of opposition (v. 52), a sweetness of joy we will experience only as we encounter opposition for living faithfully to Jesus (cf. 5:41).

In adversity we have the opportunity to advertise the power of the gospel. When some people see Christians standing firm in the face of demonic opposition, it affects them! We show the world the worth of Christ when we follow Jesus in the face of conflict.

You're not alone when you face opposition for making the gospel known! The Lord of heaven and earth is with you and for you (Matt 28:16-20).

It's important you don't assume you're in the wrong place when you face opposition. In fact, it may indicate that you're exactly where you should be! In this case the Spirit led the missionaries into a war zone, much like the Spirit led Jesus into the wilderness to be tempted by the devil (Luke 4:1). This passage, like others in Acts, helps us understand opposition.

Speak boldly. I don't suggest we go around talking to our opponents exactly as Paul addresses Bar-Jesus, but we should seek to boldly tell people the whole gospel, which includes sharing what the terrifying consequences will be should they refuse to bow the knee to Christ. Sharing this truth is an act of love! Notice Paul doesn't say, "Now, Elymas has his perspective, and I have my perspective. Both are acceptable." No! Paul challenges us to speak boldly in our tolerant, postmodern world.

Trust wholeheartedly in the triumphant power of the Word and Spirit. John Polhill reminds us, "Christianity has nothing to do with the magic and superstition of this world; its power, the power of the Word and Spirit, overcomes them all" (*Acts*, 294). The gospel really is the power of God unto salvation (Rom 1:16). John Stott says,

[T]he Holy Spirit overthrew the evil one, the apostle confounded the sorcerer, and the gospel triumphed over the occult. (*Message of Acts*, 220)

Let this story encourage you in your witness! Maintain an unshakable confidence in the gospel. And maintain an unshakable confidence in the Spirit's power to overcome obstacles and to open people's hearts to the gospel.

Some People Will Embrace God's Word (13:12)

Luke concludes by telling us a great report (v. 12). While the darkness of judgment came on Bar-Jesus, the light of salvation burst on the Gentile ruler Sergius Paulus! As in the early chapters of Acts, a miracle provided an occasion to proclaim the gospel, and this prominent Roman official, who had "no religious background in Judaism"(Stott, *Message of Acts*, 320), became a member of the family of God.

Let this conversion story encourage you as you seek to make the gospel known to unbelievers. Some people will repent and turn to Christ when a bold witness makes the good news clear to them. God is at work in the world, bringing all sorts of people to faith in Christ through the witness of faithful missionaries! Your Sergius Paulus is waiting!

Stop 2: Paul and Barnabas in Perga
ACTS 13:13-14A

The missionary squad leaves Cyprus and sails northwest to Perga in Pamphylia, which is present-day Turkey. Perga was twelve miles inland, between the Tarsus Mountains and the Mediterranean Sea. The missionaries probably first landed at Attalia and traveled by foot to Perga (Polhill, *Acts*, 296). It seems they didn't stay in Perga long, as Luke records only one detail about the stop: "John left them and went back to Jerusalem" (v. 13). Then they continued on to Pisidian Antioch (v. 14). Allow me to point out two brief applications.

Be Ready for Relational Conflicts Within Your Ministry Team (13:13)

Why did John, also known as John Mark, leave the team? Was he scared of the journey across the mountains? Did he miss his mother's home in Jerusalem? Did he protest the shift of leadership from his cousin Barnabas to Paul (Col 4:10)? Did he contract an illness, like malaria, in the Pamphylian lowlands? Did he disagree with Paul's zeal for reaching the Gentiles? Was Paul ill, leading Mark to think it foolish to cross the mountains? We know that when Paul arrived in the cities of South Galatia he was suffering from an illness, which apparently affected his eyesight (Gal 4:13-15).

Luke simply says that Mark "left them." He resurfaces later in the narrative when Barnabas tries to persuade Paul to take Mark on another trip. Luke records Paul's negative reaction to that suggestion (15:38).

Based on this text, it seems that Mark abandoned the team, and some of the reasons mentioned above don't really fit into the desertion hypothesis. I doubt that his departure was due to illness or theology. My guess is that it probably had to do with homesickness or fear. Originally, he may have been enamored by the allure of travel, and since he was Barnabas's cousin, he may have also had connections in Cyprus that made the trip sound appealing. But over time the shine of the trip began to fade—an experience you likely know something about if you've ever been on a lengthy mission trip. My first mission trip, for example, was to Australia. During the first few days I couldn't get over the fact that I was in Australia. Our earliest days of ministry were thrilling. But after five or six days passed, I couldn't wait to get back on home soil and sleep in my bed. Perhaps Mark was overcome by such feelings.

One thing is absolutely clear: the team was rocked by a relational conflict. We will experience them as well. And while such disputes are unfortunate distractions, it helps to remember that even Paul and Barnabas had them.

Conflict doesn't have to end in failure. The good news about Mark is that he finished well. After all, he ended up writing the Gospel bearing his name. When Paul writes his last letter, he says, "Bring Mark with you, for he is useful to me in the ministry" (2 Tim 4:11). That mention gives insight into the grace and restoration that had to follow what happened here in verse 13. At this point in Acts, Paul wants nothing more to do with Mark. Later he will want Mark to visit him, commending him as "useful." So, while you may have conflicts on your team, rest assured that restoration can occur.

Be Ready for Physical Challenges as You Make the Gospel Known (13:14a)

Luke's brief mention of the team's trip to Antioch in Pisidia makes no mention of the arduous nature of the trek. Polhill helps us imagine it:

Antioch lay some 100 miles to the north across the Taurus
mountain range. The route was barren, often flooded by
swollen mountain streams, and notorious for its bandits,
which even the Romans had difficulty bringing under control.
Antioch itself was in the highlands, some 3,600 feet above sea
level. (*Acts,* 297)

Add to that the likelihood of some physical illness plaguing the group's
leader, and you have one extremely challenging venture.

Ministry isn't for the faint of heart. Advancing the gospel will cost
us. If you ever imagine that pioneer evangelism and church planting are
glamorous, just read about some of Paul's afflictions in 2 Corinthians
11:23-28. Then read about the church's larger history; you will find
some of God's choicest servants like Charles Spurgeon, Martin Luther,
and William Wilberforce suffering from all sorts of health problems.
Others, like George Whitefield and David Livingstone, suffered under
violent threats.

Paul's desire to reach the Gentiles reminds us of part of the reason
we have so many unreached people in the world: *they live in extreme,
hard-to-access places*—on steep hillsides, in deserts, and out in the middle
of nowhere. Many other unreached peoples live in *dangerous places*, in
locations where society is violently hostile to Christianity. But here in
Acts 13 we see an example of the type of grace-enabled endurance that
must reside in the hearts of gospel-centered, Spirit-empowered, Christ-
exalting missionaries.

Stop 3: Paul and Barnabas in Pisidian Antioch: Proclamation Suitable for Their Audience
ACTS 13:14B-52

Although it is referred to as "Pisidian Antioch" to distinguish it from
other places such as Antioch in Syria, this town was actually in Phrygia,
just across the border from Pisidia in the Roman province of Galatia
(Polhill, *Acts*, 297). In Paul's sermon in this section, he strikes a major
theme in his letter to the Galatians—namely, justification by faith alone
(vv. 38-39). Many Jews also resided in this city, so he follows his typical approach of beginning his evangelistic efforts in the synagogue.
Pisidian Antioch was an influential political and economic region.
Paul's approach to fulfilling the gospel mission involved evangelizing
important cities like this one.

Perhaps word spread that Paul had been taught under the great rabbi Gamaliel, leading to his invitation to give the exposition for the day (vv. 14-15). Paul has been preaching already, but here Luke records one of Paul's sermons—to a Jewish audience. This sermon has a lot in common with Peter's Pentecost sermon, especially in the way it shows Jesus as the promised Messiah and in that both cite Psalm 16. It also bears similarity to Stephen's sermon in Acts 7, although Stephen emphasized Israel's rebellion while Paul emphasizes God's grace to Israel.

From this sermon we learn to proclaim Christ in a way that is suitable for a particular audience. To be sure, Paul always proclaimed Christ in evangelism. He never changed the fixed gospel. But Paul was flexible in approach. His sermon to this primarily Jewish crowd differs from his evangelism efforts to pagans. We will see this much more in 14:15-17 and 17:16-34. In addition, Paul's sermon to a group of pastors also bears a distinct flavor (20:17-35). And his speeches before Felix and Agrippa (24; 26) were also situational. The way Paul addresses the Jews in a synagogue in Acts 13 makes sense. They were familiar with David, the law, and the Old Testament story.

At issue here is the same challenge every missionary has today, whether speaking to large crowds or to individuals, to locals in their hometowns or to those who live among unreached peoples. They don't try to evangelize a sixty-year-old grandma who spent some time in American Sunday school the same way they speak to a Chinese college student who has absolutely no clue about what is in the Bible. Similarly, your Muslim neighbor has a different worldview from the teenager that goes to the private Catholic school. This will require you to share the fixed gospel with flexible communication if you intend to reach them effectively.

Evangelizing people with this kind of sensitivity is the task of *contextualization*, making the gospel known in a way appropriate for the context. Steve Timmis says,

> In every situation, there needs to be a point of contact with
> the people (understand their values, history, communication
> style) and a point of conflict that reveals how their own
> narrative conflicts with that of the Gospel. ("How to Plant a
> Church")

This requires both faithfulness to the gospel and an effectiveness and awareness in communication. Here in Acts 13 it's a Jewish setting, so Paul exalts Jesus from the Old Testament. He uses his audience's existing grasp of Scripture to show them that Jesus is the hero of their Bible.

Rabbinic sources show that the synagogue service was typically opened by a reading of the Law of Moses and one of a related text from the Prophets, a recitation of the Shema (Deut 6:4-5), and the praying of prescribed prayers (Johnson, *Let's Study Acts,* 161). An exposition then followed, sometimes given by a visiting rabbi (cf. Luke 4:16-30). This word of encouragement or exhortation (v. 15; Heb 13:22) was a sermon based on the readings for the day and the application of the texts to the people. It was basically what we call expositional preaching (cf. 1 Tim 4:13).

Paul's Christ-exalting sermon contains three parts. It received a mixed reaction.

Introduction: Preparation for the Coming of Christ (13:16-25)

Paul begins by emphasizing God's grace to Israel as he briefly summarizes Israel's history. God is the subject of nearly every verb he chooses (Stott, *Message of Acts,* 223). John Piper notes, "This text [vv. 17-30] is utterly saturated with God. Sixteen times Paul presses home the truth that God is the central Actor in history" ("History Is God's Story"). Indeed, this sermon is Scripture saturated, God centered, and Christ exalting. Notice the initiating work of God. God "led them out . . . put up with them . . . gave them their land . . . gave them judges . . . gave them Saul . . . [and] raised up David." None of their history is random because God doesn't do random. He is accomplishing his purposes in history.

After mentioning David the king, Paul then jumps to Jesus, the promised Messiah and descendent of David (v. 23), showing the continuity of the Bible and setting his emphasis on Jesus as the risen and reigning King. He then mentions the King of king's forerunner, John the Baptist (vv. 24-25).

With this brief sketch of history leading up to the coming of Christ, Paul, like John the Baptist, exalts Jesus with great boldness. And like John the Baptist, he tells his audience that Jesus is the climax of biblical history. It culminates in the arrival of David's greater Son, Jesus—God's promised Messiah and the world's Savior.

Proclamation: The Death and Resurrection of Christ (13:26-37)

Paul's focus is to herald "the word of this salvation" (v. 26), or "the good news" (v. 32), which centers on the person and work of Jesus.

Paul says that *Jesus's identity has been confirmed by his resurrection victory* (Ferguson, "Acts 13:13-57"). The residents of Jerusalem and their rulers "did not recognize him," and even though they found no guilt in him, they condemned him (vv. 27-28). The people actually thought Jesus was the opposite of who he really was, so they had him executed. Further, the fact that Jesus was crucified was proof to his opponents that he was an imposter since the Scriptures teach that God sets a curse on any who hang on a tree (v. 29; Deut 21:23-23). But Paul tells his audience that such a view of Jesus is a man-centered judgment. In raising Jesus from the dead, God confirmed Jesus's identity as the Messiah (v. 30). Resurrection is verification. The resurrection proved that Jesus's work on the cross was sufficient. And God's raising of Jesus proved Jesus's words true. Paul adds that many still-living eyewitnesses can testify to Jesus's bodily resurrection (v. 31).

Paul adds that *Jesus fulfills biblical prophecy.* God fulfilled his plan through the hands of those who had no desire to see Jesus as the Messiah (vv. 27,29). Jesus didn't self-engineer the fulfillment of prophecy. It was carried out through the evil deeds of others. Contrary to the executors' own purposes, they fulfilled God's purposes.

Paul goes on to cite several texts (Pss 2:7; 16:10; Isa 55:3), showing that in these specific ways prophecies about Jesus have been fulfilled. For instance, Jesus, the Holy One and universal King, did not see decay—unlike David (vv. 36-37).

This sermon highlights Paul's own words in 1 Corinthians 15:1-11: we must preach the things that are "most important." We must keep the crucifixion and resurrection of Jesus—as recorded in the Scriptures— the main message of our ministries. Christ is the hero of the Bible, and he must remain the hero of our teaching and preaching.

Application: The Promise of Forgiveness and Justification for All Who Trust in Christ (13:38-41)

Paul shifts to application at this point, as indicated by the transitional word "therefore." What do Christ's death and resurrection mean for them (and us)?

In effect Paul says, "Here's the good news of the gospel: You can have the forgiveness of sins through Christ! You can be justified—that is, declared righteous in God's sight through Jesus. We, who can't be perfectly obedient to God, can be counted righteous through placing faith in Jesus. We can't earn righteousness; we must receive it. We can receive justification—meaning not only 'just as if I never sinned,' but also 'just as if I always obeyed'—when we trust Christ alone."

People will try everything to get rid of the guilt they feel, to deal with their unsettled consciences. They try therapy, exercise, diets, medicine, and countless other remedies. And while these things can treat some of the symptoms of underlying issues, they won't ultimately heal a person of his or her real problems. Some religious types even try to deal with guilt by religious performance, but that only leads to pride or despair. Other religious types practice self-mutilation, physically whipping themselves in a hopeless attempt to make atonement for their sin. Some even try to dismiss their guilt by saying, "I won't worry about it. That way it will go away." But that doesn't work either.

God has provided only one solution for the problem of guilt: we must trust in Christ alone. We must trust in the One who bore our curse on the cross, setting us free from condemnation. Jesus says to repentant sinners, "You are forgiven. You are free from condemnation" (cf. Rom 8:1). Each person, then, must come to Jesus and be "justified" from everything from which they could not be freed by following the law of Moses (13:39; cf. Gal 3:10-14). Everyone can exchange condemnation for justification and the experience of peace, learning to sing wholeheartedly, "It [really] is well with my soul!"

How do people receive this forgiveness? It is through *faith* in Christ. Paul says, "Everyone who believes is justified through him" (v. 39, a theme he unpacks in Galatians in particular; e.g., Gal 2:16). So rest the weight of your sin, guilt, and restless conscience on him. Rest in the grace of Jesus. Stop trusting in anything else. Think you have done too much to be forgiven? Think again. Even those who put Jesus to death were not beyond the reach of God's saving grace (Acts 3:15,19; 1 Tim 1:13).

Paul adds a warning for all who would scoff at and reject the gospel, quoting Habakkuk 1:5. He says, in effect, "Don't set this matter aside. This is a matter of eternal life or eternal judgment!" He warns against the hardness of heart that keeps people from believing the message. He warns against the cynic who scoffs at the truth. Often people assume that it's because of some lofty intellectual argument that people make fun of the message of salvation. But accepting or rejecting what Jesus accomplished at Calvary is not about one's intelligence; it's about one's heart. Previously in Acts an intelligent man, Sergius Paulus, became a Christian. But here many in this crowd refuse Paul's message because of nothing more than hard-heartedness.

A Mixed Reaction (13:42-52)

One group wanted to hear more on the following Sabbath (vv. 42,45). Others "followed Paul and Barnabas," not just physically but spiritually

(v. 43). The missionaries urged these new disciples to "continue in the grace of God" (cf. 11:23; 14:22), meaning that just as they entered the faith by grace, they must persevere in the faith while relying on God's grace—a needed warning in light of rising persecution in the town.

"Almost the whole town assembled" to hear that forgiveness is available for anyone who will simply trust in Christ—a message just as applicable to Gentiles attracted to Jewish monotheism as to those immersed in paganism. Upon seeing the crowds gather to hear the missionaries on the Sabbath, however, the Jews were filled with "jealousy" and "began to contradict what Paul was saying, insulting him" (13:45; cf. 5:17; 17:5). Sadly, the people who knew the Bible best became the most hostile. And when they didn't have an argument, they attacked the messenger.

Paul and Barnabas answer their opponents by telling them it was by divine necessity that they preached to the Jew first, just as they will do in other cities (14:1; 17:2; Rom 1:16), being mindful of God's promise to the patriarchs. But the Jewish community in Pisidian Antioch in general rejected the Word, so Paul and Barnabas declared, "We are turning to the Gentiles" (13:46). Thus, they fulfilled the calling that was given to Israel through the prophet Isaiah: "I have made you a light for the Gentiles to bring salvation to the end of the earth" (v. 47; Isa 49:6).

This announcement causes the Gentiles to rejoice, worship, and believe (v. 48). Israel rejects its Messiah, but God still has his chosen ones, who will feast at his banquet (Luke 14:21-24). The book of Acts is filled with expressions of God's sovereign plan at work in the salvation of sinners (2:23,39,47; 3:16,18; 4:27-28; 5:14,31; 11:18,24; 15:8-9; 16:14; 18:27).

The Word then spread beyond the city into the region (v. 49). Its success reminds me of some basil we planted last year. It just grew like crazy. Perhaps you've seen some vegetables in your garden take off in a similar way. That's the picture I get when reading this passage.

Sometimes missionaries endure persecution; sometimes they move on as a result of it. On this occasion, they leave town, shaking the dust off of their feet as a sign of God's indictment against the place (cf. Luke 9:5; Acts 18:6). But they leave "filled with joy and the Holy Spirit" and head east to Iconium (v. 52), remaining on mission. Once again, we see the connection between suffering for the sake of the gospel and Christian joy. That's a joy many haven't tasted because they haven't suffered for the Name (cf. 5:41).

Some were intrigued by the message the missionaries shared. Some were enraged by it. Some believed it completely. And the messengers were filled with joy. We should expect to encounter similarly mixed results when we make the gospel known.

Conclusion

Perhaps you are familiar with the Bible but have never trusted in Jesus (John 5:39). Recognize that these Jews knew the Bible also, but they remained unconverted. You need to know more than a few hundred Bible verses to have the assurance of spending eternity in heaven. You must come to faith in the living Savior.

Perhaps you are a genuine Christian. Can you explain the gospel from the Bible? Be ready to explain the good news to people because you never know who may be open to embracing the message.

And perhaps you're zealous to share the good news—but are you ready for opposition? It's inevitable, but along with persevering in spite of it comes a deep joy that comes from obedience to Jesus. So go in the power of the Holy Spirit, telling the nations how to find forgiveness through Christ—even though it will cost you. Grab your Bible, your passport, and your first-aid kit and make the light of the gospel known in this dark world.

Reflect and Discuss

1. What can we learn from the church in Antioch about making the gospel known to the world?
2. Why should Paul's ministry to Sergius Paulus encourage us in our witness?
3. What does this chapter teach about opposition?
4. How does this chapter highlight the overcoming power of the gospel and the Spirit?
5. Why do you think John Mark went back to Jerusalem? What does this relational conflict teach about ministry teams?
6. What does this first missionary journey teach about the physical challenges of making the gospel known among the nations?
7. Explain how Paul was faithful and flexible in evangelism.
8. What do we need to know in order to present the gospel to different types of people?
9. What about Paul's sermon in Pisidian Antioch most resonates with you?
10. What do you learn from the people's reaction to Paul's sermon in Pisidian Antioch?

The Holy Spirit, a Bible, a Passport, and a First-Aid Kit, Part 2

ACTS 14:1-28

Main Idea: The completion of the first missionary journey of Paul and Barnabas provides us with an instructive and inspiring model of Christian perseverance.

I. **Perseverance in Iconium (14:1-7)**
   A. Persevere with courage (14:1).
   B. Persevere in reliance on the Lord (14:2-4).
   C. Persevere with prudence (14:5-7).
II. **Perseverance in Lystra and Derbe (14:8-21a)**
   A. Persevere in faithful and flexible evangelism (14:8-20a).
   B. Persevere through physical trials out of love for the gospel (14:20b-21a).
III. **Perseverance in the Return Trips (14:21b-28)**
   A. Persevere by being devoted to the local church (14:21b-28).

In chapter 14 the missionaries simply keep on doing what they were doing previously. This chapter contains stories of more sacrifice; it includes more examples of the Spirit at work; it notes more gospel proclamations suitable for a particular audience; it mentions more mixed responses to the gospel as well as more opposition. Paul saw these events as stories of endurance. In his last letter Paul spoke of his sufferings on this missionary journey, encouraging Timothy (who was from Lystra) to persevere:

> *But you have followed my teaching, conduct, purpose, faith, patience, love, and endurance, along with the persecutions and sufferings that came to me in Antioch, Iconium, and Lystra. What persecutions I endured—and yet the Lord rescued me from them all. In fact, all who want to live a godly life in Christ Jesus will be persecuted.* (2 Tim 3:10-12)

In a day when many were abandoning the faith, Paul was to Timothy a godly example of perseverance to be followed. These stories should spur us on to endure for the sake of the gospel too, as we consider not only Paul's endurance but also the faithful help of the Lord, who rescued the apostle from every trial.

Perseverance in Iconium
ACTS 14:1-7

The journey to Iconium wasn't easy. The city was about ninety miles southeast of Pisidian Antioch and is currently called Konya. Paul and Barnabas traveled along the famous Via Sebaste, through rolling countryside, then past the snow-capped peaks of the Sultan mountain range. The strenuous nature of this trip is obvious.

Iconium attracted lots of people since it was along an east-west trade route. John Stott tells us, "It was still a Greek city when Paul and Barnabas visited it, and was a center of agriculture and commerce" (*Message of Acts*, 228). In Scripture we see Paul's pattern of proclaiming the gospel to large, influential cities in a region and then working outward from there.

Luke records three stages of the missionaries' visit in Iconium. In stage 1 they minister in the synagogue (v. 1). In stage 2 they minister outside the synagogue (vv. 2-4). In stage 3, in response to physical threats, they flee to the cities of Lycaonia (vv. 5-7). In each of these stages we see a particular aspect of the missionaries' perseverance.

Persevere with Courage (14:1)

The missionaries begin, as usual, by engaging people in the synagogue. Paul and Barnabas were very successful (v. 1). Based on the recorded synagogue sermon in Pisidian Antioch (13:17-41), we can imagine Paul telling the story line of the Bible, which climaxes on the person and work of Jesus, the Messiah.

Even though Paul was committed to reaching the Gentiles (13:46), he still sought to win his fellow Jews to Christ. Not all of them opposed Paul's message. Also present in the synagogues were Gentile proselytes and God fearers, many of whom were also open to the good news and some of whom had at least a rudimentary understanding of the Scriptures.

What's more striking than Paul's pattern of starting at the synagogues, however, is Paul's *perseverance*. Remember, he just left a situation where those from the synagogue attacked him! He was driven out of town. Yet here he is again, back in a synagogue. He courageously goes right into a place of likely opposition.

Have you ever known that you would be opposed for speaking faithfully for Christ in a certain situation and yet did so anyway? The type of courage needed for encounters like that comes from the enabling power of the Spirit (4:29-31).

Persevere in Reliance on the Lord (14:2-4)

In verses 2-4 the missionaries encounter resistance from nonbelieving Jews. Effectiveness and opposition go together in the missionary enterprise. Tim Keller notes this general ministry principle: "The greater the effectiveness of a ministry, the greater the resistance and opposition" (*Evangelism,* 117). Not only did the Jews reject the message, they "poisoned [the] minds" of the Gentile population (v. 2). The opponents engage in "anti-evangelism" with slander and false teaching. Tensions are clearly rising.

Instead of being intimidated, however, the missionaries are inspired to even bolder witness (v. 3)! They stay several months! And as they rely on the Spirit, they preach the "message of his grace" (cf. 20:24; Gal 1:6-7). What upset their religious opponents? Grace. They were mad enough to kill the missionaries over the good news that God extends unmerited kindness to all who will turn to him by placing faith in Christ. Grace tends either to give people an unspeakable sense of relief and joy or produce hostility and anger. The default mode of the heart is works-based righteousness; that's why people generally either embrace grace or oppose it.

To some in the crowd, a statement like, "Sinners aren't qualified to receive God's grace," would've been as welcome as a drop of poison hitting their eardrums. But in that teaching is the beauty of the gospel. Paul told the Colossians that it is "the Father who has enabled you to share in the saints' inheritance in the light" (Col 1:12). No one is qualified. Yet by God's work through Jesus, sinful men and women can be forgiven, freed, and transferred into the kingdom of God's beloved Son (Col 1:13-14).

Recently my son and I were traveling home and got to the airport earlier than anticipated. So I called the airline and asked to be put on standby for an earlier flight. Since I fly so often, I qualify for free standby access. In other words, if seats are open on a particular flight and I'm at the top of the standby list, I can get on a different flight from the one I booked free of charge. But in this case I had to pay $50 for my son to get on the earlier flight with me. Why? He doesn't have enough points to merit the free access. He doesn't qualify for the perk I enjoy.

Aren't you glad the gospel doesn't work like that? We don't have to earn enough moral points with God or pay a certain price for the wrongs we've done before gaining access into the kingdom through the salvation Christ offers! Praise God that through Jesus we can have access to God by grace through faith, apart from works (Eph 2:8-9). This scandalous message of grace enrages self-righteous legalists.

The missionaries preached grace with great boldness (cf. 4:29-31) for an extended period of time, and the Lord accompanied their verbal witness with signs. These signs were also acts of God's grace, authenticating the missionaries' teaching.

These men weren't fragile. But their determination didn't come from their own strength and willpower. They were strong because they were *reliant* on the Lord. They preached about the grace of Jesus, while they relied on the grace of Jesus. Jesus uses people who depend on him (cf. John 15:5; 2 Cor 12:9-10). These missionaries are giving us a picture of grace-enabled grit that's necessary for enduring hardship in gospel ministry (cf. Eph 6:1; 2 Tim 1:8; 2:1). This boldness and stick-with-it-ness come from the Lord of heaven and earth, who promises to be with us as we make the gospel known (Matt 28:18-20).

In verse 4 we see people divided. While the gospel unites people who would never otherwise be united (cf. 1 Cor 1:10), it also divides the human race (cf. 1 Cor 1:18). If the gospel message shared is not both uniting and dividing, in fact, you can be sure that the true gospel isn't being preached.

Persevere with Prudence (14:5-7)

Soon the verbal opposition the missionaries encountered deteriorates into physical threats. Jews and Gentiles plot to stone Paul and Barnabas (v. 5). Upon learning about this plan, the missionaries flee to the nearby towns of Lystra and Derbe in Lycaonia. Lystra was about twenty miles south of Iconium, and Derbe was about sixty miles southeast of Lystra; both towns were within the Galatian province.

In verses 8-20 Luke describes the ministry in Lystra, a "quiet backwater town" (Stott, *Message of Acts,* 230). The ministry in Derbe is mentioned briefly in verses 20-21. John Polhill says, "There were no other significant towns in the region, but the reference to the 'surrounding country' in v. 6 might indicate that they evangelized the smaller towns and countryside of Lycaonia as well" (*Acts,* 311–12). In these places "they continued preaching the gospel" (v. 7).

In this act of relocating, we should notice the combination of *prudence* and *perseverance*. The missionaries were brave but not stupid! In fleeing danger, they lived to preach another day. Sometimes the best way to make the gospel known may mean remaining; at other times it may mean relocating. For such matters one must seek the Father, who promises to give his children wisdom when they ask him (Jas 1:5).

Perseverance in Lystra and Derbe
ACTS 14:8-21A

Lystra was a small country town in Paul's day, a frontier outpost of the Roman Empire. I like to imagine it as the Wild West. The Lystrans were generally uneducated and, it also seems, gullible. Kent Hughes says, "The people were half-barbarous." He adds, "The Romans ruled the land, the Greeks controlled the commerce, and the Jews had little influence" (*Acts,* 184–85). It was, then, a much different place from Iconium. Apparently there was no Jewish synagogue there, but we do know of at least one family of Jewish origin who lived there, that of Timothy and his Jewish mother (16:1). Overall, however, Lystra seems to have consisted mainly of Gentile pagans.

The events in Lystra take place in four parts. In the first section a miraculous healing occurs as Paul commands a lame man to stand up and walk (vv. 8-10). Next, this healing leads the native Lystrans to honor the missionaries as gods (vv. 11-13). Paul and Barnabas protest this idolatrous attempt, and Paul preaches a mini sermon to the crowd (vv. 14-18). Finally, this same crowd is gathered under the influence of Jews from Antioch and Iconium, and they attempt to stone Paul to death (vv. 19-20).

Persevere in Faithful and Flexible Evangelism (14:8-20a)

We find Paul preaching the gospel in a way fitting for this audience, once again giving us a model for effective evangelism. This brief abstract of his sermon is important, as John Stott notes, because it's "his only recorded address to illiterate pagans" (*Message of Acts,* 231). In the previous chapter Paul preached in a synagogue to the Jewish audience who were familiar with the Old Testament, but with this crowd Paul has to start with what they can see in creation instead of what they can read in the Scriptures. This doesn't mean Paul ignored the Bible. Everything he says is consistent with its message. Stott says, "One can't help but admire the flexibility of Paul's evangelistic approach" (ibid., 231–32).

A man who had been lame from birth was listening to Paul's words. The Holy Spirit gave Paul the ability to see what was happening in the spiritual realm, allowing him to perceive this lame man's faith. The apostle thus commands him to stand up (vv. 8-10; cf. 3:2-10). The man immediately leaps up and walks, a sign of the already/not-yet kingdom (cf. Isa 35:5-6).

Then, in ignorance, the locals react wrongly (vv. 11-13), assuming Paul and Barnabas are gods. Initially, Paul and Barnabas don't realize it because the Lystrans are speaking their native Lycaonian language. The wild Lystrans called Paul "Hermes," the Greek god of oratory and the inventor of speech. They call the noble Barnabas "Zeus," the chief god.

It's possible that this superstitious and fanatical declaration came from a local legend. The Latin poet Ovid describes how the gods descended to this region, seeking hospitality, but everyone rejected the gods except for one poor couple, Philemon and Baucis, who took them in and treated them kindly. The gods rewarded them by transforming their cottage into a magnificent temple and making them guardians of it. The gods punished the unwelcoming residents with a severe flood. The superstitious people of Lystra may want to escape disaster, so they laud Paul and Barnabas.

In verse 13 the missionaries recognize that something is brewing as they see the priest of Zeus arrive with garland and bulls for a sacrifice. Paul and Barnabas rush out into the crowds and rend their garments. This act was a sign of mourning (Gen 37:29,34), distress (Josh 7:6), or protest of perceived blasphemy (Mark 14:63; Polhill, *Acts*, 315). Here the missionaries are urging the people to stop their sacrifice.

Ministers today must take note of the missionaries' intense deflection of glory. Herod would have enjoyed such praise, but faithful Christians understand that only God is to be worshiped.

Paul then preaches a sermon to this group (vv. 15-17). The best commentary on this sermon is in 17:22-31, where Paul preaches to the Athenians—it's another sermon preached outside a synagogue to superstitious pagans. But Luke expands the Athenian sermon for us, and we see where Paul was going with some of these themes he alluded to in this sermon brief in Lystra.

Paul's main theme is the *nature and work of the living God*. The Lystrans believed in many gods and had no knowledge of the only true

God, who created and sustains the world. If Paul would have jumped straight to Jesus's life and ministry, many may have accepted Jesus as one god among the many other gods in their polytheistic worldview. Paul needed to establish that there's only one God over all things.

Paul's introduction includes a question: "People! Why are you doing these things?" (v. 15). In other words, he wants them to stop the madness. This reminds us of a similar scene when Cornelius bowed down to Peter in worship. Peter told Cornelius, "Stand up. I myself am also a man" (10:26). Here Paul says, "We are people also, just like you" (v. 15). Both men emphasize the insanity of worshiping humans.

Next, Paul tells the crowd of his desire to share the "good news" with them. Once again, Paul's preoccupation with the gospel is apparent. Unfortunately, for one of two reasons, we don't get to see Paul expound on the work of Christ. Either (1) Luke simply didn't record the sermon entirely, or more likely, (2) the sermon gets cut short because of the mob (v. 18). If it was simply cut short, we should have no doubt that Paul was moving toward the resurrection of Jesus. He simply didn't have a chance to finish the story, but we can see how he got there in 17:22-31. We must also keep in mind that Paul had already been preaching in the public square (v. 9), where he had been proclaiming the gospel.

What's stressed here in this sermon, as in previous sermons in Acts—and as in the sermon to the Athenians—is the call for *repentance*. Paul urges the listeners to "turn from these worthless things to the living God" (v. 15). Paul calls the gods of the Lystrans "worthless" (cf. Jer 2:5; Rom 1:21-23). Paul exhorts the people to abandon these nongods and turn to the one true and *living* God. That's why repentance is good news! People can know and worship the living God, instead of worthless idols, through repentance and faith in Jesus. Repentance may not sound like good news to some people, but it is! By turning from dead idols and trusting in Jesus, anyone can experience the Father's merciful, full forgiveness; they can be set free from slavery to sin; and they can have eternal life. A similar gospel summary is stated in Paul's letter to the Thessalonians:

> *They themselves report what kind of reception we had from you: how you turned to God from idols to serve the living and true God and to wait for his Son from heaven, whom he raised from the dead—Jesus, who rescues us from the coming wrath.* (1 Thess 1:9-10)

As in Thessalonica, Paul longs to see idol worshipers converted, so he communicates repentance in a way that's intelligible to the audience.

Conversion requires abandoning functional saviors and embracing the real Savior, Jesus.

Paul tells the Lystrans some things that set the living God apart from worthless idols. First, *God is Creator* (v. 15). He may have been alluding to Psalm 146:6. Paul is definitely starting with something to which they could relate and see. And he stresses the universal scope of God's creation.

Then Paul emphasizes *God's goodness and providence* (vv. 16-17). Who sent the rains for the crops? The only true and living God (cf. Ps 104). Who nourishes the body and satisfies hearts with good things? The only true and living God, who showers common grace on even his enemies (cf. Ps 145:9,16; Matt 5:45). In making a contrast with the harsh pagan gods, Paul emphasizes the goodness of God in everyday life. Every good thing the people had ever experienced was owed to the mercy and grace of the one true God.

Are you aware of the goodness of God in your daily life? Every time you eat a good meal, relax in a comfortable chair after a day's work, laugh with friends and family around a campfire, listen to the ocean, watch a sunrise, and breathe in the fresh air, you are experiencing the kindness of God.

But do you talk about the goodness of God to unbelievers over meals or in other venues as you talk about the beauty of creation? As believers, we should delight in God's goodness with gratitude and describe his goodness in evangelism.

Signs of God's goodness are all "witnesses" from God of his existence, wisdom, and benevolence. Creation itself is preaching an ongoing sermon (Ps 19:1-6). It wasn't God's purpose in the past to provide specific revelation to everyone about himself and his ways, as he did for Israel. Yet God revealed himself to the nations through creation, and consequently, everyone remains accountable to God and without excuse before him. Paul develops this concept more in Romans 1, where he says that sinful humanity exchanges worshiping the glory of the Creator for worshiping created things. Consequently, all are in need of redemption.

Perhaps you're thinking, *I can't use this approach because most people today believe in evolution. They don't even believe in God.* But we must remember that the reality of God's existence is planted inside of every person (Rom 1). When you hear the statement, "Atheists don't believe in God," remember this: God doesn't believe in atheists! When you talk to unbelievers, don't feel you must prove to them the existence of God. Paul presupposes God's existence in his preaching in Lystra. He starts with what is visible in creation and attributes it to God.

It seems like this sermon was cut short (v. 18). The crowd was determined to offer their sacrifices. They hear Paul preach, but they are underawed by his words.

Paul, however, would have a chance to develop his message further in Lystra at a later time, for Luke mentions the "disciples" in the town (vv. 20,22). Timothy and his mother were among those. This means that eventually many in Lystra heard the gospel and believed it. This opening scene, though, shows the challenge that the missionaries faced. But this is just the beginning.

We have no right or need to edit the gospel, but we do need to understand our audiences. We must begin by establishing a point of contact with people, and then we must lead them to the gospel conflict. Often points of contact can be made by simply observing what all humans see and experience and then working from there. Below are a few of those points of contact to consider as you work toward proclaiming the gospel effectively. Most people share . . .

a hunger for love and community,
a search for freedom,
a need to be rid of guilt and shame,
a quest for meaning,
a longing for significance,
a thirst for satisfaction and joy,
an attraction to beauty in creation, and
a love for creativity and innovation.

Starting with a verbal walk down any of these roads can get us into the story line of the Bible. The key is to know the Bible and to know people. "Wherever we begin," John Stott says, "we shall end with Jesus Christ, who is himself the good news, and who alone can fulfill all human aspirations" (*Message of Acts*, 232).

In verses 19-20 we see the fickleness of this Lystran crowd and the determination of the Jewish opponents from Antioch and Iconium. A group of angry Jews traveled twenty miles from Iconium, and about a hundred miles from Pisidian Antioch, in order to persecute Paul. These guys were vicious. Many of them gave up days of pay in order to throw rocks at Paul.

Unfortunately, the opponents are able to persuade the fickle locals to join them, and as a result of mob violence, they "stoned Paul" (v. 19).

One wonders while reading this account whether Paul reflected back on the stoning of Stephen, and even Stephen's prayer for the murderers, during the ordeal (Stott, *Message of Acts*, 233). One also wonders if young Timothy witnessed it. This was probably one event Paul had in mind when he wrote,

> *Five times I received the forty lashes minus one from the Jews. Three times I was beaten with rods. Once I received a stoning. Three times I was shipwrecked. I have spent a night and a day in the open sea. On frequent journeys, I faced dangers from rivers, dangers from robbers, dangers from my own people, dangers from Gentiles, dangers in the city, dangers in the wilderness, dangers at sea, and dangers among false brothers; toil and hardship, many sleepless nights, hunger and thirst, often without food, cold, and without clothing. Not to mention other things, there is the daily pressure on me: my concern for all the churches.* (2 Cor 11:24-28)

To the Galatians he simply summarized his sufferings like this: "I bear on my body the marks of Jesus" (Gal 6:17). And he wasn't exaggerating. Paul imitated the sufferings of Christ as he carried the good news to people who often rejected and even assaulted him (cf. Acts 9:16; Mark 8:34-35).

Every Christian who wishes to follow Jesus faithfully and desires to see people come to know the Savior will have to bear some measure of suffering. It's what I like to call the missions law. We simply won't reach people without sacrifice. Although for some reason Barnabas wasn't stoned alongside Paul, he was also enduring many trials along this journey—his agony over the beating his friend endured no doubt being one of them.

Everyone thought Paul was dead, but as the disciples surrounded him—as a sign of love, protection, and surely in a spirit of prayer—Paul suddenly got up! Then he accompanied the disciples back to the city where the people had stoned him, and he stayed the night. This scene reminds me of another of Paul's classic statements about grace-enabled endurance:

> *Now we have this treasure in clay jars, so that this extraordinary power may be from God and not from us. We are afflicted in every way but not crushed; we are perplexed but not in despair; we are persecuted but not abandoned; we are struck down but not destroyed.* (2 Cor 4:7-9)

Paul was struck down, but he didn't stay down! What tenacity! And what a testimony of God's grace!

Persevere through Physical Trials out of Love for the Gospel (14:20b-21a)

Although he was bruised and battered, Paul and the others began a sixty-mile trek to Derbe the next day. What would motivate a person to endure such physical trials? It was the gospel (v. 21)! Paul cared more about the salvation and sanctification of people than his own well-being (cf. 2 Tim 2:8-10).

Paul's persistence can encourage us in the ministries in which God has placed us. As a discouraged young pastor, Art Azurdia once asked a pastor of thirty years, "How have you made it in ministry so long?" The older pastor replied, "You know, Art, my dad once told me, 'Never decide to leave the ministry when you're tired or depressed,' so I've never left the ministry!" (Azurdia, "Progression by Intention, Part 5"). I love the humor and truth in the statement, but the story makes me wonder whether enduring in the ministry implies that we must live in a perpetual state of depression and disappointment. How could anyone persist in the face of that?

The thread that runs throughout chapter 14 tells us the answer: remembering the importance of the gospel keeps us fueled (vv. 7,15,21). Paul could not get over all the gospel meant—forgiveness, freedom, justification, the presence of the Holy Spirit, adoption, reconciliation, future resurrection, and participation in the kingdom that will have no end. Because of the glorious nature of the gospel, Paul couldn't stop preaching it—even if that meant suffering. The good news compelled him.

Some Christians put off engaging in ministry, telling themselves, "I'll serve Jesus when it's convenient." But when we are truly captivated by the gospel, when the truth of who Jesus is and what he did for us becomes the most important thing in our lives, we will gladly sacrifice comfort and selfish desires to make sure we help others know him. We must never get over the gospel. We must never let our affections for the Savior cool.

Paul and Barnabas could have kept traveling east to Paul's hometown of Tarsus and then back to Antioch of Syria. That route would have been the easiest. Scheduling some rest, relief, and fellowship there would've been understandable. But instead of going east, the dynamic duo courageously and persistently heads in the opposite direction, backtracking through previous places of challenging ministry! In doing this, they demonstrate an amazing love for the gospel and the church.

Perseverance in the Return Trips
ACTS 14:21B-28

In this final section we see the necessity of following up initial ministry efforts and are reminded of the critical importance of establishing healthy congregations. From Paul's passion to establish churches rather than just evangelizing the masses and from Paul's own commitment to the Antiochean congregation, we should learn devotion to a local church.

Persevere by Being Devoted to the Local Church (14:21b-28)

God has given us a wonderful gift in the fellowship of brothers and sisters in Christ. Together we can stir one another up to love and good deeds as we do life together and as we see the day of Christ drawing near (Heb 10:24-25). Paul knew new believers needed local church fellowship. Even he needed the support and strength of fellow believers.

Establishing new churches (14:21b-23). Notice Paul's commitment to helping form new congregations (vv. 21b-25). Paul wasn't interesting in getting *decisions for Christ.* He was interested in making *disciples of Christ.* So, in spite of possible danger, he retraced his steps to Lystra, Iconium, and Pisidian Antioch. Making return visits to strengthen new Christians was part of Paul's future ministry as well (cf. 15:41; 16:5).

Here we see a great model for church planting. John Stott says,

> In little more than ten years St Paul established the Church in four provinces of the Empire: Galatia, Macedonia, Achaia and Asia. Before AD 47 there were no Churches in these provinces; in AD 57 St Paul could speak as if his work there was done. (*Message of Acts,* 235)

Paul's church-planting paradigm rested on three foundations: (1) *apostolic instruction,* (2) *pastoral oversight,* and (3) *a confident trust in God.*

Regarding apostolic instruction, Paul encouraged the believers to "continue in the faith" (v. 22). The phrase *the faith* indicates they were in possession of a body of doctrine already developed (cf. Jude 3-4). Paul ensured that these new believers understood the basic biblical doctrines. In establishing these doctrines he not only fortified the church against heresy, but he also encouraged the hearts of believers, reminding the kingdom citizens of the inevitability of facing "many hardships" for holding these beliefs. Later, in his letters, he could expand on the basics.

Regarding pastoral oversight, Paul made sure every single local church had a *plurality* of elders. John Stott points out that the modern pattern of one pastor over the church was simply unknown in Paul's day (*Message of Acts*, 236; for more examples of plurality of elders, see Acts 11:30; 15:2,4,6,22-23; 16:4; 20:17-18; 1 Tim 5:17; Titus 1:5; Jas 5:14; 1 Pet 5:1,5). Instead, each church—depending on its size—had a pastoral team made up of full-time and part-time pastors, some of whom were paid and others who served voluntarily (ibid.). These elders were chosen from within the local congregation. Paul later expanded on pastoral qualifications in his letters (1 Tim 3:1-7; Titus 1:5-9).

Raising up elders from among the ranks of new converts surely required Paul to spend considerable time overseeing their training, demonstrating the need for leadership development within the church (cf. 2 Tim 2:2). All believers need biblical doctrine. They need pastoral care. They need one another. Paul doesn't make sure that each congregation has a specialized building in which to meet. Instead, he makes sure the people are built up through truth, pastoral care, and community. He equips them.

Finally, the missionaries prayerfully entrust the congregation to the Lord. Since Jesus is committed to his bride, the church, Paul can confidently rest in his nourishment of these congregations.

Rejoicing with the sending church (14:24-28). On the final leg of the trip the missionaries travel again through the rugged mountains until they reach the lowlands of Pamphylia. Upon arriving at Perga, they spend some time evangelizing the area. On their first stop in Perga, they had spent little time there (13:13-14). From Perga they go to Attalia and then finally back home to Antioch of Syria.

Verse 26 forms an *inclusio*, a bracket, with 13:2 (Polhill, *Acts*, 320). The Spirit initially directed the church to set apart Paul and Barnabas "for the work" to which he called them (13:2). Then eventually the bruised and battered missionaries return to the church "where they had been commended to the grace of God *for the work* they had now completed" (14:26; emphasis added). The mission wasn't finished, but the work of this trip was completed.

The missionaries rejoice with their brothers and sisters, who had no doubt been praying for them persistently. The missionaries give testimony of all God did through them. They celebrate that God "opened the door of faith to the Gentiles" (v. 27).

Paul and Barnabas remained in Antioch for some time, enjoying fellowship, sharing stories, and perhaps seeking some medical treatment (v. 28). While there, Paul may have penned his letter to the Galatians around AD 48.

This passage leaves me with two closing questions: (1) Do you need to look to Jesus for persevering grace today as you seek to make the gospel known? Remember, he empowers those who depend on him. (2) And do you truly love Jesus's church? Timothy Dwight, the late minister and eighth president of Yale, expressed the proper attitude about the church when he wrote,

> For her my tears shall fall
> For her my prayers ascend,
> To her my cares and toils be given
> Till toils and cares shall end. (Hughes and Chapell, *1 &*
> *2 Timothy and Titus*, 89)

Such devotion to the church certainly characterized the apostle Paul's ministry. May it also characterize ours until that day when we see the Lord of the church face-to-face.

Reflect and Discuss

1. What key lessons did you take away from this first missionary journey (Acts 13–14)?
2. What do these missionary stops teach about prudence?
3. Why do we need to hear this story about grace-enabled perseverance?
4. What about Paul's ministry in Iconium most resonates with you?
5. What does Paul's brief message in Lystra teach about communicating the gospel to different types of people?
6. What do Paul's return visits teach about discipleship?
7. What do Paul's return visits teach about church planting?
8. What does Paul's return trip to Antioch of Syria teach about "sending churches"?
9. Why is it beneficial to have a plurality of pastors/elders in a local church?
10. Take a moment to pray for some believers who are making the gospel known in difficult places. How else might you demonstrate support of missionaries today?

Grace Alone

ACTS 15:1-35

Main Idea: In this important meeting held to discuss the conditions for Gentile membership in the church, the gospel of grace is affirmed unanimously and the unity of the body is maintained charitably.

I. **Grace Disputed (15:1-5)**
II. **Grace Defended and Displayed (15:6-21)**
    A. Peter's defense (15:7b-11)
    B. The defense of Paul and Barnabas (15:12)
    C. James's defense (15:13-19)
    D. Grace displayed (15:20-21)
III. **Grace Delivered and Described (15:22-35)**

At some point during my growing-up years, I learned that there are occasions on which it is right to fight and occasions on which fighting is wrong. Unfortunately, I often chose to fight on the wrong occasions. I got in all sorts of scraps throughout my school days, frequently for stupid and childish reasons, and I deeply regret it.

As Christians, we will find that there are times to take a stand over particular issues regarding the faith and times to avoid quarreling. As I did in my rebellious school-yard days, many Christians want to fight over everything—from the location of the piano, to worship service times, to the order of the worship service, to the style of music played at church, to whether homeschool or public school is the right education route for Christian kids. On the other hand, a culture of tolerance has produced another type of Christian who thinks Christ's followers should never have a heated debate over even the most important theological matters. One group fights over everything while the other group won't stand up for anything.

Acts 15 shows us that there are times that require serious theological debate. Simply put, *we should always go to battle when the gospel is at stake.*

Just how a person gets saved *really* matters! The topic has been at the forefront of many famous debates in the history of the church. The reformer Martin Luther, for instance, wasn't fighting over small-group philosophy or the format of the bulletin when he nailed a list of grievances to the door of Wittenberg church. The man was willing to risk his life over *the gospel itself.* He contended earnestly for the truth that people are saved by grace alone, through faith alone, in Christ alone.

Long before Luther made this great stand in Germany, the apostles and leaders of the church had to make a great stand in Jerusalem. They had to contend for the exclusivity of salvation in Jesus. Verse 11 captures the major affirmation of the chapter: "We believe that we are saved through the grace of the Lord Jesus in the same way they are."

Christians today need to be ready to "contend for the faith" as well (Jude 3). If we lose the gospel, we lose everything that matters (1 Cor 15:3-4). We should, of course, contend with civility, gentleness, and respect, but we must contend.

Additionally, this chapter shows us the need for extending Christian charity in maintaining unity within the body. When matters don't involve the essentials of the faith, Christians should be flexible. They should be sensitive to others' consciences and, in love, avoid offending the weaker brother or sister by arguing nonessentials.

Lastly, Acts 15 sits between the first and second missionary journeys of Paul. One can only imagine what would have happened if this conference had not ended in wholehearted agreement over the gospel. This issue had to be settled for the gospel to continue to spread to the Gentile world. Fortunately, everyone was unified in spirit and truth, and the rest of Acts shows Paul proclaiming the gospel of grace with passion.

Grace Disputed
ACTS 15:1-5

God's opening "the door of faith to the Gentiles" (14:27) sparked serious theological controversy. Not everyone rejoiced over the Gentile mission gaining great momentum. Some Jewish believers didn't like the idea that the Gentiles were retaining their own identity as they joined the community of faith. In other words, they thought a Gentile needed to become a Jew in order to become a Christian. Luke wrote of their resulting insistence on the Gentiles adhering to the law of Moses, especially to circumcision, before becoming Christians (vv. 1-5).

Many Gentiles existed in the church in Antioch, but there's no indication Paul said anything about them becoming proselytes to Judaism before becoming Christians. This stance posed a serious problem to some conservative Jewish Christians, who adamantly made circumcision a condition for salvation (v. 1). These men could have been sent by

James, but they ended up misrepresenting him in their insistence on circumcision. It's also possible they were "false brothers [who] had infiltrated" the church (Gal 2:4; Bock, *Acts,* 495).

In all fairness to the Jewish critics, they raised a natural question. The first Christians were Jewish; Jesus was Jewish; the old-covenant people were Jewish. Christianity was a messianic movement that was foretold in the Old Testament. And since Jews had always demanded that Gentile converts be circumcised and adhere to the rituals of the Torah in order to be accepted into the community, it was probably difficult for them to understand the sudden change. They failed to realize that with the incarnation of Christ, everything had changed (Polhill, *Acts,* 321)!

This doctrinal issue also posed a practical problem: how could Jewish Christians enjoy table fellowship with Gentile Christians if the Gentiles failed to adhere to the same ritual laws the Jews did? The Jewish Christians could be defiled by the Gentiles' eating habits! Because the issue was so serious—potentially leading to the formation of two separate churches, one Gentile and one Jewish—a conference was held to deal with the matter.

The church in Antioch sent Paul and Barnabas and some others to Jerusalem to meet with the apostles and elders. As they traveled some 250 miles to Jerusalem, they visited the congregations in Phoenicia and Samaria. The believers in these places didn't have the same concerns as the Jewish critics, so they rejoiced with Paul and Barnabas. When the pair arrived in Jerusalem, the mother church gladly welcomed the delegates, and they also rejoiced over the testimonies of God's grace at work among the Gentiles.

Not everyone welcomed them warmly, however (v. 5). Some from the Pharisee party argued that the Gentiles must not only be circumcised but also keep the Mosaic law. Circumcision, in fact, represented a commitment to keep the whole Mosaic law, including its ritual aspects. The Pharisees were prepared to debate their objection to a grace/faith-based, circumcision-free gospel.

Sadly, even today we see people disputing the idea that salvation is by grace alone. Many adhere, sometimes without even realizing it, to a Jesus-plus-something-else gospel: Jesus plus baptism, Jesus plus church attendance, Jesus plus quiet times. But if we add anything to the gospel, we lose the gospel. Gospel math works like this: Jesus plus nothing equals everything. The work of Jesus Christ is totally sufficient.

This gospel of the saving exclusivity of Jesus by the grace of Jesus will always be disputed because the default mode of the human heart is works-based righteousness, not faith-based righteousness. But we can't earn righteousness; we simply receive it by faith alone. So rejoice in the grace of God! You have been saved by sheer grace (Eph 2:8-9), not by doing works of the law but through placing faith in Jesus (Gal 2:16-17).

Salvation by grace alone distinguishes Christianity from every other world religion. Religion is built on human performance, but no one has ever been saved by human performance or religious observance. The Lord has always desired our faith. The gospel, therefore, is not "do this to earn God's favor"; it is, "Jesus paid it all, so trust in him." In relying on this grace, we live our lives to the glory of God.

Grace Defended and Displayed
ACTS 15:6-21

The apostles and elders gathered to discuss this crucial matter. The solution didn't come through a new word of revelation from a prophet but through careful reasoning based on Scripture's teaching. Three speeches that defend the gospel of grace are recorded. First, Peter reported his experience in his evangelization of the Gentiles. Next, Paul and Barnabas reported how God used them to reach the Gentiles. Then, James interpreted their experiences in light of the Scriptures. These men were shepherds biblically caring for the flock.

Peter's Defense (15:7b-11)

Peter steps up first (surprise, surprise!). He alludes to the events with Cornelius, which took place about ten years before the Jerusalem Council. His defense of the Gentile mission can be outlined in three parts.

First, Peter says his preaching to the Gentiles wasn't his idea but part of God's sovereign plan (v. 7). Second, he reminds his hearers that God has given the Gentiles the Holy Spirit (v. 8; cf. 10:44,47; 11:17). This too is proof that Jews and Gentiles were on equal footing. Finally, he reminds them that God makes no distinction between Gentile and Jew (v. 9); he shows no partiality (10:34). Therefore, God's declaration has already been made, and no one should put any additional burden on Gentile Christians (v. 10).

Peter shows that the real boundary marker between alienation from God and salvation is not circumcision but *faith* (Johnson, *Let's Study Acts*, 185). The Gentiles heard the gospel and *believed it* (v. 7). Therefore, God cleansed their hearts *by faith* (v. 9; cf. 10:15; 11:9). Jewish Christians too are saved by *believing*, just like the Gentiles (v. 11). Cornelius had been accepted by faith, not by circumcision. That's the only way anyone is accepted by God. Salvation is by faith alone; it has nothing to do with the circumcision of one's flesh.

Peter sounded a lot like Paul. In Paul's letter to the Galatians, one finds many of the same themes mentioned:

> But even if we or an angel from heaven should preach to you a gospel contrary to what we have preached to you, a curse be on him! As we have said before, I now say again: If anyone is preaching to you a gospel contrary to what you received, a curse be on him! (Gal 1:8-9)

Getting the gospel right is a matter of first importance, so the apostle tells the Galatians to watch out for false teachers, who should be cursed for preaching a different gospel. He concludes his letter by saying, "Both circumcision and uncircumcision mean nothing; what matters instead is a new creation" (Gal 6:15). Because everyone is saved by grace through faith, familial fellowship is possible—although Paul even had to confront Peter on the matter on a different occasion (Gal 2:11-14). We too must defend the gospel, never emphasizing external ritual but always internal transformation.

The Defense of Paul and Barnabas (15:12)

After Peter's speech, Paul and Barnabas pick up the mike. They have already shared their experiences with the leaders (v. 4), but now they speak before the entire congregation. Essentially, they say that God endorsed their trip to the Gentiles by extending his grace. By only recording this brief verse, Luke draws attention to the fact that the main appeal they made in the debate wasn't based on their experiences alone. They interpreted their experiences in light of Scripture, which James offered next.

James's Defense (15:13-19)

This James was first mentioned in 12:17, after the martyrdom of the apostle James. He was Jesus's half brother and became author of the Bible book bearing his name. He was recognized as a pillar of the Jerusalem church, along with Peter and John (Gal 2:9). James affirms the others' defense of a circumcision-free gospel and goes on to offer a suggestion about establishing fellowship between Jewish and Gentile Christians. He begins by affirming the words of "Simeon" (another name for Simon Peter), who said the Gentile mission was God's plan. James provides scriptural support to strengthen Peter's claim that God's plan includes having a people for himself from all nations.

Prior to quoting Amos 9:11-12, he says, "The words of the prophets agree with this," implying that this Amos text reflects what the prophets teach in general (Bock, *Acts*, 503). He could have cited a whole slew of prophetic texts about the Gentiles (Isa 2:2; 45:20-23; Jer 12:15-16; Hos 3:4-5; Zech 2:11; 8:22; and also Paul in Rom 15:7-13). The point is that James stresses fulfillment; all the prophets agree with Peter's claims (ibid.).

John Stott summarizes James's citation of Amos:

> God promises first to restore David's fallen tent and rebuild
> its ruins (which Christian eyes see as a prophecy of the
> resurrection and exaltation of Christ, the seed of David, and
> the establishment of his people) so that, secondly, a Gentile
> remnant will seek the Lord. In other words, through the
> Davidic Christ Gentiles will be included in his new community.
> (*Message of Acts*, 247)

Since the Gentiles are now in fact turning to the Messiah as the prophets foretold, James argues that the Gentiles shouldn't be burdened with issues of the law (v. 19). So now we have Peter, Paul, and James in agreement. All obstacles to the gospel of grace should be removed, and the Gentiles should be welcomed to trust in Christ alone and join the community of faith.

Grace Displayed (15:20-21)

Having established the doctrine of salvation by grace alone, through faith alone, in Christ alone, apart from works of the law, James suggests an appeal to the Gentiles to avoid some practices that may offend Jewish believers. (His goal is to encourage healthy fellowship.) James wants the Gentiles to know that where Moses is read and respected, Jewish believers might be understandably sensitive about certain things; thus, out of love for their brothers, the Gentiles should avoid certain practices. And if they aren't familiar with Jewish practices, they can hear

Moses's writings for themselves. Here James models how one should display grace toward other Christians who may be offended by particular practices.

The four requirements James outlines are all basically *ritual* matters aimed at making fellowship possible between Jewish and Gentile Christians (Polhill, *Acts*, 331, so Stott and Bock). He asks the Gentile believers to avoid contact with (1) pollution that comes from idols, (2) immorality (probably the kind associated with pagan rites and temple prostitution, though he may also have intrafamilial relations in view; Lev 17–18), (3) strangled things (probably a reference to what happens to animals consumed among the Gentiles), and (4) blood (Leviticus prohibits eating meat with blood that hasn't been properly drained; cf. Lev 17:10-14; Acts 15:29; 21:25).

James provided a wise policy that would uphold the gospel of grace while helping preserve Jew-Gentile fellowship. Grace is defended and displayed.

Grace Delivered and Described
ACTS 15:22-35

The entire council agreed with James, so the apostles, elders, and the whole church decided that some men should accompany Paul and Barnabas to Antioch to give a report on the meeting. They select Judas, also called Barsabbas, and Silas, who probably was the "Silvanus" who became closely associated with Paul and Peter (15:40; cf. 2 Cor 1:19; 1 Thess 1:1; 2 Thess 1:1; 1 Pet 5:12). These were "leading men among the brothers" (v. 22). They were sent to deliver the letter.

This piece of correspondence contained three points. First, the council rejected the circumcision party's insistence on circumcision as a condition for salvation. Second, the delegates, who would not only deliver the letter but also give an oral description of the matter, had the council's full approval and authorization. Finally, they emphasized the Spirit-directed unanimous decision not to burden Gentiles with anything (like insistence on circumcision) but to request that the Gentiles abstain from four particular matters out of respect for Jewish scruples. The fellowship matters were not conditions for salvation.

With this letter, the messengers head to Antioch. When those in Antioch heard it, they rejoiced that the Gentile Christians were accepted into the family of God; they didn't need to adopt a Jewish way of life. Judas and Silas, who are noted as "prophets," stayed in Antioch for a

while and provided much encouragement and comfort to the church
(v. 32).

The section concludes with a peaceful and joyful display of unity
among different groups of Christians. Paul and Barnabas continue to
proclaim God's Word in Antioch (vv. 34-35), setting the stage for the
second missionary journey.

Conclusion

We must learn at least two lessons from the Jerusalem Council, one
regarding Christian truth and the other Christian love.

We Must Never Abandon the Gospel of Grace

Salvation is by grace alone through faith alone in Christ alone. It comes
apart from works of the law (cf. Phil 3:1-11). We must never bend on
this truth. Jesus's work is sufficient. We need to rest in his grace and
proclaim it to the world.

We Must Lovingly Preserve the Unity of the Body

There will be times in which Christians should abstain from certain
liberties in order to maintain peaceful social interactions with others.
Christians with strong consciences should never violate the consciences
of weaker brothers and sisters. We should limit our liberty out of love
for the weaker Christian (Stott, *Message of Acts*, 257; Rom 14; 1 Cor 8-9).
John Newton said this about Paul's dual commitment to the gospel
and charitable flexibility with other Christians: "Paul was a reed in
non-essentials; an iron pillar in essentials" (quoted in Stott, *Message of
Acts*, 257). Let's be an iron pillar on the gospel, and let's be charitable
to others regarding nonessentials, for the good of the church, for the
advancement of the gospel among all nations, and for the glory of Jesus.

Reflect and Discuss

1. Why do people have a difficult time embracing the message of
   grace?
2. What "Jesus-plus" gospels have you heard taught? How might this
   passage help you formulate a response to them?
3. What about Peter's speech most resonates with you?
4. Who is James, and what sort of role does he play in the council?
5. Why is the use of Scripture important for mediating conflict?

6. Why does James give these four restrictions to the Gentiles?
7. What does this passage teach about one's conscience? What freedoms might you need to limit in order not to violate the consciences of those in your circle?
8. What does this passage teach about essentials and *nonessentials* of the faith?
9. Read through the book of Galatians and list some of the issues there that are also found here in Acts 15.
10. Take a moment to pray for occasions to share the gospel of grace with others.

Jesus's Power Displayed in Philippi

ACTS 15:36–16:40

Main Idea: In the first part of Paul's second missionary journey, the gospel advances to Philippi, and a new church is established as Jesus's power is displayed in various ways.

I. **The Journey to Philippi (15:36–16:10)**
   A. Paul's missionary companions (15:36–16:5)
   B. Paul's Macedonian calling (16:6-10)
II. **New Converts in Philippi (16:11-34)**
   A. Jesus transforms a wealthy woman (16:13-15).
   B. Jesus transforms a slave girl (16:16-18).
   C. Jesus transforms a jailer (16:19-34).
III. **A New Congregation in Philippi (16:35-40)**

This week I have seen numerous pictures on social media of my friends lounging at the beach. I even have one friend cruising to Alaska. A sea adventure sounds nice, doesn't it? Well, in this chapter we're going to sail across the Aegean Sea with the apostle Paul. But we won't be riding on a cruise ship. Paul was on a *battleship* of sorts. In chapter 15 we see him and his companions on another mission to make the gospel known in new territories, and it's difficult to find a section of Scripture any more convicting, exciting, and encouraging than this one. So, all aboard! Let's go.

In Acts 15:36–18:22 we read of Paul's second missionary journey, during which Paul and his companions reach the people of Macedonia and Achaia. Then, after taking a brief furlough in 18:22, the team sets out on the third missionary journey to the Greek cities of the Aegean, giving special attention to Ephesus (18:23–21:14). Luke's description of the trips, however, is selective. He doesn't describe the founding of every church; instead, he presents many of the high points of the journeys and gives us their basic framework. Luke gives particular attention to the influential cities in which Paul spent most of his time evangelizing and establishing churches.

The text under consideration sheds light on the first time the gospel seed was planted in European soil. While the lines between Asia and

Europe didn't exist in Paul's day, we can see how epoch-making this event really was when we consider it with the benefit of hindsight. The gospel would eventually spread throughout Europe, and Europe would become a base for missionary outreach around the world (Stott, *Message of Acts*, 258).

The Journey to Philippi
ACTS 15:36–16:10

Trips require planning: Who is going and how will they reach the intended destination? In the following three paragraphs Paul's companions rely on God's guidance to answer those questions. In many of our journeys, we often experience the unexpected. So it is here. We probably wouldn't predict the change in companions or the strange route to Philippi that contributed heavily to what would happen in the journey to come.

Paul's Missionary Companions (15:36–16:5)

Paul's second missionary journey also started in Antioch. Paul and Barnabas had been ministering there after delivering the Jerusalem Council's letter to the church. After a period of time, Paul decides that it would be a good idea to revisit the churches established on the first missionary journey. As it happened, however, Paul didn't actually follow up with all the churches from the first trip. He neglected to visit Cyprus, but his companion Barnabas goes to Cyprus because of a division in the team.

Barnabas wanted to take John Mark with them on the journey, perhaps to give him a second chance. Paul rejected the proposal because he considered Mark's desertion in Pamphylia totally unacceptable. We previously covered in 13:13 some of the reasons Mark may have left the mission. Regardless of what happened, Paul would eventually be reconciled to Mark, seeing him as a beloved coworker (Col 4:10; 2 Tim 4:11; Philemon 24).

As a result of competing views, Paul and Barnabas have a "sharp disagreement" (15:39), which in Greek carries the idea of violent action or emotion. The team had an intense conflict. Who was correct? Kent Hughes states the feeling of many of us: "Our judgment goes with Paul, but our hearts go with Barnabas" (*Acts*, 203).

So Barnabas, the consummate encourager, takes Mark to Cyprus. Paul takes Silas after the two were commended by the church "to the grace of the Lord" (15:40; cf. 14:26), for the work of strengthening the churches in Syria and Cilicia (15:41). The two would, among other things, deliver the report from the Jerusalem Council to these churches.

What should we make of this separation of Paul and Barnabas? First, they were men, not angels. Flawed humans, even these mighty missionaries, will sometimes face moments of contention. I'm thankful for this dose of harsh reality here in Acts because many dream of doing ministry in a perfect church, certain that a perfect pastorate or lay leader role is out there. But it's not. To fix our thoughts on the idea that there might be is ministerial pornography, which appeals to the lustful heart of idealists, whose thirst is never satisfied as they bounce from one church to the next in hope of finding the ideal post. We will all encounter relational challenges while doing God's work, so let's walk humbly and graciously before God and one another.

We should also be encouraged that God sovereignly worked through the conflict to achieve his purposes. The result of the split is that instead of one mission journey there are two. This doesn't imply that all Christian arguments are justified! This text doesn't give us a warrant to complain, murmur, and quarrel with other brothers and sisters—these are sinful behaviors (1 Cor 10:10; Phil 2:14). But it tells us God can work through all sorts of means to advance his gospel; he can even bring about growth through separations. This split surely wounded both men, for through it Barnabas lost the companionship of the most powerful missionary of all time, and Paul may have lost the friendship of a man to whom he was greatly indebted. Yet through pain and the conflict, the gospel marches on.

In 16:1-5 another companion is added. Traveling from east to west this time, Paul and Silas arrive in Lystra and Derbe and encounter a young Lystran named Timothy, who stands out to Paul. The boy's father was an unbelieving Greek, but his mother and grandmother were Jewish and brought him up to know the Scriptures (2 Tim 1:5). These two ladies, along with Timothy, probably became Christians during Paul's first missionary journey (Acts 14:19-23). Timothy apparently displayed tremendous spiritual maturity (16:2). As a result, Paul desires that the young man accompany him and Silas (v. 3).

Paul has Timothy circumcised out of sensitivity to Jewish audiences. Some argue that this act compromised the Jerusalem Council's decree, but it didn't. Paul resisted circumcising Titus, who was a pure Greek (Gal 2:3,5), when the gospel was at stake. But Timothy's situation was different. Timothy was both Jew and Greek. And because rabbinic law taught that a child born of a Jewish mother and a Greek father was considered to be Jewish, Paul knew Timothy would have constantly offended the Jews if he didn't get circumcised. So as a matter of missionary strategy, as a sign of respect to Jewish heritage, and as an attempt to maintain Jew-Gentile unity, Timothy undergoes painful surgery. In time Timothy's Jew-Greek background would allow him to bridge different cultures effectively.

A wonderful relationship developed between Timothy and Paul. Paul considered this young man from Lystra a "son" (1 Cor 4:17; Phil 2:22; 1 Tim 1:2; 2 Tim 1:2) and a "coworker" (Rom 16:21).

In this passage we once again find a missionary application for today. Paul was willing to "become all things to all people" in order to reach them with the gospel (1 Cor 9:22). He wanted to adapt to different audiences without changing the gospel. We should be willing to do the same. As long as adapting doesn't mean adopting a sinful action, we should be willing to follow certain cultural customs in order that hearers may receive the gospel. Our goal, after all, isn't to press our culture on another culture but to press the gospel into various cultures. So if people reject your ministry, make sure it's the gospel—and not your cultural biases and practices—that's the stumbling block to effectiveness. If you need to wear a yarmulke when speaking to Jews, then do it. If you need to sit on the floor with Muslims in order to converse, sit on the floor. If you need to wear a particular type of robe in a village in order to address the unreached, then put on the robe. If you need to abstain from certain foods, do it. Put no stumbling block in the way of the gospel.

Paul, Silas, and Timothy continue their journey, visiting the churches and reporting the Jerusalem Council's decision. One can't help but admire Paul's concern for ensuring the stability of local congregations. He went on these arduous trips through the rugged mountains, through many dangerous territories, out of love for Christ and his church. As a result of his efforts, by the grace of God, the churches were strengthened and continued growing. What an inspiring picture of God-given resilience and passion he provides!

Paul's Macedonian Calling (16:6-10)

After visiting the churches, the mission team travels north, probably from Antioch in Pisidia. Somewhere along the journey, they decide to go to Asia, but the Holy Spirit had "forbidden" them from speaking there (16:6). We don't know for certain what is meant by "Asia" here since it had two meanings. John Polhill points out that it could mean the Roman province of Asia (Lycia, portions of Phrygia and Mysia, as well as ancient Asia), or in a more narrow sense, it could refer to the cities along the Aegean coast (*Acts,* 334). If Luke intended the latter, it may indicate that the team attempted to preach in Ephesus, among other places (ibid.). But Paul wouldn't reach that important city until his third journey.

We also don't know exactly *how* they were forbidden. Did they receive a divine vision? Did the Lord withdraw their sense of peace? Did they experience transportation difficulties? Did sickness hinder them? We don't know. All we know is that they were blocked. God may prevent us from doing certain things and going certain places in a whole host of ways. So should doors close, don't despair (2 Cor 4:8; Phil 1:12). Keep trusting in the Lord, who leads his children.

Another closed door is mentioned in the next verse. The team travels northward in an attempt to go to Bithynia to reach cities like Nicea and Byzantium, but they aren't permitted to go there either.

Next the team is led away from the cities of Bithynia, through the wild backwoods of Mysia, over to the coast and down to Troas (Polhill, *Acts,* 345–46). Luke records an epic calling given there (vv. 9-10). God intended to get the mission team to Macedonia, and he chose to use a vision to make his plan known. Many have speculated about the identity of the Macedonian man who appears in the vision—some even suggest he is Alexander the Great, but we aren't told who he is. Regardless, when Paul related this vision to Silas and Timothy, they agreed that God purposed for them to evangelize the Macedonians.

Verse 10 is the first certain occurrence of what people call the "we passages" of Acts. The use of "we" here most likely refers to Luke's joining the team at this time. All four men set out to cross the Aegean to engage people in Macedonia who need the gospel.

Several things are left unclear in this paragraph. We know little about the geography, about how exactly the doors were closed, about the nature of the vision, or even why the "we" passage appears. The thrust of the paragraph, though, is clear: God is guiding these missionaries. We shouldn't miss the Trinitarian nature of this Macedonian call. In verse 6, *the Holy Spirit* prevented them from going to Asia. In verse 7, *the Spirit of Jesus* didn't permit them to go to Bithynia. Later, in verse 10, God the Father called them to go to Macedonia.

While this story is descriptive and not prescriptive, we can still draw from it some safe and helpful points for how to perceive and follow

God's guidance. Even without receiving divine visions in the night, we too can make decisions that honor him.

God guides us through both closed doors and open ones. God blocked Paul and his companions from going to Asia and Bithynia but appealed to them to travel to Macedonia. In the first two instances the missionaries receive a divine no. In the last case they receive God's yes. This double guidance of restraint and prompting typifies many missionaries' experiences. David Livingstone, for instance, wanted to go to China but was sent to Africa instead. William Carey wanted to go to Polynesia but was sent to India. Adoniram Judson went to India first but then went on to Burma. Let us rejoice that God both restrains us and prompts us; he prevents and he permits (Stott, *Message of Acts,* 261).

God's guidance isn't just circumstantial; it's also rational (ibid.). Understanding what the Lord desires involves thinking over matters as this text illustrates. It's not about guessing but about using godly wisdom. The verb translated "concluding" in verse 10 carries the notion of "putting the pieces of a puzzle together"—that is, gathering information and drawing a conclusion (Keller, *Evangelism,* 136).

God's guidance is personal and communal. It may involve researching data, pondering things with other godly individuals (notice the plural terms *them, we,* and *us* in this section), and trying to come to the right conclusion based on what is known about God's character and overarching plan. Don't seek God's will apart from listening to the counsel of other godly Christians.

God's guidance often comes gradually and unpredictably. The missionaries' trip doesn't follow a neatly ordered formula, as if the men completely understood God's will from day one (Hughes, *Acts,* 202). The whole experience started with a simple idea to go revisit the churches (15:36). There was nothing dramatic about that decision. The missionaries just used wisdom to make it. But once they got into the trip, the Lord began to expand their plans, and the men must have been perplexed by traveling an extremely circuitous route.

You probably have experience with this feeling. In some seasons of life Christians can feel they are going nowhere and accomplishing nothing, but in reality they are waiting on God's guidance. The Lord often prompts us gradually. Of this experience Timothy Keller says,

> It is often like a mountainous road, on which you often labor hard, doubling back and seeming to get nowhere, until you come to some vantage point where you can see the "big"

picture and see how much progress you've made and where you are going. (*Evangelism*, 136–37)

When it comes to following God's guidance, begin by obeying God's revealed will in the Bible. Then remain sensitive to the Spirit's prompting. Seek godly counsel when you aren't certain what to do, and think over a situation carefully before making a decision. Also, don't grow discouraged along the way. Sometimes doors open; other times they shut. The Christian's life goal is to be faithful wherever the Lord leads and to maintain a humble and open heart along the journey. As missionary David Livingstone said, "Without Christ, not one step; with him, anywhere!" As long as God is with us, we have reason to rejoice—whether we're in a season of perplexity and wandering or in a season of certainty and fulfillment. After their own wandering days, this mission team enjoyed some unforgettable days of ministering in Philippi. There they endured different kinds of trials, but they did so with confidence that they were in the right place.

New Converts in Philippi
ACTS 16:11-34

Samothrace, a mountainous island, was on the direct route between Troas and Neapolis, the port of Philippi. Scholars point out that travelers must have had the wind to their backs to make it to Neapolis in just two days; it was 150 miles away from Troas. From Neapolis the mission team would have walked along the famous Via Egnatia about ten miles to Philippi.

Philippi was a Roman colony and a leading city of the district. Philip of Macedon, the father of Alexander the Great, had seized the city in the fourth century BC. Philip named the city after himself and enlarged the gold-mining operations there. It came under Roman domination in 168 BC and was enlarged in 42 BC, when Antony and Octavian defeated Brutus and Cassius (Polhill, *Acts*, 347). In 31 BC Octavian granted the city the status of a colony. A number of military veterans settled there (ibid.). Thus, Roman influence was heavy in Philippi—as one can see from Paul's letter to the Philippians. Archeological evidence also shows why the city was a "little Rome."

The missionaries may have stayed a number of weeks (Stott, *Message of Acts*, 262). While probably several people were converted during this time (see v. 40), Luke only records three conversions—probably to display "how God breaks down dividing barriers and can unite in Christ people of very different kinds" (ibid.). These encounters should *encourage* us as we behold Jesus's power and grace in transforming people. They should also *instruct* us as we consider how three different types of people, in three different events that led to their conversions, were reached by the one and only Savior. Consider this chart adapted from Tim Keller's *Church Planter Manual* (102):

Converts	Ethnically	Economically	Spiritually	Event
Lydia	Asian	wealthy	a God fearer	public exposition
slave girl	native Greek	poor	tormented by evil spirits	dramatic exorcism
jailer	Roman	blue-collar	practical and indifferent	powerful miracles and example

Jesus Transforms a Wealthy Woman (16:13-15)

Apparently Philippi lacked a Jewish synagogue, so on the Sabbath day the missionaries go to the closest thing to a synagogue. It was a "place of prayer" (v. 13) outside the city gates and was located by a river (probably the Gangites). The men speak to some women there, one of whom was named Lydia.

She was from the city of Thyatira, which was on the other side of the Aegean, within the province of Asia. Lydia was a seller of purple, which makes sense because Thyatira was the center of the purple dye trade (Polhill, *Acts*, 348–49). She was most certainly wealthy, for purple goods were expensive, often associated with royalty, and the business was profitable. Her hosting people in her home also implies that she was indeed a woman of means. Lydia was an entrepreneur, setting up business in Philippi. But despite professional success, she was still searching for more.

Luke also says that she was "God fearing"; she was like Cornelius. The description doesn't mean she was a Christian, but she was seeking God. Perhaps she had read Ezekiel 36:26-29, in which the Lord promises to give a new heart and a new spirit to people. Regardless of whether that prophecy was something she had thought about, she was a beneficiary of it: "The Lord opened her heart" (v. 14).

What does this mean? It means that the God of all grace opened her spiritual eyes so that she could embrace Jesus as Lord (cf. 2 Cor 4:5-6). God worked in Lydia's heart and gave her new life as she heard the gospel. She wasn't *ultimately* won over by Paul's effective communication skills but by God's gracious and saving initiative. Lydia was saved in the same way anyone else is converted (cf. Acts 11:18; 13:48; 14:27; 18:27).

So here we have the first mention of someone converting to faith in Jesus on European soil, and that convert is a wealthy lady named Lydia. I can't help but admire the *quietness* of this world-changing event. In a setting that may well have resembled more of a picnic than a prayer meeting, Paul explained the gospel and the Lord transformed an individual into a follower of King Jesus. While the scene no doubt lacked drama from the perspective of passersby, the Lord was at work in a big way. He opened Lydia's heart, and she—like a flower opening to the sun—embraced Paul's message.

If you aren't a Christian, let me encourage you to listen to the gospel being preached or at least to read the message on your own in the Bible books of John and Acts. See if the Lord might do something in your heart as a result of your encounter with the good news to cause you to confess Jesus as Lord. If you are a Christian, remember that the Lord still does converting work through faithful messengers of the gospel. Your Lydia is waiting! Trust that when the Bible is taught, God does work in people's lives.

After Lydia's conversion, and based on her confession of faith, she is baptized, along with her household—which probably included her servants. The latter must have believed through the witness of Paul and Lydia. If we use the Cornelius narrative to help us understand this household baptism (and the conversion of the Philippian jailer's household; v. 33), those who were baptized both heard the gospel and believed the message prior to baptism (10:44; 11:14,17). A scan of the baptism accounts in the book of Acts reveals that baptism is based on personal faith.

Lydia not only shared her faith with her household, but she also shared her home with the missionaries. The apostles affirmed her profession of faith and accepted her invitation to come to her home, the location of which eventually became the gathering place for the entire church in Philippi (v. 40). This woman provides a wonderful example of generosity and hospitality at work (cf. 4:32-37). Later Paul would write about the wonderful generosity and support of the church in Philippi (Phil 4:10-20), and it's not difficult to imagine Lydia as one of the main contributors to whom he referred.

Once again in Acts we see the use of one's home as a wonderful tool for ministry. This is a reminder that we should all seek to practice hospitality in order to serve the church. Extending hospitality isn't the same as entertaining, however. Entertaining shows off; hospitality shares. Use your home to serve others, not to wow them with your financial success or decorating abilities or as an escape from socializing.

I can't help but admire the number of godly ladies in the book of Acts; some of them are mentioned by name. Soon we will read of the leading women of Thessalonica (17:4), women of high standing in Berea (17:12), Damaris in Athens (17:34), and Priscilla in Corinth (18:2). All of these inclusions remind us that the early missionary movement was not directed only at males. This also means that Christianity was never intended to reach only the ladies who stay home, raising families and concerning themselves with household matters. Lydia and the other women I mention appear to have been strong ladies with influence. They played huge roles in extending the ministries of their local churches. The book of Acts highlights the need for all people—male and female—to find their places in God's mission and to join the work for the good of others and for the glory of God.

Jesus Transforms a Slave Girl (16:16-18)

Next Luke highlights the missionaries' encounter with an exotic figure, a young tormented girl. The contrast between this slave girl and Lydia couldn't be greater. F. F. Bruce suggests Luke made this stark contrast "in order to show how the saving name of Jesus proved its power in the lives of the most diverse types" (*Book of Acts*, 332).

The phrase "spirit by which she predicted the future" literally reads, "spirit python." According to mythology the Python guarded the temple of Apollo. Over time the word *python* came to mean a demon possessed person through whom the Python spoke (Hughes, *Acts*, 214). Luke and Paul obviously understand the girl to be demon possessed.

A "pythoness" made clairvoyant predictions and uttered words in all sorts of strange voices. Because the locals considered such fortune-tellers to be inspired by Apollo and the Python, many sought them out to hear their predictions about the future. There was "large profit" in this business (v. 16). Perhaps that's why instead of feeling sorry for this demon-possessed girl, the owners used her to make money.

Don't miss that the poor girl featured in this chapter is in double bondage. Her slave owners treat her like property, and she is abused by a demonic spirit.

Satan tried to derail the missionaries' work in Philippi by attempting to form an alliance with the missionaries for his own devilish purposes.

Satan tried to use the slave girl to associate Paul's message with the occult (v. 17), but the missionaries obviously needed to distance their ministry from this evil work. For many days the slave girl uttered things that were entirely true, but the missionaries didn't fall prey to the evil scheme behind the girl's words. In the Gospels demon-possessed people say true things about Jesus, but Jesus rebukes them every time (e.g., Mark 1:24-25; 5:7-8; Luke 4:34-35).

After becoming "greatly annoyed" by Satan's attempt to associate with the team through the girl—or perhaps out of deep grief for her— Paul frees her with a word in Jesus's name. In a moment, Jesus casts out the demon at work through the girl; Jesus masterfully crushes serpents.

With this move the power of Christ is displayed. The pythoness is delivered. What a relief this must have been to the girl! She, like the Gadarene demoniac, was suddenly in her "right mind" (Mark 5:15) following an encounter with Christ. We presume that she too—like the Gadarene man—became a follower of Jesus after deliverance (so say Stott, *Message of Acts,* 265; Hughes, *Acts,* 215; et al.). She suddenly had a new owner, the only good Shepherd, the Lord Jesus Christ, who freed her from spiritual and physical bondage and gave her peace, joy, freedom, and rest.

Contrast the two conversions. Lydia is wealthy; the slave girl is poor. Lydia is a community member of high standing; the slave girl was exploited and abused. Lydia is religious and moral; the slave girl is broken and tormented. Lydia comes to faith through a quiet Bible study; the slave girl gets transformed through a dramatic power encounter. Lydia was presented with Jesus as the Messiah of Israel; the slave girl met Jesus as the mighty Deliverer. These two different ladies both were brought to faith in Jesus—a reminder that the gospel can transform all sorts of people from all sorts of backgrounds. The power that brought the evil spirit out of this girl is the same power that opened Lydia's heart: it's the power of Jesus.

Perhaps you want to distance yourself from the powerful encounter involving the girl because you assume it doesn't relate to you. But this passage should give you hope. If Jesus can free a pythoness, he can break your addictions. He can set you free from negative thinking. Jesus Christ is Lord over all—believe it!

Jesus Transforms a Jailer (16:19-34)

As in the case of the Gadarene demoniac, the slave girl's deliverance upset the economy (Mark 5:16-17; cf. Acts 8:19-21; 19:24-28), leading to a major disturbance in Philippi. The owners of the girl were about to lose a lot of money, so the angry profiteers made false charges against Paul and Silas. They claimed the missionaries were disturbing the city and advocating unlawful customs. Soon the crowd joined the attack, and the magistrates ordered the men beaten with rods.

It is difficult to imagine undergoing the excruciating torture Paul and Silas endured next. The jailer beat the missionaries, leaving them swollen, lacerated, and sticky with blood. It would have been impossible for the wounded evangelists to lie down on their backs after that. The jailer kept the prisoners as secure as possible in what we might call the dungeon, adding to the punishment by putting their feet in stocks. John Polhill describes this particular device:

> Their feet were placed in wooden stocks, which were
> likely fastened to the wall. Often such stocks were used as
> instruments of torture; they had a number of holes for the
> legs, which allowed for severe stretching of the torso and thus
> created excruciating pain. (*Acts*, 353)

All of this makes the deliverance of this pair all the more dramatic. Peter slept in prison (12:6); Paul and Silas sing in prison. Both sleeping and singing are expressions of faith and peace in the Lord (cf. Job 35:10). Those hearing the men's raised voices were surely astonished by their example of faith in the midst of suffering. Silas and Paul probably lifted their voices in singing psalms, in quoting Scripture, and in pouring out their hearts in prayer. To all of this the prisoners listen eagerly, and then it happens. God shakes the earth!

Breaking chains is our Lord's specialty. When chains fall off in this scene, the jailer panics. In fear of the consequences of having to report an empty prison, the jailer prepares to commit suicide. But while Paul and Silas could flee in the chaos following the earthquake, they pause to save this man's life (v. 28). As the jailer calls for light, he rushes to fall before the missionaries with one question: "Sirs, what must I do to be saved?" (v. 30). This jailer knew of the deliverance of the pythoness, and he had handled the incarceration of the missionary pair. He had probably been listening to their songs when the earth rocked beneath him. This question, then, makes sense.

Paul points the jailer to the only name that saves, to Jesus the Savior of Lydia and the Savior of the slave girl (v. 31; cf. 11:14). He effectively tells this man, "Jesus can transform you, and he can transform your whole family too." That's what we must keep telling people: all who believe in the Lord Jesus Christ will be saved.

Soon the jailer's whole household hears the gospel, believes it, and is baptized. The jailer, in an act of humility and repentance, not only washes the wounds of the missionaries but also serves the two a meal. This is a sweet picture of transformation! No longer does the jailer view the wounded men as prisoners; he cares for them as brothers in Christ. In this wonderful picture of gospel hospitality, the jailer and his family rejoice in their new life. Perhaps they even sing a few songs from the *Prison Hymns Collection* Paul and Silas advertised.

This blue-collar Roman jailer, jolted by a miracle, was converted to faith in Jesus through the proclaimed gospel. His story is another reminder that no one is beyond the *reach* of God's saving grace. This account also highlights the gospel's unifying power. Jesus incorporates all kinds of people into his family, intending that the individuals he saves then serve one another as brothers and sisters on a common mission.

A New Congregation in Philippi
ACTS 16:35-40

Verse 35 records that at daylight the magistrates order the release of Paul and Silas. We aren't told why. Likely they just want them to leave town. But when the jailer reports the order to Paul and Silas, Paul declares his Roman citizenship and demands due respect. The officials, he knows, have stepped beyond the boundaries of their authority—a serious offense.

Why does Paul respond by insisting on an official escort? He's certainly not known for trying to humiliate people. So in all likelihood Paul did it to ensure the safety of the church he was leaving behind in Philippi. By showing that he and Silas had done nothing wrong and that Christianity was no threat to the Roman way of life, Paul helped the church's relationship with the Roman authorities. He wanted to make sure the church had a good reputation and to protect it from future harassment. Once again Paul's actions shout of his love for the church.

The magistrates were the lawbreakers in this story. Out of fear they came and apologized to Paul and Silas before escorting them out of the jail.

The missionaries make a visit before heading out of town. They stop at Lydia's, where those comprising the local church had gathered.

Don't miss that, before this journey to Philippi, there were no spiritual brothers or sisters in Philippi. But now, because of the power of Jesus, Paul and Silas could meet with several members of their spiritual family. Among them, in all likelihood, were Lydia, the slave girl, the jailer's family, and other converts too. Prior to meeting Christ, these individuals likely spent no time together. But accepting Jesus as Lord changes everything. In Christ people from all types of backgrounds are united as fellow citizens of heaven.

Thus, the first church on European soil is established! In Philippi, in the middle of the "Little Colony of the Kingdom of Rome," there was suddenly a "Little Colony of the Kingdom of God." Later Paul would write these words to this beloved church:

> *I give thanks to my God for every remembrance of you, always praying with joy for all of you in my every prayer, because of your partnership in the gospel from the first day until now. I am sure of this, that he who started a good work in you will carry it on to completion until the day of Christ Jesus.* (Phil 1:3-6)

Who knows? Maybe it was the slave girl who read the letter aloud to the congregation. Perhaps the jailer read it. It's possible that Lydia did. What's certain is that God did indeed begin a good work in Philippi, bringing many people to faith in Jesus and establishing a beachhead in Europe as he did so.

What a privilege to hear and receive this gospel! What a joy to partner in advancing the gospel with other brothers and sisters who confess Jesus as Lord! Let's seek God's guidance. Let's trust in his power. Let's declare his salvation day to day, from shore to shore, until the day when Christ returns.

Reflect and Discuss

1. What does this passage teach about relational conflict?
2. What missional lesson do we learn from Paul's decision to have Timothy circumcised?
3. What can we glean about God's guidance from Paul's journey to Philippi?
4. Why should the conversion of Lydia encourage us?
5. Compare and contrast the spiritual transformations of Lydia and the slave girl.
6. What can we learn about suffering from the afflictions Paul and Silas faced in Philippi?

7. What did the Lord use to convert the Philippian jailer?
8. What were some of the signs of the jailer's transformation?
9. What does this chapter teach about the importance of opening our homes in hospitality?
10. How does Paul display a love for the church in this chapter? Take a few moments to pray for those trying to engage the lost and plant new churches around the world.

Turning the World Upside Down

ACTS 17:1-15

Main Idea: Luke briefly records Paul's stops in Thessalonica and Berea, and both stories give us some important lessons about how to receive and teach the Scriptures.

I. **The Word Taught and Received in Thessalonica (17:1-9)**
    A. Establish a point of contact with people (17:1-2a).
    B. Expound the Scriptures for people (17:2b-4).
        1. Christocentrically
        2. Boldly
        3. Intelligently
        4. With personal integrity
    C. Expect various responses from people (17:4-9).
II. **The Word Taught and Received in Berea (17:10-15)**
    A. The Bereans studied the Scriptures openly.
    B. The Bereans studied the Scriptures eagerly.
    C. The Bereans studied the Scriptures carefully.
    D. The Bereans studied the Scriptures daily.
    E. Result 1: Conversions
    F. Result 2: Conflict

Someone once offered me a job by saying, "Tony, I want to change the world. And I want you to help me." That sounded like a great goal, but it wasn't unachievable. Not in that case.

Some think talk of world change is triumphalistic, idealistic, and naive. They believe the world is fine the way it is. Comedian Stephen Colbert, in a parody of the traditional commencement address, told Princeton grads, "You can change the world. . . . Please don't do that, OK? Some of us like the way things are going now" (Mulvihill, "Stephen Colbert"). And while others may admire the idea of changing the world, they are too complacent to go about it.

Christians, though, are expected to be a part of a Christ-centered, kingdom-advancing movement. We are to give ourselves over to impacting the nations for Christ's sake. We, like the missionaries of Acts, should be dedicated to influencing world change.

This idea is at work in Acts 17. According to verse 6, Paul and his mission team had already "turned the world upside down" by the time they reached Thessalonica. New Testament Professor C. Kavin Rowe titles his work on Acts *World Upside Down*, and I believe that's an apt title for the book of Acts as a whole. Rowe writes, "Acts narrates the formation of a new culture" (ibid., 140).

In the first half of Acts 17, we see the primary way they went about upending the world: they proclaimed Christ, not Caesar, as King. The preaching and teaching of the Christ-centered Scriptures impacted the world in a big way because if Jesus is Lord—and he is—then everything changes.

In this section we find the Word of the Lord spreading into two more cities. In Thessalonica and Berea King Jesus was proclaimed, embraced, and exalted. John Stott comments on the centrality of Scripture in these short stories:

> Luke chronicles the Thessalonian and Berean missions with surprising brevity. Yet one important aspect of them, to which he seems to be drawing his readers' attention, is the attitude to the Scriptures adopted by both *speaker* and *hearers*. (*Message of Acts,* 274; emphasis added)

Indeed, these passages provide a wonderful example of how to teach and receive the Scriptures faithfully. We have already noted some unique strengths of Paul's teaching; what's particularly exciting about these stops is the way the churches received the Scriptures. Their willingness welcomed whatever changes God desired.

Many today speak of the need to be "Berean Christians"—that is, Christ followers who carefully examine what's being taught rather than just accepting everything that a teacher says. In light of the fact that many Western Christians spend little time in the Word and are largely dependent on hearing one sermon a week in order to receive biblical training, a "Berean revival" could be wonderfully helpful.

In time Paul would commend the Thessalonians for their exemplary reception of the Scriptures, too:

> *We constantly thank God, because when you received the word of God that you heard from us, you welcomed it not as a human message, but as it truly is, the word of God, which also works effectively in you who believe.* (1 Thess 2:13; cf. 1:6)

Both the Berean and Thessalonian churches, then, have much to teach us—particularly in terms of how we should hear, consider, and obey God's Word.

To visit Thessalonica, Paul and his mission team first travel about a hundred miles southwest from Philippi. Due to opposition, the mission in Thessalonica gets cut short, so the team travels onward about fifty miles west to Berea. Accounts of ministry in these two cities are brief. In fact, we find out much of what can be known about the church in Thessalonica from Paul's letters to them. Despite the brevity of the visits, however, helpful applications and needed inspiration for Scripture-saturated, Christ-exalting ministry exists within these passages.

The Word Taught and Received in Thessalonica
ACTS 17:1-9

Following the Via Egnatia, the interstate of the ancient world, the missionaries passed through Amphipolis and Apollonia. Even though Amphipolis was a prominent city, Paul was eager to get to Thessalonica, which was an important seaport in Paul's day and remains so now. Thessalonica, capital of the province of Macedonia, was the second largest city in Greece; it boasted an estimated population of two hundred thousand.

Let's consider four applications for gospel ministry from this passage.

Establish a Point of Contact with People (17:1-2a)

Paul's first point of contact is made, as usual, in the Jewish synagogue. This move was theological, as we have noted, but it was also practical. Paul engages the congregation there for three consecutive Sabbaths. He encountered Jews and God-fearing Gentiles who were familiar with religious things, including the Old Testament.

Paul's habit of finding a quick way to connect with those in a new location should make us identify points of contact within our own neighborhoods and cities. Often Christians find that *serving the city* provides a great way to make connections leading to gospel conversations. Volunteering at a youth center, a homeless shelter, a tutoring program, in a home for the abused, in crisis pregnancy centers, or at a local school can lead to wonderful opportunities for sharing the gospel. Doing so demonstrates neighbor love; it demonstrates care for the whole person. Similarly, *coaching sports* provides a great way to get to know players and parents and to win opportunities to speak truth into their lives. *Hosting events* in our homes—book clubs, Bible studies, or barbecues—can lead to wonderful chances to talk about Jesus, too. Even *taking walks in your neighborhood* or frequenting the *same restaurants* your neighbors do can provide you with ways to connect with people so that you can have gospel conservations with them. The idea is to work, play, and enjoy life with gospel intentionality.

Expound the Scriptures for People (17:2b-4)

Paul's approach involved the consistent exposition of Scripture in the synagogue. First and foremost Paul did this **Christocentrically**. As Jesus did with the disciples on the Emmaus road, Paul set before his hearers this message: it was necessary for the Christ to suffer and rise from the dead (vv. 2-3; Luke 24:26). Jesus's disciples couldn't see this truth until the Savior opened their minds to understand the Scriptures (Luke 24:44-46). Paul, then, knew he needed Jesus to open the Thessalonians' eyes to this fundamental truth as well. We don't know what texts Paul presented—maybe Psalms 16 or 22 or Isaiah 53—but we do know Paul didn't merely teach facts about the Bible; he shared its story line, which climaxes in the person and work of Jesus.

A lot of people know stories from the Bible, but they don't know the story line of Scripture. So, as we have opportunity, let's tell people about the greatest story in the world. Let's show them the flow of redemptive history and Jesus Christ, the Redeemer who died on behalf of sinners in order to reconcile them to God.

Paul also expounded the Scriptures **boldly**. As the apostle showed this suffering-to-glory agenda in the Bible, he affirmed, "This Jesus I am proclaiming to you is the Messiah" (v. 3). Paul made the hero of the Bible, Jesus, the hero of every message. He taught about Jesus's nature, life, death, resurrection, ascension, reign, and coming kingdom. Doing this took incredible courage. Paul had experienced great persecution from the Jews for doing just this kind of Christ-exalting exposition, yet he won't stop exalting Jesus as the Messiah! The man was willing to endure countless afflictions for proclaiming Jesus as the Christ.

Reflecting on his ministry at Thessalonica, Paul commented on his trials and God-given boldness:

> *For you yourselves know, brothers and sisters, that our visit with you was not without result. On the contrary, after we had previously suffered and were treated outrageously in Philippi, as you know, we*

were emboldened by our God *to speak the gospel of God to you in spite of great opposition.* (1 Thess 2:1-2; emphasis added)

In our modern age of so-called tolerance and increasing hostility toward Christianity, we need to ask the Lord to give us this holy boldness to speak the gospel faithfully.

Paul also expounded the Scriptures **intelligently**. I don't mean to suggest that he taught in an academic way; rather, he used a judicious, thoughtful, and logical approach. I draw this from the verbs in verses 2-4: *reason, explain, prove, proclaim,* and *persuade* (Stott, *Message of Acts,* 247). Paul is reasoning from the Scriptures to make his arguments. He's not using the Bible in a superficial or mystical way. Instead, he is speaking rationally, logically, and cogently to his audience. The writer of Proverbs underlines the power of well-prepared, thoughtful teaching: "The heart of a wise person instructs his mouth; it adds learning to his speech" (Prov 16:23).

Evangelicals often have an anti-intellectual spirit, but we shouldn't. While we should always bathe our work in prayer, we need to observe Paul's approach carefully. Paul helped people *think* about the Bible—to consider what it meant, what it implies, and how it all points to Jesus. When doing Scripture-driven evangelism, don't leave your brain at home—and don't expect your hearers to, either.

It sometimes takes a long time for some people to be persuaded that the good news is true and applicable to them. So be patient. Be winsome. Hear unbelievers' questions. Answer them kindly, in a way that's faithful to the Bible and effective in communication.

Paul lived an exemplary life in front of the people. It's important that we also expound the Scriptures **with personal integrity**. After commenting on his God-glorifying motivations and his loving pastoral care in 1 Thessalonians 2:3-9, Paul reminds the believers of his godly lifestyle, including his hard work in both manual labor and in ministry of the Word:

For you remember our labor and hardship, brothers and sisters. Working night and day so that we would not burden any of you, we preached God's gospel to you. You are witnesses, and so is God, of how devoutly, righteously, and blamelessly we conducted ourselves with you believers. As you know, like a father with his own children, we encouraged, comforted, and implored each one of you to live worthy of God, who calls you into his own kingdom and glory. (1 Thess 2:9-12)

Paul didn't say these things to brag but to defend his ministry in Thessalonica. He was assuring the church that he and his coworkers had acted in conformity with both God's law and human law while they were in Thessalonica. They hadn't "defied Caesar's decrees." They weren't lawbreakers. They weren't rebels. They weren't greedy moneymakers. Instead, they were role models who set an example of what it looks like to obey God. By reminding the church of this fact, Paul was also instructing the believers on how they should live out God's Word.

Paul's life illustrated his teaching; his teaching explained his life. We must constantly evaluate both our lives and our teaching for our good and for the good of others (1 Tim 4:16).

Expect Various Responses from People (17:4-9)

Some Jews "joined" Paul and Silas, and a large number of God-fearing Greeks believed. A number of "leading women" also believed. John Polhill says,

> That Luke singled out the influential female converts in the
> Macedonian congregations (cf. 16:14 and 17:12) is very much in
> keeping with inscriptional evidence that in Macedonia women
> had considerable social and civic influence. (*Acts,* 360–61)

We should be encouraged here. God still converts people through faithful, Christ-exalting exposition. Trust in the power of the gospel and proclaim it!

The conversion of so many made many Jews "jealous" (v. 5), something that had also happened in Pisidian Antioch (13:45; cf. 5:17). The disgruntled Jews recruited some thugs in order to stimulate public outrage against Paul and Silas. They stormed the house of Jason, who had opened his home as a gathering place for the new church and had extended hospitality to Paul and Silas. When the attackers couldn't find the missionaries (Johnson, *Let's Study Acts,* 321), they attacked Jason and other brothers and brought them out before the crowd (cf. 1 Thess 2:14-15).

The mob leveled three charges against the Christians. First, they essentially called Paul and Silas troublemakers (v. 6). Second, they condemned Jason for harboring the pair. And third, they declared that the men were acting contrary to Caesar's decrees. This was untrue, but it was a strategic ploy. Rebellion against Caesar was pure treason. The mob believed that, in saying Jesus was King, Paul and Silas defied Caesar.

This, John Polhill points out, was virtually the same charge leveled at Jesus in Luke 23:2-4 and John 19:12,15 (*Acts,* 362).

James Boice clarifies that instead of turning the world upside down as charged, Paul and Silas were actually setting it right (*Acts,* 290). They did affirm Jesus as the King, but Jesus's rule dictated not revolution against Rome but respectful submission to human rulers (Johnson, *Let's Study Acts,* 214). Accusations stemmed from jealousy over the fact that the Gentiles were becoming Christians rather than Jews. The opponents couldn't refute Paul's arguments, so they resorted to mob violence.

The city officials were disturbed but responded to the charges with caution (v. 8). It's possible they were aware of the events in Philippi and didn't want to commit a similar embarrassing error (Johnson, *Let's Study Acts,* 214). They forced Jason to post bond, depositing money that would be forfeited if there were any more disturbance. That meant Paul and Silas had to go. During the night the brothers sent Paul and Silas (along with Timothy) fifty miles west to Berea.

Thus, the team was "forced to leave" the believers and would later long to return to see them (1 Thess 2:17-19). The team would make plans to revisit the believers but encountered Satanic opposition in the process (1 Thess 2:18). Nevertheless, they did send Timothy back to the church to encourage them in the faith (1 Thess 3:1-2), and they continued praying earnestly for the church (1 Thess 3:10). Paul had a deep pastoral love for these believers.

James Boice lists five results of Paul's Christ-exalting exposition in Thessalonica, based on Paul's later assessment of the experience (*Acts,* 291):

1. The preaching was blessed by God (1 Thess 1:5).
2. The people received God's Word eagerly (1 Thess 2:13).
3. The believers tried to model their Christian lives after Paul (1 Thess 1:6).
4. They became models themselves (1 Thess 1:7).
5. The church at Thessalonica became a missionary church (1 Thess 1:8).

This, then, was a worthwhile trip! May the Lord grant us a measure of this fruitfulness as we make known the Word of Christ and the Christ of the Word.

The Word Taught and Received in Berea
ACTS 17:10-15

Paul traveled about fifty miles to Berea at night. The journey would have taken about three nights to complete. Luke records Paul's visit with great brevity, noting the Bereans' devotion to the Word. As usual, Paul starts off in the synagogue proclaiming Jesus as the Messiah. The response of the Bereans to the teaching of the Scriptures is exemplary. Notice four commendable qualities in their actions.

The Bereans Studied the Scriptures Openly

Verse 11 says the Bereans were more "noble" than the Thessalonians. On this John Polhill comments,

> He [Luke] used a word (*eugenesteros*) that originally meant *high
> born* but came to have a more general connotation of being
> open, tolerant, generous, having the qualities that go with
> "good breeding." Nowhere was this more evident than in their
> willingness to take Paul's scriptural exposition seriously. (*Acts,* 363)

The Bereans, then, had a teachable attitude. Their hearts were open, not hardened. Here is the first step in becoming a student of the Bible: approach God's Word with humility, saying, "Teach me, oh God." Psalm 119 is filled with similar cries (e.g., vv. 12,18,27,33-36,66,125). James told the Christians, "Ridding yourselves of all moral filth and the evil that is so prevalent, *humbly* receive the implanted word, which is able to save your souls" (Jas 1:21; emphasis added).

The Bereans Studied the Scriptures Eagerly

These Berean citizens were serious about what they were learning. Peter urged Christians to study the Bible with the same "eagerness" and passion a baby has for milk:

> *Like newborn infants, desire the pure milk of the word, so that you may
> grow up into your salvation, if you have tasted that the Lord is good.*
> (1 Pet 2:2-3)

Oh, that churches would be filled with people longing more for biblical food than for Sunday-morning cotton-candy entertainment, funny stories, and pithy anecdotes! May God grant us a Berean appetite for the Scriptures.

The Bereans Studied the Scriptures Carefully

Luke also commends the Bereans for their spiritual discernment. They weren't gullible. They listened to Paul and then proceeded to do their own homework. They examined Paul's claims about the Messiah to see whether they were true. It's easy to be drawn in by a charismatic teacher. Paul, in fact, rebuked the Galatians for accepting the false gospel of false teachers rather than weighing their messages against the Word. The Bereans provide us a positive example of examining what is being taught (cf. 1 Tim 4:1-5; 6:2-10; 2 Tim 3:1-9; 2 Pet 2:1-22; 1 John 2:18-27; Jude 3-23).

The Bereans Studied the Scriptures Daily

This group of people did more than study the Bible on the Sabbath. They met every day (cf. Acts 2:42-47). Because Paul's claims had eternal ramifications, they spent time pondering them daily.

What were the results of doing so?

Result 1: Conversions

As a side effect of such devotion to Paul's teaching, many of the Bereans believed (v. 12; cf. John 5:39-40). Not only did many Jews believe but many Greeks as well—not just men but Greek women of high standing (cf. Acts 2:18; 5:14; 9:2,36-42; 12:12-17; 16:13-15; 17:34; 18:18-26). Thus, a church in Berea was born.

Let this passage encourage you if you are a Bible teacher. Not everyone will be changed when you teach, but the seed of the Word will bear fruit in some hearers' lives.

Result 2: Conflict

Unfortunately, the great movement among the Bereans was disrupted because Jews from Thessalonica traveled to Berea, stirring up a mob against Paul (v. 13). This isn't the first time we have read of such hostility, and it won't be the last (cf. 16:20-21; 17:6-7; 19:40; 1 Kgs 18:17-18). Apparently Paul was the main object of persecution since Silas and Timothy didn't leave town when he did (v. 14). They stayed and strengthened the new congregation as the "brothers and sisters" sent Paul off by sea. Paul eventually ends up in Athens where he engages another audience with the gospel (v. 15).

The Word of God is central in these stories. Paul and his companions turned the world upside down by turning the Word loose! Keep teaching and learning the Christ-centered Scriptures, and ask God to use you to change neighborhoods and nations for the glory of King Jesus.

Reflect and Discuss

1. In what ways might you establish new points of contact in your community?
2. What can we learn about expounding the Scriptures from Paul's example in Thessalonica?
3. Take some time to read 1 Thessalonians. What strikes you about what Paul says regarding the Thessalonians' heart for the Word? What about Paul's attitude toward the Thessalonians resonates with you?
4. Why do you think some of the Jews were jealous?
5. How does the story of Paul's trip to Thessalonica encourage you? How does it challenge you?
6. What does it mean to live as if "there is another King, Jesus"?
7. How did the Bereans study the Scriptures?
8. What challenges you the most about the Berean approach to God's Word? What might happen if churches today developed the same habits?
9. How does the Berean visit encourage you?
10. In light of these two stories, take a few moments to pray for those who teach in your congregation and for those who hear the Scriptures.

Lessons from Paul's Visit to Athens

ACTS 17:16-34

Main Idea: By observing how Paul evangelized the influential city of Athens, we find some important lessons about engaging unbelievers today.

I. **What Paul Saw (17:16)**
II. **What Paul Felt (17:16)**
III. **Where Paul Went (17:17-18)**
   A. The synagogue (17:17a)
   B. The marketplace: dialoguing with people in general (17:17b)
   C. The marketplace: dialoguing with intellectual skeptics in particular (17:18)
IV. **What Paul Said at the Areopagus (17:19-31)**
   A. God is the Creator (17:24).
   B. God is the Sustainer of life (17:25).
   C. God is the Ruler of the nations (17:26).
   D. God is knowable (17:27).
   E. God is the Father of humanity (17:28-29).
   F. God is both Judge and Rescuer (17:30-31).
V. **What Were the Results (17:32-34)?**

In the second half of Acts 17 we join Paul in the city of Athens. Here, once again, we see his remarkable evangelistic versatility. He reminds me of the current MLB switch-pitcher, Pat Venditte, who throws with both hands and even switches hands between batters. Of Venditte's abiltiy, one sports reporter declared, "He's amphibious!" (I think he meant ambidextrous!)

Paul was an ambidextrous evangelist; he could adapt his methods to reach the Jews or pagans, throwing gospel strikes with both his right and left hand, we might say. He could switch approaches from the synagogue to the marketplace, always preaching the same gospel.

The account of Paul's visit to Athens is one of the most popular passages in Acts. John Polhill comments, "Paul's brief visit to Athens is a centerpiece for the entire book of Acts" (*Acts*, 365). Indeed, it gives us insight into the heart and ministry of Paul, thereby providing us with important lessons for engaging unbelievers today.

Luke provides a look at the city of Athens before focusing attention on Paul's speech at the Areopagus. This speech serves as an example of how Paul evangelized Gentiles who had virtually no background in Scripture. Another example is the speech Paul gave in Lystra (14:15-17). In both cases Paul starts with creation and moves forward in the redemptive story. He also confronts idolatry.

Athens was in the "late afternoon of her glory" when Paul arrived (Boice, *Acts*, 293). Corinth had become the center of commerce and politics in Greece. After achieving impressive military victories, Athens flourished economically and culturally between 480 and 404 BC. Politically the citizens there had developed the first democracy, a city-state run by elected officials who were accountable to the people. Athens also boasted important figures in almost every category of Western civilization. Great playwrights, like Aeschylus (the father of tragedy), were there. Athens was home to the fathers of history, Herodotus and Thucydides. Hippocrates, another fifth-century Athenian, has been called "the father of Western medicine." And I can't talk about Athens without mentioning Socrates, the father of Western philosophy, who taught Plato, who later taught Aristotle. Each of these philosophical giants once graced the city discussed in Acts 17. Numerous artists also called Athens home. The most celebrated of this era was Phidias, whose statue of Zeus was considered one of the wonders of the world. Phidias also designed the enormous, majestic statue of Athena. Temples designed by other artists also lined the streets of the city, with the most impressive building there being the famous Parthenon (completed around 432 BC).

In every ancient Greek city, the highest point of elevation housed a temple to some god or goddess, usually the patron god of the city (Sproul, *Acts*, 306). These locations were known as "high cities," or to the Greeks, the *acropolis*. The high elevations there gave visitors a feeling of supremacy and closeness to the gods. Athens was no different. Athena was the patron goddess of the city; her statue stood high inside the Parthenon.

About fifty yards from the Parthenon was a little hill about 50 feet high and about 150 yards long. On it a temple was built to the Greek god of war, Ares, who corresponded to the Roman god of war, Mars; hence the name *Aeropagus*, or *Mars Hill*. Paul's speech in verses 22-31 may have taken place on that platform.

Even though its golden age had passed, Athens was still an impressive city when Paul visited it. John Polhill says, "It was still considered the cultural and intellectual center of the Roman Empire, and it is in this perspective that Luke portrayed it" (*Acts*, 365–66). Athens was also still strikingly beautiful. Paul had surely heard about the majestic city since he was a boy, and in verse 16 he is wandering its streets, waiting on his companions to join him. How would he respond to such grandeur and history and introduce Christ among such competing worldviews? Athens was the home of pagan Greek philosophy. Would it welcome divine revelation from Jerusalem?

How should we, as Christians, interact with a pluralistic society? How should we engage skeptical intellectuals in particular? To find answers from Paul's visit, let's look at what Paul *saw*, what Paul *felt*, where Paul *went*, and consider what Paul *said* at the Areopagus. We'll find that each point is related. Stott, in fact, put it well: "We do not *speak* like Paul because we do not *feel* like Paul; this is because we do not *see* like Paul" (*Message of Acts*, 290; emphasis added).

What Paul Saw
ACTS 17:16

It wasn't the history, the architecture, or the beauty of Athens that first struck Paul. While the apostle surely admired some things about the city and respected its history, what struck him most was the *idolatry* rampant in Athens. Paul looked at the city *from a Christian perspective*.

In this we see an illustration of what it means to have a *Christian worldview*. Michael Goheen and Craig Bartholomew define a worldview this way:

> [It's] an articulation of the basic beliefs embedded in a shared
> grand story that are rooted in a faith commitment and that
> give shape and direction to the whole of our individual and
> corporate lives. (*Living at the Crossroads*, 23)

In other words, a worldview is a set of beliefs about the most fundamental issues in life: *origin, meaning, morality,* and *destiny*. One's worldview allows one to look for answers to questions about these subjects within a grand narrative.

When a person truly becomes a Christian, the way that person *sees* everything changes. Why? Because embedded within the story line of the Bible is a set of theological beliefs about God, creation, humanity, sin, redemption, and the kingdom. These beliefs (and other important doctrines) along with Scripture's story line shape the Christ follower's view of the world.

We as Christians enjoy many of the same things those who don't know Jesus enjoy, but we look at them through a different set of lenses. We see the arts differently; we listen to music differently; we think about sports differently; we view business differently; we view ethnicity differently; we view the poor, the orphan, and the widow differently; we view the ocean differently; we hear the birds differently; we view money differently; we view sex differently; we view marriage differently; we view food and drink differently; we view death differently. We see the world differently because we filter everything we encounter through the right perspective of God's self-revelation in creation, in Scripture, and ultimately in his Son.

Everyone has a worldview. Luke mentions two competing worldviews in particular that were at work in Athens: that of the Epicureans and that of the Stoics. These groups saw the world differently, and their opposing perspectives remind us that even today people see things in many different lights. Even next-door neighbors may see an issue in radically divergent ways because they have radically different sets of beliefs—a fact James Sire highlights in his book, *The Universe Next Door.* The question each person must ask himself, then, is this: Is my worldview true and coherent, and do I consistently apply it to everything?

One of the things a Christian worldview consistently reveals is that the world is filled with *idols.* Underneath sin problems, relational problems, and intellectual problems is a profound *worship* problem. Martin Luther's Large Catechism teaches that if a person gets the first commandment—"Do not have other gods besides me"—right, obeying the others will follow because everything follows this fundamental issue of worship.

Some say it was easier to find a god in Athens than a person. The marketplace there was lined with idols. The phrase "full of idols," appearing in verse 16, carries the idea of the city streets being "smothered in idols" (Stott, *Message of Acts,* 277). The sight of so many people exchanging the glory of the Creator to bow to such created things radically impacts Paul, leading him to engage the Athenian citizens with the gospel. His response to what he witnessed should make us long to see our neighbors and the nations replace their idolatry with worship of the living God (1 Thess 1:9-10). We, too, live in a world smothered by idols.

An idol is anything to which we turn when we need something only Jesus can provide. Idols aren't just statues worshiped at shrines; they are substitute gods and functional saviors that supplant the true and living God in the human heart. Idols can take the form of the need for peer approval, the relentless pursuit of success and money, the drive for sex, pleasure, or food, all-consuming allegiance to a sports team, to the pursuit of education, or maybe even show an obsession with an individual. Christians bear the responsibility of destroying such idols in our lives and then lovingly pointing them out to our culture so that others may also understand that the pursuit of idols won't satisfy the human heart (Ps 16:4). Bowing to them only multiplies sorrows. People desperately need the God who made them and who can redeem them through Jesus Christ.

What Paul Felt
ACTS 17:16

Becoming a Christian also entails a change in one's *feelings*. When we belong to Christ, we become deeply affected by things. In Isaiah 53:3 Jesus is called a "man of suffering, who knew what sickness was." He wept and got enraged (John 11:33-35). Paul, too, speaks of emotions in numerous places, writing things like "as grieving, yet always rejoicing" (2 Cor 6:10). So it shouldn't surprise us—but should challenge us—to read Paul "was *deeply distressed* when he saw that the city was full of idols" (Acts 17:16; emphasis added).

The Greek word translated "deeply distressed" or "provoked" (ESV) is difficult to translate into an English expression. It's *paroxynō*, from which we get our word "paroxysm"—as in a seizure, spasm, or outburst. Some try to translate Paul's reaction here as "anger." They say that Paul was "infuriated" at the idolatry of Athens, but I think that's only part of what is meant in this passage.

The best way to understand this verb is to look to the Old Testament. This term appears in the Greek version of it to describe how God feels about idolatry. When the Israelites worshiped idols, they "provoked" the Lord to righteous anger, but this anger is also mingled with *love* (cf. Deut 9:7; Isa 65:1-7). Why is it that God wanted his people to worship him alone? The answer is that he loved them. I submit that Paul experienced a mixture of righteous indignation for the name of God and brokenhearted compassion for the people who worshiped false gods. He was motivated by love for God and neighbor.

Like an Old Testament prophet (1 Kgs 17), Paul was zealous for God's name. Often overlooked in this chapter is Paul's tone and demeanor in Athens, which display compassion. Verse 17 says Paul "reasoned" with the people. Rather than allowing his feelings to lead him to angrily take a sledgehammer to the idols, he—in holy love—engaged the people, listened to and heard them, dialogued with and debated with them. That takes gentleness and compassion. And in the speech at the Areopagus, he also demonstrated respect for his audience (v. 22).

The lesson for Christians here *involves the state of our hearts.* If your life doesn't reflect both sweetness and thunder, you will either be a coward or obnoxious when it comes to sharing your faith. Some people, for example, are good at the ministry of truth, but they are terrible at the ministry of tears (Keller, "A World of Idols"). They are good at telling people that they need to change, but they aren't willing to connect with them and love them to Christ. As believers, we need both gentleness *and* boldness. No one displayed this combination approach to evangelism better than Jesus. He rebuked people boldly, but he was also gentle. Isaiah said of the truth-telling, truth-embodying Savior, "He will not break a bruised reed" (Isa 42:3).

How can you engage people effectively in your "marketplace"? You need Paul's commitment to truth and compassion for people. Then you will be effective in society as you live out a life filled with eternal meaning and profound joy. People will be drawn to that.

The psalmist captures the believer's desire to see the nations worship the Lord:

> *May God be gracious to us and bless us;*
> *may he make his face shine upon us* Selah
> *so that your way may be known on earth,*
> *your salvation among all nations.*
> *Let the peoples praise you, God;*
> *let all the peoples praise you.*
> *Let the nations rejoice and shout for joy,*
> *for you judge the peoples with fairness*
> *and lead the nations on earth.* Selah
> *Let the peoples praise you, God,*
> *let all the peoples praise you.* (Ps 67:1-5)

Do you long to see people sing for joy to the Creator and Redeemer? If not, then cultivate your feelings by meditating on the cross of Jesus. There we can see God's absolute commitment to perfect holiness, and we can also see his unfathomable compassion for sinners. The more we think about the cross, in fact, the more we will grow in truthfulness and tears; in gentleness and boldness; in holiness and love. Paul saw the world differently and felt differently about the idols of the world because his worldview was radically cross centered (1 Cor 1:17-31). If the cross is not central to your worldview, then you will end up being too accepting or too demanding. Constant awareness of the cross prepares us to lovingly engage the Athenians in our lives.

Where Paul Went
ACTS 17:17-18

Luke records Paul evangelizing in three different places: in the synagogue, in the marketplace, and finally at the Areopagus, where he delivers a formal address. He intentionally goes to the first two places; he's taken to the third.

We should admire and seek to imitate Paul's flexibility and range in evangelism. America is a nation filled with great spiritual diversity. Some parts of the country have no knowledge of the Bible or of basic Christian concepts. In other parts of America, there's a general understanding of the Christian faith—or, at least, of some Christian vocabulary and ideals. In other areas both extremes are represented. In Raleigh, for instance, some citizens are generally aware of Christian ideas, while many of our university students have absolutely no idea what is meant by words like *God, sin, heaven,* and *redemption.* D. A. Carson said that when ministering to university students, he finds that an increasing number of them don't even know that the Bible has two testaments ("The Cross and Christian Ministry").

Carson illustrated the diversity of America using the experiences of two recent seminary graduates. One planted a church in Tulsa, Oklahoma, where it took him a whole year to meet someone who would confess to *not* being a Christian! Another student went to plant a church in Washington, DC, and found things to be totally different there. In a survey he used to spark conversation, the young DC planter asked people in the area to do a word association activity. The majority of responders associated the word *Christian* with the word *bigot* (Carson, "Lessons"). The young man in Tulsa, then, had sort of a "synagogue ministry"; he could expound the Bible to those who were familiar with it. The young man in DC had a "marketplace ministry." Let's look at how Paul engaged both types of audiences.

The Synagogue (17:17a)

As was his custom, Paul began in the synagogue, speaking to the Jews and to the devout. For those familiar with the Old Testament, Paul "reasoned" from the Scriptures, explaining and proving that Jesus was the Messiah (cf. vv. 12-13). Those who minister in a churchy setting, then, should make the gospel the priority in their work as a youth minister, a children's worker, a Sunday school teacher, a volunteer, a small group leader, a pastor, a worship leader, or in whatever other capacity in which they are placed. While those encountered in such settings may well know Christian lingo, many religious people aren't Christians.

I remember preaching at a church in Mississippi several years ago when the need to keep the gospel central to my interactions with those attending church really struck me. A seventy-year-old man handed out bulletins there every week. He'd practically grown up in the church, yet one Sunday when I preached from John 3 on the necessity of being born again, the man realized he wasn't really a Christ follower. And in that moment, the Lord opened his heart, and he trusted in him. "When I was a kid," the man explained, "a man said to me, 'Don't you think it's time for you to join the church?' And so I did." But he had never repented and trusted in Christ until that day when our paths collided. If you serve an audience of Christians, proclaim the gospel to them. Even the religious need to hear it.

The Marketplace: Dialoguing with People in General (17:17b)

In the marketplace, the hub of Athenian culture, a place of commerce and public dialogue, Paul engaged the Athenians. He didn't wait for the Sabbath day to preach the gospel. Rather, day by day, he mixed things up in the *agora*. Right there in the market he dialoged with individuals. Stott says, "He seems deliberately to have adopted the famous Socratic method of dialogue, involving questions and answers; he was, in fact, a kind of Christian Socrates, although with a better gospel than Socrates ever knew" (*Message of Acts*, 280).

We Westerners don't have a good equivalent of the agora. It contained everything: town officials deliberating, artists creating, business people dealing, the media reporting, the philosophers philosophizing. Everything happened in the marketplace. It was the public space for everything.

To this busy venue Paul takes his faith. Christianity is a public faith. The Scriptures never forbid us from allowing it to impact the marketplace. The writer of Proverbs says, "Wisdom calls out in the street; she makes her voice heard in the public squares" (Prov 1:20). Paul lives out his faith and communicates it every day in the public center of ideas.

We too should take our faith public by the way we live and talk. Paul engaged people in dialogue. He didn't aim to start a riot; he meant to start a conversation.

You don't have to be familiar with the Socratic method of teaching to understand the importance of using questions in engaging those in the marketplace. Just read through the Gospels and notice how often Jesus uses questions. The art of dialogue, in fact, helps us be effective evangelists. Sometimes timid believers will admit, "I don't know what to say in evangelism." That feeling is OK. And if it describes your own experiences, just have in your arsenal some good questions to ask. You might be surprised at what happens in a conversation as people begin to open up about what they already believe.

We can take our faith to the marketplace in the ordinary rhythm of life as we go to school, to the gas station, to the grocery store, or to sporting events. We can take it on walks around the neighborhood, to our work cubicles, and to picnics held for family and close friends. Daily and even impromptu meetings provide occasions for gospel conversations. We need to get where people are and engage them day by day.

The Marketplace: Dialoguing with Intellectual Skeptics in Particular (17:18)

Luke goes on to mention others with whom Paul conversed in the city: "philosophers." Some of them called Paul a babbler, a word translated "ignorant show-off" in CSB; the term originally used here literally means a "seed picker." It was used of various seed-eating or scavenging birds (Stott, *Message of Acts*, 282). This means the philosophers compared Paul to a bird picking up an idea here or there, without having anything really coherent to say.

These philosophers prized a coherent worldview. Their name-calling doesn't indicate Paul was doing a poor job; rather, it suggests that the philosophers couldn't understand Paul's categories. They thus accused him of advocating "foreign deities." Because they couldn't grasp Paul's understanding of God, the world, and salvation—only picking up bits and pieces of his message rather than comprehending the whole— *they* smugly considered *him* a seed picker. That they didn't understand

Paul's worldview is demonstrated by the fact that they thought the *resurrection* (*anastasis* in Greek) referred to Jesus's female consort. In Greek thought, many deities bore the names of abstract qualities (like Fate, Mercy, Effort, and Shame), so these philosophers apparently assumed *resurrection* to be a similar (and lesser) deity.

With what types of philosophers was Paul engaging? While many in the city loved talking about ideas (v. 21), two schools of thought are mentioned in this passage: Epicurean and Stoic philosophies.

Epicureans were materialists. They believed the body and even the soul were composed of fine matter, which dissolves after death. They believed the gods to be totally indifferent to human actions. Epicureans didn't believe in divine providence. And they considered a person who neither feared divine judgment nor awaited eternal reward to be wise. The best way to imitate the gods, for the Epicureans, was to enjoy pleasure—not gross idolatry but pleasure itself. "You only live once" and "If it feels good, do it" capture a bit of their spirit. They pursued detached and tranquil life apart from pain and in pursuit of pleasure—an approach to existence that they felt reflected the lifestyle of the gods. Today we use the term *epicurean* to refer to things like fine food and wine or to describe a person who has luxurious tastes and habits.

Stoics, on the other hand, were pantheists. They thought a divine principle was immersed in all of nature, including humans. This spark of divinity, the *logos*, was the cohesive rational principle that bound the entire cosmic order together. They confused God with the "world soul" and thought the world was determined by fate. For them, a wise person recognized his connection with everything else in the universe, cultivating an attitude of self-sufficient contentment, regardless of circumstances. A Stoic lived with a stiff upper lip, responding calmly to everything. To pursue his highest good, he lived by reason. Stoics saw history as an unending cycle of order, followed by chaos, followed by order. They would applaud Paul's emphasis on God's nearness but would reject the notion that history was moving to a culminating point (Johnson, *Let's Study Acts*, 219–20). The phrase *que sera sera* ("what will be, will be") captures the spirit of Stoicism.

Stott says, "To oversimplify, it was characteristic of Epicureans to emphasize chance, escape and the enjoyment of pleasure, and of the Stoics to emphasize fatalism, submission and the endurance of pain" (*Message of Acts*, 281). In other words, one group said, "If it feels good, do it; there are no consequences," while the other group said, "Grin and bear it; there's nothing you can do about it anyway." Both worldviews were hopeless and meaningless.

Today's world is plagued by a similar intellectual climate. One prevailing view, *skepticism*, rejects ultimate truth, the idea that life has meaning, and humanity's need for salvation. Adherents live for the here and now. Importantly, culture often accepts the skeptical viewpoint as the *intellectual one*. Thus, anyone who believes in the God of the Bible and accepts his or her need for salvation must therefore be unlearned, naive, and primitive.

The growing number of "nones" in Western culture illustrates society's general lack of desire for eternal, ultimate matters. The "nones" are those people who classify themselves as having no religious affiliation. About one-third of American adults under the age of thirty align themselves with this category, the highest percentage of people ever to do so, according to Pew Research. These men and women live without any real sense of God. Thankfully, Paul gives us a mighty example of how to engage such a culture.

Skeptical intellectuals need the church to speak up for truth, to share the gospel in spite of their stated aversion to it. Obviously, good Christian thinkers are needed who can argue with the intellectuals in colleges and universities. But skepticism infects every arena of culture, making the need to preach the Christian worldview in an appealing way necessary across every sphere. Whatever your point of influence—the world of filmmaking, music writing, journalism, science, education, law, politics, art, or parenting—do not retreat from culture. Like Paul, engage it humbly, boldly, and intelligently.

What Paul Said at the Areopagus
ACTS 17:19-31

In light of Paul's teaching, the philosophers lead him to the Areopagus in order for Paul to further explain himself and give a defense of his message. The *Areopagus*, or Mars Hill, can refer to either a *court* or a *hill*. Sometimes it may refer to both since the court traditionally met on that particular rise (Polhill, *Acts*, 367). Athenians would often assemble here to debate and decide affairs. The sermon or defense in verses 24-31 is a response to the question, What do these ideas mean?

Like many in our modern era, the Athenians loved *new* things (v. 21). But they didn't need new ideas; they needed new life! People today love to watch the daily *news*, listen to *new* music, see *new* movies, buy the *newest* clothing styles, and make *new* discoveries. And enjoying new things isn't necessarily wrong. The problem, however, is that some things are unchanging. The gospel is an unchanging, old message; it cannot be edited, expanded, or updated. A man at the University of Manchester got his PhD in New Testament with the thesis that Jesus was the founder of a phallic mushroom cult; apparently the doctoral candidate thought it a good idea to put a new twist on the gospel. But on this R. C. Sproul wisely commented, "That is new, but it is also ridiculous" (*Acts*, 310). The new ignored the true. Be careful, then, of overemphasizing new things. Remember that the gospel is the old, old story that has the power to give people *new life*. If we change it, we destroy it.

Paul has the opportunity to give the Athenians the unchanging message about Jesus. He first establishes *a point of contact* with them. He identifies with their religious interest. He understands that man is incurably religious. Wherever you go today, in fact, you will find some sort of religion.

Though the atheist may say, "God does not exist," creation and conscience testify to God's existence; the atheist's words reflect his own dislike for God (Sproul, *Acts*, 310). That he feels the need to address the topic of God at all suggests something is wrong with his theory. As Romans 1:18-23 states, he suppresses the truth about God though God's existence is evident to him. As someone quipped, "The common atheist is really saying, 'There's no god, and I hate him.'"

Paul moves on to establish *a point of conflict*. In the synagogue Paul's text was the Old Testament; in Athens it was an inscription (v. 23). A number of ancient visitors to Athens reported seeing altars with the inscription he mentions (Boice, *Acts*, 297). Paul's point of conflict was obvious: God has revealed himself! God is not unknowable. Paul's speech then describes *the revelation of God* and how the problem is not that people *can't* know God but that we *don't want to* know him.

Then Paul preaches about "what these things mean." D. A. Carson says that Areopagus speeches had a reputation for lasting a long time, as in two to three hours. With that in mind, it's likely that every clause the Bible records here is just part of the outline. If we read the rest of Paul's writings, however, we gain a pretty good clue as to how Paul would have filled in the rest (Carson, "The Cross"). Paul essentially explains a Christian worldview here. He puts the gospel into the bigger story of the Bible, showing the reasonableness of the faith, the exclusivity of the faith, and the necessity of repentance and placing faith in the Redeemer. He shares several core beliefs embedded in the Christian story.

God Is the Creator (17:24)

Paul begins his address with creation, asserting that God made the world and everything in it. Regarding the Stoics, Paul states that God is distinct from his creation; regarding the Epicureans, Paul states that God is not aloof but involved in creation.

We, too, are surrounded by the revelation of God, who spoke the world into existence (Gen 1; cf. Pss 33:6; 146:6). This fact makes it absurd to suggest that God can be contained in a shrine or temple. Even when Solomon's temple was dedicated, the wealthy ruler realized God couldn't be domesticated (1 Kgs 8:27; Isa 66:1-2). No one can lock up the Creator (cf. Ps 115:3).

The whole earth, in fact, is a theater of God's revelation. As theologian Herman Bavinck stated, "In an absolute sense, therefore, nothing is atheistic" (*Reformed Dogmatics*, 56–57). Though some might suppress the truth of God's existence, they can't escape it (Ps 139:7-8). One persecuted Christian, facing the threat of having his congregation's church building destroyed, said this: "You can pull down our steeples, but you can't pull down the stars." His comment draws attention to the fact that God's glory *surrounds* us (Ps 19). Echoes of his reality permeate the world. He has made himself known in creation, and this is why no one can claim to be completely without revelation of God (Rom 1:18-32).

Have you ever noticed how many modern items are stamped with the words "Made in China"? It's laughable. I can buy a T-shirt with an American flag on it, but the tag inside will most likely read "Made in China." The reality is that everything in the world is similarly stamped with the undeniable truth that God the Creator formed it. That's why the psalmist declares, "How countless are your works, LORD! In wisdom you have made them all; the earth is full of your creatures" (Ps 104:24). The Athenians, like many others, believed in many gods—a god over the sea, a god over the sun, a god over business. And Paul starts his speech to them by clarifying that there's one God who created everything. All of the beauty of nature was made by the triune God for his glory (Rom 11:36; Col 1:16-17).

God Is the Sustainer of Life (17:25)

Paul says that the God who created the world sustains the world. If Jesus weren't holding the world together, everything would fall apart (Col 1:17). This idea too stood in contrast to the beliefs of the Epicureans and Stoics. God is distinct from creation yet is intimately involved in it, sustaining it moment by moment (cf. Gen 2:7; Isa 42:5).

God doesn't need people—we need him (cf. Ps 50:10-12). God is entirely independent, and we're dependent. God needs no oxygen, no sleep, and no food. Such self-sufficiency should humble us, reminding us that we're not God, but it should also give us hope. If we know God through Jesus Christ, then we have everything we need (2 Pet 1:3). A. W. Tozer said, "[God] needs no one, but when faith is present he works through anyone" (*The Knowledge of the Holy*, 36). When God called Moses, he told him that "I AM" was sending him (Exod 3:14). Moses rightly saw himself as insufficient for the task, and he learned to see "I AM" as totally sufficient for the task. Learn to cast your insufficiencies on God's total sufficiency.

God Is the Ruler of the Nations (17:26)

Paul goes on to say that God's independence doesn't mean disengagement. God is intimately involved in the lives of humankind, the pinnacle of his creation. God, in fact, created diverse ethnic groups from one man (cf. Gen 5; 10). This means that the diversity in the human family is God's design! He delighted in creating people of different ethnicities.

The reference to determining "times" and "boundaries" either refers to God's sovereignty over seasons and the borders between habitable regions and wilderness (Ps 74:17) or to God's sovereignty over the rise and fall of nations and the boundaries between them (Deut 32:8). In either case God is sovereign over history and geography.

God Is Knowable (17:27)

In contrast to the teachings of Epicureans, who viewed the gods as being detached and uninvolved in daily affairs, Paul teaches that God's purpose in creating humans was that "they might seek God." He lovingly desires that people discover their Creator.

Paul's language, though, also suggests the doctrine of sin. The image he gives is that of blind people groping after God. James Boice says the word used here for "reach out" or "feel" (*pselaphesian*) is the word the Greek poet Homer used in the well-known story of the Cyclops. The one-eyed giant captured Odysseus and his men, but Odysseus got the Cyclops drunk and blinded him with a sharp stake. Though Odysseus wanted to get out of the cave and find his men, doing so was difficult because the Cyclops was "groping around" to find and kill the hero. In using this word, then, it's as if Paul is saying, "In our sin, we are as unseeing as the blinded Cyclops." We instinctively know God is there, but because of sin's blinding effects, we need divine grace to give us the new spiritual eyes to find him (Boice, *Acts*, 299). God is not detached, disinterested, or unengaged. He is near to us, but we need the work of Jesus Christ to know him (Heb 10:22).

God Is the Father of Humanity (17:28-29)

In verse 28 Paul quotes two pagan poets who, by the common grace God offers, caught a glimpse of the intimate relationship between God and man. He first quotes Epimenides of Crete, who wrote of the nearness and sustaining power of God. Then Paul quotes from a Stoic author, Aratus, who wrote of man's creation in the image of God.

Paul quotes these men to describe the truth about human nature to his audience. We humans are like our Creator in many ways. He not only sustains us, but his resemblance is reflected in us. If you have ever said or done something that left you commenting, "I sounded just like my father," you know firsthand that people tend to resemble their parents. In a similar way we as creatures made in God's likeness bear similarities to God. This doesn't mean we are God; rather, we can think, act, feel, choose, love, and work like he does. And even more amazingly, we can know and worship him through Jesus, who enables us to call God "Father" (1 Pet 1:17), even "*Abba* [Daddy or Papa], Father" (Gal 4:6).

These writers caught a glimpse of the fact that humans are invaded by the revelation of God (Ferguson, "Acts 17:16-34"). As Abraham Kuyper stated, "If the cosmos is a theatre of God's revelation, in this theatre, man is both actor and spectator" (*Encyclopedia of Sacred Theology*, 265). We are an expression of God's creation. We are made in God's likeness. We are made to know and worship him. That means God's revelation isn't just echoing outside of us; it's echoing inside of us, too.

Paul adds in verse 29 that since we're made in God's image, it would be utter folly to worship something made by human hands (cf. Ps 115:4-8; Isa 44:9-20). While the Epicureans and Stoics realized this, they failed to see that their own mental conceptions of God were also the products of human invention (Johnson, *Let's Study Acts*, 221).

Before moving on, let me make a few applications. We have already noted Paul's ability to adapt his methods to reach different audiences. Let's not miss the fact that with this biblically illiterate audience he begins by making a *comprehensive presentation of biblical truth*. Paul starts in creation to tell the story line of the Bible. This is important because even in our day and culture, many people know virtually nothing of the Bible. (Just watch what happens when someone is asked a scriptural question on a game show, and you'll see what I mean.) Paul recognizes the biblical illiteracy of the Athenians and doesn't speak to them in the same manner he uses with those in the synagogue. To start his address by quoting John 3:16 would only confuse the Athenians, so Paul wisely begins by sharing foundational basics that come from the beginning of God's written revelation.

We too must learn to present the gospel within the framework of the larger biblical story line. Simply telling someone, "Jesus loves you and died for you, so make him Lord of your life and be forgiven of your sins" is confusing and even alienating to those who can't define sin and don't understand who Jesus is or what his death has to do with anything. Even Easter Sunday morning gospel presentations, then, are helped when we first begin with a little "preevangelism." We need to lay a basic framework in which Jesus makes sense to those who know little about him.

D. A. Carson tells this story about a friend who served in India as a missionary for twelve years. His main task was to teach in a seminary, but he was also an energetic evangelist. The missionary learned to speak Hindi fluently and spent hours preaching in villages, which were places of great religious diversity and syncretism. In every case the missionary took pains to emphasize the exclusiveness of Christ as he taught. But over the years, while he saw *many* profession of faith, he was unable to plant a single church. The problem was that while people said yes to Jesus based on the gospel presentations the man made, they basically just absorbed Christ into the greater pantheism that underlies Hinduism. In other words, they didn't fully understand Christianity. They didn't really understand Jesus. After twelve years the missionary returned home in discouragement. He decided he needed a new strategy.

When he retuned to India, he made some changes to his approach. This time all of his evangelistic activity was restricted to only two villages. And he began his outreach to the inhabitants in them by sharing Genesis 1:1. He thus began by teaching his hearers the doctrine of God, the truth about who humans are, and the reality of God's relationship to creation. As the people began to grasp those basics, he moved on to share the Bible's story line. And eventually he moved on to share about the cross and Christ's resurrection. Then, when all of that was done, he focused on establishing congregations. And while at the end of four years, he saw *few* converts to Christianity, he had planted two churches (Carson, "Lessons").

In the past Western Christians communicating the gospel to next-door neighbors assumed people basically shared our worldview. We assumed they had an understanding of God. We assumed they had heard of Jesus. We assumed they knew he died on the cross and rose from the dead for the benefit of humanity. We assumed they viewed sin as offensive to God and destructive to people. We assumed people believed history is moving somewhere. In days gone by, even atheists were "Christian atheists" in that the deity they claimed to deny was clearly the Christian God. But the time for making assumptions in evangelism has passed. In order to be effective, we have to begin sharing the truth of the gospel by anchoring our teaching in the creation account. We must describe the nature of God and move through the biblical story line.

Paul's address also reminds us that the spiritually ignorant don't have a mental "blank hard drive" (Carson, "Lessons"). People already have a worldview in place that will compete with the biblical truth we share. Wrong ideas must be lovingly countered and replaced with the new categories and meaning of a Christian worldview before they can be completely destroyed.

Next we should consider Paul's *cultural relevance.* He worked to connect with his hearers in meaningful ways. He even quoted pagan philosophers. As we consider how to apply the principle of cultural relevance to our own outreach efforts, we should remember this point from John Stott:

> [Paul's] precedent gives us warrant to do the same, and indicates that glimmerings of truth, insights from general revelation, may be found in non-Christian authors. At the same time we need to exercise caution, for in stating that "we are his offspring", Aratus was referring to Zeus, and Zeus is emphatically not identical with the living and true God. (*Message of Acts,* 286; other Greek writers also quote a similar phrase)

Today's pop music lyricists are the poetic theologians and philosophers of culture. The writers of popular TV shows and movies are also responsible for teaching worldview to the masses. While we certainly don't need to be experts on pop music and film, we do need to be aware of popular worldviews presented through these mediums.

I find myself regularly quoting songs and shows as I teach, and I find that doing so receives a mixed response. One audience enjoys and learns from contemporary connections; another expresses concern that it's dangerous or silly for a minister to quote from pagans. (Once, a guest to our church never returned because I quoted the TV comedy

The Fresh Prince of Bel-Air.) Stott's word, then, is instructive. Christians can use cultural sources as we strive to connect with those who don't know Jesus and who aren't familiar with God's Word, but we must always do so with caution and discretion. We must also take care not to allow a love of entertainment to divert us from spending quality time in prayer and in Scripture. Paul was aware of popular writings, but nothing about his life suggests he would have been watching hours of Netflix if given the opportunity—much less allowing his mind to play in the gutter as he considered hours of explicit pop lyrics. We must guard our minds (Phil 4:8), but we should also seek to understand culture. Doing so can help us build bridges to the gospel.

God Is Both the Judge and the Rescuer (17:30-31)

Paul tells the Athenians that, despite the revelation of God in creation, they have become spiritually ignorant. But that ignorance doesn't give them an excuse before God. Instead, Paul warns them of judgment. His use of "overlooked" in this case doesn't imply that God ignored human rebellion. In God's great mercy he didn't immediately visit humanity with the judgment they deserved (Stott, *Message of Acts,* 287). With the coming of Jesus, however, a decisive turning point is taking place in redemptive history: now everyone must repent or face God's just judgment.

The fact that God will judge has been clearly expressed through the resurrection of Jesus. Paul tells the Athenians that God has committed this judgment to his Son, Jesus, who will judge everyone on a fixed day, in perfect righteousness. If people will *repent,* however, this same Judge can save them. Salvation comes through this *man,* the Second Adam, who lived the life we fallen humans couldn't live, died the death we deserved, and rose on our behalf. We come from one man: Adam (v. 26), but we must turn to this man: Jesus, the Lord. He is not only our Judge but our Savior.

The appeal to repent is clear and consistent in Scripture (cf. Isa 45:22; Matt 4:17). All are under the wrath of God because they have rebelled against him. But if they will turn from their sins and turn to Christ, "sins [will] be wiped out" (Acts 3:19); he will give them life. Paul moves from the realm of philosophical debate to personal responsibility (Johnson, *Let's Study Acts,* 222). Everyone must repent or perish.

Several ideas were perceived as outrageous by many in Paul's audience: (1) the exclusivity of salvation in Jesus (which flew in the face of pluralists); (2) the suggestion that Jesus rose bodily (which flew in the face of many Greek philosophies based on the idea that matter is principally bad); and (3) the notion that history is going somewhere (which flew in the face of the Stoics). These truths, in fact, still offend people today. And because Paul's hearers found them so offensive, Paul's speech was halted.

Some have stated that Paul failed to mention the cross to the Athenians, and thus they give this speech a failing grade. Some go further and say that Paul was so moved by the failure recorded here that he changed his tactics when he went to Corinth, resolving to know nothing but "Jesus Christ and him crucified" (1 Cor 2:2). But we shouldn't make that leap. We must remember a few things, chiefly that we have in Acts only the outline of Paul's speech. (I doubt Paul ever talked about the resurrection apart from the cross!) Further, we know from verse 18 that Paul was preaching "Jesus and the resurrection." Are we to imagine Paul talking about these subjects apart from the cross? The idea is absurd. Even more, when Paul said that God overlooked times of ignorance but has *now* commanded everyone to repent, he seems to be pinpointing the hinge point in redemptive history—namely, the events surrounding Good Friday and Easter. These are a few reasons to assert that Paul did indeed mention the cross.

What Were the Results?
ACTS 17:32-34

Some also assert that Paul proved to be a failure at Athens because his words brought about so few conversions, but I think Paul had a good day! Ultimately, we shouldn't evaluate Paul—or any other evangelist—based on results, but by his or her faithfulness to preach the gospel. Paul was a bold witness in Athens! Sure, some mocked his message. But others wanted to hear more. And most importantly, some believed. The latter group included Dionysius, a member of the council, and a woman named Damaris.

In his work Paul encountered religious pluralism, a great diversity of worldviews, and intelligent yet biblically illiterate people. And so will we. May God grant us grace as we make the truth of the gospel and the glory of the crucified and risen Christ known to the world. Our message may turn out to be a "stumbling block to Jews" and "foolishness to the Gentiles," but to others it will turn out to be the power of God unto salvation (cf. Rom 1:16; 1 Cor 1:18,23).

Reflect and Discuss

1. What does it mean to have evangelistic versatility? Why is it important?
2. What does it mean to have a Christian worldview? What does Paul teach about this concept?
3. What are some of the idols worshiped in your city, neighborhood, or nation?
4. Describe what Paul felt when he saw the idolatry in Athens. Why is this important?
5. What does Paul's evangelism in the marketplace teach?
6. What about Paul's speech at the Areopagus most resonates with you?
7. Explain why Paul started with creation before moving to the resurrection and judgment.
8. In what context might we need to establish the basic framework of the Bible before talking about the need for repentance and faith in Jesus?
9. Do you think Paul was successful in Athens? Why or why not?
10. Take a few moments to pray for opportunities to imitate Paul's evangelistic mission this week.

Gospel Ministry in an Immoral Culture

ACTS 18:1-22

Main Idea: Tired saints can draw much hope from the account of Paul's visit to the influential and immoral city of Corinth. There the apostle was absorbed in work, weakened by trials, and then rejuvenated by the sovereign Lord.

I. **Stage 1: Tent Making (18:1-4)**
   A. Paul's coworkers (18:1-3)
   B. Paul's work ethic (18:3-4)
II. **Stage 2: Full-Time Ministry (18:5-8)**
   A. Support (18:5)
   B. Opposition (18:6)
   C. Fruitfulness (18:7-8)
III. **Stage 3: Weakness and Fear (18:9-10)**
   A. The Lord's Gentle Rebuke (18:9a)
   B. The Lord's Strong Mandate (18:9b)
   C. The Lord's Sovereign Promises (18:10)
IV. **Stage 4: Long-Term Discipleship (18:11-17)**
V. **Paul Returns to Antioch (18:18-22)**

A friend sent me a picture of a chuckling man who must be in his eighties. Below the photo a caption reads, "Who said ministry was stressful? I'm 35 and I feel great!" Anyone who knows anything about ministry laughs at this because the joke highlights truth: gospel ministry is difficult and stressful not only for pastors but for every disciple-making Christian.

By Acts 18 Paul has already been through a long list of terrible challenges, and the trials in Corinth will only add to his list of afflictions. As we will see, however, the Lord rejuvenates his servant in some wonderful ways. The Lord gives him companions. He blesses Paul's work. He gives Paul an assuring word. And the Lord fulfills promises to his faithful servant. Tired saints, then, can find a lot of hope in this passage about Paul's absorption in work and weakness in trials that are eclipsed by rejuvenation by the sovereign Lord.

Corinth was another major city of Paul's day, and it was the last *major* place of witness on his second missionary journey. John Stott is surely right in saying, "It seems to have been Paul's deliberate policy to move purposefully from one strategic city-center to the next" (*Message of Acts,* 293). After proclaiming the gospel in the intellectual city of Athens, Paul moves forty-six miles west to proclaim the good news to the commercial and immoral metropolis of Corinth.

Today the need to plant the gospel in major cities remains urgent. Thus these chapters in the book of Acts, which highlight Paul's ministry in Athens, Corinth, and Ephesus, are instructive.

Julius Caesar built a new Corinth after the Romans destroyed the old city. It was the largest and most cosmopolitan city of Greece. John Stott says that while the population of Ephesus was over a half a million, Corinth's numbered nearly 750,000 (Stott, *Message of Acts,* 293), but others estimate the population lower. Timothy Keller helpfully says Athens was like Boston, an intellectual center; Corinth was like New York City, a commercial center; Ephesus was like Los Angeles, a popular culture and occult center; and Rome was like Washington, DC; it was the political center (*Evangelism,* 161).

No building was more than one hundred years old when Paul arrived in Corinth (Polhill, *Acts,* 381). The city sat on the southern end of the isthmus, a narrow land bridge, about three and a half miles wide, that connected the Peloponnese peninsula with the mainland of Greece to the north. Until a canal was dug there in the nineteenth century, ships were dragged across a wooden railroad connecting one harbor to the other.

Corinth was a flourishing center of political power, commerce, and sexual immorality. Politically, Corinth was a Roman colony, and it was the capital of the province of Achaia. Commercially it had "location, location, location" working for it. There north-south land routes intersected with east-west sea routes. Corinth had two ports, Cenchreae to the east, opening into the Aegean Sea, and Lechaeum to the west, giving access to the Adriatic. One could sail goods to Cenchreae, transport the goods by land over the isthmus, and then send them on ships to places like Italy. Morally, as in many port cities, Corinth was known for sexual promiscuity. In fact, the word translated "to live like a Corinthian" (*korinthiazesthai*) came to mean to live immorally (Polhill, *Acts,* 381). Despite the moral depravity, however, the city also had a well-established synagogue.

All of these factors made ministry to the city challenging; outreach required strategy. And those who became part of the church in this location soon found that living a godly life in the midst of Corinth was a major challenge. The temple of Aphrodite, the goddess of love, was at the city's center; it stood on a nineteen hundred-foot tall hill overlooking the city. Thousands of female slave-priestesses related to the cult at this temple walked through the city as prostitutes in search of "worshipers." Paul thus had to give the church much-needed instructions about sexual purity (cf. 1 Cor 6:12-20). In spite of such things, however, the city was a strategic spot for gospel advancement due to the city's influence and to the mobility and diversity of the people there.

While Paul wrote his letters to the Corinthians after this initial visit, his letters still shed light on his early ministry and the Corinthian context. (He wrote 1 Corinthians from Ephesus near the end of his three-year ministry in Ephesus—see Acts 19:21-22; 20:31—and 2 Corinthians about a year later, probably from Macedonia—see Acts 20:2-3.) Most notable in these missives are Paul's feeling of "weakness and fear" and his resolute commitment to preaching the cross in Corinth. In his first letter to the young believers there he said,

> When I came to you, brothers and sisters, announcing the mystery
> of God to you, I did not come with brilliance of speech or wisdom.
> I decided to know nothing among you except Jesus Christ and him
> crucified. I came to you in weakness, in fear, and in much trembling.
> (1 Cor 2:1-3)

These words make us wonder what could have possibly weakened and intimidated the apostle Paul. For starters, the *immorality of Corinth* surely impacted him: sin was rampant there. The *idolatry* could have also affected him as many "gods" and "lords" were worshiped in Corinth (1 Cor 8:5). The *arrogance* of the city too could have rocked him because the Corinthians were proud of their intellect, wealth, political power, and culture. (The world-famous Isthmian Games were hosted in Corinth every other year, and many professional orators who charged a fee for offering wisdom on how to advance socially were hosted by Corinth.) But it could also be that the cumulative effect of traveling and facing various trials that preceded Paul's visit to Corinth had taken a deep emotional toll on him by the time he reached this stop. No matter what was behind Paul's admission, he clearly had no allusions about being a superhero and wasn't comfortable being surrounded by persistent evil. He thus admits weaknesses and fears.

Paul tells the Corinthians that the great solution to human pride and sexual perversion is the cross work of Jesus Christ (1 Cor 2:2). And it's this message of the Substitute that Paul carried with him. The solution the apostle offered tells us what should we do about sexual perversion and human arrogance in culture today. We must preach the fully sufficient, self-humiliating, self-denying cross of Christ. We mustn't proclaim it in arrogance but in desperate reliance on the Spirit's power as Paul did (cf. 1 Cor 2:4-5).

We will probe more deeply into Paul's fears soon. But for now let's consider Paul's journey to Corinth in four stages.

Stage 1: Tent Making
ACTS 18:1-4

Paul traveled from Athens to Corinth. This adds to his extensive travelogue. Between the years 49 and 52 Paul traveled approximately two thousand miles by foot and about a thousand miles by boat (Schreiner, "A God-Glorifying Ministry"). That means this nearly fifty-year-old man walked the equivalent of the distance between Raleigh, North Carolina, and Denver, Colorado, just to tell people about Jesus.

Paul's Coworkers (18:1-3)

In Corinth, Paul made new friends who not only shared his tent-making trade but also opened their home to him. Aquila and Priscilla provided wonderful strength to the missionary. The working friendship memorialized here confirms that Paul was no rugged individualist. He longed to be with his brothers and sisters, as his letters indicate. He even traveled with others as often as he could.

This couple is mentioned elsewhere in the New Testament (cf. Rom 16:3-4; 1 Cor 16:19; 2 Tim 4:19). They had much in common with Paul. They were Jews. They were tent makers. And it's possible that they were the owners of a sizable business when they employed Paul.

Aquila and Priscilla may have been Christians before their expulsion from Rome. While they could have become Christians through Paul's witness in Corinth, the text is silent on the point. According to the second-century historian Suetonius, Claudius expelled all the Jews because of an uproar instigated by "Chrestus" (probably a Latin transliteration of *Christos*, i.e., "Christ"). That means the disturbance in Rome apparently had to do with whether Jesus was the Messiah. Claudius expelled the Jews to maintain peace. Though his edict was never reversed, it evidently was not enforced carefully since many Jews, including this couple, resettled in Rome (cf. Rom 16:3-4; Johnson, *Let's Study Acts,* 225).

We as modern believers have a tendency to distance ourselves from the mighty apostle Paul, who is the main human character featured in much of the book of Acts. But the husband and wife about whom we read here were ordinary Christians, whom we can identify with and emulate.

First, it appears that the pair enjoyed a *dynamic marriage.* Each time Aquila and Priscilla are mentioned, they are mentioned *together.* At the end of this chapter we read how they together took Apollos aside and filled in some theological gaps in his thinking. They worked as a team. And it seems that Paul couldn't think of one of them without mentioning the other.

Second, it seems *Priscilla had remarkable influence* in this family unit. Of the six times this couple is mentioned, Priscilla is mentioned *first* on four occasions. This unusual fact probably indicates that her ministry in particular stood out to the Christians—though we shouldn't draw the conclusion that Aquila's ministry was insignificant or speculate that Priscilla dominated their marriage. Instead, it's possible that Priscilla, like Lydia, was an important female figure in the early church. Her inclusion provides another example of how godly ladies have played significant roles throughout church history. She's proof that the church's mission in Acts wasn't a male-dominated movement.

Third, this couple was *mobile.* Aquila migrated to Italy from Pontus, on the southern shore of the Black Sea. When forced to leave Rome, he and his wife ended up in Corinth. They later undertook another move to Ephesus with Paul, where the church (or a portion of it) met in their house (18:18-19; 1 Cor 16:3). And then they eventually returned to Rome (Rom 16:3-4)—only to appear back in Ephesus in 2 Timothy 4:19. These two were sojourners whose movements suggest they didn't think of any spot on this world as their home. Instead, they remained open to the will of God, refusing to limit their lives to whatever might happen within a certain circle they'd drawn on a map. While their vocation likely contributed to their mobility, it was ultimately their commitment to following Jesus that caused them to go from city to city. Their experiences are a reminder that while the Lord may sometimes keep a Christian couple in a certain place throughout their marriage, he takes others on complex journeys reminiscent of Aquila's and Priscilla's. So, treasure Jesus and follow him wherever he leads you. Life is good—though not always easy—when it is spent in service to the King.

Fourth, this married couple had *Christ-centered passion*. Because of that Paul held them in the highest regard. He called the pair "coworkers in Christ Jesus" who "risked their own necks" on his account (Rom 16:3-4), and this commendation was no cheap compliment. Paul knew the couple well. He worked with them. He traveled with them. He stayed with them. And whatever he meant by this phrase, "risked their own necks," he literally owed his life to these risk takers. Since Paul calls them "coworkers in Christ Jesus," we must conclude that they did what they did because of their love for the Lord.

You may work in the military, in medicine, in education, or in the tech industry. Whatever you do, follow the model Aquila and Priscilla provide us: they worked "in Christ Jesus." Whether they were making tents or planning to host people in their home, they did everything in, through, and for Jesus. The pair viewed all their work in relationship to him. May God raise up millions just like this Christ-exalting couple!

Fifth, these two were *hospitable*. Whenever Priscilla and Aquila are mentioned in Scripture, they are opening up their home to others as they did for Paul in Corinth. They instructed Apollos in their home (18:26 NIV). And when they lived in Ephesus and in Rome, churches met in their house (Rom 16:3-5; 1 Cor 16:19; 2 Tim 4:19). Likely they were people of means who chose to use their sizable dwelling for the benefit of others. These ordinary Christians sought to show hospitality (cf. Rom 12:13).

In our busy modern culture, we must fight to overcome the many challenges to practicing hospitality: (1) overcommitment, (2) intentional isolation; (3) addiction to comfort; (4) selfishness; (5) pride; and (6) wanting recognition for our acts of service. Following the lead of this first-century couple can help. Their actions demonstrate what happens when Christians understand the grace of Jesus—the grace of the One who welcomes us into God's family and is preparing a place for us (John 14:1-7). I encourage you to look for ways to practice hospitality, whether that involves welcoming orphans, hosting missionaries, or sharing a meal with your neighbors.

Paul's Work Ethic (18:3-4)

Is there a better model of hard work than the one Paul provides? The man is always on the go; he never misses a chance to preach; he's writing faith-building letters in his off hours; and oh, by the way, he makes tents!

Elsewhere Paul mentions that he supported himself (Acts 20:34; 1 Cor 4:12; 1 Thess 2:9; 2 Thess 3:7-9; cf. 2 Cor 11:7), but only here in Acts 18:3 are we told about his trade. Some of the church fathers rendered the term translated "tent maker" as "leather worker." Since tents were often made of leather, this description is likely true in a sense; moreover, tent makers probably used their skills on other types of leather products, too. Some suggest Paul was more of a cloth worker, who manufactured tents using goat's hair (*cillicium*). Regardless of exactly what his job involved, Paul, like other rabbis, knew how to work with his hands—not just with his mind. He was able to do what others have to do; he could make a living in a secular vocation. While in his letters to the Corinthians Paul encouraged believers to compensate pastors, he refused to take any support from them. He wanted to avoid any obstacle to the gospel's progress (1 Cor 9:7-14; cf. Gal 6:6).

Throughout his week Paul made tents and surely witnessed about the faith during the course of the day. On the Sabbath he preached in the synagogue (v. 4). He picked up where he left off in previous towns, testifying that Jesus is the Messiah. He "reasoned" and "tried to persuade people." He told them to repent and put their faith in Jesus and then left the results to God.

After Silas and Timothy arrived (v. 5), probably with funds, Paul would transition into full-time preaching ministry. But during the wait for such support, Paul remained *flexible*. It appears that his years of service to the church included seasons in which he was fully funded and times when he needed to resort to tent making to stay fed. Paul learned to be content in Christ no matter the season (Phil 4:11-13). That's a lesson every Christian should embrace.

Paul was not effective merely because he was a gifted teacher; by God's grace he also *worked* extremely hard (1 Cor 15:10). National Basketball Association all-star Kevin Durant once quipped, "Hard work beats talent when talent doesn't work" (http://www.nba.com/thunder /team/kevin_durant.html). I love that quote. To me it's a great reminder that Christians should value and pursue a noble work ethic, trusting God to bless their efforts even in situations in which skill alone might fall short. Paul told the Romans, "Do not lack diligence in zeal; be fervent in the Spirit; serve the Lord" (Rom 12:11). I have read lots of biographies about great saints, and they share one common denominator: they weren't lazy! (I've noticed, in fact, that no one writes biographies about lazy people.)

Please don't take this the wrong way. Each of us requires rest. In fact, we work best when we live in an established rhythm of work and rest. But we must not think that lounging by the pool or sleeping in all day or vacationing is what life is all about. We must work hard in all of our endeavors, as unto the Lord (cf. Col 3:23). We've got to stay on mission as Paul did.

In the world of ministry and mission, so-called tent making or bivocational ministry is becoming increasingly important. In fact, the SBC International Mission Board is calling for more business people and retirees to enter the mission field *in order to send more people to the nations without the burden of fully funding them first.* This approach is also a blessing as such Christians go overseas equipped to share both the gospel and valuable trades that can aid families facing financial hardships. And Ruth Simmons comments on how people are creatively using their vocations to get the gospel message into hard-to-enter countries:

> A tentmaker couple translated the New Testament for five million Muslims while he did university teaching and she tutored English! A science teacher evangelized his students in rural Kenya, and preached every third Sunday in the local church. A symphony violinist in Singapore had Bible studies with fellow musicians. A faculty person and an engineer set up a Christian bookstore in the Arab Gulf region. ("Tentmakers Needed for World Evangelization," quoted in Fernado, *Acts,* 498–99)

All Christians should consider how they might leverage their vocations for the good of the nations.

Working a secular job is no less important than working full-time as a clergyman: those in both positions can use their gifts and opportunities to help build Christ's kingdom. The Bible, in fact, is filled with mentions of godly saints who held various vocations. Your job gives you the opportunity not only to provide for basic needs but also to love neighbors, to display Christ-honoring integrity, to speak the good news (either during work or in conversations after hours), and to make the gospel known around the world using whatever means the Lord gives you.

Stage 2: Full-Time Ministry
ACTS 18:5-8

Paul is able to transition from bivocational ministry into full-time ministry once his companions, Silas and Timothy, arrive in Corinth. Let's consider three aspects of this next stage in Paul's journey: (1) support, (2) opposition, and (3) fruitfulness.

Support (18:5)

In verse 5 we see that Paul was "devoted" to the Word of God. This term carries the idea of being "absorbed" or "engrossed" in a work. Previously the apostle was making tents and preaching as he could, but with the arrival of his old friends, he's giving all of his attention to the Word. I like how the NLT translates verse 5: "And *after* Silas and Timothy came down from Macedonia, Paul spent *all his time* preaching the Word" (emphasis added).

How was Paul able to set aside the tent-making business? It seems Luke is here referring to the generous gifts given by the Macedonian churches, like Philippi, who financially supported Paul so that he could devote all of his time to making Jesus known. Consider these two texts (the first was written to the Philippians, and the second was addressed to the Corinthians):

> And you Philippians know that in the early days of the gospel, when I left Macedonia, no church shared with me in the matter of giving and receiving except you alone. For even in Thessalonica you sent gifts for my need several times. (Phil 4:15-16)

> When I was present with you and in need, I did not burden anyone, since the brothers who came from Macedonia supplied my needs. (2 Cor 11:9)

In addition to delivering financial support, Silas and Timothy probably also brought an encouraging report regarding the Thessalonians (see 1 Thess 3:6-7). Thus, the fellowship of Silas and Timothy, the news of the Thessalonians, and the generous gifts of the Macedonians strengthened the apostle.

This passage illustrates the truth that the whole body of Christ is important in fulfilling the mission of the church. You may not be a skilled Bible teacher, but if you can financially support the ministry of the Word, then you're playing a vital role in making sure the gospel is shared! You may be so busy at home that you can't help out in the children's ministry, but if you are discipling your own kids around the breakfast table, you are playing a vital role in spreading the gospel. It takes the whole body of Christ to get the gospel to the whole world.

When Paul talks about generous giving in 2 Corinthians 8–9, including the example of the Macedonians, he reminds the church that Jesus has given us the greatest motivation for being cheerful, generous givers:

For you know the grace of our Lord Jesus Christ: Though he was rich,
for your sake he became poor, so that by his poverty you might become
rich. (2 Cor 8:9)

Jesus gave everything so that we might be spiritually rich in him. The
more we understand the grace of Jesus, the more generous we will be.

Opposition (18:6)

It wasn't long before Jews opposed Paul's message about the crucified
and risen Jesus. And when they did, Paul—just as he did in Pisidian
Antioch—shifted his focus to the Gentiles (v. 6; cf. 13:45-48). He even
shook out his garments as a sign of protest against their hard-heartedness, just as he had shaken off his sandals previously in response to stubborn listeners (13:51). As he did so, he also used an image from Ezekiel's
prophecy to declare that those who refused to repent were bringing
judgment on their own heads (cf. Ezk 3:16-19; 33:1-9). Paul had done
his job, he knew, in preaching the message. Because the Jews refused to
listen, he moved on to the Gentiles (a pattern that will continue: 19:8-9;
28:23-28). Later Paul told the Ephesian elders he was innocent of the
blood of all, for he had proclaimed the whole counsel of God to Jews
and Greeks (20:18-31, esp. 26-27).

Anytime we speak the gospel to unbelievers, we must tell them
they're responsible for responding to the message. Let's do our job and
leave the results to God.

Fruitfulness (18:7-8)

Where does Paul go after being run out of the synagogue? Next door!
A man named Titius Justus, a God fearer, apparently became a believer
during Paul's synagogue ministry. Titius opened his home to Paul and
to the new church, although the Jews surely hated the idea of Christians
meeting next door to the synagogue. And they had to be even more
angered when the ruler of their synagogue, Crispus, professed faith in
Jesus! Paul mentions Crispus in his letter to the Corinthians as being
one of the few people he actually baptized (1 Cor 1:14-16). Crispus
probably had a teachable Berean spirit and, after carefully considering
Paul's teaching against what he knew from the Old Testament, declared,
"Jesus is Lord" and followed in baptism.

Many other Corinthians also believed, and presumably many
Gentiles were among them. In time the church in Corinth was made

up of many working-class people and a few "powerful" people of "noble birth" (1 Cor 1:26-31). Paul preached the message of the cross to those of every social class and regardless of ethnicity. By God's grace, many were saved (1 Cor 1:17–2:5).

The fact that the ruler of the synagogue was converted adds force to the truth that the gospel is powerful enough to transform anyone (Rom 1:16). To put Crispus's conversion in modern terms, we might imagine that Christian missionaries enter a hostile Muslim context and slowly build relationships with the people there. In time they are introduced to a local imam, and after a series of conversations, that Muslim leader becomes a Christian! Is such a thing really possible? Yes! Because the gospel is true and life changing.

The work in Corinth started off rather slowly (especially during the tent-making phase), but over time Paul's ministry produced fruit. This is a great indicator that we need to take the long view in terms of evaluating ministry effectiveness. Though it's sometimes difficult to maintain patience in this fast-food, microwave culture, where we want to see immediate results, we will need to go through slow seasons before seeing fruit. So keep being faithful to the mission, and ask God to bless your efforts.

Stage 3: Weakness and Fear
ACTS 18:9-10

Despite such remarkable success in outreach, Paul's confidence seems to evaporate by verse 9. He acknowledges his weakness in 1 Corinthians 2:3, and his condition is evident from the Lord's word of encouragement here.

Paul seems to be ready to quit at this point, even after great fruitfulness. Given his previous trials in general and his trials in Corinth in particular, maybe Paul was too tired to enjoy these evangelistic blessings. So was Paul experiencing what some call burnout? That theory is possible because when we're overworking, we tend to find it difficult to delight in our work.

We will never know all the reasons for Paul's condition here, but what most blesses me when I read this passage is that even the apostle Paul needed encouragement in order to press on.

Up to this point Paul's missionary visits have been relatively brief due to opposition. But this time the Lord encourages Paul's spirit through a gentle rebuke, a strong mandate, and some sovereign promises. Paul needed these in order to remain in Corinth.

The Lord's Gentle Rebuke (18:9a)

In verse 9 the Lord tells Paul something he has been saying to his people for centuries: "Don't be afraid." We sometimes think of Paul being immune to fear. But apparently the opposition and Corinthian context frightened him. He wasn't the first messenger to need the gentle rebuke about not being fearful, and he wasn't the last to need it either. Paul was like a boxer that needed his corner man to encourage him to get back in the ring and go another round.

How loving of the Lord to speak to Paul in this vision! Kent Hughes comments on the Lord's grace here:

> The vision and its opening words—the fact that God made the effort to encourage Paul not to fear—meant that God loved and cared for his ambassador. This assurance ministered to Paul's heart, just as 1 John 4:18 teaches us: "There is no fear in love. But perfect love drives out fear." The simple words in the vision filled Paul's heart with God's love, and fear was put to flight. Time and time again the Scriptures tell us to fear not—to stop worrying about tomorrow, to stop borrowing trouble—because we are divinely loved, and God's love is enough! (*Acts*, 241–42)

As followers of Christ, we don't need to fear man because the sovereign King cares for us. The psalmist says,

> *When I am afraid,*
> *I will trust in you.*
> *In God, whose word I praise,*
> *in God I trust; I will not fear.*
> *What can mere mortals do to me?* . . .
>
> *This I know: God is for me.*
> *In God, whose word I praise,*
> *in the LORD, whose word I praise,*
> *in God I trust; I will not be afraid.*
> *What can mere humans do to me?* (Ps 56:3-4,9-11)

God *loves* his people. We can trust him. We have no reason to fear humans.

The Lord's Strong Mandate (18:9b)

In the face of intimidation, Paul is told by the Lord to open his mouth and boldly proclaim the truth (cf. Eph 6:18-20). This suggests that Paul went through a season in which he was tempted to be silent, though that's difficult to imagine! Whatever was behind his state of mind here, he needed to be told to keep on speaking about the Messiah because only through hearing about Jesus can people come to faith in Jesus (cf. Rom 10:17).

The Lord doesn't tell Paul to keep on speaking because Paul is so good at it. Elsewhere, Paul mentions the brother who is "praised among all the churches for his gospel ministry" (2 Cor 8:18), suggesting some other preachers were more gifted than he. Paul obviously had remarkable gifts, but that's not the primary reason the Lord gives this mandate here. Instead, God told him to speak because Jesus was gathering a people in Corinth. And what he was doing in that city wasn't about Paul; it was about fulfilling the Lord's own will. God delights in using the weak to accomplish his purposes and to magnify himself (cf. 2 Cor 12:9-10).

Many Christians aren't afraid to serve, but they are afraid to speak. And many assume they're not gifted enough or powerful enough for the Lord's work of making the gospel known. Even Paul experienced timidity and weakness. But *in spite of* this, the Lord commissioned him— not *because of* his oratorical gifts and his commanding presence. So be encouraged! The Lord uses ordinary, fragile people (2 Cor 4:7). Cast your insufficiencies on the Lord's totally sufficiency, and you will find that weakness is the secret strength of God's ambassadors.

The Lord's Sovereign Promises (18:10)

The Lord first promises Paul this: "I am with you." This guarantee of God's presence basically repeats Jesus's words in the Great Commission (Matt 28:20). This same promise was made during the callings of Moses (Exod 3:2-12), Joshua (Josh 1:1-9), and Jeremiah (Jer 1:5-10). Because the Lord is with his servants, they can persevere in the mission.

The second promise was unique to Paul's situation: no one would *attack* Paul to *harm* him. In other cities Paul was attacked and harmed, but in this location the Lord made a promise of protection that would cover him throughout a certain window of time (Hughes, *Acts,* 243).

While we can't claim this protection of an attack-free witness, we too can be certain that our lives and times are in the Lord's hands. We can trust him in every situation. We can be assured that Romans 8:28 is true for every believer!

The final promise assured Paul of the Lord's sovereignty in salvation. In it he tells Paul to go on speaking because "I have many people in this city." To this Paul doesn't reply, "Well, since you already have people here, Lord, I'll go to the next town." No, Paul accepts the Lord's words to mean that some people in Corinth will be saved when he preaches the gospel to them. In other words, the Lord was letting Paul know that some people in Corinth were Jesus's property even though they hadn't realized it yet. Paul, therefore, needed to go on speaking the gospel with confidence because Jesus was determined to have a people in Corinth.

Now you might be tempted to think, *I wish I had such promises to go on when it comes to sharing about Jesus.* Take heart because you do! The Lord has already told us that he is with us (cf. Heb 13:5) and that he is drawing people to himself (cf. John 6:37,39). And while we can't claim God's final promise to Paul exactly, we do have God's promise to work for the good of his people (cf. Rom 8:28). With that in mind, we must daily fill our minds with the promises of God. That, in fact, is how we fight fear today. So saturate your mind and heart with the Lord's sovereign and sweet promises.

Several of my historical heroes experienced serious bouts of discouragement, fear, and depression. Zack Eswine recently released a book entitled *Spurgeon's Sorrows*. Consider what acclaimed preacher Charles Spurgeon had to say on the reality of sorrow:

> "I am the subject of depressions of spirit so fearful that I hope none of you ever get to such extremes of wretchedness as I go to." (Quoted in Eswine, 15)

> "I wonder every day that there are not more suicides, considering the troubles in this life." (Quoted in Eswine, 119)

> "The Road to sorrow has been well trodden, it is the regular sheep track to heaven, and all the flock of God have had to pass along it." (Quoted in Eswine, 17)

But also consider Spurgeon's counsel to look to God's promises, providence, and strength:

> An ointment for every wound, a cordial for every faintness, a remedy for every disease. Blessed is he who is skilled in heavenly pharmacy and knows how to lay hold on the healing virtues of the promises of God! ("Obtaining Promises")

To be cast down is often the best thing that could happen to us. ("Sweet Stimulants for the Fainting Soul")

It is an unspeakable consolation that our Lord Jesus knows this experience. ("The Roots of Depression")

From both Paul the apostle and Charles Spurgeon, we can learn about the necessity of leaning on the cane of God's grace. In your sorrows, meditate on the promises of God; draw near to Jesus, the Man of Sorrows; and trust in God's providence. What this means practically is that in your sorrows you don't need to skip worship gatherings. You need to listen to Scripture. When facing trials, you must not remove yourself from community. Instead, press in to God's Word, be around God's people, and allow the Lord of promises to rejuvenate you.

Stage 4: Long-Term Discipleship
ACTS 18:11-17

This is the first time Paul stays an extended period in a city. He uses the extra time to disciple this new congregation, grounding them in the Scriptures.

Then in verses 12-17 we see how the vision God provided him prepared Paul for a legal assault by the Jews. They leveled a complaint to Gallio, claiming that Paul was persuading people to worship God in ways contrary to the law. In the long run, Gallio dismisses the whole matter, refusing to get involved in some internal theological debate. Paul goes free as a result.

The person attacked by proxy is actually Crispus's successor, Sosthenes. We're not told why Sosthenes was beaten or who was behind the violence. It could be that the Jews attacked him because he, too, was on the verge of becoming a Christian or because he had already become one (cf. 1 Cor 1:1). Jews may have attacked him simply because they were upset about their loss of pubic image. Or perhaps the Gentiles attacked him in a moment of anti-Semitic rage. All we know is this: the Lord kept his promise to Paul. He really did protect him. And he protected him on this occasion in an ordinary way—not through a miraculous escape but through a judicial decision.

So Paul stays for a longer period of time in Corinth, grounding the saints in the Scriptures as he rests in the promises of God. The Lord in his grace and sovereignty may give us longer seasons of discipleship in some places than in others. Let's make sure we are expounding the

Word of Christ and exalting the Christ of the Word no matter the duration of our assignments.

Paul Returns to Antioch
ACTS 18:18-22

Here we have a travelogue that shows how Paul completed the final part of his second missionary journey, returning to the church in Antioch where it began (15:35-41).

Paul must have intended to go to Jerusalem before going to Cenchreae because he shaved his hair to conclude a Nazirite vow (cf. Num 6:2,5,9,18). Doing so may have been Paul's expression of thanks to God for protecting him at Corinth. The ritual would include offering a sacrifice at the temple and burning hair devoted to God on the altar (Johnson, *Let's Study Acts*, 230). The action shows that Paul never disregarded the law's relevance to Jews, contrary to false charges from others (ibid.; cf. Acts 18:13; 21:21-26; 1 Cor 9:20). John Stott comments,

> Once Paul had been liberated from the attempt to be justified
> by the law, his conscience was free to take part in practices
> which, being ceremonial or cultural, belonged to the "matters
> indifferent," perhaps on this occasion in order to conciliate
> the Jewish Christian leaders he was going to see in Jerusalem
> (cf. 21:23). (*Message of Acts*, 301)

Though Jerusalem isn't mentioned in the Greek here, most interpreters see it as implied by the verbs "went up" and "went down" (v. 22; cf. 11:2; 21:15). Paul visited "the church" there (v. 22).

This passage helps us look forward to what will become the primary place of ministry during Paul's third missionary journey, Ephesus. The Spirit blocked Paul's attempt to minister there previously (16:6), but on this return trip he visits briefly, teaching in the synagogue and promising to return "if God wills" (v. 21), which is a practical expression of belief in God's sovereignty. Paul left his friends Aquila and Priscilla there. They will give some important instruction to a character we'll meet in the next chapter, Apollos (vv. 24-28; cf. 1 Cor 3:5-9).

Paul finally returns to Antioch, the sending church, concluding the second missionary journey. We're reminded again that Paul wasn't an isolated missionary. He ministered in association with the church.

This chapter reminds us that Paul loved the gospel, the church, and the King's mission. So let's follow this model. Paul encountered weakness and fear but found strength in God's abundant grace. So let's look to the sufficiency of God's grace in our trials. Paul resolved to preach the cross in the midst of an arrogant and immoral culture. So by the power of the Spirit, let's do the same.

Reflect and Discuss

1. What kind of trials had Paul experienced before arriving in Corinth? What additional trials did he encounter there?
2. What facts about Aquila and Priscilla most resonate with you?
3. What does it mean for Christians to be "tent makers"? Explain why we need tent makers today.
4. What allowed Paul to switch to ministering full-time in Corinth? What does this teach about the body of Christ's role in advancing the gospel?
5. Why does Paul keep preaching to the Jews in the synagogue?
6. Why should the conversions in Corinth encourage us?
7. How did the Lord rejuvenate Paul (18:9-10)?
8. What should Christians do when experiencing weakness and fear?
9. Explain how God fulfilled his promise to protect Paul in Corinth.
10. What does Paul's return trip teach about the importance of the church? Take a few moments to pray for your local church in light of this passage.

Word-Driven Disciple Makers

ACTS 18:23–19:10

Main Idea: This section of Acts reinforces the *importance* of Word-driven disciple making and gives *illustrations* of what it looks like to teach and receive gospel-centered instruction.

I. **Paul: Following Up with New Congregations (18:23)**
II. **Aquila and Priscilla: Filling in the Gaps for Apollos (18:24-26)**
III. **Apollos: Helping Believers, Refuting the Jews (18:27-28)**
IV. **Paul: Evangelizing the Ephesians (19:1-10)**
   A. The disciples of John (19:1-7)
   B. The synagogue (19:8-9a)
   C. The lecture hall of Tyrannus (19:9b-10)

The risen Jesus gave his followers this Great Commission:

> *All authority has been given to me in heaven and on earth. Go, therefore, and make disciples of all nations, baptizing them in the name of the Father and of the Son and of the Holy Spirit, teaching them to observe everything I have commanded you. And remember, I am with you always, to the end of the age.* (Matt 28:18-20)

The book of Acts is filled with examples of God's people fulfilling this holy mandate. This section of Acts reinforces the *importance* of Word-driven disciple making and gives us some *illustrations* of what it looks like. It introduces us to a variety of teachers and students in a variety of contexts. As we observe these examples, we should examine our own disciple-making practices.

Paul: Following Up with New Churches
ACTS 18:23

In verse 23 the third missionary journey begins. After stopping in Antioch (v. 22), undoubtedly giving a report of his second journey, Paul retraces his steps (v. 23). His route most likely included a visit to the churches of Derbe, Lystra, Iconium, and Pisidian Antioch. John Polhill notes that the visits to the Galatian religion and Phrygia might have accounted for the area farther north and may indicate that Paul planted churches in the northern portion of the Roman province of Galatia on his second journey (*Acts*, 395; cf. 16:6).

Paul's burden here is much like what he expressed previously in 15:36 at the beginning of the second journey—a desire to follow up with the new churches. He desired to go to Ephesus, but he first chose to revisit his spiritual children. He agonized over the spiritual maturity of recent converts (Gal 4:19) and rejoiced at their progress in the faith (1 Thess 2:19-20). Paul's evangelistic zeal was mingled with a passion for spiritual growth and healthy congregations. We too must desire earnestly to see people converted and to see them grow in grace—in the context of healthy churches.

Aquila and Priscilla: Filling in the Gaps for Apollos
ACTS 18:24-26

While Paul was traveling, a man from Alexandria, Apollos, arrived in Ephesus. He had an impressive résumé and striking teaching abilities, but Apollos needed some further instruction in the faith. So Aquila and Priscilla, remaining in Ephesus for a time, filled in the gaps in his understanding.

Apollos was a well-educated man. His native Alexandria was an intellectual center renowned for its library. Years earlier the Alexandrian community produced a Greek translation of the Old Testament. The city was also home to famous philosophical scholars like Philo and later religious scholars like Clement, Athanasius, and Origen.

Apollos appears to be a Christian. A few clues point this direction. First, he "accurately" taught the way of the Lord (v. 25). Second, the Holy Spirit energized his passion. When Luke says he was "fervent in spirit," the Greek includes the article "the" before the word *spirit*, which seems to indicate "the Holy Spirit." This expression also appears in Romans 12:11. In both places it seems to refer to the Holy Spirit (so J. Dunn, 88, in Polhill, *Acts*, 396). In contrast, the "disciples of John" were in a different position (19:2-7). They weren't believers yet.

The reason some feel reticent to label Apollos a believer is that Luke says Apollos "knew only John's baptism" (18:25), and since the Holy Spirit is the distinguishing mark between the baptism of John and that of Jesus (1:5), they contend Apollos must not have been a Christian. But I'm not persuaded.

Nevertheless, something was indeed deficient in his understanding. I take Luke's mention that Apollos knew only the baptism of John to mean that he didn't know about the new covenant baptism *practice* established by Jesus. Aquila and Priscilla thus needed to explain baptism "more accurately" (v. 26). This godly couple would have taught him how, in Christian baptism, the triune God places his name on his people (Matt 28:19). The ordinance vividly illustrates our union with Christ in his death and resurrection (Rom 6:3-4; Gal 3:27). It seems to me that Apollos understood, believed, and preached the gospel of Christ, but he knew nothing of this ordinance in which the use of water preaches the gospel (Johnson, *Let's Study Acts*, 232). Apollos lived in a unique historical situation that caused him to need some clarification on this point.

Priscilla and Aquila give us a good model of how a high-capacity teacher should be corrected. They don't rebuke Apollos publicly. They don't embarrass or shame him. They demonstrate humility and compassion in addressing him, but they also demonstrate *conviction*. That is, they don't just let the matter of his deficiency go. Instead, they address the gap in his instruction in a Christ-honoring way. They take him aside, perhaps to their *home* (v. 26 NIV), and gently explain baptism fully. Every Christian should take note of this couple's *gentle persuasion method*, which is advocated elsewhere in the New Testament and demonstrated by Jesus, the Servant of the Lord (Matt 12:17-21; 2 Tim 2:24-26). We shouldn't try to correct brothers and sisters by using an argumentative, critical spirit; rather, we need to use an open Bible and a loving tone.

Sometimes disciple making will resemble this scene involving Apollos, Aquila, and his wife. You may not need to correct a teacher, but you may need to pull a brother or sister aside to discuss a doctrinal matter privately. Perhaps you will have the opportunity to disciple a younger believer in private, showing him or her what Scripture says about the essentials of the faith in a setting that invites questions. Remember, this type of personal disciple making is important. No one needs to stand behind a pulpit to teach.

Apollos's attitude in this passage is instructive, too. Think about it. This guy probably had far more education than Aquila and Priscilla combined, but he maintained a teachable heart. He listened to their counsel and adopted their position. This is a reminder that we should never think we are beyond the need for further instruction in God's Word—no matter how long we have been Christians or how many degrees we hold.

Apollos: Helping Believers, Refuting the Jews
ACTS 18:27-28

Regardless of whether you consider Apollos a Christian prior to his meeting with Aquila and Priscilla, he is clearly a believer after it. In verse 27 Apollos is powerfully teaching others. Apollos decides to go to "Achaia," that is Corinth, where Paul recently ministered the Word for an extended time. Apollos is mentioned in several places in 1 Corinthians (1 Cor 1:12; 3:4-6,22; 4:6), and it's possible that some Corinthian believers invited him there. But more likely, Aquila and Priscilla stimulated his interest in Corinth by passing along a report of how God had been at work in that city (Polhill, *Acts,* 397). The believers of the early church in Ephesus wrote a letter of recommendation to the saints in Corinth, which was a common early church practice (cf. Rom 16:1; 2 Cor 3:1-3).

When Apollos arrived, he "was a great help to those who by grace had believed" (v. 27). The saints in Corinth believed not just because Paul's teaching had been powerful but because of God's saving grace at work among them (cf. 3:26; 11:18; 13:48; Eph 2:8-9). Apollos watered what Paul had planted in Corinth, but Paul was quick to point out the real hero behind their efforts: "God gave the growth" (1 Cor 3:6). The Lord greatly used Paul and Apollos in the lives of the young believers at Corinth (1 Cor 3:8). They served as "God's coworkers" (1 Cor 3:9). But Paul assigned all glory to God, not to the messengers (1 Cor 3:21-23).

While we should honor faithful teachers, we should not deify them. First Corinthians rebukes believers for such idolatry. If you don't think this issue is a real problem today, just listen carefully to some Christians talk about certain speakers, share stories about how they went to great trouble and expense to visit a big conference featuring a particular individual, or most sadly, consider what has happened to a few congregations who lost their own "Apollos" to another assignment. To the Corinthians who were arguing over who was the best preacher, Paul wrote, "Let the one who boasts, boast in the Lord" (1 Cor 1:31), and, "Let no one boast in human leaders" (1 Cor 3:21). Be thankful for Word-driven disciple makers, but worship and adore the triune God alone.

Apollos also had a powerful evangelistic ministry in Corinth (v. 28). Like Paul he explained how the Messiah must suffer and rise and that Jesus was this Messiah (cf. 17:3; 18:5). Apollos's thorough knowledge of the Old Testament equipped him to be an effective evangelist to the Jews in Corinth.

Later, when Paul wrote 1 Corinthians from Ephesus, he mentioned Apollos being there with him (1 Cor 16:12). Apollos's ministry blessed many, and Paul must have appreciated having another laborer in the harvest field (Matt 9:37-38).

Paul: Evangelizing the Ephesians
ACTS 19:1-10

While Apollos was watering the seed in Corinth, Paul arrived in Ephesus, the major stop on this third missionary journey. Paul expounded the Scriptures and exalted the Savior (1) to the disciples of John, (2) to the Jews in the synagogue, and (3) to many residents of Asia in the lecture hall of Tyrannus.

The Disciples of John (19:1-7)

In chapter 19 we find Paul first encountering "some disciples" (v. 1). Unfortunately, these people weren't true disciples of Jesus; rather, they were "twelve almost Christians" (Begg, "About Twelve Almost Christians"). They resembled Apollos in some ways, but the differences outweigh the similarities (Johnson, *Let's Study Acts,* 235). Apollos taught accurately about Jesus and was fervent in the Holy Spirit, but the same can't be said for this group.

Perhaps Paul observed something in their behavior and demeanor, leading him to ask them some important spiritual questions. This is a good possibility since it's clear that this group didn't possess the Holy Spirit, who indwells all believers (e.g., John 14:17; Rom 8:14-16; Gal 3:1-5; Eph 1:13-14; 3:16; 4:30). Paul wrote to the Romans clearly and emphatically: "If anyone does not have the Spirit of Christ, he does not belong to him" (Rom 8:9).

After a discussion about the Spirit, baptism, and the Christ (vv. 2-4), they were baptized "into the name of the Lord Jesus" (v. 5). Paul then laid hands on them, and they experienced the Spirit's presence and power in a mini-Pentecost sort of way, speaking in tongues and prophesying (v. 6).

Surely these disciples had at some level heard of the Spirit since they were familiar with John the Baptist, who spoke of the Holy Spirit (cf. Matt 3:11). But they hadn't heard of the fulfillment of John's ministry—that the Holy Spirit had come into people's experience (Johnson, *Let's Study Acts,* 235). They were ignorant of Pentecost (Stott, *Message of Acts,* 304). John Stott describes their condition well:

In a word, they were still living in the Old Testament which culminated with John the Baptist. They understood neither that the new age had been ushered in by Jesus, nor that those who believe in him and are baptized into him receive the distinctive blessing of the new age, the indwelling Spirit. (Ibid.)

But after Paul explained the gospel to them, they believed by the grace of God.

Later Paul wrote to the Corinthians, urging them to "examine" themselves to see if they were of the faith (2 Cor 13:5). In 1 John we also see tests: every believer will pass a "doctrinal test," an "ethical test," and an "experiential test." Doctrinally, they will believe in the real Jesus and what he did (1 John 1:1-4; 2:2,22-23; 4:2-3,10,15; 5:1,5). Ethically, they will walk in light and love (1 John 1:6; 2:6,9-11,29; 3:6-10,14; 4:8). Experientially, they will know the abiding presence of the Spirit (1 John 3:24; 4:6,13). Paul forces John the Baptist's disciples to examine themselves, and doing so leads to their conversion.

Often religious people, like these disciples, are unconverted people. One need only look at popular cults—like Mormonism, Jehovah's Witnesses, and Christian Science—to find examples of what I mean. Those who often attend Christian religious events but can't articulate the basic truths of the gospel and who give no signs of regeneration also serve as examples. This is why we must explain the true gospel to religious types; they too are in need of salvation.

What should we make of these disciples speaking in other tongues and prophesying after believing? These signs, like those experienced by the believers in Samaria, were visible and public indicators that they possessed the Spirit. But this pattern is not universal in Acts. Not every convert experiences such manifestations. The norm is repentance and faith in Jesus and possession of the Spirit. And the visible profession of faith is baptism.

The disciples of John at first had some external form of religion, but until Paul told them about the gospel, they had not been changed truly and internally. But praise God, he changes all sorts of people—from the hedonists to the religious types.

I have always been moved by the story of John Wesley's conversion, which bears some similarity to what we see here. Wesley was the son of a minister, Samuel Wesley, and of a godly mother, Susanna. Wesley attended Oxford and became double professor of Greek and logic at Lincoln College. He served as his father's assistant and was later ordained by the church (Hughes, *Acts,* 245). While at Oxford, Wesley was a member of the "Holy Club," a group dedicated to wholeheartedly pursuing godliness. He then became a missionary to the American Indians in Georgia.

After failing in his work among them, he was forced to return to England. He wrote, "I went to America to convert the Indians; but, oh, who shall convert me?" (cited in Hughes, *Acts,* 245). By God's grace, however, in America he had encountered some Moravians, *a Christian group that emphasized Bible reading, prayer, and worship.* Their spiritual vitality had a tremendous impact on him. He sought out one of the leaders, having become convinced of his own unbelief. Wesley wrote in his journal about his conversion the night of May 24, 1738:

> In the evening I went very unwillingly to a society in Aldersgate Street where one was reading Luther's preface to the Epistle to the Romans. About a quarter before nine, while he was describing the change which God works in the heart through faith in Christ, I felt my heart strangely warmed. I felt I did trust in Christ, Christ alone, for salvation; and an assurance was given me, that he had taken away my sins, even mine, and saved me from the law of sin and death. (Quoted in Hughes, *Acts,* 245)

Prior to that experience, Wesley was a committed religious man who even traveled overseas as a missionary. But in spite of his theological knowledge, he wasn't truly born anew. He needed to experience and embrace the reality of the living Savior. Many religious people are in a similar position today. May God grant us grace to proclaim the gospel to them so that they too may come to saving faith in Christ.

The Synagogue (19:8-9a)

As was his custom, Paul evangelized in the synagogue, proclaiming Jesus as Messiah. He had already visited the Ephesian synagogue briefly (18:19-21), but now he's able to stay longer. Unlike some other synagogue experiences, Paul taught this time for "three months" before opposition ensued. That suggests the Ephesians were more open to Paul's message than previous Jewish audiences. Some of them became believers, but others persisted in unbelief. The latter slandered the Way publicly, as Paul once did (22:4), bringing opposition once again (cf. 1 Cor 16:8-9). The "hardened" Jews were rejecting the only way to God (John 14:6).

The Lecture Hall of Tyrannus (19:9b-10)

As in Corinth (18:7), Paul took the new converts to a different location in order to continue his evangelistic exposition. They went to the lecture hall of Tyrannus. Some traditions claim Paul taught during the typical siesta times in Ephesus, between 11:00 and 4:00. This would make sense if Paul made tents in Ephesus (see 20:34). I like to imagine Paul taking a break from tent making to expound the Word, once again displaying his exemplary work ethic. This went on for "two years" (v. 10), a long stay for Paul.

Since the hall was a public place, Paul could evangelize all sorts of people, both Jews and Greeks, there. It's possible Epaphras became a Christian there during this time and then helped establish the congregation in Colossae and probably many others (Col 1:7; 4:13; Rev 2–3). The origins of many of the churches in Revelation, in fact, probably date from this period (Rev 1:4,11; Johnson, *Let's Study Acts*, 236). Here then is another example of the benefit of planting the gospel/churches in major cities, as Paul did in Ephesus. From city centers other churches in other areas are often started.

Conclusion

Luke presents to Theophilus a range of people who need Christian instruction. Some people know Christ and simply need encouragement and reinforcement, as Paul's return visits in verse 23 illustrate. Others may be genuine Christians, but they lack doctrinal clarity on a particular matter, as Apollos did. Still others are religious but have no understanding of the gospel, as the disciples of John demonstrate. Further, some have heard the gospel but refuse to believe in Christ, as was the case with many unbelieving Jews in Ephesus.

The great news is that many people—of great diversity—will believe the gospel when it's taught to them. The world needs thousands of Bible-teaching, Christ-exalting, Spirit-empowered, prayer-soaked, gospel-centered teachers. The world needs Word-driven disciple makers who will teach others one-on-one in homes, in public settings, in marketplaces, and everywhere in between. So, by the power of the Spirit, with the Word of Christ, let's go make disciples of all nations.

Reflect and Discuss

1. What do Paul's follow-up visits (v. 23) teach about the importance of follow-up discipleship and the value of the local church?
2. What can we learn about instructing leaders from the example of Aquila and Priscilla?
3. What can we learn about how to receive instruction from the example of Apollos?
4. What about the ministry of Apollos most resonates with you?
5. Why do you think Paul thought it necessary to ask these spiritual questions of the "disciples of John the Baptist"?
6. What does Paul's encounter with the disciples of John teach about the need to evangelize religious people?
7. Compare Paul's ministry in the synagogue in Ephesus to previous synagogue experiences.
8. What might a contemporary "lecture hall of Tyrannus" ministry look like today? Where might we have opportunity to publicly evangelize large numbers of people?
9. What were some of the results of Paul's ministry in the lecture hall of Tyrannus?
10. What does this passage teach about making disciples through teaching?

Exalting Jesus Instead of Idols

ACTS 19:10-41

Main Idea: In Paul's extended Word-driven ministry in Ephesus, many Ephesians turned from idols to the living Christ; Luke records some significant events surrounding this spiritual awakening.

I.   The Word Increased and Prevailed (19:10,20).
II. God Displayed His Power (19:11-12).
III. People Magnified Jesus (19:13-17).
IV. Believers Confessed/Renounced Sin (19:18-19).
V.   The Gospel Impacted Social Norms (19:21-41).

When a person is genuinely converted to faith in Jesus, he or she gets *new affections*. Old loves, desires, and interests are replaced with new ones. Those who have become new creations in Christ (2 Cor 5:17) experience a new love for Jesus, his church, and his mission. The converts in Ephesus illustrate this dynamic. The Ephesians loved many things—sports, theater, idols (especially their famed goddess, Artemis), and wealth. But when Paul preached the gospel and the Holy Spirit opened the eyes of many in the city, they experienced a change in affections (v. 17).

If you have ever seen a young man in his late teens get a crush on a girl, then perhaps you have seen how this works. All of a sudden the smitten lad's interests change. He washes the car—like twice a week. He starts wearing cologne—enough to overpower your nose. He gets a job—maybe two jobs. Why? Because he has a new love! His parents may have told him a hundred times before to wash the car, to freshen up, and to get a job, but with his change in interest, they no longer have to tell him! He wants to do these things because he has experienced a change in affections. And that's the sort of thing that happens when we meet Jesus, only in a much greater sense. When affections change, everything changes.

Ephesus was a mighty city with many points of interest. Most notably, Ephesus was the keeper of the renowned temple of Artemis (also known as Diana), the pagan goddess of fertility. Her worshipers believed her image had fallen from heaven and was housed inside her temple.

But with Paul's arrival, a Christian was walking around town preaching a message about a crucified and risen Savior with far more power than Artemis could claim. So some Ephesians exchanged their idols for the worship of the living Christ (cf. 1 Thess 1:9-10).

A phrase that captures Paul's extended ministry in Ephesus is found in 19:23—"a major disturbance about the Way." Indeed, Christ's work through Paul was causing a number of disturbances. Early in the chapter we see the disturbance in the synagogue community when Paul preached about the Messiah (vv. 8-9). Then there were disturbances in cities around Ephesus as residents from various places took the gospel back to their towns and "all the residents of Asia . . . heard the word of the Lord" (v. 10). There were disturbances in the demonic realm, too; we will read of some extraordinary miracles in verses 11-19. Finally, there was a major disturbance in the city center; in response to the gospel's impact on the social customs of Ephesus, a group of protestors opposed the Way (vv. 23-41).

From one point of view, these things created "a major disturbance." But from our point of view, what happened in Ephesus is better called "a great awakening." This chapter has all the signs of a great awakening. In an essay on Jonathan Edwards and *the* Great Awakening, J. I. Packer notes ten elements:

1. God comes down.
2. God's Word pierces.
3. Man's sin is seen.
4. Christ's cross is valued.
5. Change goes deep [which Packer illustrates with 19:18-19].
6. Love breaks out.
7. Joy fills hearts.
8. Each church becomes itself. . . . God is felt to be there, present to bless, in the midst of those who are his.
9. The lost are found.
10. Satan keeps pace. ("The Glory of God and the Reviving of Religion," 100–104)

When we read Acts 19–20 and the book of Ephesians, it's easy to see that Ephesus experienced such a movement as Packer describes. So let's look at some of the notable events surrounding Paul's ministry in Ephesus and this great spiritual awakening.

The Word Increased and Prevailed
ACTS 19:10,20

The awakening in Ephesus began and continued with the proclaimed Word, as discussed previously. Later, when Paul reflected on his ministry in Ephesus, he emphasized how his primary task there involved expounding the Scriptures to everyone (20:20-21,27,31-32).

Luke brackets verses 10-20 with references to "the word of the Lord." In verse 10, a transitional verse, he says, "This went on for two years, so that all the residents of Asia, both Jews and Greeks, heard the word of the Lord." Then, in a summary verse, he says, "In this way the word of the Lord flourished and prevailed" (v. 20). This bracket highlights the major emphasis in Paul's ministry in Ephesus: the Word of the Lord. Additionally, the later report of Paul's critic, Demetrius, also underscores Paul's persuasive teaching (v. 26). Paul's preaching was causing a major disturbance.

All of this points to the fact that what turned Ephesus upside down was Paul's message. The miracles confirmed the validity of Paul's message, displayed the superior power of Jesus over all other forms of power, and were, indeed, impressive. But let's not lose sight of what was primary: the exposition of the Word.

Repeatedly in the book of Acts, Luke reports on how the early church impacted the nations: through the Word of the Lord (cf. 2:41; 6:7; 12:24; 13:49). So if want to know how we can see cities changed and wonder how the affections of idolaters can be changed, we need to preach the Word of Christ. Doing so is key.

I know it *seems* like a hopeless exercise. A little guy going into a massive, powerful city and deciding to teach in the synagogue and then lecturing daily for two years doesn't sound world changing. But just read Acts 19–20. The gospel changed lives then, and it does so today. God has always used the intense preaching of the Word to stimulate spiritual awakening. John Calvin preached once each day, and twice on Sunday during the Geneva reformation (Ferguson, "No Little Disturbance"). Through the Spirit-empowered preaching of Calvin, the city was transformed.

I'm not talking about merely preaching sermons like those you hear from the pastor on Sunday. I am talking about Christians meeting Christ in *his Word* and helping others meet him through the exposition of Scriptures. Intense preaching of the Christ-exalting Scriptures transformed the city of Ephesus. And it can transform our nation today. So let this passage increase your confidence in the power of the proclaimed Word. Just keep explaining and applying it—in small groups, in large groups, one-on-one, in lecture halls, in homes, under a tree in Ethiopia, or anywhere else. For hearing it really does "renew one's life" (Ps 19:7).

God Displayed His Power
ACTS 19:11-12

Luke tells of some wonders that accompanied Paul's message. Unfortunately, passages like these have been misapplied. Religious hucksters on television have told gullible people bizarre things like, "Get this prayer hankie that I have prayed over, and it will heal you. . . . Order yours now for only $99.99." Tom Schreiner told a story about how one such person was marketing prayer carpets. He told superstitious customers that previous buyers had prayed on the carpet and received wonderful things, including vacations to Hawaii and mobile homes (Schreiner, "Power of Lord Jesus")! Such applications are abuses of this passage.

Here Luke is *describing* historical events; he is not *prescribing* an activity that we should mimic. Paul is simply the instrument here. He's not walking around handing out facecloths. In fact, Luke emphatically states that it was "God" who was doing extraordinary miracles. God may choose to do the miraculous today too, but we must not expect him to do so—much less demand it. In this case, in a city steeped in superstition and interest in magic, God kindly condescended to show the Ephesians his sovereign power in a way that would get their attention and draw them to the Savior.

Many Christians want to see a miracle every moment, but little of the typical Christian life involves visible displays of miraculous power. Just read the book of Proverbs. Most of life involves submitting to God's revealed will in the Bible, walking by the Spirit, and pursuing godly wisdom.

So let's have a balanced view of miracles. We must not rule miracles out. God can do whatever he pleases (Ps 115:3). But we must not assume God isn't working when we don't see visible miracles. The greatest miracle, after all, is the new birth. God raised Jesus from the dead, and all who are in Christ will also vacate a tomb! So while we shouldn't start a miracle sweatband ministry, we should keep trusting in the God who raises the dead. We should keep pouring out our hearts to him in prayer, even asking for healing, as James 5:14-16 says. We must keep believing that he will change lives as the gospel is proclaimed.

People Magnified Jesus
ACTS 19:13-17

"The Seven Sons of Sceva" sounds like the name of a modern rock band. Sceva, the biological father of this group, is called a Jewish chief priest. He may have simply claimed this position without actually occupying it. Another possibility is that Sceva really was a chief priest, and his sons turned away from traditional Judaism to practice exorcism.

Jewish exorcists were known for offering strange Hebrew incantations. The Ephesians were attracted to sorcerers, looking to them to provide cures and blessings for a price. It was common for charlatans to borrow names to use in their incantations. So after observing Paul's ministry, this particular group of pretenders decided to cash in on Jesus's name (much like Simon Magus wanted to do in 8:9-24), but their attempt backfired. A better title for these guys, as Alistair Begg quipped, would be "The Seven Streakers of Sceva" ("Reaching the City")!

After trying to add Jesus's name to their hocus-pocus act in order to cast out evil spirits, the seven sons get utterly humiliated. As demons often do in the New Testament, this one testifies to the power of Jesus—this time to his power working through Paul (Polhill, *Acts*, 404; cf. Acts 16:17). The demon essentially says, "I know I can't best Jesus or Paul, but you guys have no power to do anything to me." Because these wizards didn't belong to Jesus, the demon wasn't forced to relinquish control to them. And instead of being exorcised of the evil spirit, the tormented man becomes supernaturally strong and proceeds to whip the sorcerers (cf. Mark 5:3-4). Things got so bad, in fact, that the sons fled the house naked and dripping with blood. So who won the battle? As Matt Chandler commented, "If when the fight started you were wearing pants and when it was over you were no longer wearing pants, you lost" ("Like a Wildfire").

People should magnify Jesus's name in worship, never trying to misuse it for witchcraft. Only Jesus's people have the Spirit of God. This episode shows us the reality and influence of the devil but also the superior power of Jesus over all forms of power (cf. Mark 5:6-7).

The people certainly recognized Jesus's superior power (v. 18). After the sons of Sceva failed in their attempt to combat demonic powers, both Jews and Greeks began revering Jesus's name and esteeming him all the more.

Believers Confessed/Renounced Sin
ACTS 19:18-19

The story continues with a vivid picture of confession and repentance. Luke says "believers" were confessing and disclosing their practices. Apparently some of them realized for the first time that faith in Jesus and participation in magic and the occult were incompatible (Johnson, *Let's Study Acts*, 238). So they burn their books—the scrolls prescribing occult rituals.

It shouldn't shock us that "believers" were burning books. After all, salvation leads to a process of growth—a work of sanctification in which the Spirit shapes us into the image of Christ over time. After believing in Christ, then, there are often practices and ideas that new converts realize they must abandon as they come to understand more about Jesus.

In the Louvre there's a painting by Eustache Le Sueur that dates to 1649. It's entitled "The Sermon of Saint Paul at Ephesus." It shows Paul addressing a crowd while people beneath him burn books. It's one of my favorite pieces in the famed museum, as it conveys a powerful picture of repentance. Those who practiced sorcery confessed their evil practices and burned occult books publicly.

I love that they don't just give the books away or sell them; they destroy them. That was a costly thing to do, considering the total expense of those burned volumes. I've read suggestions of their value ranging from thousands of dollars to millions. Yet the believers wanted a radical break with all that was ungodly in their lives because the Spirit of God produced a deep change in their hearts. Selling the volumes would've only spread the poison of what they contained: Christ's followers are to spread the good news instead.

These Ephesian believers had a new affection. They had a new love for Jesus. Their actions shouted that he was more valuable to them than any god, power, false source of trust, or any amount of money. In Revelation the church in Ephesus is rebuked for abandoning "the love [they] had at first" (Rev 2:2-4). We may begin with passionate adoration of Jesus, but we must not grow cold in our love for the Savior. Continue to cultivate your love for him by confessing secret sins and forsaking ungodly practices (Rev 2:5). Seek his Word and remember that he is your greatest good and your highest joy. Reject all rivals and revere the Son of God, who loved you and gave himself for you (Gal 2:20).

The Gospel Impacted Social Norms
ACTS 19:21-41

After summarizing how the power of Jesus was displayed in Ephesus and spotlighting the triumph of the Word (v. 20), Luke tells about the protest in Ephesus. But before we see how the gospel impacted social norms, we get two verses about Paul's travel plans (vv. 21-22). This gives a glimpse of what's to come in the book of Acts. Paul plans on returning to Jerusalem via Macedonia and Achaia. Then he hopes to fulfill his desire to preach in Rome (cf. Rom 1:13). The Spirit prompts this decision, even though he lets Paul know that trials await him in Jerusalem (20:22-23; 21:10-11). Paul apparently wrote 1 Corinthians during his time here in Ephesus. He sent the letter ahead with Timothy and Erastus (1 Cor 16:5-10), and he later visited Corinth himself (Acts 20:1-2).

Paul's purpose for visiting Jerusalem was to give the poor Jewish believers an offering from the Gentile churches. The gift is a wonderful picture of unity and generosity (cf. Rom 15:25-28; 1 Cor 16:1-4; 2 Cor 8–9). Paul sent his companions, Timothy and Erastus, ahead of him while he remained in Ephesus for a while to allow for these preparations (Johnson, *Let's Study Acts,* 239). We should observe in this passage Paul's heart for evangelism and also his care for the church and for the poor. Let's follow his example.

In verses 23-41 we read the last recorded event in Paul's stay in Ephesus. It's a vivid picture of what happens when people exalt Jesus instead of idols. Paul's gospel-centered, Jesus-exalting, Spirit-empowered ministry impacted the local economy and caused an uproar. The "disturbance" begins with a man named Demetrius, a leader among the silversmiths (v. 24). These craftsmen made silver replicas of the temple of Artemis. People would purchase them as souvenirs and for home altars. These have been found throughout the Mediterranean world. John Polhill describes this temple:

> The temple of Artemis was indeed a hub of Ephesian economic life. It was an impressive building, some 165 feet by 345 feet in dimension and built on a platform 240 by 420 feet. The entire edifice was elaborately adorned in brilliant colors and gold leaf. The altar area was 20 feet square and contained a massive image of the goddess with a veiled head, with animals and birds decorating her head and lower body and numerous breasts from her waist to her neck. The animals

and breasts were symbolic of her status as the ancient Asian Mother Goddess, the goddess of nature who was believed to protect and preserve the fecundity of all living things. (*Acts*, 408–9)

This temple grew so wealthy that it became the main financial institution of Asia, receiving deposits and making loans (ibid.). Clearly, Artemis and the god of money were tied closely together in Ephesus.

The angry Demetrius gathers a crew of craftsmen and delivers his speech (vv. 25-27). Here's his argument: Paul's preaching threatens the craftsmen's idol-making business—both its profitability and its reputation; Paul is misleading people by proclaiming that gods made with hands aren't gods (cf. 17:24,29). To these claims he adds a third argument: Paul's preaching threatens to rob our world-renowned goddess of her rightful glory. This assertion was meant to stir up the emotions of patriotic Ephesians. In making it, he essentially said, "To attack Artemis is to attack Ephesus" (Polhill, *Acts*, 410).

Demetrius has no interest in trying to learn what Paul is teaching. He's driven ultimately by greed ("which is idolatry," Col 3:5), not by his love for the goddess. He's driven by dollars, not doctrine. Many today may not bow down to a statue, but millions bow to the idol of money—oblivious to the fact that it can never satisfy or provide ultimate security (Eccl 5:10; 1 Tim 6:6-10).

What do people do when their idols are threatened? If they don't repent and look to Jesus instead of idols, then they get angry. That's what happens in this story. Instead of saying, "Jesus is Lord. Let's either find a new profession or make some new products," the craftsmen decide to assault the messenger. Chaos ensues. Since the wild rioters can't get to Paul, they take Paul's companions into the amphitheater, which seated around twenty-four thousand people (v. 29). Paul tries to enter the scene and speak on behalf of his brothers Gaius (cf. 20:4) and Aristarchus (cf. 27:2), but Paul's friends (including some high-ranking officers) plead with him to avoid the mob (vv. 30-31). The scene is one of total chaos, with one group shouting one thing and another group shouting something else and some people not even knowing why they are assembled (v. 32)!

The Alexander moment adds to the confusion (v. 33). We aren't told why the Jews put him forward. It was probably to distance themselves from the Christians. But before he can deliver his speech, his voice is drowned out by a two-hour chant: "Great is Artemis of the Ephesians!" (v. 34).

Paul and his companions encountered much persecution in Ephesus from the Jews (20:19) and from the Ephesians (1 Cor 16:8-9; also consider 1 Cor 15:32 and 2 Cor 1:8-9 as possible allusions to this riot). But the Lord delivered his ambassador. On this occasion God used the city clerk—the chief administrative officer—to prevent this ordeal from turning into a violent riot. The clerk was the city's liaison to the Roman provincial government of Asia, which had its seat in Ephesus. If local authorities couldn't control the citizenry, then some of the city's self-governing privileges—enjoyed under the empire's authority— would be jeopardized.

The clerk basically says the worship and glory of Artemis stand secure. The rise of Christianity, he feels, poses no threat to Ephesus's reputation as keeper of the grand temple. He asserts that no earthly movement can threaten one whose image dropped from the heavens. Then he deals with the legal ramifications of the gathering. He states that the two Christians whom they had seized were not guilty of any crime, but if anyone was guilty, it was the Ephesians who were running the risk of being charged with unlawful assembly (Polhill, *Acts*, 413). The assembly is thus dismissed, and the uproar ceases (20:1).

This story shows us how we advance the kingdom of Christ. It's not by weapons, force, or violence. Paul preaches the gospel; people get converted; they renounce sin and idolatry; and by the power of the Spirit, the whole social order is impacted. Don't underestimate the power the gospel. Keep exalting Christ in cities filled with idols.

When Paul writes his letter to the Ephesians later, he says the believers in Christ are joined together, growing "into a holy temple in the Lord" (Eph 2:21). The church comprised of individuals on common mission is God's real temple! He says, "In him you are also being built together for God's dwelling in the Spirit" (2:22). The power of Christ in his people stood in stark contrast to the renowned Ephesian temple. One had life. The other was lifeless.

We are made to worship but not to worship idols. Exalt Jesus, who comes to reside in repentant people, transforming them from the inside out.

Reflect and Discuss

1. How have you experienced or witnessed a change in affections through conversion?
2. How does this chapter display the idea of a great awakening?
3. Explain in your own words the culture of Ephesus.
4. Explain how Paul's exposition of the Scriptures impacted Ephesus.
5. What are some common misapplications of the story of people being healed by contact with Paul's facecloths?
6. What does Paul's encounter with the "sons of Sceva" teach about the Holy Spirit? What does it teach about the evil one?
7. What does the story about believers burning books teach?
8. What does Paul's decision to go to Jerusalem teach about loving the church and loving the poor?
9. Why were the craftsmen in Ephesus upset?
10. How might the preaching of the gospel impact your city's social norms?

Encouraging One Another

ACTS 20:1-12

Main Idea: This passage illustrates some of the ways believers can give and receive Christ-exalting, Spirit-empowered encouragement.

I. **Encouraging the Saints in Macedonia and Greece en Route to Jerusalem (20:1-6)**
   A. How can we encourage the saints this week?
   B. Why don't believers encourage other believers?
II. **Encouraging the Saints in Troas in Corporate Worship (20:7-12)**
   A. Gather weekly to celebrate the Lord's resurrection (20:7-12).
   B. Gather weekly to experience the Lord's Supper (20:7,11).
      1. The privilege
      2. The pattern
      3. The power
   C. Gather weekly to hear the Lord's Word (20:7-12).

This passage is famous for the story of Eutychus falling asleep during Paul's sermon. The young man, whose name means "lucky" or "fortunate," was *unfortunately* sitting by a window when he nodded off as Paul spoke. After his deadly three-story fall, God restored his life, and Paul continued preaching until daybreak.

The story is humorous because many of us can identify with the slow drift toward sleep that can overtake us during a lecture, sermon, or film. My good friend David Platt once fell asleep during *prayer* time at our mentor's house! This poor brother, a committed disciple maker, had worked himself to the point of exhaustion and just couldn't stay awake. Our spirit is often willing, but our flesh is weak. Such weakness reminds us that God alone is self-sufficient and doesn't need sleep (cf. Ps 121:4).

But this story in Acts 20 isn't mainly about how to stay awake during corporate worship. This section of Scripture opens and closes with the concept of *encouragement* in verses 1 and 12, though most versions have "comforted" in verse 12. Luke uses the same basic term (*parakaleō*; cf. "Counselor" in John 14:16) three times in this section (vv. 1,2,12). It appears numerous times in the New Testament, showing the importance of encouraging others in the mission. Here, in a Christlike and Spirit-like way, Paul comes alongside the saints in various places, strengthening them in word and deed.

The author of Hebrews tells us that all believers have the privilege and responsibility of encouraging other brothers and sisters in Christ:

> *Watch out, brothers and sisters, so that there won't be in any of you an evil, unbelieving heart that turns away from the living God.* But encourage each other daily, *while it is still called today, so that none of you is hardened by sin's deception.* (Heb 3:12-13; emphasis added)

We must encourage one another constantly. Our hearts are fickle; sin never sleeps; Satan is at work; and the gospel is of first importance.

Knowing the reality of the spiritual war and the need to fan the flame of Christians' passion for the King, Paul makes several trips to build up the believers. This indicates to me that we need to elevate our concept of encouragement. George Adams said, "Encouragement is the oxygen of the soul" (in Thomas, *Acts*, 562). It's a great privilege to give Christ-exalting encouragement to fellow soldiers and to receive it from others! Let's look at how we can both give and receive encouragement.

Encouraging the Churches of Macedonia and Greece en Route to Jerusalem
ACTS 20:1-6

After the riot in Ephesus, Paul executed his plans to visit Jerusalem via Macedonia and Achaia (19:21). We can fill in some of the details from Paul's letters of 2 Corinthians (esp. chs. 1–7) and Romans, which he composed during this time. Paul went to give an offering to the poor saints in Jerusalem (see 24:17), a gift that no doubt brought much encouragement to the believers there.

Paul collected offerings from the Gentile congregations of Macedonia and Achaia (Greece), and presumably from Galatia and Asia Minor, in order to support the brothers and sisters in Jerusalem. This offering would serve as a concrete expression of love, support, and solidarity. Paul tells the church in Rome that those in Macedonia and Achaia were pleased to make this offering (Rom 15:26-27). They were "cheerful giver[s]" (2 Cor 9:7).

While making the swing from west to east, Paul had an opportunity not only to collect funds but also to encourage the saints in the faith, as he had done earlier in his ministry (see 14:21-22; 15:36,41).

During Paul's ministry in Ephesus, Paul and the Corinthians became embroiled in some drama. Paul apparently wrote a "painful" letter to the church during this time (2 Cor 2:1-11). Some believers in Corinth opposed Paul and attacked his apostolic credentials. So Paul sent a letter by way of Titus. Paul then waited for Titus's report before visiting Corinth himself. When Paul traveled to Macedonia (Acts 20:1), he hoped to meet up with Titus to see how the Corinthians received his strong letter. He had stopped first at Troas and had an opportunity to minister there (2 Cor 2:12-13), but because Corinth was on his mind, and because Titus didn't meet him at Troas, Paul moved on to Macedonia—most likely Philippi. When they met, Titus brought Paul good news: the offenders had been disciplined, and the church in Corinth had become reconciled to Paul (2 Cor 2:5-11; 7:5-13, Polhill, *Acts,* 415).

When Paul reached Macedonia (v. 1), having received this report, he then wrote 2 Corinthians. He sent it ahead of his own visit to the church in Corinth. We see in Acts 20:2-3 that Paul made it to Corinth, called a three-month stay in "Greece." This would be Paul's final visit to Corinth, and it happened in the winter of AD 55–56. While there, Paul wrote his majestic letter to the Romans.

But Luke only chooses to highlight Paul's personal *encouragement* to the saints (vv. 1-2). Paul encourages the saints *in person*, spending a great deal of time with them. Paul told the Romans,

> *For* I want very much to see you, *so that I may impart to you some spiritual gift to strengthen you, that is, to be mutually encouraged by each other's faith, both yours and mine.* (Rom 1:11-12; emphasis added)

Paul's letter to the Romans was a special, inspired epistle, yet he still wanted to visit the saints in person. John also related his desire to see the saints face-to-face (3 John 13-14).

We too must remember the value of encouraging others in person. We can do this through small groups and in a thousand other ways. When we love and encourage one another, the unbelieving world sees that we are Jesus's disciples (cf. John 13:34-35).

Because Paul was about to be attacked at sea (v. 3), he changed his plans and decided to go north by land. Luke mentions a long list of traveling companions, which expresses the nature of ministry partnership. These guys probably are all delegates from the Gentile churches. They joined Paul as official representatives of their churches. Their presence and gift represented partnership. They also served to help protect Paul and the offerings. Paul mentioned the representatives in his letters (cf. 1 Cor 16:3; 2 Cor 8:18-24). He valued these coworkers (cf. Acts 27:2; Eph 6:21-22; Phil 2:19-24; Col 4:7-10; 2 Tim 1:2,8).

At least a few of these men went ahead to Troas (v. 5), but Paul and Luke observed the Passover with the Philippian congregation—as is evidenced by the "we" mention in verse 6; Luke had probably stayed in Philippi since the second journey (16:40). The Passover carried more meaning to Paul once he saw its fulfillment in Christ, the ultimate Passover Lamb (1 Cor 5:7-8). Jesus's ultimate sacrifice gave the Christians not only salvation but also grace-generated motivation for sacrificial giving (2 Cor 8:9).

Consider two questions and some answers that emerge from this passage.

How Can We Encourage the Saints This Week?

First, we need to give to others. Paul collected funds to support the church in Jerusalem. This encouraged the saints in both word (as the representatives passed on a good word to the saints) and deed (in terms of the financial gift). Be on the lookout for needs in the body of Christ and give material possessions when possible (cf. Gal 6:2,10).

Second, we need to visit with others. Paul went to great pains to visit churches previously established. Follow his example. Don't settle for e-mail or Skype contacts with your Christian friends. Be present with people. It's dangerous to live in isolation. We're made for biblical community. Sharing lunch is one of many things we can do to support one another.

Third, we must serve with others in ministry. These delegates surely brought Paul (and one another) great encouragement on this trip. One way to forge deep, uplifting relationships is by going after a common goal together.

Why Don't Believers Encourage Other Believers?

I suspect the main reason believers often fail to encourage one another is that we think we're too busy to do so. To this, I say, look at the apostle Paul for a moment! Even in his busyness he thought about others.

It could also be that we are often too self-absorbed to encourage other brothers and sisters. To this, I say again, look at Paul's example. Great concerns about the future must have filled his mind. Death threats loomed. He desired to go to Jerusalem. Yet he thought about others and encouraged them rather than spending all of his energy focusing on his own problems.

We must realize that our failure to encourage is a sign that we really don't love our brothers and sisters. We love our plans. We love ourselves. So may God break our hearts, leading us to repentance and showing us how we can encourage others this week.

Before moving on from this point, I want to touch on ten things that serve to *discourage* fellow brothers and sisters. They are things we should avoid:

1. Being harsh toward or critical of one another
2. Being angry with one another
3. Envying one another
4. Disrespecting one another
5. Avoiding one another
6. Being too busy for one another
7. Puffing ourselves up in front of one another
8. Squeezing the life out of one another
9. Showing no patience with one another
10. Gossiping about one another

Instead of falling into one of these traps, give yourself to the ministry of building up other believers in a spirit of love for Christ and for his people.

Encouraging the Church in Troas in Corporate Worship
ACTS 20:7-12

Paul and his companions spent a week in Troas, probably awaiting the departure of their ship. While there they were able to worship with the church. Luke records an unforgettable worship service. Luke's last phrase, "They . . . were greatly comforted," expresses how much the service encouraged the people of God in Troas. Our worship gatherings too can serve as wonderful means of encouragement when we follow the pattern set forth here.

F. F. Bruce notes the significance of this gathering: "The reference to meeting for the breaking of bread on 'the first day of the week' is the earliest text we have from which it may be inferred with reasonable certainty that Christians regularly came together for worship on that day" (*Book of Acts*, 384). From this gathering we get an inside look at some of the priorities of the church gathered.

Of course, we shouldn't try to apply everything here to our modern context. I don't think that insisting on oil lamps or demanding a super long sermon would prove a good idea! Neither should we necessarily neglect what's not mentioned here, like *prayer*. Rather, we should seek to transfer from this account what's transferable.

Since Luke was present ("we," v. 7), he could report several details. The gathering probably began around sunset, after the workday was complete. Paul prolonged his speech until midnight and later went on to speak until daybreak. The length of the sermon highlights the special occasion. The church and Paul knew they had limited time together, so they wanted to use every minute of it.

Further, the meeting took place in a home on the third floor. Lamps were in the room, and Eutychus (who may have been a young boy) sat in the window, trying to get some air. It seems as though Luke is trying not to attach blame to the sleepy young man as he shares what happened. Eutychus was fighting to stay awake as Paul "kept on talking" (v. 9).

After the deadly fall, Paul, by the power of Jesus, was able to raise this young man back to life (v. 10). His actions are not unlike those of Elijah, Elisha, and Peter (cf. 1 Kgs 17:17-24; 2 Kgs 4:32-33; Luke 7:11-17; John 11:1-44; Acts 9:36-41).

The church then had a meal (which included the Lord's Supper), and Paul continued speaking until daybreak (v. 11). Luke then makes another comment on Eutychus, saying "they brought the boy home alive," bringing great comfort to the church.

Let's consider three applications.

Gather Weekly to Celebrate the Lord's Resurrection (20:7-12)

Luke says the church met "on the first day of the week" for corporate worship. This day had been set apart by the Lord's resurrection as the Lord's Day (cf. Luke 24:1; 1 Cor 16:1-2; Rev 1:10).

The way Luke describes these events gives the impression that this was simply the norm for churches. Several ancient documents also describe how early Christians gathered on Sundays to celebrate Jesus's resurrection. Each time they did, they were reminding one another that the tomb is empty and the heavenly throne is occupied. This congregation in Troas met in the evenings. Sunday mornings became the more popular gathering time as culture and leadership changed.

There's something special and significant about assembling together. There's always more going on at a church gathering than meets the eye (cf. Heb 12:18-24). They give us a glimpse of the great gathering to come (Rev 4–5). And we never know what might happen at a church service! Imagine, for instance, how wonderful it would have been to attend the meeting at which Paul spoke and one of the guys in the youth group got raised from the dead! Meeting together for worship encourages us, and it reminds us that our greatest problem has already been solved: death has been defeated.

Yet there remains a spirit of indifference to weekly gatherings among many professing Christians. Many feel they're too important to make time for Jesus Christ and his people. They think they should invest their time elsewhere. But gathering with the church is the best investment of time you could possibly make! If you aren't prioritizing the assembly of the redeemed, beware! It may indicate that your relationship with Jesus isn't what it should be.

Understand that there's a *vertical* and *horizontal* dimension to our Christian meetings: both have tremendous benefits for the individual and for the crowd. Every believer needs the encouragement that comes not only from the risen King (vertical) but also from the King's people (horizontal). The writer of Hebrews says,

> And let us watch out for one another to provoke love and good works, not neglecting to gather together, as some are in the habit of doing, but encouraging each other, and all the more as you see the day approaching. (Heb 10:24-25)

You have a role to play in the weekly assembly. You come not to be entertained but to encourage and receive encouragement. For the good of your own soul and for the good of the souls of your brothers and sisters, protect corporate worship times.

Gather Weekly to Experience the Lord's Supper (20:7,11)

Luke mentions the Lord's Supper in the same way, as a common event in the life of the gathered church (see 1 Cor 11:17-34, "when you come together"). It was probably shared in the context of a meal. John Stott says, "Word and sacrament [the Lord's Supper] were combined in the ministry given to the church at Troas, and the universal church has followed suit ever since" (*Message of Acts*, 321). Let's consider three aspects of the Lord's Supper.

The Privilege. Paul was able to remember Jesus's substitutionary death through the Lord's Supper with individuals who couldn't have been Christians for long. It must have been an encouraging experience to see former pagans take the bread and the cup. It must have also been an incredibly joyous experience for the believers in Troas to take the bread and the cup with the apostle Paul. He had sacrificed so much for the cause of the gospel.

Imagine a modern missionary's joy at serving Communion to new believers in his area of outreach. How much excitement would fill such a person's heart as he held out the emblems of the Savior's death to repentant believers? Just thinking about it reminds me of the missionary John Paton (1824–1907), who took the gospel to the people of the New Hebrides islands. After many trials and difficult seasons, Paton reported the unspeakable joy he experienced when he served the first Communion to a group of new believers at Aniwa:

> For years we had toiled and prayed and taught for this. At the moment when I put the bread and wine into those dark hands, once stained with the blood of cannibalism but now stretched out to receive and partake the emblems and seals of the Redeemer's love, I had a foretaste of the joy of glory that well-nigh broke my heart to pieces. I shall never taste a deeper bliss till I gaze on the glorified face of Jesus himself. (*John G. Paton*, Ch. LXXIII)

Every time I read this story, I feel tears pool in my eyes. What a powerful picture it paints! What a privilege to memorialize the Lord's forgiveness in the Lord's Supper and to share the meal with other believers. Each of us was dead in sin and unworthy to take the Table until God made us alive in Christ. May we never get over the wonder of the gospel—the wonder of taking the bread and the cup, reminders of the Lord's torn flesh and precious blood shed on our behalf.

The Pattern. So how often should we take the Lord's Supper? It seems the early church took the Lord's Supper weekly. After the church spread out from Jerusalem, became more stabilized, and began meeting weekly for worship, the Lord's Supper became a weekly experience. John Stott says, "The disciples met on the Lord's Day for the Lord's Supper. At least verse 7 sounds like a description of the normal, regular practice of the church in Troas" (*Message of Acts*, 321).

Allow me to mention a few leading biblical scholars on this subject. Ray Van Neste says of Acts 20:7,

> The breaking of bread is the term used especially in Acts for the celebration of the Lord's Supper (2:42; cf. 1 Cor. 10:16), and this passage is of particular interest in providing the first allusion to the Christian custom of meeting on the first day of

the week for the purpose. . . . This passage need not mean the Lord's Supper was the only purpose of their gathering, but it certainly is one prominent purpose and the one emphasized here. The centrality of communion to the weekly gathering is stated casually without explanation or defense, suggesting this practice was common among those Luke expected to read his account. These early Christians met weekly to celebrate the Lord's Supper. (*The Lord's Supper*, 366, kindle)

Similarly, James Hamilton says,

I would suggest that Acts 20:7 (with 1 Cor. 10:16, 11:23-24) indicates that the celebration of the Lord's supper was central to the early Christian gatherings—look at it again: "On the first day of the week, when we gathered to break bread . . ." (Acts 20:7). They gathered to break bread (Paul also preached all night, so the gathering probably started in the evening, 20:7-11), and the gathering happened on the first day of the week. . . . Everywhere the apostles went to make disciples, they planted churches. They always baptized new disciples into membership in those churches, and those churches met on the first day of the week to celebrate the death and resurrection of Jesus, looking for his return, by partaking of the Lord's supper. ("How Often Should a Church Take the Lord's Supper?")

Hamilton applies this to us today:

This means, I think, that if we become convinced that the earliest church took the Lord's supper every Lord's day— and if this was so widespread that when Paul and Luke are traveling from one place to another, they know that if they find a church gathered on the Lord's day that church will have gathered to break bread—if we become convinced that the earliest church in every place took the Lord's supper every Lord's day, we will want to do the same. (Ibid.)

And finally, Van Neste concludes,

From these passages, a clear pattern emerges of a weekly celebration of Communion in the NT. . . . [T]his is the pattern in the NT and therefore would be the best practice. (*The Lord's Supper*, 367, kindle)

I agree wholeheartedly.

My experience, and the testimony of many others, is that regular Communion is more meaningful, not less meaningful, than periodic observances. Charles Spurgeon believed this as well:

> My witness is, and I think I speak the mind of many of God's people now present, that coming as some of us do, weekly, to the Lord's Table, we do not find the breaking of bread to have lost its significance—it is always fresh to us. . . . Shame on the Christian church that she should put it off to once a month, and mar the first day of the week by depriving it of its glory in the meeting together for fellowship and breaking of bread, and showing forth of the death of Christ till he come. They who once know the sweetness of each Lord's-day celebrating his Supper, will not be content, I am sure, to put it off to less frequent seasons. ("Songs of Deliverance")

I don't want to be overly critical on this matter. To be fair, in Scripture we don't find an explicit command to take the Lord's Supper weekly. If we did, I'm sure most Bible-believing churches would be doing so. Nevertheless, this does seem to be the pattern of the early churches. And it's a wonderful privilege to enjoy!

The Power. The Lord's Supper is powerful in its *reception*. While we shouldn't go so far as to view the elements as transforming into the actual body and blood of Jesus, it's also wrong to minimize the experience of the Table. Many Christians grow up only hearing what the Lord's Supper is *not*. In hearing such negativity associated with it, they tend to have a low view of the Supper, assuming nothing special happens when we take it. In truth we should experience profound delight and deep joy when we come to the Table. We should take it repentantly, prayerfully, gratefully, and joyfully. J. I. Packer notes, "At the Holy Table, above all, let there be praise" (cited in Van Neste, *Lord's Supper,* 363). Yes indeed. May we take Communion with holy praise to the Lamb!

The Lord's Supper is also powerful in its *proclamation*. Sermons preach to the *ear*. The Lord's Supper preaches to the *eye*. And the preached Word has great power. In the Lord's Supper people get to see and hear the gospel proclaimed through the explanation of the elements. We shouldn't minimize this fact.

When my youngest son was only six years old, I asked him about the worship service. He couldn't remember much about my sermon, but he could remember the presentation of the Lord's Supper. I was thrilled because what he remembered was *the gospel!*

The Lord's Supper is also powerful in its *unification*. In his letter to the Corinthians Paul speaks much about the call for unity at the Table because the "haves" weren't treating the "have-nots" appropriately (1 Cor 11:17-34). At the Table we Christians confess our unity in Christ. The Lord's Supper is a powerful way to build community within the church because it illustrates that we are all one in him. We all come as repentant sinners, having placed faith in the same Savior and thus sharing the same hope. In Jesus we're family. There are no distinctions. Skin color doesn't matter. Paycheck size doesn't matter. What matters is Christ's blood, reconciling us to God and one another. Consider this powerful illustration of unity:

> At the end of the Civil War in Richmond, Virginia, on the Sunday after Appomattox and the surrender, a worship service was held in the historic Episcopal church there. It was an old church that had a balcony where the slaves of the owners had sat for many years, with their masters and their families sitting downstairs. The practice in this church had been to have two calls for the Lord's Supper, one first for the whites downstairs, and then one for the slaves upstairs. But on this given Sunday at the first call to communion an older black man, a former slave, began down the central aisle, right after the call. Naturally enough there was surprise and shock downstairs, but what was even more of a shock was when an elderly, white, bearded gentleman got up, hooked his arm in the arm of the former slave, and they went forward and took communion together. That man was Robert E. Lee. There was forgiveness and healing and reunion at the Table that day, and thereafter there was no more segregated communion. This is indeed one of the functions of communion—the receiving and sharing of forgiveness. Jesus sacrificed himself so that our sins might be forgiven and so that we might be forgiving as well. (Witherington III, *Making a Meal of It*, 132)

What a powerful picture of grace, forgiveness, and *togetherness* at the Table!

This togetherness is also a powerful sign of what's to come. The Lord's Supper is the sign of the messianic reign and a foretaste of the future, for in the Table, we're proclaiming the Lord's death "until he comes" (1 Cor 11:26). Soon we will feast with the King and all the redeemed (cf. Matt 8:11).

Gather Weekly to Hear the Lord's Word (20:7-12)

The church in Troas also gathered to hear the apostle Paul teach. Paul "kept on talking" until midnight (vv. 7,9), and then he "talked" with them until daybreak (v. 11). The first part of the evening may have been a lecture, an argument based on Scripture that could have included some questions and answers, whereas the latter address was more of a casual conversation. Regarding the latter, John Stott says, "It was clearly more free and open than a formal sermon" (*Message of Acts*, 321).

Obviously this was a unique event. But we should see from this text (and the rest of the Bible) that the preaching and teaching of God's Word is to be taken *seriously*. Paul gave Timothy this instruction about corporate worship: "Until I come, give your attention to public reading, exhortation, and teaching" (1 Tim 4:13). Dr. D. Martyn Lloyd-Jones underscored the importance of preaching in his classic book on the subject:

> Is it not clear, as you take a bird's eye view of Church history,
> that the decadent periods and eras in the history of the
> Church have always been those periods when preaching
> has declined? What is it that always heralds the dawn of
> a Reformation or of a Revival? It is renewed preaching.
> (*Preaching and Preachers*, 31)

However, we should not draw from this text that a speaker should preach ten-hour sermons! John Newton wisely said, "When weariness begins, edification ends" (in Hughes, *Acts*, 270).

How, then, should you listen to a sermon? Here a few pointers:

1. Listen *humbly*. Realize that you need God's Word. Don't listen with a grudge or with a spirit of arrogance. Don't allow familiarity with the text or even with the speaker's general message to block your desire to meet Christ in the Scriptures.
2. Listen *intently*. Do whatever you must to stay engaged with the message. Say "amen," sit in the front, or take notes. Listen attentively, like the audience in Nehemiah 8. Fight the urge to fall asleep or to mentally check out.
3. Listen *biblically*. Use your mind to weigh what is taught against what you already know of the Bible, as the Bereans did.
4. Listen *personally*. Listen for yourself, not just for someone "who needed to hear that."

5. Listen *communally*. Listen for the good of your brothers and sisters. Who knows? It could be that you'll hear something within the message that you can later use to encourage someone.

6. Listen *missionally*. Don't merely be a receiver of the Word; be a reproducer of the Word. Listen in order to make disciples of all nations.

7. Listen *practically*. Think about ways you should change your behavior based on what you hear.

8. Listen *gratefully*. Be thankful that God speaks to his people, including you!

Remember, too, that it's important to get adequate rest before corporate worship. Prepare for corporate worship as you would prepare for other important events.

In summary, Acts 20:1-12 illustrates the ministry of Christ-exalting, Spirit-empowered encouragement. We may encourage people in personal meetings, through financial offerings, in gospel partnerships, and in our weekly worship assemblies. In all things let's commit ourselves to building up one another. And let's be thankful that we have the Comforter, the *Holy Spirit*, with us, in us, and working through us for this ministry.

After all, we have the greatest news in the world to share. Our God raises the dead! The living Christ gives us power to persevere in the faith, to advance the gospel in the midst of persecution, and to sing in days of discouragement. Keep pointing your brothers and sisters to Jesus Christ, the resurrection and the life. The gospel message is not only for the unrepentant sinner but also for the redeemed saint.

Reflect and Discuss

1. How can we encourage other Christians based on this passage?
2. Why do we often fail to encourage other saints?
3. What about verses 1-6 most stands out to you? Why?
4. Why is it important to be reminded of the resurrection weekly?
5. Why is it important to gather corporately with God's people?
6. What does the Lord's Supper communicate? Why is participating in it a privilege?
7. Why is hearing the Word corporately important?
8. How should we listen to sermons?
9. What does the raising of Eutychus teach us?
10. Take a moment to pray for your weekly gatherings in your local church.

Caring for the Blood-Bought Church of God

ACTS 20:13-38

Main Idea: Paul's farewell address to the Ephesian elders highlights the nature and importance of the church and the role of its overseers.

I. **Paul's Example (20:13-27)**
   A. He identified with the people (20:18).
   B. He served the Lord with humility and passion (20:19).
   C. He taught the gospel (20:20-21).
   D. He lived by the Spirit and treasured Jesus supremely (20:22-24).
   E. He served with a clear conscience (20:25-27).
II. **Paul's Exhortations (20:28-32)**
   A. Watch your life (20:28a).
   B. Watch the flock (20:28b-32).
III. **Paul's Example—Again (20:33-38)**
   A. He avoided greed, worked hard, and practiced generosity (20:33-35).
   B. He loved the flock (20:36-38).

The book of Acts is filled with speeches. Some are addressed to non-Christians (Acts 13; 14; 17), and others are defenses (Acts 22–26). But this address in Acts 20 is different. It's addressed to the Christian leaders of the church in Ephesus. To be even more specific, it's a farewell speech. The Bible contains several important farewell speeches that prepare people for the future (Gen 49–50; Deuteronomy; Josh 23:1–24:27; 1 Sam 12:1-25; John 13–17; also 2 Timothy and 2 Peter).

In this speech Paul highlights the nature of pastoral oversight and the importance of the church. A good one-sentence summary of Paul's charge is given in verse 28:

> *Be on guard for yourselves and for all the flock of which the Holy Spirit has appointed you as overseers, to shepherd the church of God, which he purchased with his own blood.* (Acts 20:28)

This text sounds a lot like Paul's later charge to Timothy, in which Paul essentially summarizes the nature of pastoral ministry in one verse. He urges Timothy to watch both his *life* and his *teaching* for the good of his soul and the good of others:

> *Pay close attention to your life and your teaching; persevere in these things, for in doing this you will save both yourself and your hearers.* (1 Tim 4:16)

Indeed, this speech in Acts is very Pauline. It sounds like Paul's pastoral letters and is consistent with what Paul said to both Timothy and Titus.

In Charles Spurgeon's *Lectures to My Students*, the seasoned pastor provides several exhortations to aspiring pastors. The first lecture is drawn from 1 Timothy 4:16. It is titled "The Minister's Self-Watch." After urging each student to examine his own salvation, Spurgeon transitioned to the need for the minister to guard his own personal character:

> We have all heard the story of the man who preached so well and lived so badly, that when he was in the pulpit everybody said he ought never to come out again, and when he was out of it, they all declared he never ought to enter it again. . . . Too many preachers forget to serve God when they are out of the pulpit, their lives are negatively inconsistent. Abhor, dear brethren, the thought of being clockwork ministers who are not alive by abiding grace within, but are wound up by temporary influences; men who are only ministers for the time being, under the stress of the hour of ministering, but cease to be ministers when they descend the pulpit stairs. True ministers are always ministers. . . . It is a horrible thing to be an inconsistent minister. (17)

Spurgeon's charge is a call to *consistency*. Not perfection but consistency. We who are overseers must live a consistent life of godliness. We must consistently care for the flock in word and deed.

Paul's address to the Ephesian elders is a mingling of both *example* and *exhortation*. His example serves to both inspire and instruct the elders who will be leading the church from this point forward. His exhortation includes some important matters related to pastoral oversight.

Obviously, pastors/elders/overseers (synonymous terms in the New Testament; see vv. 17,28; Titus 1:5,7) should pay careful attention to Paul's words here, but they're beneficial for all God's people. Every Christian should care about the church and should seek to follow Paul's example, just as he followed after Christ (1 Cor 11:1; Phil 3:17). Further, even those who are not Christians, but are exploring the Christian faith, will find that by studying the church, they will learn a lot about Jesus.

While this address is difficult to outline, as John Polhill notes (*Acts*, 423), we will look at it in three parts.

Paul's Example
ACTS 20:13-27

In verses 13-16 we see Paul rushing to get to Jerusalem to make it for Pentecost. Perhaps Paul wanted to present the offerings from the Gentiles during the Feast of Weeks, which Jewish tradition also associated with Gentiles' hearing God's Word at Sinai, alongside Israel (Johnson, *Let's Study Acts*, 251; see Exod 19:1; 34:22; Deut 16:9-12; Acts 2:1). Seven weeks separated Passover from Pentecost. Paul can't risk a long delay in Ephesus—either fruitful ministry or continued opposition could keep him there for a while—so the apostle bypasses Ephesus and lands farther south in Miletus (vv. 13-15). Despite Paul's hurry, he still makes the time to invest in elders, demonstrating his care for the Ephesian church and its leaders. In Miletus, Paul gives them this powerful charge, which we have in summary form, and the apostle begins with his own example. As a good leader Paul offered more than words. His life illustrated his teaching.

He Identified with the People (20:18)

According to verse 18, Paul had lived among and identified with the people of Ephesus. In writing to the Thessalonians, Paul said something similar: "You know how we lived among you" (1 Thess 1:5; cf. 2:7-11). Because Paul was with his people, he knew their needs and how to apply God's Word to those needs (v. 20).

Many pastors today are isolated from their people. But good pastors know the sheep by name and by need. This requires involvement as well as transparency. Ajith Fernando commented, "[Paul] obviously had what might be called an openhearted approach to ministry. This is why he could spend a whole night chatting with believers in Troas (vv. 9-10), and this is why he shed so many tears among the Ephesians (vv. 19,31)" (*Acts*, 533). Paul didn't have a celebrity ministry that allowed him to hide out in an office after delivering his speeches. He was with his people.

I don't want to be slavish in applying this to pastors because I know every pastoral setting is different. But I would ask this question of each career minister: If you aren't spending time with your people outside the pulpit, then are you really following Paul's pattern? As pastors, let's find ways to be involved in people's lives and avoid merely being the sages on the stages.

He Served the Lord with Humility and Passion (20:19)

Verse 19 makes clear that Paul saw his ministry as *serving the Lord*. Whether he was ministering to the new believers or evangelizing in the lecture hall of Tyrannus or in the synagogue, he ultimately did everything unto the Lord Jesus. Everyone serves something or someone, so who or what are we serving? Even the most mundane activities should be done for the Lord (Col 3:23-24). Because Jesus takes everything done in his name seriously, this gives our lives and ministries great meaning. And we don't have to have a big platform to serve the Lord.

Most importantly, Paul says he served the Lord with *humility, tears,* and during *trials.* His humility denotes his posture before God and people. His trials remind us of his courage and faithfulness. His tears call attention to his tenderness (cf. v. 31). I would submit that this kind of service to the Lord is a direct result of a proper grasp of the gospel. The gospel—when applied deeply—humbles us, makes us tender, and makes us courageous.

It humbles us because we know we don't deserve grace. We were beggars in need of salvation when the Savior brought us into the kingdom. That should make us willing to do whatever needs to be done in order for the gospel to be proclaimed effectively.

The gospel makes us tender because the Spirit of God makes us loving and gentle people. It makes us begin to live like the ultimate weeping prophet, Jesus. Spirit-empowered servants are brokenhearted servants. God rarely blesses a tearless ministry because it's difficult to operate by the Spirit without deep emotion (cf. 2 Cor 5:20).

And the gospel makes us courageous because we have no need to fear man. What can man do to us? Kill us? Paul says to that threat, "To die is gain" (Phil 1:21). The gospel causes us to live with an unstoppable boldness when it comes to sharing the truth of who Jesus is and what he came to accomplish.

Therefore, let's invite the gospel to work deeply into our hearts that we too may become humble, tender, and courageous. In a world filled with bullies and cowards, we desperately need men and women to be transformed by the gospel so that they too may become humble, tender, and courageous.

He Taught the Gospel (20:20-21)

Paul, who had been so deeply changed by grace, taught the gospel of grace to everyone, everywhere. Here, then, is another wonderful example for us to follow. Don't shrink back from teaching anything that's profitable—even if it's in the Old Testament! Be bold in your exposition in this age of tolerance. Don't cave in to culture, but lovingly and courageously teach the "whole plan of God" (v. 27).

There's not really a bad place to teach the gospel! And everyone needs the gospel! As we teach the gospel—behind pulpits, in homes, in coffee shops, in parks—let's call people to repentance and faith just as Paul did. He and others simply continued the preaching ministry of the Lord Jesus himself (Matt 4:17).

He Lived by the Spirit and Treasured Jesus Supremely (20:22-24)

Paul knew that going to Jerusalem would involve suffering, but because he valued Jesus above comfort and even his own life, he was willing to go. His desire was to finish the ministry Jesus gave him (cf. 2 Tim 4:7).

The goal of life is not to have a long life but a full life, one lived to the glory of Jesus Christ. For some Christians such faithfulness will involve hardship, persecution, and even martyrdom. Paul's example here shows how one can endure such experiences: We must value Jesus above everything, and we must rely on the Spirit.

He Served with a Clear Conscience (20:25-27)

How could Paul say he was innocent of the blood of all his hearers? Because he didn't shrink back from comprehensively declaring God's Word to them. He preached the redemptive plan of God, promised in the Old Testament, fulfilled in the gospel (1 Cor 2:2; Col 1:27-29).

Paul's faithful exposition exonerated him from responsibility for the blood of his hearers (Johnson, *Let's Study Acts*, 252). Paul may have been alluding to Ezekiel's prophetic ministry. God called Ezekiel to be a faithful watchman (Ezek 3:18-19; 33:1-9). The prophet's job, then, was to sound the alarm when he saw danger. If the citizens failed to heed the warning, then they would have no one to blame for the consequences except themselves (ibid., 253). Paul could say that he sounded the alarm. He faithfully preached the life-and-death message of the gospel; therefore, his conscience was clear.

Paul's ministry was both comprehensive and consistent. He didn't view the ministry as a career. He didn't punch a clock. His ministry was an all-consuming task, and he fulfilled it in Ephesus daily. He fulfilled it with humility and passion, with faithfulness and courage. He set the pace for the elders who would build on his foundation (Johnson, *Let's Study Acts*, 255). This is how leaders should hand off a ministry to others.

Paul's Exhortations
ACTS 20:28-32

After looking back, Paul looks ahead. He announces his departure for Jerusalem, along with his expectation never to see the elders again. He also predicts future dangers to the church. In light of these things, he exhorts the elders to watch their own lives and to watch over the flock. Paul raises a number of important concepts here.

First, the Holy Spirit ultimately appoints elders (v. 28a). A man can't call himself into the ministry. The Spirit of God works in the heart of a man, giving him a desire for the task (1 Tim 3:1). The local congregation then affirms his Spirit-initiated calling (cf. Acts 13:2-3). No one, then, should take the office of elder lightly.

Importantly, you don't have to be an elder to do significant kingdom work. If the Spirit of God isn't calling you to this task, then find other ways to make a gospel impact in the world. The Spirit uses every Christian to do ministry (Eph 4:7-16).

Second, God paid the highest possible price for the church (v. 28b). How valuable is the church? She was purchased by the blood of Jesus (the title "God" here probably referring to "Jesus"; cf. Rom 9:5). This means we should never have a low view of the church. We should love the church deeply, and shepherds should care for the church carefully.

With this in mind, consider Paul's two charges to the elders.

Watch Your Life (20:28a)

Paul reminds the elders of the utter necessity of godly lives (cf. 1 Tim 4:16). Charles Spurgeon said this to his students:

> When we say to you, my dear brethren, take care of your life, we mean be careful of even the minutiae of your character. Avoid little debts, unpunctuality, gossiping, nicknaming, petty quarrels, and all other of those little vices which fill the ointment with flies. (*Lectures to My Students*, 20–21)

Robert Murray McCheyne said it well: "My people's greatest need is my personal holiness" (in J. I. Packer, *Rediscovering Holiness*, 33).

Holiness is necessary for faithfulness in ministry. You may be gifted to do the work to which God has called you, but if you aren't godly, then you won't have a ministry. Just ask the countless pastors who have fallen morally and are no longer serving in the pastorate. Many of them are incredibly gifted and bright. But it doesn't matter how good your theology is or how dynamically you speak if your character doesn't match your teaching. If you don't have holiness, you won't have a ministry. I'm not talking about living in sinless perfection. I'm talking about living "above reproach" (1 Tim 3:1-7).

Holiness is also necessary for compensating for deficiencies in ministry. There are many faithful pastors who aren't great speakers, but they're godly. As a result of their holiness, people find them interesting, and their ministries bless the people. As a pastor, I can't separate my life from my vocation as those in other vocations may be able to do. My life will inevitably impact my ministry. If I'm following hard after Jesus, it will show in the way I teach and serve. So in the words of Paul to Timothy, watch your life *persistently* (1 Tim 4:16). Don't ever stop putting sin to death and pursuing Christlikeness, no matter your job. As a Christian, you are also a minister.

Watch the Flock (20:28b-32)

Paul warns the elders about what will happen after his departure. Not only do churches face the threat of wolves on the outside, but sometimes wolves will "come in among" the believers, too. Paul predicts that some teachers—for their own devious reasons—will try to attract disciples to themselves rather than to Christ (v. 30). They will pose as pastors but will actually be predators (cf. Matt 7:15).

Paul thus tells the elders to keep a watch on *themselves*—to watch *one another* for the good of the flock. Paul is not only emphasizing personal accountability (1 Tim 4:16) but also *mutual accountability*. And this is one of the reasons a *plurality* of elders/pastors is so important (see Acts 14:23; Jas 5:14). Leaders need to be held accountable for how they live and for what they teach. They need to "guard each other from *error* and *arrogance,* and the flock from *abuse*" (Johnson, *Let's Study Acts,* 256; emphasis added).

By the time Paul writes to Timothy, who was leading the church in Ephesus, wolves had already entered (2 Tim 2:17-18; 3:1-9; 4:3). Wolves were teaching deviant doctrines (Acts 20:30) and doing great damage to the churches of Asia (cf. Eph 5:6-14; Col 2:8; Rev 2:2). So here Paul wasn't exaggerating the threat. The leaders needed to "be on the alert" so that the flock would be protected from such savages. The overseers needed to follow Paul's own example of faithful and passionate teaching (v. 31). They needed to teach sound doctrine and rebuke those who contradict it (see Titus 1:9).

After this serious warning, Paul gives the elders a wonderful word of assurance: "I commit you to God and to the work of his grace, which is able to build you up and to give you an inheritance among all who are sanctified" (v. 32). This transitional verse highlights two important concepts.

First, it highlights the Word of God, centrally a message of grace, which grants believers a share in the heavenly inheritance (cf. 26:18; Eph 1:13-14; Col 1:12). Paul reminds the leaders of the power of the gospel, which saves the lost and builds up believers.

Second, it draws attention to the fact that God himself is the ultimate *watchman*. He is the faithful protector of his church (cf. 2 Tim 2:19). Previously in Acts, when Paul appointed elders in each church, he committed the elders "to the Lord in whom they had believed" (14:23; cf. 13:3; 14:26; 15:40). Paul is reminding the elders that they don't shepherd alone. Jesus is with them (Heb 13:5), and Jesus will build his church (Matt 16:18). God's promises, God's presence, and God's powerful gospel bring much needed comfort and assurance to pastors who feel the weight of their shepherding task.

Paul's Example—Again
ACTS 20:33-38

While it seems like the speech concludes with verse 32, Paul doesn't stop there. He wants to take up one more important matter: the leader's relationship to material goods. Every Christian—not just elders—should pay careful attention to Paul's theology and practice of work and wealth here.

He Avoided Greed, Worked Hard, and Practiced Generosity (20:33-35)

Paul's testimony here is consistent with what he says elsewhere regarding work and wealth. Paul avoided greed and never used ministry as a means to cover it up (1 Thess 2:5). He supported himself by working with his hands, as we observed in Corinth (Acts 18:2-3; cf. 1 Cor 4:12; 9:12,15; 2 Cor 11:7). We read of the same pattern in Thessalonica, where Paul described his work ethic (1 Thess 2:9; 2 Thess 3:7-8) and also urged his readers to imitate him (1 Thess 4:11; 2 Thess 3:9).

Greed can pose a major problem for everyone, and pastors aren't exempt from the temptation (1 Tim 3:3,8; 6:3-10; Titus 1:7,11), so it's fitting that Paul would include this subject in his address to a group of overseers.

One of the major incentives for hard, honest work is noted here in the Miletus speech: so that one may "help the weak" (v. 35). In a speech that deals so much with preaching and teaching, Paul also includes this note about caring for the poor (cf. Rom 15:1; Gal 6:21; Eph 4:28; 1 Thess 5:14). Paul truly had a well-rounded, comprehensive ministry that serves as a wonderful model. Even though Paul was mighty in the Word, he didn't neglect practical deed ministry to the poor. Tim Keller writes,

> The apostle Paul viewed ministry to the poor as so important
> that it was one of the last things he admonished the
> Ephesian church to do before he left them for the last time.
> In his farewell address, Paul was able to ground this duty
> in the teaching of Jesus. "We must help the poor," he said,
> "remembering the words the Lord Jesus himself said, 'It is
> more blessed to give than receive'" (Acts 20:35). You don't
> use your "last words" without saying something that is all-
> important to you. For Paul it was: "Don't only preach—help
> the poor." (*Generous Justice*, 73)

Modern-day preachers should pay attention to Paul's model of both teaching and showing mercy to the weak.

Paul quotes the saying of Jesus, reminding the elders that they should be givers, not takers. They should also remember that one experiences tremendous *blessing* when practicing generosity. Church leaders should set the example of grace-motivated generosity. Jesus himself, the chief Shepherd, modeled this concept. He gave everything in order to help us in our poor, weak condition (2 Cor 8:9). The more we understand the grace of Jesus, the more generous we become.

He Loved the Flock (20:36-38)

Verses 36-38 are transitional; they conclude Paul's Ephesian ministry and connect to the narrative of Paul's journey to Jerusalem (21:1-16). The warmth and love between believers expressed in these verses are expressed again in this next section.

Looking back over the Miletus address, one can't help but ponder the richness and relevance of the *shepherding* metaphor for pastoral ministry. A pastor isn't a cowboy, he's not a CEO, he's not a rock-star celebrity; he's a shepherd. Faithful shepherds know the flock, care for the flock, pray for the flock, feed the flock, and protect the flock from wolves. We should be careful to build our philosophy of pastoral ministry, then, from *the Bible*—not from popular leadership books (though we can learn from them). Pastoral leadership is unique and important; therefore, let everyone who aspires to the office of the overseer do so with humility and dependence on the great Shepherd (Heb 13:20). He purchased the church with his own blood.

Reflect and Discuss

1. How is this speech different from Paul's other speeches in Acts? How is it similar to other speeches in the Bible?
2. What does it mean for pastors to live among the sheep? Why is doing so important?
3. What about the way Paul served the church most resonates with you?
4. Explain where and what Paul taught. What can we learn from his priorities and approach?
5. How can you apply verses 22-24 to your own life?
6. Why must pastors keep a close watch on their own lives and on the lives of other pastors?
7. What does this passage teach about spiritual "wolves"?
8. Explain why verse 32 is a word of comfort and assurance.
9. What can we learn from Paul's work ethic in verses 34-35?
10. Take a moment to pray for your elders/pastors. In what specific ways might you encourage them?

Paul's Journey to Jerusalem

ACTS 20:36–21:16

Main Idea: Paul's trip to Jerusalem illustrates the gift of Christian friendship and powerfully portrays the cost of Christian discipleship.

I. **The Gift of Christian Friendship (20:36–21:16)**
  A. The need for Christian friendship
  B. How Christian friendship is established
  C. How Christian friendship is experienced
    1. Practicing hospitality
    2. Showing affection
    3. Praying together
    4. Discussing important decisions

II. **The Cost of Christian Discipleship (20:36–21:16)**
  A. Perspectives on Paul's decision
    1. The perspective of Paul (21:1-3)
    2. The perspective of the Christians in Tyre (21:4-6)
    3. The perspective of the Christians in Caesarea (21:7-13)
    4. The perspective of Luke (21:12,14)
  B. Principles to apply
    1. Love people, but love Jesus more.
    2. Value input, but follow God's will.
    3. There's something worse than dying: not living.
    4. When you follow Jesus down the Calvary road, you're not alone and you won't regret it.
    5. Following Jesus is costly, but not following Jesus is more costly.

This passage caused me to reflect back on a personal experience that occurred about fifteen years ago. I had finished my college degree in secondary education, and I was offered a job to be a high school teacher and baseball coach at a local school. The position came with a decent salary, good benefits, summers off, and lots of baseball. But there was one problem: the job clashed with what I knew to be the will of God for my life.

A few years prior Jesus had transformed me. Soon after my conversion I sensed a call into the ministry of the Word. Because of that calling, I thought I should go to seminary following graduation. And so, determined to follow through with the urge in spite of those who argued against it, I sold my beat-up car, packed a trunk, and flew to New Orleans to study theology. A friend's family graciously housed me in a spare bedroom there and helped me secure a job on campus. Instead of the good salary that had gone with the teaching position I turned down, this job came with little money and had no benefits. But I was convinced I was following Jesus in enrolling in that seminary and trusting him with my future.

Looking back now, I'm so grateful for the Lord's grace in guiding me through the difficult decision-making process that came on the heels of college. Back then some questioned my calling, and others thought me a fool for not accepting the teaching position. But had I listened to them, I would've missed out on the wonderful adventure God planned for me.

If you seek to follow Jesus, you too will come to various crossroads in your life. You will have to make many difficult decisions—some that may even make your loved ones question your sanity!

In Acts 21 the apostle Paul's life illustrates the painful pleasure of following Jesus. Paul is a man on a mission, headed to Jerusalem. His friends think he's crazy for going there. But Paul is "resolved" (19:21) and "compelled by the Spirit" (20:22), so he must go.

Before we examine the dominant theme in this text—*the cost of discipleship*—another theme stands out and deserves attention: that of *Christian friendship*. Paul's trip is punctuated by a chain of hellos and good-byes, which underscores the value of relationships within the body of Christ and provides some insight into how to interact in Christian love.

The Gift of Christian Friendship
ACTS 20:36–21:16

We pick up the story with Paul saying good-bye to the Ephesian elders. Farewells tend to be memorable and special, and this one certainly was. After studying Paul's ministry in Ephesus, and in light of everything Paul said in his farewell speech, we can understand that Paul loved these men. And these elders loved Paul. So they displayed understandable affection and emotion. They knelt on the beach and prayed together. Then the group escorted Paul to the ship, perhaps comforting one another with the reality that they would see Paul again in glory. It's a moving picture of Christ-centered community.

The heart-wrenching farewell is memorialized once again in the following verse before Luke lists ports and lengths of stay along the journey to Jerusalem. In the midst of all these names and places, Luke provides some vivid illustrations of genuine Christian fellowship and friendship at work. (I'll mainly use "friendship" as opposed to "fellowship" in the following discussion because it may be more challenging and practical for us.) The important thing to remember about chapter 21 is that we must not get overwhelmed by all the names and places it records. Rather, we need to look at the strength of Christian friendship expressed there.

The team first took a small vessel around the southwest tip of Asia Minor. They briefly stopped at the islands of Cos and Rhodes before reaching the port of Patara on the mainland. Then they booked a trip on a larger cargo ship as they headed toward the major port in Tyre. There Paul and his companions "sought out the disciples" (21:4) and stayed with them for a week. The Tyre group deeply loved Paul and urged him not to go to Jerusalem. Yet when the week ended, the Christians in Tyre accompanied the missionaries to the beach (v. 5), and as was done in the Ephesus scene, the believers knelt down to pray before saying farewell (v. 6).

Paul then traveled south to Ptolemais and enjoyed a day of fellowship with the "brothers and sisters" (v. 7) there before proceeding down to Caesarea (v. 8), the seaside capital of the province of Judea and the location of Peter's meeting with Cornelius (10:1–11:18). Paul stayed with Philip, one of the "Magnificent Seven" who distributed food to widows (6:1-7). This same Philip evangelized Samaria, the Ethiopian eunuch, and the coastal towns of Philistia (8:4-13). Philip rightly earned the title *evangelist* (21:8), a term rarely used in the New Testament (cf. Eph 4:11; 2 Tim 4:5). Even more unusual are Philip's daughters. They were unmarried and they "prophesied" (v. 9). This means they were living proof of the Spirit's coming at Pentecost (see 2:17). Luke, however, doesn't draw attention to their prophecies. He focuses on the prophecy of Agabus of Judea (21:10-11), which we will look at in a moment.

After Paul's resolute commitment to go to Jerusalem (vv. 11-14), the final scene of Christian fellowship is found in verses 15-16. Some of the believers accompanied Paul and his crew to Jerusalem. As they journeyed, they stayed with Mnason, a Cypriot and early disciple (cf. 11:19-20).

The Need for Christian Friendship

It's remarkable to observe how often Paul is surrounded by Christian friends as he does the work God called him to do. Paul travels with friends. He stays with them. He visits them. He works alongside them. Here in Acts 21 we see this trait on display again. His friends surround him. They journey together. They spend time together. They talk together. They weep together. They no doubt laugh together. And they pray together. Is Paul's constant contact with friends due to a weakness in his life? Is this merely the result of Paul's personality? I don't think so. I believe Paul surrounded himself with friends because he, like every person, is created in the image of God. And we humans are made for community. God exists in a perfect triune relationship, and we, who are made by him and in his likeness, are built for friendships.

Even the mighty apostle Paul needed friends. But the biblical importance of friends isn't limited to what we can read about Paul. Look at Jesus—he was the "friend of sinners," and he called his disciples "friends" (John 15:12-15). To live apart from others is not only to be unlike Paul, but it's also to be unlike Jesus. Tim Keller rightly says,

> To need and to want deep spiritual friendships is not a sign
> of spiritual immaturity, but of maturity. It's not a sign of
> weakness, but a sign of health. ("Spiritual Friendship")

Think back to Genesis 2. Prior to sin entering the world, when everything is perfect, God declares everything he made as being "good." He notes just one exception: Adam is *alone* (Gen 2:18). Keller notes,

> Adam was not lonely because he was imperfect, but because he
> was perfect. The ache for friends is the one ache that's not the
> result of sin. . . . God made us in such a way that we couldn't
> even enjoy paradise without friends . . . human friends. . . .
> Adam had a perfect "quiet time" every day, for twenty-four
> hours a day. Yet, he needed friends. . . . If you are lonely,
> you aren't dysfunctional, you're fine. You're lonely because
> you're not a tree. You're lonely because you're not a machine.
> You're lonely because you're built this way. . . . Now I have to
> be careful about this because one of the reasons you may not
> have friends is because of sin, but the passion for it, the need

for it, the sense of lack of it, is not wrong at all. ("Spiritual Friendship")

Keller goes on to challenge believers to see this need and to be open to cultivating new friendships:

> Friends, let yourself need people. . . . Here's the trouble. When you're in trouble, it's too late. You know, very few people walk around saying, "Ah, I love air. Ah. Air! Air! What good is my brain without air? What good would my life be without air?" . . . You only sound that way when you're under water! Then you start to say, "Wow. Air!" And you don't walk around saying, "I need friends" until you emotionally and personally go *under*, and then it's too late—if you don't already have them. You need spiritual friendships. (Ibid.)

How Christian Friendship Is Established

When you become a Christian, you not only enter into a new relationship with God through Jesus, but you also enter into new relationships with other believers (1 John 3:11-15). We see this reality illustrated in Acts 21.

As Paul journeys through these various places and meets with various groups of people (some of whom he probably hadn't previously met!), we see a beautiful truth at work: the gospel creates spiritual friendships. What on earth would unite diverse people in diverse towns? A common Savior. The Christians in Tyre had such a bond with Paul, though they hardly knew him, that they could challenge Paul's decision making! And Paul lets them! How could this happen? Because they all shared the deepest possible commonality with him: they too called Jesus "Lord" (vv. 13-14).

Christians are united in the Holy Spirit. Paul told the Ephesians, "[Make] every effort to keep the unity of the Spirit through the bond of peace" (Eph 4:3). Paul didn't say to "attain" the unity of the Spirit, but to "keep" it. We can't ultimately create Christian fellowship; God establishes it. It's our job then to cultivate it, to work on it, to maintain it.

Just think about these scenes of Christian brothers and sisters bowing on the beach before the Lord (20:36; 21:5). Here are two vivid pictures of what brings people, who would otherwise never be together, into deep intimate friendship. They bow before the same Savior.

Friendships happen when two people share something in common. And in the case of Christian friendships, the common denominator couldn't be greater. Because Christians share a common passion in Christ, people who may not have otherwise spent time together can become great friends—no matter who they were before meeting Jesus. Young techies, then, can become friends with retirees; rock stars can become friends with doctors; hip-hoppers can share a deep bond of friendship with farmers; businessmen can be friends with hipsters; valley girls can enjoy friendships with home girls. And when diverse individuals kneel down before Jesus and do life together, it's a powerful testimony to the life-changing, friendship-forming power of the gospel. And it gets the world's attention. Jesus creates remarkable spiritual friendships.

How Christian Friendship Is Experienced

I see at least four ways Christian friendship gets expressed in this text.

Practicing hospitality. "Fellowship" means *to share.* The believers shared time and possessions with one another in general and shared their *homes* in particular. In at least four places, Paul stays with fellow believers: in Tyre (v. 4), in Ptolemais (v. 7), in Caesarea (v. 8), and finally in the home of Mnason of Cyprus at Jerusalem (v. 16). This indicates that early Christians didn't say, "*My* home is *my* refuge," as we often hear people today do in trying to justify self-indulgence and people avoidance. These believers viewed their homes as gifts from God (cf. Jas 1:17) and as places to be used for ministry and as a blessing to others.

Hospitality means "love for strangers," or "love for new people" (Keller, *Evangelism,* 198; cf. Lev 19:32-33; Heb 13:2). Practicing it is required of church leaders (Titus 1:8), commanded of all Christians (Rom 12:13), and seems to be a spiritual gift for some saints (1 Pet 4:9-10). We shouldn't practice hospitality with "complaining" (1 Pet 4:9), but with joy because, after all, Jesus himself has welcomed us (cf. John 14:2-3; Rom 15:7). Our displays of hospitality should be motivated by the gospel. Because God has welcomed us—new people—into his family, we should gladly welcome others into our homes and into our lives, as Lydia did (Acts 16:15).

While we must practice hospitality, some seasons of life will make extending it more difficult than others. But still we should seek to welcome others as much as possible. In transient areas there's a deep need for hospitality because more new people are always coming into the region and feeling disconnected (Keller, *Evangelism,* 198–99). Some, in fact, have no natural family living nearby. Therefore, if you live in such an area, remember that hospitality requires two basic things: (1) a spirit of welcome and openness to making new friends, and (2) the actual sharing of resources.

It's so important that the Christian resist the urge to avoid making new friends. It's difficult for some to be open to new relationships, especially if they have already invested much time and energy in previous friendships that were interrupted by a move, a job change, or even by death. But not having friendships is hard on the heart, and it's out of step with the relational nature of Christianity. You're made for biblical community. And you have no idea how sweet and precious new friendships may become. Don't cut yourself off from community.

Importantly, sharing resources is not limited to sharing your home. You can show a new person around town, give advice on shopping places, greet him or her at Sunday worship gatherings, and extend a lunch invitation after the service. And should you and the new person both have small children, you may want to schedule a playdate.

Showing affection is the second expression of friendship. I have already mentioned the emotion conveyed in the scenes in chapters 20 and 21. These friends displayed *visible, physical affection* for one another. We see them weeping, embracing, and kissing. In 21:5 we see that whole families accompanied Paul to the ship and knelt down with him in support. I don't want to push this too far, but we should somehow show our love for one another visibly. We should shake hands, offer hugs when appropriate, even give an encouraging shoulder pat. Paul tells the Romans, "Love one another deeply as brothers and sisters" (Rom 12:10).

Praying together. We see the Ephesian elders praying for Paul (20:36), and then the Christians in Tyre pray for him (21:5). John Polhill comments, "The reference to prayer is not incidental. Everyone was fully aware of the difficulties facing Paul at Jerusalem. They were also aware that prayer was the disciple's best fortification in a time of suffering and trial" (*Acts*, 434). Let's learn from this example. Deep Christian friendship involves times of fervent prayer for one another (cf. Rom 12:12). So pray for protection, blessing, guidance, healing, relationships, and all other aspects of life and ministry when you gather with believing friends.

Discussing important decisions. Acting on God's will wasn't merely a private matter for Paul. Others weighed in on his decision to go to Jerusalem. Following God's guidance involves allowing others to give you counsel. It doesn't mean their counsel is always right. In this case the Christians had really good intentions. They urged him not to go to Jerusalem. Paul, however, had to make the difficult decision to reject their counsel because he sensed God was leading him—like Jesus—to face suffering in Jerusalem.

So then, basic Christianity involves experiencing Christian friendships that are created by Jesus and cultivated through practices like those we see in 20:36–21:16.

The Cost of Christian Discipleship
ACTS 20:36–21:16

Paul is confident that God is leading him to Jerusalem. At the same time, other Christians are equally as confident that God has *not* called Paul to go to Jerusalem. So what do we do when we hear conflicting voices concerning the will of God? Let's consider the perspectives on Paul's decision and draw some practical guidance for following Jesus.

Perspectives on Paul's Decision

Let's consider four views on Paul's resolution to go to Jerusalem.

The Perspective of Paul (21:1-3). Paul is in a hurry. Luke uses phrases like "the next day," "another boat," and "we boarded another ship" to tell us about this stage of the journey. The apostle is moving quickly because he wants to be in Jerusalem by Pentecost (20:16), even though he knows it will involve suffering (20:22-24). He is determined to give a love offering from the Gentile churches to the Jerusalem churches and to testify there about the gospel of the grace of God (20:24). Paul doesn't care about the danger; he cares about obeying God's will, regardless of the cost.

The Perspective of the Christians in Tyre (21:4-6). "They told Paul not to go to Jerusalem" (v. 4). However, Paul didn't heed their counsel (vv. 5-6). How do we reconcile this text with the previous texts about the Spirit leading Paul to Jerusalem (19:21; 20:22-23)? Let's read on before handling this matter.

The Perspective of the Christians in Caesarea (21:7-13). As Paul stays with Philip, he meets the prophet Agabus (v. 10; cf. 11:28-30), who gives Paul an object lesson in the tradition of Old Testament prophets (e.g., 1 Kgs 11:29-32; Isa 20:2-6; Jer 13:1-11). Agabus took Paul's long belt, normally wrapped several times around the waist, and tied up his hands and feet with it. Then the prophet predicted that the Jews would tie Paul up and deliver him over to the Gentiles (v. 11). Though Agabus didn't forbid him from going to Jerusalem, he did warn Paul of the events to come. Following this dire prediction, the concerned saints in Caesarea (like the saints in Tyre) urged Paul not to go to the city (v. 12). But their counsel also proved fruitless (v. 13). Paul wouldn't be deterred.

The Perspective of Luke (21:12,14). Luke even included himself in the dissenting number. His presence is denoted by the "we" references at work throughout this passage. Apparently Luke also pleaded with Paul to change his plans. But after Paul rejected these pleas, too, the disciples surrendered (v. 14). The Christians respected their beloved leader's firm conviction.

Commentators have pointed out how the apostle's submission to God's will sounds a lot like Jesus's prayer in Gethsemane. Jesus didn't look forward to the suffering on the cross, but he submitted to the Father's plan for it by saying, "Not my will, but yours, be done" (Luke 22:42). Paul's deep anguish expressed in verse 13 has caused some to say that this moment was "Paul's Gethsemane" (Polhill, *Acts,* 436).

What should we make of these various perspectives? Some have tried to argue that Paul was being disobedient in going to Jerusalem.

Luke, however, believed Paul was right in going to Jerusalem, as indicated by the references to the Spirit in 19:21 and 20:22. The Spirit led Paul to make the decision to go to Jerusalem, and he also provided the compulsion to go (Stott, *Message of Acts,* 333). Further, Luke clearly sees Paul as following in his Lord's footsteps (ibid.).

With that said, what should we do with verses 4 and 11—these references to the Spirit? I like Stott's explanation: "[We should] draw a distinction between a *prediction* and a *prohibition*" (*Message of Acts;* emphasis added). Agabus simply predicted what would happen. The conclusions Paul's friends made based on that information weren't infallible. They were human deductions. All of this, then, helps us understand 21:4. It's probably best to take Luke's statement as a "condensed way of saying that the warning was divine while the urging was human" (ibid.). This is consistent with the Spirit's previous word to Paul. John Stott notes, "After all, the Spirit's word to Paul combined the compulsion to go with a warning of the consequences (20:22-23)" (ibid.).

Paul's decision should be admired. It was a difficult decision. But such is the cost of following Jesus. We can understand the dissenting voices. These people loved Paul. They were well intended. When they considered the inevitable suffering that awaited him, they naturally urged him to choose another path.

Indeed, it's not difficult to see the parallels between the journeys to Jerusalem made by Paul and his Savior. In a pivotal point in Luke's Gospel, Paul's loyal friend says that Jesus "determined to journey to

Jerusalem" (Luke 9:51; cf. Isa 50:7). Luke later mentions this dire destination frequently (cf. Luke 9:53; 13:33; 18:31; 19:11). Prior to the cross, Jesus told the disciples that he would be handed over to the Gentiles:

> "See, we are going up to Jerusalem. Everything that is written through the prophets about the Son of Man will be accomplished. For he will be handed over to the Gentiles, and he will be mocked, insulted, spit on; and after they flog him, they will kill him, and he will rise on the third day." (Luke 18:31-33)

Because of these foretold sufferings, Peter, like the Christians in Acts 21, tried to persuade Jesus to avoid such pains (Matt 16:21-23). But the Savior marched on. Praise God that he did! Now we like Paul must follow in our Master's footsteps, wherever he leads, in the strength he provides, keeping our eyes fixed on him (cf. Heb 12:1-2).

Principles to Apply

The Lord Jesus bids Christians to follow him, regardless of the cost, by the power of the Spirit. Let's consider a few lessons on what it means to count the cost to follow Jesus.

Love people, but love Jesus more. Paul clearly loved people in general, and his Christian friends in particular. Yet Paul treasured Jesus more than anyone. And so must we (cf. Matt 10:37). We must resist the urge to be people pleasers, choosing instead to be Jesus pleasers. We need to be able to say, like Paul, "I am ready . . . to die. . . for the name of the Lord Jesus" (21:13). No one or no thing is more valuable than Jesus. And we are ultimately accountable to him. So treasure the Lord supremely.

Value input, but follow God's will. Paul listened to the counsel of others. The book of Proverbs teaches the value of heeding godly counsel (e.g., Prov 15:22; 20:18). Refusing to allow other Christian friends to speak into our lives is foolish. But at the same time, there may be occasions when following Jesus will make us look foolish.

Missions history is filled with the accounts of missionaries who left people and possessions for dangerous places, even though friends and family urged them to choose different paths. These condensed stories of Jim Elliot, David Livingstone, William Carey, Adoniram Judson, C. T. Studd, and John G. Paton are just a few examples of what I mean:

> Jim Elliot, who decided to give his life to serve the Auca Indians in Ecuador even though people told him he was "too gifted" to consider such a thing, said: "Consider the call from

the throne above. 'Go ye, and from round about, come over and help us.' And even the call from damned souls below, 'Send Lazarus to my brothers that they come not to this place.' Impelled, then, by these voices, I dare not stay home while these Indians perish. So, what if the well-fed church in the homeland needs stirring? They have the Scriptures, Moses and the Prophets and a whole lot more. Their condemnation is written on their bankbooks and in the dust on their Bible covers. American believers have sold their lives to the service of mammon, and God has His rightful way of dealing with those who succumb to the spirit of Laodicea." Elliot and four other heroes gave their lives for the Auca Indians.

David Livingstone, who went into the heart of Africa, wrote a letter to the London Missionary Society: "So powerfully convinced am I that it is the will of the Lord that I should go to Africa, I will go no matter who opposes me." Later, after countless afflictions, he still wouldn't return home, even though others, like Henry M. Stanley, tried to persuade him to do so. Livingstone told Stanley, "God has called me to Africa, and I am staying here."

William Carey, "the father of modern missions," rose up in Europe and said to a group of ministers, "I am going to go to India and make the gospel known there." A minister in the audience rebuked him: "Sit down, young man. You are an enthusiast. When God pleases to convert the heathen in India, he will do it without consulting you or me." But Carey wouldn't be persuaded—and praise God he wouldn't!

Adoniram Judson, a Baptist missionary who had a desire to go to Burma (present-day Myanmar), a "closed country," against the pleas of others, took his new wife into the heart of Burma. He labored for thirty-eight years, suffering through cholera, malaria, dysentery, and unknown miseries that would claim the lives of his first wife and second wife, as well as seven of his thirteen children and numerous colleagues. As a result of his resolve, today there are close to four thousand Baptist congregations in the middle of Buddhist Burma. Over half a million believers are represented in those congregations.

C. T. Studd, a wealthy Englishman, came to faith in Christ and, soon thereafter, sensed God's call to go to China. His family brought a Christian worker in to dissuade him. Studd said, "Let's ask God then. I don't want to be pig-headed and go out there of my own accord. I just want to do God's will." He sought God's will and decided that he should indeed go. Then later, when he was fifty years old, he resolved that he should spend the rest of his life in Sudan, when others again urged him to do otherwise! In the next twenty years, he founded the Worldwide Evangelization Crusade through his work in Africa, which has planted gospel seeds all over Africa, Asia, and South America.

John G. Paton served for ten years as the pastor of a church in Glasgow, Scotland, but God began to burden his heart for the New Hebrides. These were Pacific Islands filled with cannibalistic peoples with no knowledge of the gospel. Twenty years earlier, two missionaries had been cannibalized there. Paton received opposition from everywhere. The church offered him more money to stay. When one older man protested, Paton famously said, "Mr. Dixon, you are advanced in years now and your own prospect is soon to be laid in the grave there to be eaten by worms. I confess to you if I can but live and die serving and honoring the Lord Jesus, it will make no difference to me whether I am eaten by cannibals or by worms. And in the great day, my resurrection body will arise as fair as yours in the likeness of our risen Redeemer." Paton wouldn't be persuaded, and soon he would be putting the Lord's Supper elements into the hands of former cannibals that had repented and trusted in Jesus. (Paraphrased from Platt, "A Mission Only the Church Can Stop")

The costly obedience of these missionaries, and others like them, blessed millions and set an inspiring example for a host of future missionaries. So value input but follow God's will.

There's something worse than dying: not living. Life is short. Don't waste it! Pour yourself out for the good of others, and then you will actually find life (Mark 8:34-35). This may involve risk and hardship, but it's worth it. Let us say with Paul, "I consider my life of no value to myself; my purpose is to finish my course and the ministry I received from the Lord Jesus, to testify to the gospel of God's grace" (Acts 20:24).

When you follow Jesus down the Calvary road, you're not alone and you won't regret it. Jesus—our unfailing friend—is with us as we make disciples of all nations (Matt 28:18-20). And even though suffering may be inevitable, following Jesus is worth it. This life is not the end. The best is yet to come (Phil 1:21-23). As John Piper commented on Acts 20:24, "Lord, keep me faithful to the job, then let me drop and go to my reward" (in Chandler, "My Heart Is Full"). When we see Christ, we will not regret having followed him.

Following Jesus is costly, but not following Jesus is more costly. I can see how an unbeliever could look at Paul's life—and Jesus's for that matter—and say, "What a waste!" But Scripture gives us a different view. Jesus said these words to his disciples about the disastrous result of pursuing material gain instead of him:

> *What does it benefit someone to gain the whole world and yet lose his life? What can anyone give in exchange for his life? For whoever is ashamed of me and my words in this adulterous and sinful generation, the Son of Man will also be ashamed of him when he comes in the glory of his Father with the holy angels.* (Mark 8:36-38)

The only thing more costly than discipleship is the cost of "nondiscipleship." Follow Jesus now, and you will experience unspeakable joy later. Reject him now, and you will experience eternal suffering later. He bids us to come and follow him. Let's surrender to his lordship.

Reflect and Discuss

1. How does this passage highlight the need for Christian friendship?
2. How are Christian friendships established?
3. How are Christian friendships experienced?
4. In what ways can you show hospitality to new people?
5. In what ways have you found it difficult to show affection to or to pray with your Christian friends? Explain.
6. Do you find it difficult to discuss important decisions with Christian friends? Why or why not?
7. What were Paul's friends telling him about going to Jerusalem? Do you think Paul made the right decision? Explain.
8. How does Paul display a supreme love for the Lord Jesus?
9. What do the experiences of Paul and other missionaries teach about the cost of following Jesus?
10. Take a moment to pray for your Christian friends, asking the Lord to empower you to fulfill the purposes of Jesus. What can you do today to be a good friend to another believer?

Paul in Jerusalem, Part 1

ACTS 21:17–22:21

Main Idea: Paul gets attacked by a Jewish mob while participating in a vow, and then he gives a defense speech before the crowd.

I. **Humility and Love Displayed in James and Paul (21:17-26)**
    A. A God-centered celebration (21:18-20a)
    B. A Grace-motivated gift
    C. A Gospel-driven plan (21:20b-26)
II. **Hostility and Lies Displayed in the Jewish Mob (21:27-36)**
III. **Honesty and Loyalty Displayed in Paul's Defense (21:37–22:21)**
    A. Former zeal (22:3-5)
    B. Encounter with Jesus (22:6-11)
    C. Commission (22:12-16)
    D. Vision in the temple (22:17-21)

Every year in college football a few schools have dominant offenses, while a few others have phenomenal defenses. So-called Monday morning quarterbacks debate which teams are better. One group says, "Defense wins championships!" Others declare, "A good defense is a good offense!" Actually, both offense and defense are important. The same is true in the Christian faith.

Believers must be effective on *offense*, taking the gospel to the nations. But we also have to be effective on *defense*, "ready at any time to give a defense to anyone who asks . . . for a reason for the hope that is in [us]" (1 Pet 3:15). Usually the focus of fulfilling our Christian mission is on offense—initiating gospel conversations with unbelievers. But sometimes unbelievers may actually start gospel conversations with us, and in those situations we must be ready to explain why we're Christians.

For the last decade of his life Paul has intentionally engaged strategic centers with the gospel during his three missionary journeys. But now we'll observe Paul playing defense. The apostle becomes a prisoner, and the rest of his ministry recorded in Acts is basically a set of reactions to opposition and assaults.

In Acts 21–26 we read of five defense speeches given by the apostle Paul and also learn what happens in between them. In the first two speeches Paul defends himself in Jerusalem before the Jewish crowd (22:1-21) and before the supreme Jewish council (23:1-6). His next three defenses are given in Caesarea. He goes before Felix in chapter 24, Festus in chapter 25, and finally King Herod Agrippa II in chapter 26. Because we, too, will face opposition, and because we must be good defenders of the faith like Paul, these chapters are relevant.

In what follows we will consider Paul's welcome in Jerusalem (21:17-26), the hostility of the Jewish crowd (21:27-36), and Paul's defense before the Jewish crowd (21:37–22:21). In these we will see an example of humility and love that we should pursue; an example of hostility and lies that we may face; and an example of the type of honesty and loyalty that should characterize our lives and conversations.

Humility and Love Displayed in James and Paul
ACTS 21:17-26

When Paul arrives in Jerusalem, things get interesting on day two. A formal meeting takes place between Paul, James (Jesus's half brother and primary spokesman of the Jerusalem church), and the Jerusalem elders. In this meeting we find a few wonderful expressions of humility and love.

A God-Centered Celebration (21:18-20a)

James and Paul together praise God for the victories achieved among the Gentiles. "God had done" the work among them (v. 19). Paul didn't brag; he gave glory to God. He also related "in detail" what God did on his journeys. It's a good practice to recount the evidences of God's grace and to share them with others. The psalmist says, "My soul, bless the LORD, and do not forget all his benefits" (103:2 ESV). So don't forget them. Don't take what God does for granted. Treasure it. Tell others about it.

When the Jewish brothers heard these things, they too "glorified God" (v. 20). The report concerned what God did among *the Gentiles*. And to it the Jewish Christians respond with joy, not jealousy or suspicion. This worshipful reaction is similar to previous reactions when the Jewish Christians received reports of God's grace shown to Cornelius, the Greeks in Antioch, and in the first missionary journey (11:18,22-23; 14:27; 15:12).

At times it's difficult for some Christians to rejoice when God is working through someone else or through someone else's church. But that's an attitude from which the follower of Jesus must repent. We must take note of the united praise that takes place here in Jerusalem. When God is at work in other places, saving sinners by his amazing grace, it's always a reason to rejoice! We are never in competition with other like-minded Christians; we're on the same team!

A Grace-Motivated Gift

At some point, in response to the grace of Jesus, certain Christians presented a love offering to the church in Jerusalem. This gift accomplished two purposes. It served as a means of helping the poor (cf. Acts 11:27-30; 20:35; 2 Cor 8:9; Gal 2:10; 6:10), and it also served as a symbol of unity. In sending it, the Gentile Christians were humbly and lovingly expressing their solidarity with the Jewish Christians.

Providing resources to others is a tangible way of expressing love and support. Christians should regularly display acts of generosity because we have received such amazing grace from Jesus. Let us look for ways to bless others through tangible gifts.

Unfortunately the gift in this case didn't actually accomplish the unifying purpose Paul hoped it would (Rom 15:31). It's possible that the "more right-winged elements in the church were distinctly cold towards it" (Marshall, *Acts of the Apostles*, 342). The reason? Paul's reputation was suffering. James gives Paul an interesting proposal in hopes of disarming the suspicions.

A Gospel-Driven Plan (21:20b-26)

The great news was that thousands of Jews trusted in Christ (v. 20b). But what hurt Paul's reputation was that many of these believers were zealous about continuing to keep Jewish customs while the word on the street was that Paul was urging Jewish Christians who lived in Gentile communities to abandon their heritage, giving up practices like circumcision.

James's concern wasn't about *salvation*—he and Paul agreed that salvation was by grace alone through faith alone in Christ alone, apart from works of the law (see Acts 15; cf. 1 Cor 7:19; Gal 6:15). He wasn't concerned about what Paul was teaching the *Gentiles either*—the Jerusalem Council had agreed on what should be communicated to them (see 21:25; cf. 15:20,29). James's concern didn't involve Paul's view of the *moral law*. Both James and Paul agreed that regenerate people should pursue holiness by walking in God's ways. The concern, rather, had to do with *Jewish cultural practices* (Stott, *Message of Acts*, 341). Should Jewish

Christians cease from following certain cultural traditions? Word had spread that Paul was teaching them to avoid customary activities. But this was untrue. He never demanded that the Jews abandon circumcision. In fact, his hurry to reach Jerusalem by Pentecost revealed that he still valued Israel's calendar (Johnson, *Let's Study Acts*, 266).

Though Paul proclaimed that Christ was the end of the law (Rom 10:4), he didn't insist that Jewish believers give up Jewish customs (Rom 14–15; 1 Cor 8–10). From Paul's writings one can understand how such rumors could develop (see Rom 2:25-30; Gal 4:9; 5:6). Nevertheless, the conclusions drawn were false (Marshall, *Acts of the Apostles*, 344).

Paul clearly loved his countrymen. In Romans 9:1-5 he said that he would trade places with unbelieving Jews if that would accomplish their salvation. Many of his countrymen loved Paul too, but sadly, many others distorted his views. They smeared him and misrepresented him. And that had to hurt the apostle deeply.

So James proposed that Paul demonstrate his respect for traditional Jewish Christianity by participating in a vow, which involved the presentation of an offering at the temple (21:20b-25). He suggested that Paul go with four brothers who were soon to complete a Nazirite vow (20:23; cf. Num 6:1-21). James asked Paul to pay for the animals for their sacrifice. And by fulfilling this request (v. 26), Paul showed that he didn't object to Jewish converts following Jewish customs as long as the gospel wasn't compromised and the customs weren't required of Gentiles. Paul gave notice that in seven days he and the brothers would appear at the temple to conclude the vow and make the offerings.

Since the minimum period for the vow was thirty days, it seems that Paul didn't undergo the Nazirite vow. However, he did previously do so in 18:18 as a traditional Jewish expression of thanksgiving or petition, which in the words of I. Howard Marshall would be "theologically acceptable" and not a violation of the gospel (*Acts of the Apostles*, 300). Paul's seven-day purification (v. 26) was probably due to the fact that Paul was returning from Gentile territory:

> Often a Jew on returning to the Holy Land after a sojourn
> in Gentile territory would undergo ritual purification. The
> period involved was seven days (cf. Num 19:12), which fits the
> present picture (v. 27). Paul thus underwent ritual purification
> to qualify for participation in the completion ceremony of the
> four Nazirites which took place within the sacred precincts
> of the temple. This would be a thorough demonstration of
> his full loyalty to the Torah, not only in his bearing the heavy

expenses of the vow but also in his undergoing the necessary purification himself. (Polhill, *Acts*, 449)

Was this a compromise of the gospel? I don't think so. Paul's actions are in keeping with his missionary policy of becoming "all things to all people" for the sake of the gospel's spread (1 Cor 9:22-23). In the book of Acts, we see that Paul remained true to his Jewish heritage in his own relations with Jews (cf. 18:18; 20:6; 23:5). He previously had Timothy circumcised (16:3), not as a matter of salvation but for unity and mission. Here Paul is willing to undergo some purification rituals in order to appease Jewish consciences.

Previously, Paul said the gospel was his ultimate motivation (20:24). In this episode Paul sacrifices his safety and his freedom for its sake. So don't miss Paul's gospel centrality, humility, and desire for unity here. Paul could have said, "Let the haters hate. I'm going to do what I want!" But he didn't. He submitted to James's proposal in hopes of unifying the church and advancing the gospel. He lived out his words, "To the Jews I became like a Jew, to win Jews; to those under the law, like one under the law—though I myself am not under the law—to win those under the law" (1 Cor 9:20).

This passage reveals the heart of this great missionary. Paul's passionate about God's glory, the unity of the church, and the evangelization of all people. He's literally willing to do anything for the sake of the gospel—as long as he doesn't compromise it. Paul offers a powerful picture of Christian liberty in this passage, showing us spiritual maturity. Paul wouldn't use his liberty to show everybody all he could do because of the freedom he enjoyed in Christ. Instead, he became a "slave to everyone" (1 Cor 9:19) like Jesus, who humbled himself, looking on the interests of others in selfless, redeeming love (cf. Phil 2:3-11).

We too should be flexible when ministering to various cultures. Some cultures are more traditional, while others are more progressive. When outside your immediate sphere, you may find it necessary to learn to adapt to the ways of another group for the sake of the gospel's spread. *Never compromise the gospel* and *never participate in sin* when you are attempting to reach people, but don't convey the impression that everyone must first be like you before they can take your invitation to accept Christ seriously. Some Christians struggle with this aspect of missionary living. But when the gospel is our main thing—when we find our identity in Christ rather than in an ethnic group, social class, or particular culture—then we will be able to minister humbly and lovingly with Pauline flexibility.

Hostility and Lies Displayed in the Jewish Mob
ACTS 21:27-36

From its focus on humility and love, Acts 21 turns to hostility and lies. What a stark contrast between the spirit of Paul and the spirit of the Jewish crowd in verses 27-36. Some Asian Jews—probably from Ephesus (see 21:29)—recognize Paul and respond violently to him (vv. 27-28). Their wild accusations against him are designed to generate mob violence. The charges sounded like what Stephen's accusers said about him before stoning him to death (6:13-14). And the accusations are ironic given that Paul was actually undergoing a purification ritual in order to enter the temple (in Stott, *Message of Acts,* 343). Paul did teach, however, that the Messiah is the fulfillment of the law, the people, and the temple—not in a way to denigrate them but in a way to reveal their true glory as Christ himself taught (ibid.).

The Jews assumed that Paul was defiling the temple by bringing Trophimus the Ephesian (v. 29; cf. 20:4) beyond the wall that separated the court of the Gentiles from the inner sanctuary, which was off limits to Gentiles (cf. Eph 2:14). Of course, he had done no such thing. Paul knew the consequence of this violation was the death penalty.

As a result of these claims, the crowd became hostile and tried to kill Paul. Fortunately, the Roman soldiers (stationed nearby, knowing that the temple area could be a volatile place) hear the wild uproar. Lysias, the commander, had the responsibility of maintaining peace in the city, and he proceeds to arrest Paul and put the apostle in "two chains" (v. 33), perhaps indicating that he bound him hand and foot, as Agabus predicted (v. 11). Claudius inquired about Paul and what he had done to stimulate the riot, but due to the shouts of the crowd, he couldn't discern the facts, so he ordered Paul be taken into the barracks (v. 34). When the men reached the steps of the Antonia fortress, the soldiers had to lift Paul up and carry him in order to protect him from the angry mob (v. 35). The crowd continued to chant, "Get rid of him!" (v. 36), just as an earlier crowd in Jerusalem demanded of Pontius Pilate, "Take this man away!" (Luke 23:18) and "Crucify him!" (Mark 15:13).

This ugly scene makes us wonder whether James's plan backfired. But I don't think it did. Paul didn't expect to have a pain-free experience in Jerusalem, for he knew afflictions awaited him there (cf. Acts 20:23; 21:4,10-11). His submission to James's plan was designed to show his support to Jewish Christians who were committed to their Jewish heritage, not to escape hardship. While the immediate outcome of his actions looks like a failure, we have to take the longer view. Paul's actions would eventually put the suspicions of many Jewish Christians to rest. Further, this event would be one link in the chain of sovereign events that would deliver Paul to Rome (Johnson, *Let's Study Acts*, 268).

We must always make the right decisions in the sight of God and let things unfold as they may. Obedience to Jesus will involve hardship (2 Tim 3:12), so we shouldn't be surprised should intimidation, hate, and false accusations come our way. Many Christians have been, and will continue to be, victims of hostility and lies. Early Christians were accused of incest, cannibalism, and atheism simply because they greeted one another with a holy kiss, took the Lord's Supper, and refused to worship the emperor. Today we're accused of immorality and bigotry because of our views on marriage and life.

When falsely accused and persecuted, remember that the Suffering Servant is with you. Jesus stands ready to grant you grace in time of need, and he will have the last word.

Honesty and Loyalty Displayed in Paul's Defense
ACTS 21:37–22:21

When Paul and the Roman soldiers reach the top of the stairs, before entering the barracks, Paul asks the tribune for permission to speak (21:37). The soldiers express surprise at Paul's proficient Greek skills. Lysias assumes Paul might be the Egyptian assassin who had stirred up a revolt recently (v. 38). According to Josephus, this false prophet presented himself as a new Moses or Joshua, gathered together thousands of followers, and lived in the desert. He predicted that Jerusalem's walls would fall like Jericho when surrounded by his men, leaving Roman forces exposed. Instead of this happening, four hundred of his rebels were killed, two hundred were captured, and the Egyptian and the rest fled (in Polhill, *Acts*, 455).

Paul informs Lysias that he is neither a terrorist nor an Egyptian but a Jew and a citizen of the honorable city of Tarsus (v. 39), one of the great university cities in the Roman world (Stott, *Message of Acts*, 347). Lysias assumed Paul was a rabble-rouser and may have associated him with an Egyptian due to Paul's shaved head. But upon learning of Paul's distinguished background, Lysias grants Paul permission to speak. Paul stands at the top of the steps, and the crowd falls silent as Paul addresses them in their own language ("Hebrew dialect" can mean Aramaic; 21:40; cf. 22:2; 26:14).

In Paul's "defense" (*apologia*, 22:1), he provides a respectful and honest account of life and conversion in response to the charges made against him. He has almost been killed. He has been arrested and chained. But he speaks calmly. If I were to speak in that situation, I'm afraid my words would be tainted by anger.

Paul had two purposes in addressing the crowd. First, he wanted them to hear that he was loyal to his Jewish heritage. He saw himself as standing in continuity with it though he confessed Jesus as Messiah, the Righteous One foretold by the prophets. Second, Paul wanted them to know the facts about his conversion. His life and ministry weren't the result of his own imagination and wild ideas. They were the result of the sovereign, transforming grace of Jesus. Paul used this defense opportunity as an occasion to speak the good news.

His loyalty is conveyed in the careful way he addresses the crowd ("Brothers and fathers"), in his choice of language (22:2), in his mention of being raised in Jerusalem and educated under Gamaliel, in his reference to Ananias's ministry (vv. 12-16), in his reference to the "God of our fathers", and in his statement of his vision in the temple (vv. 17-20). Paul respects his Jewish heritage.

The apostle's honesty is simply displayed in the telling of his testimony. We can observe it in four sections.

Former Zeal (22:3-5)

Paul begins by identifying with the crowd, reflecting on his former life. He was born a Jew in Tarsus and had been brought up in Jerusalem. He sat at the feet of Gamaliel. He had been a strict Pharisee, indeed a Pharisee of Pharisees (Phil 3:4-7). His zeal was expressed in the violent persecution of Christians, both men and women, whom he had handed over to death (cf. 8:3; 26:10). Paul wanted to destroy Christianity. The high priest and council of elders would confirm his story (22:5). They knew that at one time Paul had even sought to travel all the way to Damascus to persecute followers of the Way.

Encounter with Jesus (22:6-11)

But then something happened: Paul met the living Christ, and that changed everything.

The light blinding Paul around noon implies it outshone the sun at its strongest time (cf. 26:13, perhaps echoing Deut 28:28-29). Paul fell to the ground and heard Jesus speaking to him. Paul includes in his defense speech that it was Jesus of *Nazareth* who confronted him. Before this Jewish audience, Paul wanted to be clear about Jesus's identity. Jesus informed Paul that he had not only been persecuting the church but also the Lord himself in his eagerness to stamp out Christianity (cf. 9:4-5; 26:14-15). This truth highlights the special relationship between Christ and the church.

Jesus didn't execute Paul on the Damascus road. Instead, he turned the terrorist into an evangelist by his amazing grace (cf. Gal 1:13-17; 1 Tim 1:12-17). Paul was commissioned, not consumed, as he would later get instructions in Damascus when meeting Ananias (cf. 9:10-17).

Commission (22:12-16)

Paul goes on to describe Ananias's devotion to the law, adding the note that Ananias "had a good reputation with all the Jews" (v. 12). Paul's omission of some of the story about Ananias that is recorded in Acts 9 reveals part of Paul's purpose in this defense speech. Paul wants to emphasize his respect for Israel. The person who led Paul into the Christian faith (Ananias) was himself well known for keeping God's commands.

Let's consider four parts to Paul's commission.

The "God of our ancestors" called Paul (22:14). This is the language God used in Moses's burning bush experience (Exod 3:15-16). The same God who commissioned Moses also commissioned Paul. In making this connection, Paul also highlights God's marvelous grace. Did Moses deserve to hear God's voice and be used to bring people into freedom? No. Did Paul deserve such grace? Did he deserve the privilege of proclaiming liberty to the nations? No. Both men were dependent on grace.

God appointed Paul to see "the Righteous One" (22:14). This too is an allusion to the Old Testament, stressing the continuity between the Old Testament and the work of Jesus the Messiah. Isaiah speaks of this Righteous One as the obedient Servant who was wounded for our transgressions (Isa 53:5-6,11; cf. Acts 3:14; 7:52). The only way for a person to be righteous is through the Righteous One—not through religious effort. Paul's life and ministry would be devoted to proclaiming this message (e.g., 2 Cor 5:21; Phil 3:9). So then Paul is pointing out that Judaism, rightly understood, should culminate in faith in this Jesus, the Righteous One of whom Isaiah spoke.

God called Paul to be his "witness" to "all people" (22:15; cf. v. 21; 26:17; Gal 1:16). The man would give eyewitness testimony (1 Cor 9:1) to people of all ethnicities and social classes. He told the Corinthians that he was compelled to preach this message (1 Cor 9:16).

Paul received instructions on how to act on his commission. Ananias tells Paul to "get up and be baptized, and wash away your sins, calling on his name" (22:16). Baptism is the expression of one's faith in Jesus. Calling on the name of Jesus is a cry for salvation, rescue, cleansing, and new life. Paul became a new creation in Christ Jesus (2 Cor 5:21), as can anyone else who calls on the name of the Lord (Rom 10:13).

Vision in the Temple (22:17-21)

In the last part of Paul's defense speech, he tells of the vision he had in the temple. This part of Paul's story doesn't appear in Acts 9 (cf. 9:26-30). He probably included it here in order to answer the mob's charge that he had defiled the temple. He had no interest in defiling the temple; he prayed in it.

In some ways Paul's vision sounds similar to Isaiah's vision (Isa 6:1-13), once again showing continuity between Judaism and the Christian faith. Both men were called through a vision and were commissioned (22:18-21). Both were told that people would reject their messages. Isaiah was told to stay in the city to face the rejection, but Paul was told to leave (22:18; Polhill, *Acts,* 462).

Paul describes how he protested the vision, another element common to calling narratives in the Old Testament. Paul argued he should stay in Jerusalem because while he previously persecuted Christians in Jerusalem, he was now the Lord's convincing witness (vv. 19-20). Despite the argument the Lord persisted and said, "Go, because I will send you far away to the Gentiles" (v. 21). This calling to the Gentiles wasn't merely for the sake of safety but as a matter of purpose. The Lord had raised Paul up specifically so that he would be a witness to the Gentiles (cf. 9:15-16).

With the mention of the Gentiles, the mob's suppressed emotion erupted (22:22). Paul didn't get to deal with the charges of defiling the temple.

Several features stand out from Paul's defense. Let me highlight three final applications.

First, we can learn from Paul's calmness. In this intense moment Paul responds with meekness, gentleness, and compassion. He doesn't respond in anger. He doesn't attack. He reasons. When you are in a pressure-filled conversation, ask the Father to calm you and give you grace to speak the message with gentleness and respect (cf. Gal 5:22-23; 2 Tim 2:24-25; Jas 4:17-18; 1 Pet 3:15).

Second, we can learn from Paul's courage. In the face of opposition, Paul didn't bend. He stood his ground. Such boldness also comes from God (cf. 4:29-31). Many Christians can remain calm, but that's because they cave in and fail to speak truth when pressed. We need both truth and love (cf. Eph 4:15). Only churches that love people *and* stand firmly on the gospel against the winds of culture will have anything to offer this broken world.

Third, we can learn from Paul's calling. Paul knew his assignment: proclaim the good news. That's our job too. On this particular occasion, the crowd is enraged against the apostle. On other occasions in Acts, however, people respond to his words in faith. We aren't responsible for the results of what happens when we lovingly proclaim the good news; we are responsible for sharing it.

My friend Todd told me about a young man at his school. I'll call him Kyle. Kyle was an outspoken atheist in their predominantly Christian academy. His parents were also atheists. They sent him to the school only because its academic record was so good. When my friend Todd first met Kyle, the boy boldly declared, "I'm an atheist." To this Todd replied, "Well, I'm glad to meet you. I'd love to talk to you sometime about how you arrived at your belief system."

Over the years, from Kyle's first day at kindergarten to his senior year of high school, he saw the gospel on beautiful display. His friends and teachers weren't like the hypocrites about whom he often complained. They loved him well. He also heard the gospel over and over from people like Todd. Yet Kyle remained resistant to the message of what Jesus did for him—until the senior class trip, which involved walking in the places where the apostle Paul once walked.

Todd told me that as their group went from one city to another in the Mediterranean world, Kyle became more and more fascinated by what he was experiencing. He asked tons of questions—not to debate what he heard but out of genuine interest. In those days he didn't leave the side of the student chaplain. And eventually, at the island of Patmos, and after an emotional conversation, Kyle placed his faith in Jesus.

Soon after that Todd shared this story about Kyle with a wealthy group of people at a country club in North Carolina. When he finished, a man in his nineties tearfully approached Todd and thanked him for the message. Todd didn't know then that the older man was dying of cancer and was, in fact, not a Christian. He learned the news on the way home.

"We have to turn around," Todd announced as the car sped away from the club. "I need to visit with that man."

Soon Todd and the elderly fellow settled in for a conversation. The man told Todd that he had little interest in religion. His life had been devoted to making money. He had made billions. "But," he said after a pause, "what good is all that now?"

You are probably hoping that before Todd left the country club that afternoon the wealthy man gave his heart to the Lord. But that's not what happened. Instead, the two men parted amicably and have continued to stay in touch through letter writing. While Todd has the man's word that he is reading the Bible, Todd is less sure about the man's thoughts on what he's shared with him regarding Jesus. "At least I know he has heard the gospel," Todd says. "I can't make him respond."

These stories reveal that while some plant the seeds of the gospel through proclamation and others water it through loving actions and deeper teaching that reinforce the message, only God gives growth (1 Cor 3:6). Sometimes people will be enraged by a presentation of the gospel; sometimes people will hear it and inquire for more information; and sometimes people will surrender to the lordship of Jesus—though they, like Kyle, may take their time doing so. We must remember that no one is beyond the reach of God's converting grace. Just look at Paul! Just look at us! Be faithful to sow the seed and beg God to send rain to nourish it as you humbly and courageously give an answer for the hope within you.

Reflect and Discuss

1. What does it mean to defend the faith?
2. When might you need to defend the faith?
3. How do Paul and James display humility and love?
4. Compare Acts 21:20b-26 with 1 Corinthians 9:15-23. Are Paul's actions and his missionary policy consistent? Explain your answer.
5. Why were the Jewish people enraged at Paul?
6. In what modern contexts might Christians face hostility and false accusations? How should we respond to them?
7. Generally speaking, what does Paul try to accomplish in his defense speech in Acts 22:1-21?
8. How is Paul's calling similar to the callings of Moses and Isaiah? How is it different?
9. Do you think Paul's speech was effective? Explain.
10. Take a few moments to pray for God to help you present the gospel this week. Ask God to bring your hearers to faith in Christ.

Paul in Jerusalem, Part 2

ACTS 22:22–23:11

Main Idea: Jesus was with Paul when he testified before the authorities, and Jesus is with us when we speak the gospel before unbelieving and unfriendly audiences.

I. **Reactions (22:22–23:10)**
   A. "Paper"—Paul reveals his Roman citizenship (22:22-29).
   B. "Rock"—Paul rebukes the high priest (22:30–23:5).
   C. "Scissors"—Paul divides the Pharisees and Sadducees (23:6-10).

II. **Reassurance (23:11)**
   A. The Lord knows us.
   B. The Lord is with us.
   C. The Lord is for us.
   D. The Lord isn't finished with us.

Now we come to the second of Paul's five defense speeches. At the end of his trials, we're reminded where to find the *strength* to speak before unbelieving and unfriendly audiences. It's one thing to know what to say about Jesus and how to say it, but there's also the challenge of finding the strength and encouragement to proclaim it. In this passage we see that the same Jesus who stood for Paul at the cross now stands by Paul in his trials (23:11).

We too need this encouragement. Jesus stood for us, and he now stands with us. The Jesus who was with Paul when he testified before the authorities is the same Jesus who stands with us when we speak the gospel before hostile audiences.

In the previous chapter we observed how Paul lived out several ideas he taught in his letters. We reflected on 1 Corinthians 9, in which Paul attempted to "win Jews" (Acts 21:17-26; 1 Cor 9:20). Romans 8:28—"All things work together for the good of those who love God"—could be considered in each of these concluding chapters of Acts as we observe how God is accomplishing his sovereign purposes. In this portion of Paul's afflictions in Jerusalem, the message of the book of 2 Corinthians comes to mind: "strength through weakness." Paul told the Corinthians,

Now we have this treasure in clay jars, so that this extraordinary power may be from God and not from us. We are afflicted in every way but not crushed; we are perplexed but not in despair; we are persecuted but not abandoned; we are struck down but not destroyed. (2 Cor 4:7-9; cf. 2 Cor 6:3-10; 11:23-28; 12:9-12)

We indeed see Paul afflicted, perplexed, persecuted, and struck down; but he's not crushed, driven to despair, abandoned, or destroyed. He knows Jesus is with him. This section of Acts points us to the all-sufficient grace of Jesus, who uses wounded soldiers to accomplish his mission.

We pick up the story in 22:22. After Paul mentions his ministry to the Gentiles before the Jewish mob (v. 21), the riot resumes. To say this was a tough crowd would be a massive understatement. This unwilling audience wants to kill Paul! Both their words and actions express outrage (v. 23). Paul never even gets a chance to address the accusation that he had defiled the temple (21:28). Of course, as I. Howard Marshall says, "The real issue is not whether Paul defiled the temple, but whether Judaism was prepared to tolerate Christianity" (*Acts of the Apostles,* 360). It seems it was not.

Paul, thankfully, is rescued from the mob (22:24). We then see how Paul continues to respond to more trials in Jerusalem in the remainder of our selected text (22:25–23:10).

It's not an easy task to understand or teach this passage because Paul's actions are simply reported here. Luke offers no appraisal of them. What I can say for certain is that Paul is clearly intelligent, savvy, bold, and passionate in front of the commander and the religious council. But are his responses filled with integrity and gospel witness? Bible teachers go in various directions when it comes to answering this question—especially with regard to 23:1-10. One thing is for sure: Paul is a man with feet of clay. In this chapter we see his humanity and his need for the Lord's grace. It's a need we all share.

Before we examine Paul's reactions, consider the humanity of the Roman commander named Lysias (23:26). He can't seem to get the facts about Paul. We read of his first attempt in 21:34. At that point Lysias took Paul to the barracks to question him. Lysias's second attempt to get the facts comes here in 22:24. Once Paul reveals his Roman citizenship, making it unjust to examine him by flogging, Lysias tries a third approach. He decides to let the religious council examine Paul (22:30)—apparently as he listens in. Just thinking about this chapter makes me imagine Lysias and his wife sitting down for dinner and talking about his day. "How's it going with that Paul fellow?" she might ask. "I can't get anywhere with this case," he'd probably reply in frustration. "I've tried everything!"

Now we have the flow of the story. Paul is on trial. In response to Paul's gestures of love in Jerusalem, the crowd rejected him, like those who previously rejected Jesus, the Suffering Servant. All the while, Lysias is trying to figure out what all the commotion is about.

That brings me to the exposition. First we will observe how Paul responded to his trials. In 23:11 we will see how the Lord comforted his afflicted servant.

Reactions
ACTS 22:22–23:10

Paul's reactions to his escalating trials intrigue me. First, he reacts to Lysias by revealing his Roman citizenship (22:22-29). Paul then rebukes the Jewish high priest who had ordered Paul to be physically assaulted (22:30–23:5). Finally, Paul divides the Pharisees and Sadducees by bringing up the subject of the resurrection (23:6-10). I find I better remember Paul's reactions when I mentally note them as "paper," "rock," and "scissors."

"Paper"—Paul Reveals His Roman Citizenship (22:22-29)

After the crowd rages at Paul, expressing their desire to rip him to shreds, Lysias takes him away for examination (vv. 22-24). It appears that Lysias means to employ a "Jack Bauer" method of examination, planning to have the apostle flogged. John Polhill notes the violent nature of this form of torture:

> This was a particularly cruel manner of scourging that
> consisted of a beating across the raw flesh with leather thongs
> in which were inserted rough pieces of bone or metal. The
> thongs were set in a stout wooden handle. This was a much
> more severe manner of beating than that of the rods which
> Paul and Silas underwent at Philippi (16:22f., 37; cf. 2 Cor
> 11:25). It was not uncommon for the victim to die as a result
> of the flagellum. (*Acts*, 464)

But just before the beating begins, Paul asks a centurion an attention-grabbing question: "Is it legal for you to scourge a man who is a Roman citizen and is uncondemned?" (v. 25). Paul knew, of course, that it was illegal to flog a Roman citizen prior to allowing him a formal trial or sentencing (cf. 16:37). His claim of citizenship could have been verified in the public records of Tarsus (Johnson, *Let's Study Acts*, 278).

The attending centurion, knowing the danger of transgressing the law, immediately halts the plans and quickly reports the problem to the commander (22:26). Lysias is really perplexed now! He finds out that Paul is actually a Roman citizen—not just a Johnny-come-lately to citizenship, like himself, who became a citizen *by bribe*, but a man who became one *by birth* (Johnson, *Let's Study Acts*, 465).

How was Paul a Roman citizen by birth? There are several theories, including the idea that the Romans may have awarded Paul's family citizenship because their tent-making trade proved useful to the military. Whatever the case, Paul's citizenship proves to be significant to what happens next.

This marks another swing and a miss by the Roman commander. The examination ceases, and Lysias still doesn't know the truth about Paul. Added to his frustration is a sense of fear (v. 29). He will put a positive spin on his actions later (see 23:27), but at this point Lysias moves to another approach.

Paul urged Christians to submit to the governing authorities as God's ministers of justice (Rom 13:1-7), but he also expected the government to exercise its duties rightly. Paul challenged those in power to wield their authority honorably. This suggests there's a difference between humbly suffering for Christ and being a victim of injustice. We live in a land of laws, and if the laws protect us, then we should appeal to them. If these laws prevent us from following Jesus, then it's better to obey God than man (Acts 5:29).

"Rock"—Paul Rebukes the High Priest (22:30–23:5)

Paul encounters more hostility as Lysias sets him before the Jewish Sanhedrin. The Sanhedrin included the high priestly aristocracy and the ruling elders, who were mainly Sadducees. The minority of members were Pharisees, who were represented among the scribes (Polhill, *Acts*, 470). Paul "looked straight at" the Sanhedrin and offered his opening statement (23:1). First, he notes his own character—his actions are upright.

When it comes to defending the faith, our Christian character really matters (cf. 1 Tim 1:5; 1 Pet 3:14-16). We come to Jesus for a clean conscience (Heb 10:22). Paul told the Corinthians, "I am not conscious of anything against myself, but I am not justified by this. It is the Lord who judges me" (1 Cor 4:4). We should pursue a blameless life, and when we're made aware of sin, we must humbly repent in order to maintain a good conscience and glorify God (see 24:16).

No sooner did Paul testify to the uprightness of his own character than did the high priest, Ananias, command those near Paul to "strike him on the mouth" (23:2; cf. John 18:22). What a bizarre interruption! One would expect a leader in the Jewish high court to display civility and justice. Ananias's response was totally unacceptable and unbiblical (see Lev 19:15), and it makes his character stand out in stark contrast to Paul's.

Why such anger and aggression? First, Ananias thought Paul a wicked man. He thought him a troublemaker. But Paul wouldn't admit to any guilt. In what he said, Paul didn't mean that he was sinless but that he lived above reproach and that he had done nothing to provoke the riot (see Acts 25:8). This claim sounded absurd to Ananias so he lost his temper. Second, Ananias was a wicked man. According to historical records, he was known for greed, a quick temper, violence, and pro-Roman sentiments.

Being struck in the face tends to raise a reaction! Paul responded to the unnecessary violence by rebuking the high priest (23:3). We can certainly sympathize with this reaction.

Paul knew the law, and he knew that Ananias's order was unjust (Lev 19:15). He therefore threw a verbal rock back at him, calling out the hypocrisy of the high priest (cf. Deut 28:22; Ezek 13:10-16; Matt 23:27), who was likely dressed in his fine religious attire. Paul's language of a "whitewashed" wall was an insult. He was saying that the priest outwardly looked clean and stable but was actually corrupt and flimsy. Paul's statement was more prophetic than he probably realized. In less than ten years, Ananias's Jewish freedom fighters would assassinate him (Polhill, *Acts*, 468).

While Paul spoke the truth, and while his cause was just, he did seem to regret speaking to the high priest in such a way, based on the manner in which he steps back from his statement in verse 5. Many correctly point out that Paul's initial heated reaction doesn't reflect the spirit of passages like 1 Corinthians 4:12: "When we are reviled, we bless; when we are persecuted, we endure it" (cf. Matt 5:39). Jesus and Paul both condemned hypocrisy, but at the time of his trial, our Lord responded to his accusers with restraint (see Luke 22:63-71; John 18:19-23). This indicates that while we must speak out against injustice, we must always do so with respect and restraint.

The assembly was definitely provoked by Paul's words (23:4). Paul responded to their outcry, citing Exodus 22:28 (v. 5). What should we make of this statement?

The first main view is what I call the *sincerity* view. It could be that Paul genuinely didn't know he was speaking to the high priest. Maybe (1) Ananias wasn't dressed with his religious garb since this wasn't a regular meeting of the Sanhedrin; (2) Paul didn't know who gave the order because of the commotion in the meeting; (3) Paul's eyesight caused him to see only a blurry white-robed figure; or (4) because Paul had been away from Jerusalem for so long, he didn't know Ananias.

Another option is what we may call the *sarcasm* view. Perhaps in his quip, Paul was using irony, as if to say, "Brothers I see nothing priestly in this man" (Lev 19:15; Deut 25:1; Calvin, "Christ the End of the Law," 318). If that is the case, Paul is here ministering in a prophetic sense. He first offers the rebuke, and then he makes this strong statement about Ananias's character.

But I hold (lightly!) to the idea that Paul sincerely didn't know that the high priest gave the order. He sought to address people respectfully, and when he crossed the line, he admitted it. We too should pursue the proper tone with ruling authorities as we address them (Bock, *Acts*, 674–75), refusing to mimic the disrespect so rampant in our culture. And should we fail to speak as we ought, we should emulate Paul's humility.

One thing is for certain, Paul was in need of the Lord's grace. He had been beaten by a Jewish mob, almost flogged by the Romans, and at his hearing he was punched in the face by religious leaders. In spite of these many challenges, however, he was never alone.

"Scissors"—Paul Divides the Sadducees and Pharisees (23:6-10)

The trial takes a sharp turn when Paul, still in the middle of his speech, brings up the reason for his arrest: "the hope of the resurrection" (v. 6). His words end up "dividing and conquering."

Was Paul trying to divert attention away from himself in this move? Perhaps. But I don't think we should jump to that conclusion. Paul did indeed point out the real issue behind his trials. It was a theological dispute. His belief in Jesus's *resurrection* separated him from the rest of the Jews, and throughout his defense speeches, he constantly brings up the resurrection (cf. 24:14-16; 26:6-8; 28:20). Further, at the end of this trial Jesus commended Paul for testifying about him here in Jerusalem

(23:11). So I think Paul was simply stating the facts. His belief in the risen Christ made him intolerable to many of the Jews. With that said, Paul may have anticipated the division that would follow his statement. And those who hold to the idea that Paul was thinking, *This whole trial is going nowhere, let me bring up the resurrection and show them that even they have disagreements,* may not be that far off.

Was Paul correct in calling himself a Pharisee and a son of Pharisees? Well, he was in fact educated in the pharisaic tradition (cf. 22:3; Phil 3:5). His assertion doesn't have to be taken as a claim that his literal father was a Pharisee. And he wasn't necessarily claiming to endorse everything the Pharisees taught, but with respect to their eschatological hope revealed in Scripture (cf. Ezek 37:1-14; Dan 12:1-3), he still identified with them. Jesus was the fulfillment of that hope.

The Sadducees didn't believe in the resurrection. Nor did they embrace the existence of *angels,* nor the *spirit*—a fact probably referring to the eschatology of the Pharisees. But the Pharisees embraced these ideas (23:8). The Sadducees only recognized the books of Moses as authoritative, and they argued that such ideas weren't found there. Jesus, however, showed them on one occasion that denying the resurrection contradicted God's covenant faithfulness to the patriarchs (Luke 20:27-39; Johnson, *Let's Study Acts,* 283). The Pharisees believed the resurrection was Israel's ultimate hope. Paul knew what these groups believed. He identified with the Pharisees, essentially saying that Jesus is the fulfillment of their shared hope.

The effect of the theological controversy was sharp division. The Pharisees actually defended Paul in this case! As the apostle's story unfolds, others will make the same conclusion about Paul's innocence (e.g., 23:29; 25:25-27; 26:32). But here the shouting soon turned to violence, and Lysias once again had to intervene and rescue Paul, delivering him back to the barracks. Still the commander lacked the answers he desired.

The resurrection remains central to the Christian faith. Paul said, "If Christ has not been raised, then our proclamation is in vain, and so is your faith" (1 Cor 15:14). We must keep heralding the good news of the empty tomb, and we should expect various responses to it.

Once Paul is back in the barracks, left to nurse his wounds and ponder what just happened, the Lord Jesus appears to the discouraged apostle. Having appeared to him in Corinth previously, he now shows up in Jerusalem to comfort and energize Paul for his upcoming trip to Rome.

Reassurance

ACTS 23:11

We can only speculate what was going on in the apostle's mind before Jesus comforted him, but surely we can assume Paul was at a low point in his life. The Lord often appeared to Paul with encouragement and guidance in important moments in his career (cf. 16:9; 18:9-10; 22:17,21; 27:23-24). Paul had found an unsupportive church in Jerusalem. He had suffered physically and emotionally before rulers and crowds. And he may have questioned or regretted some of his actions. He was in need of the Lord's grace. That's just what he received.

While Jesus's words here were specifically for Paul in this moment, we still find in them reassuring application for our lives. Jesus told Paul that he must go on to testify about him in Rome as he did in Jerusalem. That was a reminder that Paul's task wasn't mainly to defend himself; he was to testify about Jesus. We too are commanded to testify to the gospel in front of unbelieving and sometimes unfriendly audiences. Here, then, are four encouragements.

The Lord Knows Us

Jesus knew Paul's situation and condition, and he knows what we face, too. We are never outside his gaze. Jesus knows his sheep by name and by need (John 10:14).

Charles Spurgeon commented on this passage:

> One is reminded of the Quaker who came to see John Bunyan in prison and said to him, "Friend, the Lord sent me to you and I have been seeking you in half the prisons in England." "No, verily," said John, "that cannot be! For if the Lord had sent you to me, you would have come here at once, for He knows I have been here for years!" ("Paul Cheered in Prison")

Indeed, the Lord knew Paul's condition, and he knows ours.

The Lord Is with Us

Jesus's presence comforted Paul (cf. 18:9-10). While Paul felt alone, the reality is that Jesus was with him (cf. 2 Tim 4:17-18). Jesus stood for Paul at the cross; here he stands with Paul in the barracks. Be encouraged: the Lord will never leave you or forsake you (Heb 13:5).

The Lord Is for Us

The Lord displays his support of Paul in two ways. First, the Lord gave him an exhortation: "Have courage!" If you have ever coached young kids in baseball, you know some tend to back away from the baseball out of fear of being hit. To these kids I often say, "Don't bail out! Stay in the box!" In similar fashion the Lord Jesus exhorted Paul to endure courageously against the wild pitches of the opponents. He gave Paul the same exhortation in Corinth (Acts 18:9). Jesus gives his followers this wonderful word of comfort and challenge: "Have courage!" (cf. Matt 9:2,22; 14:27; John 16:33). He is with us, and he is for us, as we do his will.

Second, the Lord gave Paul a commendation: "You have testified about me in Jerusalem." What an encouragement to hear the Lord, your Savior and hero, say, "You did it. You told people about Me!" Charles Spurgeon said that Paul was "too humble to console himself with that fact till his Lord gave him leave to do so by acknowledging the brave deed!" ("Paul Cheered in Prison").

Paul asked the Romans, "If God is for us, who is against us?" (Rom 8:31). That's a great question with a fabulous answer. We can press on, in view of this reality.

The Lord Isn't Finished with Us

Paul may have wondered if he would make it to Rome. But in telling Paul it was "necessary" that he testify there, the sovereign Lord let the apostle know that he would make sure he arrived. Though Paul would encounter many trials en route, he could face everything that happened to him over the course of the next weeks knowing that the Lord's purposes would prevail.

Jesus wasn't finished with Paul. The prospect of future service must have been a great encouragement to the war-weary apostle. The psalmist said, "The course of my life is in your power" (Ps 31:15). While we still have breath, we should believe that Jesus has work for us to do.

All this good news—that Jesus knows us, is with us, is for us, and isn't finished with us—leads me to ask a question: How should we expect to experience the reassuring comfort of Jesus if we don't experience visions like Paul's? Let me remind you that the Lord still speaks to us by his Spirit, through the *Christ-centered Scriptures*. Jesus meets us in his Word. By marinating our thoughts and hearts in the gospel, we find great strength. So don't neglect the Scriptures. John Calvin wrote,

"This is the whole of what we should seek in the Scriptures: to be well acquainted with Jesus Christ, and the infinite riches which are contained in Him; and which are, by Him, offered to us from God His Father" ("Christ the End").

The Pharisees had a category for resurrection but failed to rely on Jesus, who is himself the "resurrection and the life" (John 11:25). Let your study of Scripture lead you to the hero of Scripture (John 5:39-40,46).

Reflect and Discuss

1. Read 2 Corinthians 4:7-12. What is your reaction to this text? How did Paul live out this passage?
2. How does it encourage you to know that the Lord uses wounded soldiers in the mission? Explain.
3. Do you think Paul should have allowed himself to be flogged instead of playing his Roman citizenship card? Explain your reasoning.
4. Read Luke 22:63-71 and John 18:19-23. Compare Jesus's reactions with Paul's reaction to Ananias. Do you think Paul responded appropriately? Why or why not?
5. Read Acts 24:14-16; 26:6-8; and 28:20. Notice how Paul emphasizes the resurrection. How do these passages relate to what Paul told the Sanhedrin in 23:6-10?
6. Why must we emphasize the resurrection when sharing the gospel?
7. Have you ever shared the gospel before an unfriendly and unbelieving audience? If so, what were your biggest challenges? What can you learn from Paul's defenses that may prepare you to do this task more faithfully and effectively?
8. How does verse 11 encourage you? Explain.
9. How can we experience the reassuring presence of Jesus on a daily basis?
10. Take a few moments to pray for gospel-sowing opportunities. Ask the Lord to give you boldness and wisdom as you declare and defend the faith.

Paul in Caesarea, Part 1

ACTS 23:12–24:27

Main Idea: This portion of the narrative demonstrates the sovereignty of God and the character of a faithful Christian witness.

I. **God Is in Control Even When We're Going through Trials (23:12-35).**
   - A. God uses an unnamed nephew to thwart a plot (23:12-22).
   - B. God uses Lysias to protect Paul (23:23-30).
   - C. God uses a Roman army to transport Paul (23:31-35).
II. **We Can Be Faithful Witnesses Even in Stressful Situations (24:1-27).**
   - A. Enemies of the gospel will oppose Christians (24:1-9).
   - B. Faithful witnesses of the gospel speak calmly and courageously (24:10-27).

These two chapters have much to teach Christians who are seeking first the kingdom of God. One of the most obvious truths is that we can keep calm because God is in control—even when we're witnessing in stressful situations.

Paul finds himself in some stressful situations in Acts 23–24. We tend to like watching suspenseful shows on television while preferring not to encounter suspense in real life. In this passage Paul is first the object of a terrorist attack, and then he's a defendant in a tense court case that looks unwinnable. John Stott said Paul's chances of surviving the attacks of the angry Jews and mighty Romans resemble that of a butterfly before a steamroller (*Message of Acts*, 358)! Yet the apostle remains calm and courageous, submitting to the sovereign plan and power of God.

I remember going to court in Ukraine some years ago and giving a defense as to why the judge should grant my wife and me the privilege of adopting our children. Knowing what was at stake, I prepared my thoughts and had my speech memorized long before we walked into the courtroom. But when we entered, the judge asked my wife to speak instead of me! Then he talked to the kids before he finally asked me only a few questions. I'm happy to report that we received a good verdict even though things didn't proceed as I'd planned.

What happens when you imagine the future? Does it stress you out? Could it be that you find it easier to affirm the sovereignty of God *theoretically* rather than resting in the sovereignty of God *experientially*? This passage shows us that we can rest the whole weight of our concerns on God our Father, who holds the whole world in his hands.

God Is in Control Even When We're Going through Trials
ACTS 23:12-35

The names of God, Jesus, and the Holy Spirit aren't mentioned in these verses—it's a notable absence that reminds me of the book of Esther. In that book, too, the name of God is missing, but his fingerprints are everywhere within the story. God works in various ways to accomplish his purposes, even when we can't see him. In this passage the same Lord who promised that Paul would get to Rome works through people and circumstances to accomplish his agenda (cf. v. 11).

We sometimes think God isn't working when we don't see visible signs of his sovereignty. But never mistake the lack of the spectacular for the inactivity of God. His quiet, invisible hand is always at work.

God Uses an Unnamed Nephew to Thwart a Plot (23:12-22)

The day after Jesus reassured Paul in the barracks, more than forty angry Jews hatched a plot to kill him (vv. 12-13; cf. 9:24; 20:19). Their oath not to eat or drink until they had murdered the apostle meant they intended to act quickly. They approached the chief priests and elders (avoiding the minority Pharisees, who had defended Paul) and told them of their plan. The Sanhedrin, apparently cooperating, agreed to act as if they were reconvening to discuss Paul's crimes. The plan meant that as Paul approached the meeting, the assassins would intercept and execute him. So much for justice and law within the Sanhedrin (Gangel, *Acts*, 390)! These terrorists, like many modern-day terrorists, would stop at nothing to achieve their selfish, religious goals. Such an evil plan would appeal to Ananias the high priest, who was known for such violence. God, however, would thwart the scheme.

God uses a young man to do it. John Polhill says it's anyone's guess how old the nephew featured in this passage was, but perhaps he was in his late teens (*Acts*, 472). In light of how Lysias takes him "by the hand" in verse 19, he may be just a little boy (Schreiner, "Living as Disciples"). Regardless, this unnamed nephew becomes an incredibly important advocate, one clearly raised up for "for such a time as this" (Esth 4:14).

This is the only mention of Paul's family found anywhere in the New Testament. We get the impression from his writings that he lost connection with them after his conversion (cf. Phil 3:8), but here we learn that he had a sister and a nephew. We aren't sure how the nephew was able to hear of the plan. Perhaps the zealots underestimated him and were just speaking freely in front of him (Schreiner, "Living as Disciples").

Marvel at the sovereignty of God here. The Lord often uses little things and even little children to accomplish his great purposes. This story illustrates the seamless integration between God's sovereign agenda and human decisions made by responsible people (Johnson, *Let's Study Acts*, 288). The Lord already promised Paul that he would get to Rome, but God would preserve Paul through the actions of individuals. The nephew hears of the conspiracy. He relates it to Paul. Paul acts wisely. The Roman centurion does his job. And Lysias acts to protect Paul. There are no burning bushes involved in Paul's rescue. No light shows. Paul's life is spared as a result of people doing what's in front of them. God uses their actions to accomplish his purposes.

God Uses Lysias to Protect Paul (23:23-30)

Lysias immediately responds to the threat when he hears about it. He makes plans to transfer Paul to Caesarea. Named after Augustus Caesar, Caesarea was a beautiful harbor on the Mediterranean Sea about twenty-five miles northwest of the city of Samaria. It served as the headquarters for Roman military forces.

To protect Paul, Lysias summoned the centurion to prepare two hundred infantrymen, seventy mounted soldiers, and two hundred "spearmen" (v. 23). This action is a reminder that God can even use secular governments to achieve his purposes. We see God's rule over the affairs of people and nations throughout the Scriptures. He turns the hearts of rulers and kings (cf. Prov 21:1).

In order to bring the governor, Felix, up to speed on the situation, Lysias wrote a brief letter to him (vv. 26-30). Here again we see how the Lord used Lysias to protect Paul as Lysias testifies to Paul's innocence.

Felix, a freed slave, was a violent, licentious, and ineffective governor (or procurator) of the Roman province of Judea (AD 52–59). He rose to this official position because of his brother Pallas, who was for a number of years the head of imperial civil service (Fernando, *Acts*, 578). He married three women of royal birth, and Drusilla—daughter of Herod Agrippa I—was his third wife. She was a woman of legendary beauty (Thomas, *Acts*, 671), who apparently divorced her husband in order to marry Felix. Eventually he would get recalled to Rome because he mishandled riots in Caesarea.

In his letter Lysias calls Felix "most excellent," but many would deny any excellence in Felix. Lysias also tries to paint himself as a top-notch soldier. He implies that his first rescue of Paul was motivated by his commitment to defend a Roman citizen, but the fact is, Lysias thought Paul was an Egyptian revolutionary. He also conveniently omits that he nearly had a Roman citizen flogged illegally.

The most important statement in the letter is the claim of Paul's innocence. The problem involving him revolved around theology; it didn't warrant death or imprisonment. In including this note here, Luke once again weaves this theme into Acts: Christians aren't dangerous law-breakers (Schreiner, "Living as Disciples").

These events remind us of Paul's experience in Corinth. After discouragement, the Lord Jesus reassures Paul of his presence and protection (18:9-10). Immediately following that encouraging word, angry Jews attempt to attack Paul (18:12-13). But when the Jews bring the charges to Gallio, he dismisses their complaints as a quibble over theology (cp. 23:29 with 18:12-17).

Some people claimed that the early Christians were criminals (Schreiner, "Living as Disciples"). People said that Christians should be imprisoned for injustice, pointing to Jesus, the leader, who died as a "criminal" to support their argument. He was sentenced by a Roman procurator and crucified. But the four Gospel writers go to great pains to say that Jesus was innocent (cf. Mark 14:55). Even Pilate recognized it (Mark 15:14-15). So here is another parallel between Paul's trials and those of the Savior.

The application for us is simple: Christians should be honorable citizens. We shouldn't be ruthless pragmatists, breaking laws for the sake of our causes and claiming we are acting in the name of God. When the laws of the land don't hinder us from living out our faith, then we should abide by the rule of law as model citizens.

God Uses a Roman Army to Transport Paul (23:31-35)

The soldiers take Paul to Antipatris the next morning by the cover of night. The seventy horsemen then ride onward with Paul to Caesarea. Though they assumed they were moving a prisoner, God was transporting his preacher safely.

Even though ruthless Felix was corrupt and incompetent (as Paul's case will illustrate and as history records), he at least begins the right way. He promises to hear Paul's case as soon as the accusers arrive from Jerusalem, sending the apostle away to be held by Herod's praetorian guard (v. 34).

So the nephew thwarts the plan. Lysias reports the plan. Soldiers transport the prisoner. And all of this occurs under the sovereign rule of the King. Kenneth Gangel comments, "Sometimes God delivers his children by the simple word of a young relative. Sometimes he has to call in the cavalry. At all times, he is ultimately in charge" (*Acts*, 391). God has an infinite number of options for working out his will in our lives. While our daily lives may not look spectacular, we can be assured that God is involved in the affairs of his people. Paul says, "I am sure of this, that he who started a good work in you will carry it on to completion until the day of Jesus Christ" (Phil 1:6). Trust him even in difficult circumstances! Thank him for his care and provision.

We Can Be Faithful Witnesses Even in Stressful Situations
ACTS 24:1-27

In chapter 24 we read of a typical court procedure; it includes the filing of charges, the prosecution of the plaintiff's spokesman, and the answer from the defendant (Johnson, *Let's Study Acts*, 293). After hearing the arguments the judge normally rendered a verdict. But this case has some unique twists to it because of the nature of the alleged crime, the defendant, and the judge. This story reminds us of some basic truths about being faithful witnesses.

Enemies of the Gospel Will Oppose Christians (24:1-9)

Paul's accusers were serious. They brought in an attorney, a professional orator named Tertullus, to prosecute him. Flattery is practically dripping from Tertullus's lips as he attempts to make a favorable first impression on the judge. Tertullus expresses gratitude for the "great peace" brought about by Felix, but the fact was, Felix's reign had been marked by constant unrest and fights between imperial forces and the oppressed Jews and Samaritans. Nevertheless, because peace was a major Roman value, the skilled attorney commends Felix for bringing it.

Tertullus strikes this topic of peace again as he brings up the first of four charges against Paul. First, he accuses Paul of being a *pest*. He calls him a pestilent fellow, a public nuisance, a "plague" (v. 5). His point is that Paul "infects" people (cf. 17:6-7).

Second, Tertullus contends that Paul is a *political agitator*. That is, he stirs up riots. There was a grain of truth to this statement. Paul's ministry often resulted in riots, although that wasn't Paul's intent. In actuality, the enemies of the gospel instigated the riots (see 13:50; 14:2,5,19; 16:22; 17:5,13; 19:23-29,37-40).

Third, Tertullus calls Paul *the leader of a sectarian movement*. This is the only place where the term "Nazarenes" is used to describe Christians (Marshall, *Acts of the Apostles*, 375). It's possible that Jewish Christians were given this nickname—especially since the word contained a condescending implication (ibid.), as illustrated by Nathaniel's question regarding Jesus: "Can anything good come out of Nazareth?" (John 1:46).

Finally, Tertullus makes a specific charge: Paul was *disruptive in the temple* (v. 6). This charge of profaning the temple, however, was false. Tertullus also claims that Paul's attempt to desecrate the temple was frustrated by the Jews. In a sentence, then, Tertullus charges, "Paul disturbs the peace as a seditious member of a dangerous sect" (Bock, *Acts*, 691).

Those who oppose Christ will go to great lengths to oppose the kingdom. They will use skill, political maneuvering, and lies. Such opposition shouldn't surprise us. We should be prepared spiritually for such attacks (cf. Eph 6:1-10).

Faithful Witnesses of the Gospel Speak Calmly and Courageously (24:10-27)

In verses 10-21 Paul speaks for the defense. He seizes this opportunity to give a **public witness** not only of his innocence but also of the gospel (cf. 9:15). He states that Christianity isn't a threat to Rome or any state (Bock, *Acts*, 697). And he shows that this "new movement" is rooted in the "old promises" of the Scriptures (cf. 13:15; 22:3; 28:17,23).

Rather than examining Paul, Felix, dramatizing his authority, gives Paul a head nod indicating his right to speak. Paul begins with a few benevolent comments. He expresses gladness to appear before the judge (v. 10). But Paul doesn't flatter Felix's fictional justice or wisdom the way Tertullus celebrated Felix's fictional peace (Johnson, *Let's Study Acts*, 296). He simply acknowledges Felix's connection with Israel and his familiarity with religious events in Judea.

Paul's public witness has three parts. In verses 11-16 Paul says, "My religious record is clear—no lawbreaking." In 17-20 Paul says, "My civil behavior is blameless—no riots." In verse 21 he concludes by once again proclaiming the resurrection, essentially saying, "My personal message is the issue—Jesus is alive" (Gangel, *Acts*, 411).

A Clear Religious Record (24:11-16). Paul goes straight to the specific charges and brings up that he has only been in Jerusalem for twelve days. It's difficult to start a riot in less than two weeks! Believing in a future heavenly judgment, Paul then says he takes pains to have a "clear conscience toward God and men" (v. 16). So Paul not only claims to be innocent, but he also claims to have a faith that is in accord with the fundamental outlook of Judaism—with a belief in God, with the Scriptures, with future judgment, and with the importance of holiness.

We should take note of Paul's seamless transition into the Christian faith. He first dealt with the charges and then gave a defense of the faith. But he doesn't merely want to defend himself; he wants to proclaim the gospel as well. This is an excellent reminder to look for ways in your daily conversations to make gospel transitions as you talk with people.

Blameless Civil Behavior (24:17-20). In verse 17 Paul returns to the issue about defiling the temple. He gives his version of the story. He first tells Felix that he brought "charitable gifts" to Jerusalem. We have mentioned this gift from the Gentile churches a number of times, and it is mentioned in Paul's letters (cf. Rom 15:25-33; 1 Cor 16:1-4; 2 Cor 8–9). Paul devoted a lot of time and effort to this collection. He also adds that he presented "offerings" while at the temple, alluding to the payments Paul made on behalf of four men (21:23-26).

Paul continues to describe how, when he was engaging in this activity at the temple, he was discovered by his opponents. He starts off mentioning "some Jews from Asia." These accusers were conspicuously absent from the trial, however. While these men should have been the ones to bring the charges against Paul, they had no case! Paul was confident that no criminal charges could be made against him.

Personal Message: Jesus Is Alive! (24:21). Paul had a wonderful ability to bring up the resurrection of Jesus in all sorts of contexts. The resurrection is indeed a central doctrine to the Christian faith that shows the sufficiency of Christ's death, the supremacy of his lordship, and his inevitable return as Judge. We do well to follow Paul's example of funneling conversations to this life-changing, world-altering event.

Consider now how Paul gives a gospel witness in a **private context**. Felix chooses to postpone a decision. He claims that he wants to hear from Lysias. His other reason for delay is that he "was well informed about the Way." F. F. Bruce suggests that this knowledge may have come through his wife Drusilla, who was a member of the Herod family (*Book of Acts,* 446).

This statement about his knowledge of the Way suggests he was acting out of sympathy for the Christians. He doesn't seem to want them to be mistreated by the Jewish authorities, although his subsequent behavior does nothing to justify this impression (Marshall, *Acts of the Apostles,* 380). While he should have released Paul, he at least refused to decide for the Jewish authorities (ibid.).

Paul was then treated in a manner consistent with Roman citizenship. Friends could visit him and bring food and other necessities during his wait (24:23). The text never says whether Lysias ever came. This suggests that the whole line about waiting for him may have been just a smoke screen; after all, Felix already had Lysias's letter giving his point of view (Gangel, *Acts,* 405).

For whatever reason (perhaps it was Drusilla's influence), Felix sent for Paul in order to hear Paul's message. Paul spoke the same message in private that he spoke in public: "faith in Christ Jesus" (v. 24; cf. 13:38-39).

He reasoned with Felix about what God's Word said about righteousness, self-control, and the coming judgment (v. 25). All three topics would have been fitting based on Felix's lifestyle. By highlighting God's holiness, man's sinfulness, and the judgment to come, Paul was showing Felix why he needed Jesus. The sermon, then, was not a nice, warm, uplifting talk. It involved confrontation with a call to repentance.

None of these points were popular then, nor are they today. The exclusivity of Jesus Christ and submitting one's whole life under the lordship of Jesus in holiness continue to offend people. But we must be more concerned about offending Christ than culture. Speak his Word in humility and love as a faithful messenger.

How did Felix respond to Paul's sermon? Sadly, not with repentance of sin and placing faith in Jesus. He rejected the message (v. 25). Felix was convicted by what he had heard but not changed.

More greedy than interested in God, Felix would continue to summon Paul over the coming weeks in hopes that the apostle would offer him a bribe (v. 26). Felix should have released Paul, but that would have upset the Jews—something he had done too frequently during his rule (Gangel, *Acts,* 406). As a side note, many believe Paul and Luke used Paul's detainment in Caesarea as an opportunity to gather information for writings, perhaps the books of Luke and Acts (ibid.).

So at the end of chapter 24, we see yet another illustration that God is in control—even when we're going through trials. If you find yourself in a perplexing season, take comfort here: God hasn't forgotten you. Paul sat in this prison for two years! The Old Testament saint Joseph can also testify to God's faithfulness in a similar situation. Our Lord is sovereign, and we can and should trust him—even when we're perplexed (cf. Gen 50:20). We live by faith, not by sight, until we get home (2 Cor 5:7).

We also see in this passage a picture of how to **deliver** the Word as well as an illustration of how not to receive it. Paul's example should inspire us to deliver the Word courageously and calmly in both public and private contexts. Paul knew how to address various audiences with the same basic message of the resurrection. He also wasn't afraid to talk about the holiness of God. We too should never shy away from telling people that "it is a terrifying thing to fall into the hands of the living God" (Heb 10:31). We must tell them that "our God is a consuming fire" (Heb 12:29) and then call them to flee to Christ for complete refuge.

In Oxford, England, one can visit the Martyrs' Memorial, an imposing stone monument acknowledging three bishops burned at the stake in October 1555 under Queen Mary's reign. One of them, Hugh Latimer, had actually been burned earlier during King Henry VIII's reign. All three were executed for the crime of being faithful to the message of justification by faith (Gangel, *Acts*, 401); that is, they held to the idea that people are made right with God only by placing faith in Jesus and not by any merit they have earned. The story goes that on one occasion, the king demanded that Latimer offer an apology for what Henry found offensive in Latimer's Sunday message. Rather than conceding his biblical views to appease the king, Latimer read the same text again and then proceeded to preach the same sermon he had preached to his congregation (ibid.).

Stories like this one remind us that regardless of the audience, we must keep pointing people to Jesus calmly and courageously. We must take every opportunity to speak this message.

Felix illustrates what not to do with regard to the Word. At first he seems curious about it. Then he's convicted by it (cf. John 16:8). But instead of repenting, Felix clutches his idols. (1) He tries to *preserve his career* by not letting Paul go. (Ultimately, however, he fails; he gets replaced by Festus.) (2) He tries to *feed his greed* by seeking a bribe. (3) He *wastes his time* on other matters, saying, "I will call on you when I get some time" (24:25, paraphrased).

Sadly, Felix isn't the only person to care more about career and money than salvation through Christ. Jesus recognizes this common but unwise choice when asking, "What does it benefit someone to gain the whole world and yet lose his life?" (Mark 8:36; cf. 1 Tim 6:9-10). Many people, especially those with influence and power, believe they are self-made men or women in control of their own lives and in need of no one. And they couldn't be more wrong!

Learn from Felix. Time isn't on your side. Repent and trust in the risen Jesus while there's still time. And tell others about him before they too run out of opportunities to embrace him.

Reflect and Discuss

1. Do you find it easier to affirm the sovereignty of God theoretically rather than resting in the sovereignty of God experientially? Explain your answer.
2. What does Acts 23:12-30 teach about the way God works to accomplish his purposes?
3. How do these assassins compare with modern-day terrorists?
4. What does Paul's life teach about living as law-abiding citizens?
5. What about Paul's defense before Felix most resonates with you?
6. Do you find it difficult to transition general conversations into gospel conversations? If so, why? What does this passage teach you about how to do that more effectively?
7. Why does Paul constantly bring up the resurrection? What does this teach about our gospel conversations?
8. What do you find most striking about Paul's message to Felix when he speaks to him privately (24:24-26)?
9. What can we learn about what not to do with the Word by considering Felix's example?
10. Take a few moments to pray for God to grant you confidence in his sovereignty and courage in your witness.

Paul in Caesarea, Part 2

ACTS 25:1–26:32

Main Idea: Paul's speech before Festus sets the stage for Paul's final defense before Agrippa; from the latter we can learn to live as faithful witnesses.

I. **Paul Before Festus (25:1-27)**
   A. Festus rejects the Jewish leaders' request (25:1-5).
   B. Festus hears Paul's defense (25:6-12).
   C. Festus seeks Agrippa's help (25:13-22).
   D. Festus presents Paul to Agrippa and the assembly (25:23-27).
II. **Paul Before Agrippa (26:1-32)**
   A. Paul's generous remark to Agrippa (26:1-3)
   B. Paul's thoroughly Jewish upbringing (26:4-8; cf. 22:3)
   C. Paul's persecution of Christians (26:9-11; cf. 22:4-5)
   D. Paul's conversion (26:12-15; cf. 22:6-11)
   E. Paul's commission (26:16-18; cf. 22:17-21)
   F. Paul's witness for Christ (26:19-23)
   G. Paul's evangelistic appeal to Agrippa (26:24-32)
III. **Application for Faithful Witnesses (26:1-32)**
   A. Address unbelievers respectfully (26:1-3).
   B. Express what it was like not to believe (26:4-11,14).
   C. Aim to exalt Jesus, not self (26:12-15).
   D. Share the need for and the benefits of the gospel with all types of people (26:16-18).
   E. Stick to the message of the resurrection and the call to repentance based on Scripture (26:19-23).
   F. Rely on the help that comes from God (26:22).
   G. Make specific application boldly (26:24-28).
   H. Be prepared for rejection and ridicule (26:24).
   I. Pray for the people you're evangelizing (26:29).

Here we come to the final defense speeches of Paul. In them we see God's faithfulness to his purposes (cf. 23:11) and Paul's faithfulness to testify to the gospel.

The apostle has addressed the crowd in Jerusalem (22:1-21), the Jewish Council in Jerusalem (23:1-6), and the Roman governor, Felix, in Caesarea (24:1-21). He will now briefly address "the new Felix," named "Festus" (25:6-12). This sets the stage for Paul's final address to Agrippa II.

This speech before Agrippa is powerful, gospel filled, inspiring, and exemplary. It gives important insights into bearing testimony to Jesus Christ. Remember, Paul's general task is the same as ours: articulating the good news about the risen Messiah and calling people to trust in him. Darrell Bock says Paul shows himself to be "the exemplary witness who calls for a response" (*Acts,* 706). Jesus has *saved* us and *sent* us, like Paul, into the world to give the good news (Matt 28:18-20). Salvation doesn't stop with us. God saved us so we would tell the world about the One who opens eyes, brings people out of darkness into the light, forgives sin, and gives strangers an inheritance (26:18). As we observe how Paul speaks to Agrippa and as we hear afresh Paul's commission, we can make some important applications for how to be Great Commission Christians.

Acts 26 has several transferable principles for modern-day witnesses. The chapter opens on a hearing designed to give King Agrippa insight into Paul's case in order that he might advise Governor Festus about what should be included in his report to Caesar (25:26-27). Festus is sending Paul to Rome, but he doesn't know what to report about him because Paul is innocent. Because Paul's speech in this case is not technically a legal defense, it is different from the previous speeches. It involves more of a personal biography with a persuasive evangelistic appeal. Here Paul is defending the foundations of the Christian faith, so we should observe Paul's passion and practice carefully.

Let's first look at Paul's trial before Festus, which sets the stage for Paul's words before Agrippa.

Paul Before Festus
ACTS 25:1-27

Festus Rejects the Jewish Leaders' Request (25:1-5)

Festus replaces Felix as governor of Judea and attempts to bring closure to this unresolved case. Not much is known about Festus, who only served in this position for two years before dying in office. He seems to be more just and moderate than his predecessor, Felix, who was fired by Nero.

Don't miss that Paul is still serving the Lord Jesus when Felix drops out of the telling and isn't mentioned again. Mary sang about how the Lord scatters the proud, brings down the mighty from their thrones, and exalts those of humble estate (cf. Luke 1:51-52). We should take heart in God's sovereign lordship. Though God's providence sometimes appears to be inefficient (Thomas, *Acts,* 675), his ways aren't our ways (Isa 55:8-9). Later, Paul would reflect on God's sovereignty from a Roman prison cell, telling the Philippians that through his imprisonment the gospel was reaching people it would otherwise not have reached, and other Christians were being encouraged to greater boldness (Phil 1:12-14). Faithfully serve the Lord Jesus and keep trusting in him to work even when you can't see what he's doing.

Festus plunged into his work immediately. Three days after reaching Caesarea, he makes a courtesy visit to Jerusalem to meet with the leaders in person. Certain Jews' feelings toward Paul haven't changed in the past two years. Some still want to kill Paul. They ask Festus to send Paul to Jerusalem to be tried, but they plan to ambush the apostle on the road. Festus, however, won't be the Jews' puppet—at least initially. He wants things done decently and in order.

Festus Hears Paul's Defense (25:6-12)

After returning to Caesarea, Festus takes his seat on the bench and makes Paul face the accusers. This time they add some physical intimidation as they stand "around him" (v. 7) while bringing the charges. Paul simply denies the accusations, and for the first time he mentions that he hasn't offended Caesar.

Festus could close the case at this point, but instead he plays politics. Festus, "wanting to do the Jews a favor," asks Paul if he's willing to change the venue (v. 9; cf. 24:27). He may have assumed that he would get more clarity on the situation in Jerusalem and clearly still plans to preside over the trial rather than putting it in the hands of the Sanhedrin.

Paul wants to silence all discussion about a possible return to Jerusalem. He strongly replies, insisting that the trumped-up charges are nonsense and Festus knows it (v. 10). Paul adds that he's not afraid to die, but a death sentence must come from Roman court, not from angry Jewish leaders in Jerusalem (v. 11). Knowing that his only hope of justice involves traveling to Rome, he makes use of his citizen's right of appeal to Caesar (cf. 25:21,25-26; 26:32; 28:19).

A. W. Tozer said, "Not death but sin should be our great fear" (in Gangel, *Acts,* 414). To die is "gain" for the Christian (Phil 1:21). This type of attitude gave Paul (and gives us) great boldness and hope.

Festus is in a tight spot now. He can't set Paul free, for that would offend the Jews. But he can't convict and sentence Paul, for that would offend Roman law (Stott, *Message of Acts,* 367). So, after consulting his advisors, he grants the appeal (v. 12).

The Caesar in view here was Nero, who reigned from AD 54 to 68. His latter reign degenerated into immoderation, weird behavior, and violence—especially against Christians—but his earlier reign seems to have been more stable (Polhill, *Acts,* 492). At this point in history, his notoriously bad behavior had not yet appeared.

Most significant to understanding this portion of Scripture is that in making his appeal, Paul would travel to *Rome* to bear witness (cf. 19:21; 23:11). Through Paul's many dangers, toils, and snares, God is working out his purposes for his apostle.

Festus Seeks Agrippa's Help (25:13-22)

Herod Agrippa II (AD 27–100), whom I. Howard Marshall calls "a petty king" (*Acts of the Apostles,* 387), and his sister pay a courtesy visit to the new governor not long after Paul's appeal. This gave Festus the opportunity to get advice on the matter. He knew Agrippa was familiar with imperial politics and Jewish disputes. He was the great-grandson of Herod the Great and the son of Herod Agrippa I. His father had killed James and arrested Peter, both Christian leaders, but was then killed under God's judgment (Acts 12). The Romans had given Agrippa II various territories in northeast Palestine to rule over, and he ruled over them with the status of a king (ibid., 387). Kenneth Gangel gives further commentary:

> [At] approximately thirty-three years of age, he had become king of Chalcis in A.D. 48 and had advanced to control over Abilene, Trachonitis, Acra, Tarichea, and Tiberias. His sister Bernice was one year younger and had come to live with her brother after the death of her husband, who was also her uncle. Throughout the Roman Empire people assumed an incestuous relationship, probably an accurate analysis of the strange situation. (*Acts,* 418)

Agrippa ruled mainly over the Gentile population. He never reigned over the main Jewish territory of Judea, Samaria, and Galilee as his father had (Polhill, *Acts*, 492). The Romans did give him custody of the ceremonial vestments worn by the priests on the Day of Atonement. Claudius also gave him the right to appoint high priests for the Jerusalem temple (ibid., 492–93).

Festus reports a Roman version of the case against Paul to Agrippa. He basically echoes Gallio (18:12-15) and Lysias (23:29). The Jews' dispute with Paul was about *theology*. It revolved around Paul's interpretation of the Old Testament and the claim that Jesus was the risen Messiah. I. Howard Marshall notes how everything has now drifted to the subject of the resurrection. "It is interesting that by this stage the question of Paul's alleged desecration of the temple has quite disappeared from sight, and the topic of the resurrection (23:6; 24:21) has replaced it," he says (*Acts of the Apostles*, 388). Festus doesn't understand the resurrection debate (cf. 26:4). His statement shows how incomprehensible such a belief was to a pagan (Polhill, *Acts*, 494). He sees this issue as an internal Jewish discussion, not a matter of Roman law (ibid.).

One can't miss the parallels to Jesus's case here. Both Paul and Jesus were prosecuted before a Roman governor (Pilate/Festus) and then brought before a Jewish king (Herod Antipas/Herod Agrippa II; see Luke 23:6-12). Both Paul and Jesus were found to be innocent (see Luke 23:4,13-16,22). But Jesus would die at the hand of Pilate, and Paul would be sent to Rome for further trial. Paul, whether he realizes it or not, is walking in the footsteps of Jesus.

Festus concluded by bringing Agrippa up to speed on Paul's appeal to Caesar (v. 21). Agrippa, like his great uncle, Herod Antipas in Luke 23:8, was curious about the matter. Festus assured Agrippa that he would hear from Paul the next day.

Festus Presents Paul to Agrippa and the Assembly (25:23-27)

The next morning, in spite of having just a day's notice, Festus, Bernice, and Agrippa were able to pull off a grand public event filled with "great pomp" (v. 23, Greek *fantasia*, our "fantasy") during which Paul would be heard. Each knew how to put on appearances. Luke mentions the many dignitaries in attendance, who would have been predominately Gentile (Johnson, *Let's Study Acts*, 307). Paul is summoned to enter when the event reaches its climax.

Festus speaks with great rhetorical exaggeration, claiming that the "whole" Jewish community was shouting for Paul's execution, but being a just governor, he delivered Paul. Festus then absolves himself from further responsibility by mentioning Paul's appeal. Finally, Festus sets the agenda. He has assembled this group of people to assist him in writing up charges against Paul. Of course, he had none to write at this point because he knew Paul was innocent.

Jesus originally promised Paul that he would testify before Gentiles and kings and the people of Israel (9:15). Jesus had also previously warned his disciples that they would be brought before kings and governors, but he assured them that he would give them words of wisdom to speak (Luke 21:12-15; 2 Cor 5:20) in order to make them bold witnesses. In the following paragraphs we see that the Lord Jesus was faithful to his word. Understand that Festus and Agrippa could decide absolutely nothing about the outcome for Paul. He had appealed to Caesar. In their view these two authorities had assembled to gather information and put on a show. But what was really happening was that the Lord Jesus was accomplishing his agenda in Paul's life. His testimony before Agrippa is gripping.

When you give a defense of the gospel, the Lord Jesus is with you. Rely on him as you make the good news known.

Paul Before Agrippa
ACTS 26:1-32

Paul's speech is stated carefully and stylistically; it's appropriate for his audience. Commentator Ben Witherington notes six elements in Greek rhetorical style at work here (*Acts of the Apostles*, 737–38). Additionally, this speech is similar to Paul's speech before the Jewish mob (22:1-21). Within this life summary, two themes dominate. First, Paul magnifies the cross and resurrection (26:6-8,22-23). Second, Paul insists that this new faith is actually an extension of Judaism (Bock, *Acts*, 705). While Paul addresses a largely Gentile assembly and alludes to a number of witnesses present, the speech is more for Agrippa's benefit than anyone else's. Paul tries to persuade King Agrippa to bow before King Jesus (Johnson, *Let's Study Acts*, 312). Paul is a man with a commission. He's not pouting, complaining, or trying to negotiate a deal in front of this monarch. He's preaching the gospel to him.

Paul's Generous Remark to Agrippa (26:1-3)

Agrippa is in charge of the meeting. Paul begins his "defense" (*apologia*) of the gospel by first stretching out his hand as a sign of respect for the Jewish king, not as a sign for silencing the crowd (Bruce, *Book of Acts*, 461). Paul then makes a generous comment to the king (*capitatio benevolentiae),* noting the king's familiarity with Jewish customs. He then respectfully asks Agrippa to listen patiently to his defense.

Paul's Thoroughly Jewish Upbringing (26:4-8; cf. 22:3)

Paul describes his strict upbringing in Judaism. He then states a major theme in the speech: his faith is not a violation of his Jewish heritage; his faith actually links to the Old Testament's promises (Bock, *Acts,* 714). Jesus's death and resurrection are fulfillments of the Jewish messianic hope. Paul, then, is saying that he has never left his Jewish tradition. His faith is rooted in a belief the Jews share.

Now Paul addresses the wider assembly, asking a striking rhetorical question: "Why do *any of you* consider it incredible that God raises the dead?" (v. 8; emphasis added). Of course the question is really a statement that the idea is actually not so far-fetched. Central to the shared Jewish hope was the resurrection. The Jews prayed for its fulfillment in their worship day and night (Polhill, *Acts,* 500). The Pharisees, in fact, only have to accept that Jesus himself was resurrected, for they already believed in a resurrection. The Sadducees would need to reverse their position, and the Gentiles—like Festus—would have to adjust the most since they generally didn't even discuss the resurrection (Bock, *Acts,* 715). Yet we have seen the Jews' opposition to this claim that God raised Jesus from the dead. In other words, both Jew and Gentile found it incredible. Not much has changed.

Paul's Persecution of Christians (26:9-11; cf. 22:4-5)

Next, Paul admits that he once found the resurrection incredible. More than that, Paul—then known as Saul—persecuted Christians (v. 9; cf. 2:22). Eventually, Paul would know Jesus as "Lord," but at first, he looked on Jesus of Nazareth and his people with contempt. He locked up the "saints" in prison and voted for their deaths (vv. 9-10). Further, Paul "punished" Christians and tried to make them deny who Jesus really is or even to curse him (Bock, *Acts,* 715).

Paul's Conversion (26:12-15; cf. 22:6-11)

But then Paul the terrorist, having been commissioned by the chief priest to continue his persecution, became Paul the evangelist when he met Jesus on the Damascus Road. To paraphrase, Paul says to Agrippa, "I saw a light; I heard a voice" (vv. 13-14). The light was brighter than the sun. Everyone fell down at its appearance, so this wasn't a private experience for Paul; it was a real, external experience (Bock, *Acts*, 716).

We find this additional comment in this telling of Paul's testimony: "It is hard for you to kick against the goads," Jesus said to him (26:14). Goads were sharp sticks used to prod and direct an animal. So Paul was kicking against the Lord's discipline and direction (Bock, *Acts*, 716). Paul seems to have been resisting the Spirit's conviction, especially during Stephen's speech and martyrdom. Jesus was telling Paul to stop rejecting his call and to end the persecution—essentially saying, "Stop fighting me and submit to me" (cf. 5:39).

Paul's Commission (26:16-18; cf. 22:17-21)

"This commission constitutes the center and climax of Paul's entire speech," John Polhill notes. "It's virtually repeated in Paul's closing words" (cf. vv. 22-23; *Acts*, 503). Paul's commission reflects the prophetic tradition. Like Ezekiel, Paul was directed to rise and stand on his feet (v. 16; cf. Ezek 2:1). As in the case of the prophets, the Lord sent Paul (cf. Ezek 2:3) and promised to rescue him from his enemies (v. 17; cf. Jer 1:6-8; Acts 27). Paul was appointed as a "servant" and a "witness" of the things associated with Christ (v. 16). "His whole story in Acts has shown his faithful witness—before Jews and Gentiles, Greeks and Romans, peasants, philosophers, and kings" (ibid.). Every Christian stands in this line of being a servant of Jesus and a witness for him (1:8).

The Lord called Paul to proclaim the comprehensive *benefits* of the gospel (vv. 18-19) to a comprehensive *audience*. The latter is referenced in verse 17: "your people" and "the Gentiles"; and in verse 22: "both small and great." This is a reminder that no one is beyond the reach of or need for God's saving grace.

The phrase "both small and great" reminds me of a story about the great British preacher, Martyn Lloyd-Jones. After he delivered a sermon at a meeting at Cambridge University, a minister invited some students over to his home to ask Lloyd-Jones questions. One student said to the guest, "I listened to your sermon. And I can see how this sort of message appeals to farmers around here, but I fail to see how it's relevant to academics like myself and my colleagues." To this Lloyd-Jones replied, "Well, the last time I checked, Cambridge students were made of the same dull clay as the farm workers in the fields" (quoted in Begg, "Persuasive Preaching"). In other words, the gospel message is the same for both small and great because people from all walks of life share the same need for a Savior.

Regarding the benefits of the gospel, Paul indirectly informs Agrippa and the audience about their own desperate spiritual condition and need for salvation. Paul could have been vague when talking about what the Lord told him to do. Instead, he leaves the king with something he should process personally. He brings up the universal need for the wonderful privileges of the gospel. First, the gospel sets people free from spiritual confusion and ignorance, a fact indicated by the phrases "open their eyes" and turning from "darkness to light" (v. 18; cf. 2 Cor 4:4,6). Second, the gospel sets people free from the oppressive tyranny of their souls (Johnson, *Let's Study Acts*, 316). By placing faith in Christ, they go from "the power of Satan to God." While not a popular concept, this is biblically true nonetheless (Eph 2:1-3; Col 1:13). Third, the gospel sets people free from guilt, condemnation, and eternal punishment when they "receive forgiveness of sins" (v. 18; cf. Rom 4:25–5:1). And finally, the gospel provides disinherited wanderers a "share among those who are sanctified" (v. 18). This concept speaks of a home of "unimaginable comfort and impregnable security" (ibid; Acts 20:32; Col 1:12).

Who is the source of these gospel blessings? Jesus Christ. Only by placing "faith in" the Lord Jesus Christ, the One who suffered and rose from the dead, do we receive new life, new identity, and a living hope.

Paul's Witness for Christ (26:19-23)

Beginning in verse 19 Paul shows how he carried out the commission Christ gave him. He preached in Damascus, in Jerusalem, in all of Judea, and to the Gentiles (v. 20). With a message of repentance reminiscent of John the Baptist's (Luke 3:8), Paul urges everyone to bear fruit in a way that reflects their new life in Christ. While good works aren't the basis of salvation, they are the fruit of salvation (cf. 2 Cor 13:5-7; Gal 5:22-23; Eph 2:8-10; Titus 2:14; 3:8).

Paul then describes that he preaches the Christ of Scripture to everyone through "help from God" (vv. 22-23). God provides the power, and God provides the message, which centers on a person, Jesus Christ.

Paul's statement about the prophets and Moses reminds us of Jesus's teaching on the road to Emmaus (Luke 24:44-47). Paul notes that he's simply a preacher of the Jewish promise and hope. His preaching, then, in a sense, isn't new; it's rooted in the old Hebrew Scriptures (Bock, *Acts*, 721). Paul didn't make up this message. He's simply preaching the fulfillment of this great hope, which culminates in the risen Messiah (cf. Job 19:25-27; Pss 16:9-11; 49:15; 73:24; Isa 26:19; Dan 12:2). Paul adds that Jesus is the light shining in the darkness (cf. Isa 42:6;

49:6; 60:3; Luke 1:78-79), which is proclaimed to both Jews and Gentiles (Acts 26:23). As a servant to the Servant, fulfilling his role as a witness of Christ, Paul was accomplishing Jesus's purpose of being light to the nations (Polhill, *Acts,* 506).

Paul's Evangelistic Appeal to Agrippa (26:24-32)

Festus can't contain himself after hearing Paul's message (cf. 25:19) and thus interrupts Paul's speech. He says Paul is insane for believing such things (v. 24; cf. 2 Cor 5:13). A belief in the resurrection was, in fact, a crazy idea to Romans. Festus's outburst serves as a reminder that the gospel really is "foolishness" to some (1 Cor 1:23; cf. Acts 17:18,32). Nonetheless, Paul defends himself respectfully and candidly, assuring Festus that he's speaking "true and rational words" (v. 25 ESV).

Paul then pivots his attention back to King Agrippa. He disarms the king, nudging him and wooing him over to his side. Paul here assumes that Agrippa is familiar with the ministry of Jesus because it didn't take place "in a corner" (v. 26). Christianity isn't a secret cult. Further, the message about the Messiah is actually rooted in the teachings of the Old Testament prophets, whom Paul assumes Agrippa trusts (v. 27). In other words, Agrippa should be able to understand and appreciate what Paul is saying (Bock, *Acts,* 723).

Agrippa, however, dodges the question. He can't say he denies the prophets, but he also doesn't want to say yes and have Paul press him further (Polhill, *Acts,* 5–8). Kenneth Gangel summarizes his response:

> This king had been in politics for over ten years. He wasn't about to change his religious viewpoints on the basis of one sermon in a Roman hall. (*Acts,* 436).

At this point Paul, growing bolder still, makes a direct evangelistic appeal (v. 29). Paul wanted everyone to believe the good news about Jesus—regardless of how long it took. He wanted them to have what he enjoyed in Christ. In this captivating scene the people listening are actually the ones in chains, in spiritual bondage. Paul, on the other hand, can still soar in joyful praise even while physically chained. He wants freedom and joy for his audience.

Paul's evangelistic desire is conveyed here as he makes a prayerful wish: "I wish before God," or "I pray to God" (NIV). Paul's statement reflects the heart of one interceding for the lost audience. The man had been beaten and persecuted by Jews and ridiculed by the Romans, but he still wanted people to know the Savior! Once again Paul gives us a model for witnessing to unbelievers—not only in words but also in heart.

Finally, Agrippa rises to his feet (v. 30). The speech is over. Agrippa, Bernice, and other prominent people meet together and privately affirm Paul's innocence (v. 31; 25:19-20,25). As in the case of Jesus, Paul is so thoroughly innocent that he isn't even worthy of imprisonment (Bock, *Acts,* 724). Agrippa thus concludes that Paul could go free if he hadn't appealed to Caesar (v. 32). But since nothing can short-circuit such an appeal, it's time to honor Caesar by asking him to render a decision in Paul's case (ibid.).

Paul faithfully delivered the gospel. Agrippa tragically rejected Israel's Messiah. It was time for Paul to continue testifying to the gospel of grace in Rome.

Application for Faithful Witnesses
26:1-32

We could draw a seemingly endless number of application points from this text with regard to being faithful witnesses in the modern world. I'll focus on nine.

Address Unbelievers Respectfully (26:1-3)

Paul's generous and courteous comment to Agrippa reflects the spirit of Peter's words to Christians living in a hostile culture:

> *In your hearts regard Christ the Lord as holy, ready at any time to give a defense to anyone who asks you for a reason for the hope that is in you. Yet* do this with gentleness and respect, *keeping a clear conscience, so that when you are accused, those who disparage your good conduct in Christ will be put to shame.* (1 Pet 3:15-16; emphasis added)

What we say is more important than how we say it, but our delivery methods and tone matter to God and to those we're addressing. Therefore, we should seek to blend truthfulness with tenderness and courage with compassion.

Express What It Was like Not to Believe (26:4-11,14)

Paul's recounting of his former way of life before his conversion illustrates this approach. Sometimes it helps people understand the gospel when we explain our perspectives and practices prior to our acceptance of Christ. In sympathizing with our audiences in this way, we may gain better hearings. To be clear, our personal stories are not the gospel, but our ability to identify with our listeners is important.

Think about ways you once "kick[ed] against the goads" (v. 14) and be prepared to summarize your experiences. Doing so can ready you to connect with hearers when you tell the good news. Plan to lovingly explain your former assumptions, misconceptions, and even sins from which the Lord delivered you. Not everyone has a story as dramatic as Paul's, but choosing personal transparency can go a long way in helping you connect with audiences of all sizes.

Aim to Exalt Jesus, Not Self (26:12-15)

Paul's Damascus road story is ultimately a story about Jesus, not one about Paul. The apostle always took care to keep Jesus the hero of his testimony, and this is a great reminder that Jesus should always be the clear hero of the personal stories we tell too. It sounds too obvious to mention, but when speaking to unbelievers, we should speak a lot about Jesus. Like Paul, we must keep talking about him again and again. Even when we begin a spiritual conversation by talking about our own lives, we need to use threads of those stories to point hearers to the Savior.

Share the Need for and the Benefits of the Gospel—with All Types of People (26:16-18)

The evangelists in Acts kept speaking about the Lord's *grace* in opening eyes, in transferring people into the kingdom of light, in transferring them into the power of God from out of the grip of Satan, and in granting them an inheritance. So, like Paul, we must speak to all people groups, "both small and great," about their need for the gospel and about the amazing benefits of embracing the gospel. We must speak honestly about the sinful condition of humans and about the amazing grace of Jesus toward sinners.

Stick to the Message of the Resurrection and the Call to Repentance Based on Scripture (26:19-23)

If you ever have any doubt about what to say when bearing witness, head for the cross, to an account of the resurrection, and then give a clear call for repentance. From the first chapter of Acts onward, Luke continues to emphasize the Messiah who suffered, died, and rose from the dead.

Present in the preaching of the apostles was the promised Messiah of the Scriptures. And also present was the call to repent and believe. Until we see Christ, let's not get tired of talking about the heart of the gospel.

Rely on the Help That Comes from God (26:22)

Paul's comment in verse 22 reminds us that our help comes from God. To be faithful servants and witnesses of Jesus, we need to rely on Jesus for power and grace.

Make Specific Application Boldly (26:24-28)

The gospel demands a response, and we should be ready to pose some probing questions to our unbelieving neighbors. We must give them clear chances to accept or reject Christ. Paul certainly did so with Agrippa. Be respectful but not cowardly.

Be Prepared for Rejection and Ridicule (26:24)

Festus called Paul insane, and we may expect similar comments to be aimed at us when we follow Paul's example. We're simply called to deliver the message about humanity's need for Jesus. Only God converts. We can thus trust him with the results of our efforts, and we can rest in his presence when attacked.

Pray for the People You're Evangelizing (26:29)

Paul's words to the crowd, "I wish before God," remind us of what kind of hearts we as modern evangelists need. Paul prayerfully desires everyone in the assembly to know Jesus. This suggests that he has a heart of compassion toward his hearers. We shouldn't see unbelievers as projects, then, but as people made in God's image who, because of sin, are in need of God's salvation. We should desire that they come to know the same saving grace that we have experienced through the Savior (cf. Rom 10:1; 1 Tim 2:1-4).

May God grant us help to make his grace known to a broken world in loving ways. That same grace that changed Paul has changed us. We must proclaim it.

Reflect and Discuss

1. Identify the similarities between Jesus's trials in Luke 23:1-25 and Paul's trials in Acts 24–25.
2. What does Festus say to Agrippa about Paul in 25:13-22? What do you find most interesting about his statements?
3. How does Paul's speech in Acts 26 magnify the resurrection?
4. How does Paul's speech in Acts 26 show Christ as the fulfillment of Jewish hope?
5. How does Paul speak both respectfully and boldly to Agrippa?
6. Explain how a person might be "kick[ing] against the goads" (26:14).
7. What do modern believers share in common with Paul's commission?
8. What does it mean to "do works worthy of repentance" (26:20)?
9. How might remembering Festus's response to Paul in 26:24 help prepare us to do evangelism?
10. Take a few moments to pray for the salvation of your unbelieving friends, neighbors, coworkers, and family members. In a paragraph or two, summarize your own before-and-after-meeting-Christ story. Then identify a thread in the story that could help you transition smoothly into a presentation of the gospel.

Rome at Last!

ACTS 27:1–28:16

Main Idea: God keeps his promises, so we should trust him and give thanks to him.

I. **Tracing the Narrative (27:1–28:16)**
   A. All aboard (27:1-5)
   B. All change (27:6-12)
   C. All over (27:13-20)
   D. All listen (27:21-26)
   E. All stay (27:27-32)
   F. All eat (27:33-38)
   G. All survive (27:39-44)
   H. All warm (28:1-10)
   I. All arrive (28:11-16)

II. **Thanking God and Taking Courage**

Many people book cruises on the Mediterranean Sea, and for good reason: it's beautiful. The cities along that coast are fascinating and historically significant, and the Mediterranean cruise ships themselves are luxurious. In Acts 27 Paul sails on the Mediterranean, but his trip is nothing like a modern cruise! His traveling companions are mainly prisoners, and their vessels hardly qualify as luxury liners. Worse, this group of men is about to be tossed in a violent, life-threatening storm without the benefits of life vests and antimotion sickness tablets.

We should take care to avoid two extremes when considering this story. One extreme is to assert that this story didn't really happen. Some suggest that Luke essentially took a preexisting storm narrative and inserted Paul into it. This view should be rejected outright (see Witherington III, *Acts of the Apostles,* 757–58). The other danger is to turn this story into an allegory in which every person and thing becomes a symbol representing some hidden meaning. People have tried to make the four anchors mentioned, for example, stand for certain things like trusting in *reason, religion, luck,* or *self.* Anchors are anchors. A ship is a ship. This story really happened. And if we can simply read through the narrative and get caught up in the story, we will find great encouragement from it. We don't need to take away from it or add to it.

The trip involves three main sections: (1) Caesarea to Myra (27:1-5); (2) Myra to Malta (27:6-44); and (3) Malta to Italy (28:1-13). The visit to Rome is then fulfilled in 28:14-16. From the drama that unfolds along this route, we see a wonderful picture of the seamless integration between God's providence and human responsibility. Indeed, the most important lesson related to this passage is that *God keeps his word* (see 27:4-26).

God told Paul that he would reach Rome. He did. In the story God tells Paul that none of the prisoners will be lost. They aren't. God tells Paul that the ship will run aground. And again God's word proves true, just as it always does! At work here is the theme that God will accomplish his purposes, so we should obey and trust him.

In order to help us trace the drama of this passage, I've built on Alistair Begg's three-part outline ("He Plants His Footsteps"). I've added six more "Alls" to his list. In the last chapter, a lead-in to a section said there would be 9 item. And those following subheads were numbered. These are not.

Tracing the Narrative
ACTS 27:1–28:16

All Aboard (27:1-5)

The story begins with a reference to "we." As we've noted previously (e.g., Acts 16; 20), the narrator who is present is *Luke*. Dr. Luke proves an intelligent, diligent, and accurate historian. He reports as an eyewitness about the stops along the trip, the nature of the ships, the sailing practices, and the sailors' experiences.

The final destination of this trip was "Italy" (v. 1; cf. "Rome," 28:16). In Paul's day Gentiles saw Rome as the center of the earth (Bock, *Acts*, 726). It was a strategic place to get the gospel out to the nations because everything went in and out of Rome—hence, Paul's desire to go there (Rom 1:10-16; 15:22-23). In the first century Rome was the most powerful political center in the world, and Paul was a Roman citizen. The apostle had spent over twenty-five years of ministry in the eastern part of the Roman Empire (Rom 15:19-20), but he had dreams of taking the gospel as far west as Spain, using Rome as a launching pad (Rom 15:22-29). About three years before this trip, Paul had written his letter to the

Romans preparing them for his visit. Later, in a time of crisis, the Lord assured Paul that he would indeed testify in Rome itself (23:11).

Under the best of conditions, and sailing straight to Rome from Caesarea, it would take five weeks to transfer Paul to his intended destination. But when this trip is over, the journey will have taken well over four months (Bock, *Acts,* 746).

Other prisoners were with the group, along with a centurion named Julius, who will display a spirit of generosity and kindness in his leadership throughout the trip. Importantly, these prisoners may have been going to Rome not to stand trial, but to serve in the arena as part of entertainment for the emperor and the citizens (Keener in Witherington III, *Acts of the Apostles,* 758n17).

Julius and the prisoners boarded a ship that was apparently returning to its homeport in "Adramyttium," east of Troas. This first ship appears to be a coastal vessel, traveling close to the shore and putting in at the various ports along the way (Polhill, *Acts,* 516). These ports offered a good prospect for finding a more suitable vessel for the trip to Rome (ibid.).

Aristarchus also made the trip (v. 2). Later, when Paul writes to the Colossians from the Roman prison, he mentions the presence of both Luke and Aristarchus (Col 4:10,14). Aristarchus had been traveling with Paul for some time and was caught up in the persecution Paul faced in Ephesus (cf. Acts 19:29; 20:4). Paul describes him as his "fellow prisoner" (Col 4:10), and in Philemon (another prison letter) he calls him his coworker. Kenneth Gangel suggests Julius and others probably viewed Aristarchus as Paul's servant, but we know him better as a member of the missionary team (*Acts,* 446).

The coastal vessel sailed about seventy nautical miles north to the ancient city of "Sidon" (v. 3). While there, Julius kindly gave Paul permission to go enjoy the fellowship of "his friends"—that is, some Christians in the area (cf. 11:19). Julius, then, didn't see Paul as dangerous. These friends cared for Paul, providing essentials for his trip. There were no restaurants or vending machines on this vessel.

Christian friendship is an important theme appearing throughout the book of Acts. Some suggest that Christians in the first century commonly used *friends* as a term for themselves (Gangel, *Acts,* 446). Paul definitely had some wonderful friends, like Aristarchus and Luke, and he also shared relationships with other believers scattered throughout the world—like those in Sidon. Important to this discussion is the fact that John ends his third epistle by referring to fellow Christians as "friends":

I have many things to write you, but I don't want to write to you with
pen and ink. I hope to see you soon, and we will talk face to face.
  Peace to you. The friends *send you greetings. Greet the* friends *by*
name. (3 John 13-15 ESV; emphasis added)

Christian friendship is a gift of God that's rooted in our relationship
with Jesus, who calls his disciples "friends" (cf. Luke 12:4; John 11:11;
15:13-15). Thank God for Christian friends.

At times we, like Paul did, must say good-bye to friends. Nevertheless,
we can have the assurance that true Christian friends will have eternity
to hang out together in the presence of the glorified Jesus. This fact
really encourages me when I think about my friends who are laboring
among the nations and in other states for the sake of the gospel. I would
love to see them more often! But we know that for now we must sacrifice
for the King's sake. Soon we can forever enjoy one another's company
in a renewed world. And I suspect that thoughts like that encouraged
Paul throughout his ministry.

Due to the western winds, the ship sailed north and east of Cyprus
(v. 4). Sailing literally "under the lee" means sailing in such a way that
the island protects the vessel from the winds. Then they sailed "through
the open sea off Cilicia and Pamphylia," before reaching "Myra in Lycia"
(v. 5).

All Change (27:6-12)

In Myra, Julius finds a ship from Alexandria that is "sailing for Italy," so
he brings the passengers on board (v. 6). John Stott notes that this vessel
was a freight ship used for transporting grain (v. 38), with Egypt being
Rome's main granary (*Message of Acts,* 387).

In verses 7-8 Luke describes the "difficulty" of the next part of the
trip as conditions deteriorated. Progress was slow due to the contrary
winds. The passengers and crew were no doubt relieved to stop at Fair
Havens to rest and make further plans.

Fair Havens, or "Good Harbor," sounds like a nice place to stay, but
it wasn't a suitable spot to face the winter season. The group had already
been delayed: "the Day of Atonement" (lit. "the Fast") was already in the
past (v. 9). The Day of Atonement was observed in late September or
early October (Polhill, *Acts,* 518), and this fact is important to the story
because the time between September and November was particularly
dangerous for sea travel. In fact, it ceased entirely between November
and mid-February or mid-March (cf. 28:11; Bock, *Acts,* 733). Paul's

counsel reflected this understanding: thinking it unsafe to venture out west to find another place to endure winter, he warns the men in what seems to be a meeting with his own personal advice rather than a word of prophecy. He tells them that if they proceed, they are likely to lose cargo and lives (v. 10).

Even though Paul was an experienced traveler, having already endured three shipwrecks (2 Cor 11:25), he was outnumbered by the majority. The crew determined to travel about forty miles or so west to a better harbor at Phoenix (Acts 27:12). Paul's counsel, however, turns out to be true in that the crew did lose the ship and the cargo. Fortunately, however, no lives were lost (Polhill, *Acts,* 519). Later, Julius learns from this mistake and listens to Paul (v. 31).

All Over (27:13-20)

Initially the journey goes smoothly. In fact, things move along so well that it's easy to imagine the sailors making fun of Paul for giving them the unnecessary word of caution. But then things change, A violent storm nicknamed with a hybrid formation of the Greek term *euros,* the east wind, and Latin term *aquilo,* the north wind (*eurakylon* or "northeaster"), comes down from the mountain and takes over the ship. The sailors are unable to do anything to fight the wind and are forced to let the ship drift southwest toward the African coastal city of Cyrene (v. 15)

Verse 16 mentions the small island of Cauda, about twenty-three miles away from Crete. There the ship ran under the lee; it sheltered on the side of the island. Luke describes the sailors' attempt to secure the ship. First they hauled in the ship's lifeboat, and then they tried to undergird the ship itself (v. 17). Next they attempted to lower "the drift-anchor," hoping to slow progress in case this great storm blew them toward the deadly shoals.

We can only imagine what the next two weeks must have been like (cf. v. 27). Verse 18 reports that the men jettisoned at least part of "the cargo," and the ship's "tackle" was thrown overboard in verse 19. Discarding any unnecessary equipment was a technique used to make the ship float higher on the water. These efforts had little effect, however, and soon great panic filled the ship. Despite all these efforts to survive the storm, "all hope was fading." The men were left with no gear, no stars, and no hope (Bock, *Acts,* 736).

This point in the narrative reminds me of the story of Jonah. That Old Testament prophet too encountered a violent storm while out at sea, and during it another ship's crew was forced to jettison equipment and despaired of life itself. In that case the prophet and the crew were delivered, but for a different reason than Paul and his crewmen. Jonah's presence in the ship caused the storm, and in his absence the others were saved. Here it's Paul's presence in the ship that leads to safety for all (Polhill, *Acts*, 522).

All Listen (27:21-26)

It's in the midst of great crisis that Paul gives his first of three intervening words, which will help bring everyone onboard to safety (vv. 21-38). John Stott summarizes,

> So far in the Acts, Luke has depicted Paul as the apostle to the Gentiles, the pioneer of the three missionary expeditions, the prisoner, and the defendant. Now, however, he portrays him in a different light. He is no longer an honored apostle, but an ordinary man among men, a lonely Christian (apart from Luke himself and Aristarchus) among nearly three hundred non-Christians, who were either soldiers or prisoners or perhaps merchants or crew. Yet Paul's God-given leadership gifts clearly emerge. "It is quite certain," writes William Barclay, "that Paul was the most experienced traveller on board that ship." . . . Yet it was more than mature experience at sea which made Paul stand out as a leader on board ship; it was his steadfast Christian faith and character. (*Message of Acts*, 389–90)

This first word from Paul is a word of encouragement, rooted in a word from the Lord. In the middle of the storm, everyone was hungry, hopeless, and directionless. Then Paul "stood up" to speak (v. 21), reflecting the posture used to deliver previous authoritative messages (e.g., 2:14; 17:22). His first words seem at first to be an "I told you so" speech, but I think he was simply encouraging the group to listen to him as a credible speaker. He tells them good news on this occasion, saying that no one will die as a result of their predicament, but their ship will be lost (v. 22). He attempts to lift their spirits with this word.

How could Paul be so confident on this point? This time his word to the crew came from the Lord, who had advised him through an angel in the night (v. 23). That means that what the apostle shares here was more than Paul's opinion or wish. The angel gave Paul two promises: (1) Paul *must* appear before Caesar; and (2) all aboard the ship would be graciously delivered with Paul (v. 24). Because of these promises, there was no need to fear.

Paul's first speech in this narrative is central. He and the others will make it safely through the storm because of *the providence of God.* The Lord will keep his promises. He will see to it that Paul gets to Rome. Even so, Paul still warns his audience that there remains more storm to endure and that they will run aground on some island before final deliverance (v. 26). Thus, *human responsibility* is also in view.

In the storm narratives of the Gospels, Jesus addresses the disciples' fear (Mark 4:35-41; 6:45-52). In these moments, Jesus shows the disciples that he is Lord of the storm. His words, "Have courage! It is I. Don't be afraid" (Mark 6:50), are words of comfort for all his saints. We are prone to have "little faith" (Matt 8:26). But Jesus can be trusted even when waves crash around us. The Lord said these reassuring words through Isaiah: "Do not fear, for I have redeemed you; I have called you by your name; you are mine. I will be with you when you pass through the waters" (Isa 43:1-2). What set Paul apart from the others on the ship was his assurance of the presence of God and the promises of God. And that's what we have too.

Fight fear by remembering God's faithful promises. Rest in his comforting presence.

All Stay (27:27-32)

Verses 27-30 set up Paul's next intervening word to the crew. We read that they were drifting in the Adriatic Sea on the fourteenth night since the storm first struck (v. 27). Luke's reference to the "Adriatic Sea" used a first-century name for the north central Mediterranean between Crete and Malta (Gangel, *Acts,* 451). The seasoned sailors sensed that land was near, so they dropped anchors and prayed to their gods for daylight (vv. 28-29). But the pagan sailors apparently didn't trust in their gods very much: some of them tried to escape under the pretense of letting out anchors. (These anchors would have to be set out at a distance from the bow using the lifeboat.) The sailors' real plan was to row the lifeboat to shore (v. 30).

Paul discerned their plan and reported it to Julius and the soldiers (v. 31). They listened to Paul's advice this time and let the lifeboat go free, ensuring that everyone stayed together (v. 32). This action reveals how respected Paul has become during the course of the journey, even though this particular course of action appeared reckless. God's promise to preserve everyone seems to have presupposed that all stay with the ship (Stott, *Message of Acts,* 391).

All Eat (27:33-38)

As dawn drew near, Paul gave his third word of instruction to the group, urging them to eat. Their failure to do so prior to this point probably had to do with the craziness of the situation and seasickness. If you've ever been in a hospital waiting room during a crisis situation, you know what this is like. We lose our appetites when under stress and fear. But Paul used good common sense when he noted their need to eat in order to have the strength to reach land. He again assured them of God's protection, using a biblical metaphor: "none of you will lose a hair from your head" (cf. 1 Sam 14:45; 2 Sam 14:11; Luke 12:7; 21:18). Once again providence and human responsibility are intermingled.

The occasion to eat gave Paul an opportunity to give a visible display of his devotion to the Giver of all good things. Taking the role of a father or a host, he offered the blessing, distributed the food, and began to eat (v. 35). This description reminds us of the feeding of the five thousand (Luke 9:16), Jesus's meal with the Emmaus disciples (Luke 24:30), and especially the institution of the Lord's Supper (Luke 22:19).

The men aboard the ship, however, were not taking the Lord's Supper; they were eating for the sake of nourishment. Paul knew that hungry men are useless men. Nevertheless, "Paul's calm consumption, and especially his public thanksgiving to the God of all grace, bears witness to the peace amid life's storms that Jesus gives through the new covenant" (Johnson, *Let's Study Acts*, 335). It wasn't a sacred meal the men shared, but it was indeed a "sacred moment" (Bock, *Acts*, 740).

The crew of 276 men was "encouraged" (v. 36; cf. vv. 22,25) and followed Paul's example by eating (v. 36). After the meal, they jettisoned the rest of the grain in order to lighten the ship (vv. 37-38). Buoyed by Paul's words, they were confident that they would obtain access to food again; it was time to lift the boat higher in the water as they were drawing near to the shore (Bock, *Acts*, 740).

In looking back over Paul's exemplary guidance, what can we learn about leadership in secular situations?

First, Paul was a man of both spiritual depth and practical wisdom. Paul wasn't a wild mystic. He had a real faith in the living God that gave him the confidence he needed to stay calm and to lead. But he also had Proverbs-like wisdom that enabled him to give basic instructions to those in need. In secular situations we really need leaders who are both wise and in step with God, men and women who will serve as agents of hope in a world of darkness. John Stott says, "[Paul] was a man of God and of action, a man of the Spirit and of common sense" (*Message of Acts*, 392).

Paul also gave a clear and appropriate testimony in the situation (Fernando, *Acts*, 620). While we don't see aggressive evangelism at work in this story, we do see Paul taking opportunities to point people to God. He spoke of his God in verse 23 before speaking God's promise, and later he gave thanks to God in prayer in front of others before taking something to eat (v. 35). Paul spoke and prayed in the midst of hopelessness, giving the crew an alternate perspective, a ray of hope, and something important to ponder. We too should look for clear and appropriate ways to bear witness to Jesus in the public sphere.

All Survive (27:39-44)

As the sun appeared on the horizon, the crew could see a place to run the ship ashore. With the storm still blowing, they cast off the anchors, freed up the rudders, and went straight for the beach. That's when the ship struck a sandbar. The bow was hung up on the sandbar, and the stern was exposed to the pounding waves. Soon the ship would be totally shattered, as Paul had warned.

At this point Julius's soldiers faced a double threat. To stay alive, they needed to swim to shore. But if they make it to land and some prisoners escaped, the guards would face execution for those losses (cf. 12:19; 16:27). In light of this fear, the soldiers prepared to kill the prisoners before jumping overboard themselves. But Julius intervened because he wanted to save Paul. This move shows that Julius's respect for Paul had grown, and he may have believed Paul's prophecy. Julius ordered everyone to head for the land by swimming or floating to shore. Luke concludes, "In this way, everyone safely reached the shore" (v. 44). All survived!

Once again God's word proves true. We can trust him.

All Warm (28:1-10)

The survivors must have breathed a massive sigh of relief when their feet hit the sand. Upon arriving on an island, they received some warm hospitality by some "local people" (v. 2)—that is, some non-Greek-speaking people (*barbaroi*, cf. Rom 1:14-15). They were rustic, preferring their own dialect, but the Maltese people weren't barbaric in their character. They displayed "extraordinary kindness" to the survivors. They kindled a fire and welcomed everyone. I can only imagine how wonderful that fire must have felt to those men who had been in an open boat on a storm-tossed sea for so long.

Right away Paul, as a servant leader, began gathering sticks for the fire. His actions remind us that no job was beneath Paul. During the whole trip he displayed a servant lifestyle. William Barclay helpfully comments: "It is only the little man that refuses the little task" (quoted in Stott, *Message of Acts,* 621).

In his search Paul picked up more than sticks. A poisonous snake bit down on his hand! From this the natives drew the conclusion that Paul was guilty of a great crime, like murder (v. 4). "Justice" in this passage is personified as a goddess, the daughter of Zeus and Themis (Bock, *Acts,* 743). But to the natives' surprise, Paul suffered no harm from what should have been a deadly bite. They thus concluded he was "a god" (cf. 14:11).

While Paul was certainly not a god, the God who rules heaven and earth, the sea and all that is in it, was with Paul. And the islanders received a visible display of God's power through his servant's immunity to the snake's venom. As we have noted previously in our study, God often revealed himself to various groups of people in Scripture in ways that got their attention and helped make his saving message known to them (cf. Acts 19). What happened to Paul, then, was an act of God's kindness displayed to the superstitious islanders. They were surprised by the event; Paul was probably surprised at the ministry opportunity the snake's bite afforded him. Since the shipwrecked group stayed on the island for three months during the winter (v. 11), Paul had time and opportunity to make God's truth known to the barbarians.

The leading man of the island, Publius, hosted the visitors for three days (v. 7). His mention provides another example in Acts of Paul's establishing a relationship with the leading figures in an area (cf. 13:7; 16:22; 17:19; 18:12; 19:31). It also serves as an example of a pagan displaying kindness and warm hospitality and of a believer receiving it! We should notice that Paul didn't act like a Pharisee and try to distance himself from those on the island who shared neither his beliefs nor his traditions. Instead, he acted like Jesus did and became a friend of sinners.

Scripture's mentions of Julius and Publius—whose combined names sound like the name of a great hip-hop group—illustrate how, in God's common grace, even unredeemed humans can display lovely virtues. While every human is sinful and in need of redemption, unbelievers do have an innate capacity to do good. Believers, then, should compliment unbelievers when such acts of kindness are displayed, perhaps even using those acts to draw attention to the characteristics of our Savior. Jesus, love itself, invites everyone—Jew, Greek, Barbarian, slave, free, educated, uneducated, kind, and unkind—to his banquet (cf. Luke 14:21-24; Col 3:11).

In verse 8 we learn that Publius's father was sick with fever and dysentery (v. 8). This kind of fever could last for months or even a few years (Bock, *Acts,* 744). Paul, apparently without invitation, visited the sick man and prayed, making clear to everyone that healing power comes from God (cf. 3:12; 9:34,40). He laid his hands on him (cf. 9:12,17; Jas 5:13-14) and healed him (cf. Luke 4:38-39). And in doing so, Paul—though held unjustly as a prisoner—proved a blessing to everyone (ibid.).

News of what happened traveled quickly, and soon sick people from all over the island flocked to Paul and received cures. They displayed their gratitude not only with words but also in deeds, offering provisions to the crew for the rest of the voyage. I love to hear about creative ways the Lord provides for his people!

All Arrive (28:11-16)

Had my kids been traveling on the journey to Rome, they would've been asking, "Are we there yet?" by verse 11. To this Paul might have responded, "Almost."

The ship that took Paul on the 210-mile journey to Italy in mid-February was also a ship from Alexandria (Bock, *Acts,* 745; v. 11). On its bow it had a figurehead of the "Twin Gods," Castor and Pollux, who were seen as protectors. It was the Lord of all creation, however, who was the real protector of those onboard. Once the travel was underway, the crew first stopped at Syracuse for three days and then went on to Rhegium, at the toe of the Italian mainland. Not long after that they finally reached Puteoli, the port of Neapolis—present-day Naples, which sits about 130 miles south of Rome.

Paul was invited to stay with the Christian brothers there for seven days. This stop was probably due to Julius's wanting to rest before making the remainder of the trip by foot. The freedom given to Paul was probably due to the level of respect Julius had for Paul and was another display of the man's kindness. It's possible that the church provided fresh provisions for the rest of the trip.

Luke's premature comment, "And so we came to Rome," in verse 14 rather than in verse 16, is explained in various ways. It may be that

Luke is eager to get to the climax of the story, as he anticipates their actual arrival in Rome (Fernando, *Acts,* 615). That is, he may be saying something like, "Here's how we came to Rome . . ." (Witherington III, *Acts of the Apostles,* 787). Or he may view Puteoli as part of greater Rome. Or better yet, related to this second option, he probably is saying that for all practical purposes, the goal for reaching Rome is *as good as attained* (Polhill, *Acts,* 536–37). To this idea John Polhill adds, "In a real sense, v. 14b can be considered as the climax to the entire Book of Acts" (ibid., 538). We can't read of Paul's arrival in Rome without reflecting on Jesus's plan for his witnesses to go "to the ends of the earth" (1:8).

After resting, the men had before them about a five-day walk to Rome by means of two well-traveled roads, the Companion Way and the Appian Way (Bock, *Acts,* 746). Word reached the church in Rome that Paul had arrived in Italy. His magisterial letter—Romans—had reached them three years earlier. Some of the Roman believers thus decided to meet Paul along the way (v. 15). Some others met him at the famous Forum, or market of Appius, which was about forty-three miles from Rome and lacked a great reputation. Others met Paul at Three Taverns (a settlement that had grown around an isolated inn by that name), ten miles closer to the capital. Cicero mentions both locations as resting places along the way (Witherington III, *Acts of the Apostles,* 787). When Paul saw these men who shared his faith, he "thanked God" and "took courage."

Here once again we can observe how sweet Christian fellowship is. The sight of other spiritual brothers and sisters in what was once faraway Rome must have filled Paul's heart with delight.

Nearly two and a half difficult years had passed since Paul was given divine assurance in Jerusalem that he would reach Rome (Fernando, *Acts,* 614), but finally he made it. Though Paul was a prisoner, he had some freedom to minister.

Thanking God and Taking Courage

Back in 27:23 Paul told the distressed ship's crew that the God to whom he belonged and whom he served assured him of safe arrival to Rome. In saying this, Paul identified what it means to be a Christian. Christians know they belong to God through Jesus and have the indwelling Spirit (cf. 1 Cor 6:20; Gal 5:24). Christians also worship and serve God, through Jesus, by the Spirit. We don't serve the idols of money, pleasure, or success. We serve and worship God in easy times and in difficult ones. So, if you aren't certain that you are serving God in this way, it's time to ask, "Do I really belong to God through Jesus?" (cf. Rom 8:9). If you can't answer in the affirmative with absolute certainty, then embrace him. Trust him. He is the Savior of all types of people (cf. Col 3:11). He will not turn you away.

Those who belong to Jesus can take courage and be thankful as they consider Paul's story. Let me encourage you with three applications from the current passage.

First, you can trust in the providence of God. God is at work, accomplishing his purposes and conforming us into Christ's image (cf. Rom 8:28-30). God keeps his promises. William Cowper reminds us in his classic hymn of these sweet words:

> God moves in a mysterious way
> His wonders to perform;
> He plants His footsteps in the sea
> And rides upon the storm.

> Judge not the Lord by feeble sense,
> But trust Him for His grace;
> Behind a frowning providence
> He hides a smiling face. ("God Moves in a Mysterious Way")

Though you may not understand everything that's happening when you consider the twists and turns of your life, know that God is working for believers' good and for his glory. You can always trust him.

Second, you can rejoice in the saving grace of God. Think about it. If you're a Christian, you are among *the reached.* The gospel came to you. That's a beautiful miracle you should never get tired of pondering! Paul wanted to get the gospel to Rome and then to Spain. Just as it took a lot for Paul to get to Rome, it took a lot for the gospel to get to you. Marvel at God's grace.

Third, you can align yourself with the mission of God. Acts 27–28 remind us of 1:8. Jesus has a mission that extends to the ends of the earth. And what a mission it is! Let's not waste our time on earth. We must use it wisely and missionally for the good of the nations and for the glory of our great King.

Reflect and Discuss

1. Have you ever been in a life-threatening situation? If so, how did you react to it? How might this passage encourage someone facing a great trial?
2. How does this narrative highlight the truth that God keeps his word?
3. Why are Christian friendships important? How do we see Paul valuing friendships in this narrative?
4. How does this narrative display both the sovereign providence of God and the responsibility of humans?
5. Explain some ways Paul displays great spiritual and practical leadership in this story.
6. Identify some of the ways unbelievers display kindness in this narrative. How should we respond to such displays from the unbelievers we encounter?
7. Explain how Paul gave an appropriate and clear witness on this trip. How might you apply some of these methods in your own interactions?
8. How did Paul respond to Julius's hospitality? What would you do if invited to spend time with unbelievers? How should Christians view such invitations, and how should we respond to them?
9. At the end of the narrative, Paul thanked God. Think about some of the ways God has provided for you in recent months and give him thanks.
10. Take a few moments to pray for God to grant you—and others—*peace* in the midst of great trials.

The End of the Beginning

ACTS 28:17-31

Main Idea: The book of Acts concludes with Paul's ministry in Rome, but the mission continues today through God's people.

I. **Make the Most of Every Ministry Opportunity (28:17-23,30-31; Phil 1:12-26).**
II. **Teach All People about King Jesus from the Scriptures (28:23-31).**
   A. From dawn to dusk (28:23)
   B. From cover to cover (28:23)
   C. From heart to heart (28:23-24)
   D. From Jew to Gentile (28:25-28)
III. **Ask God to Grant You Spirit-Empowered Boldness (28:30-31).**
IV. **Maintain an Unshakeable Confidence in the Gospel (28:31).**
V. **Pour Yourself Out for the King Until You See the King (28:30-31; 2 Tim 4:6-8,17-18).**

The concluding episode of a popular television series always creates a buzz. I remember when the show *Lost* was nearing its last episode. It seemed everyone was asking, "How will it end?" I also remember the mixed reviews that finale got. Many viewers weren't satisfied with the ending, but others liked it.

Do you like happy endings? Do you want complete closure when you reach the end of a riveting novel or movie? Does seeing the words "To be continued" typed across the last page or final screen shot drive you to insanity? Do movies and books that allow you to choose your own ending seem somehow dissatisfying?

If you like complete closure and prefer happily-ever-after conclusions, then you might be disappointed with the ending of Acts. Luke has taken us for quite a journey. His writing is remarkable, but his ending might appear surprising and perhaps even a bit frustrating. We have been leading up to Paul's trial before Caesar for many chapters now, but nothing is said about it here!

In fact, Acts closes without telling us what happened to Paul. We're not sure how long he lived. We don't know how long he was able to go on ministering unhindered. We can't even be certain he ever made it to

Spain. Can you imagine reading a novel that ended like this? If you did, you might write the publisher to say, "Hey! I'm missing a chapter! I need to know what happened to Paul!"

Acts essentially ends on a big "To be continued." Why? Because Luke didn't intend to write a biography of Paul. Luke purposed to describe the acts of the Lord Jesus accomplished by the Spirit. He set out to describe the unstoppable progress of the gospel. His first book, the Gospel of Luke, set out to tell "all that Jesus began to do and teach until the day he was taken up" (Acts 1:1-2). The book of Acts, then, is about all that Jesus *continued* to do after that point. The ministry of Jesus continued by the Spirit through the church. Luke leaves us with Paul preaching the mighty gospel of the kingdom in Rome. And in choosing to walk away from the story here, Luke masterfully keeps the King—not Paul or anyone else—the hero of Acts. Luke concludes Acts on a note of victory, with the triumph of the King. This is a fitting conclusion.

Luke's message ends up being something like this: "This book is finished, but the mission Jesus assigned to the church isn't." This means that Christians—whether in first-century Rome or in twenty-first-century America—get to enter the story! We get to participate in the next chapters of Acts! We get to join the drama of spreading the good news to the nations. While God replaces messengers over time, the message and the mission assigned to Christians will remain unchanging until the King returns.

From Scripture we can identify at least five applications as we seek to continue this mission.

Make the Most of Every Ministry Opportunity
ACTS 28:17-23,30-31; PHILIPPIANS 1:12-26

From verse 30 onward, it seems that Paul lived at his own expense in a relaxed form of house arrest, able to welcome visitors. He makes the most of the situation by ministering to the Roman imperial guard (and by extension, to those associated with the guards), to the Jews, and eventually to all who would come to him. Though technically a prisoner, Paul isn't complaining; he's proclaiming.

In his letter to the Colossians, which was written during this imprisonment, Paul said,

> *Devote yourselves to prayer; stay alert in it with thanksgiving. At the same time, pray also for us that God may open a door to us for the word, to speak the mystery of Christ, for which I am in chains, so that I may*

> *make it known as I should. Act wisely toward outsiders, making the*
> *most of the time. Let your speech always be gracious, seasoned with salt,*
> *so that you may know how you should answer each person.* (Col 4:2-6)

Don't miss that in this passage Paul's asking for prayer that he may make the message about Christ known effectively, not that he be released from prison! And he's exhorting the believers not to think about him but to make the best use of their time, living with evangelistic sensitivity toward unbelievers. Importantly, Paul is living out his own advice. He's seeking to make the most of his opportunity to minister the gospel in Rome. And he knows he needs God's help to do it faithfully and effectively.

We know of at least one person who was converted during Paul's house arrest in Rome. He was a runaway servant named Onesimus. Paul wrote a letter to Philemon, the servant's owner, during this same imprisonment. He encouraged him to be reconciled to Onesimus:

> *Although I have great boldness in Christ to command you to do what*
> *is right, I appeal to you, instead, on the basis of love. I, Paul, as an*
> *elderly man and now also as a prisoner of Christ Jesus, appeal to you*
> *for my son, Onesimus. I became his father while I was in chains. . . .*
> *So if you consider me a partner, welcome him as you would me. And if*
> *he has wronged you in any way, or owes you anything, charge that to*
> *my account.* (Phlm 8-10,17-18)

I'm sure Onesimus was grateful that Paul didn't quit ministering during his imprisonment. Because Paul kept his heart focused on the mission of sharing Jesus rather than allowing his circumstances to shut him down, Onesimus was able to hear the apostle teach the gospel and was gloriously converted.

Paul also made the most of his opportunity with the imperial guard. Paul was under a lenient form of military custody in which only one soldier guarded him (28:16). This soldier would probably be relieved every so often, creating a rotation of guardsmen who were essentially Paul's captive audience while chained to him—if indeed they were chained. These guards, in my view, had to be the most privileged guards in human history. They were able to hear the greatest evangelist-expositor in the history of the church. They were in a position to ask him anything! And perhaps some of them were converted as a result.

A survey of the New Testament leaves us with the idea that Paul's witness impacted more than just the particular soldiers who guarded him.

His witness apparently became the talk of the guards and the palace officials. Some estimate that there were as many as nine thousand Roman guards in that day. Paul's message became known to many of them, to officials, and even to pagans in the streets. In Philippians, also written during this imprisonment, Paul mentions how God was accomplishing his purposes through this incarceration:

> *I want you to know, brothers and sisters, that what has happened to me has actually advanced the gospel, so that it has become known throughout the whole imperial guard, and to everyone else, that my imprisonment is because I am in Christ. Most of the brothers have gained confidence in the Lord from my imprisonment and dare even more to speak the word fearlessly. . . . I know this will lead to my salvation through your prayers and help from the Spirit of Jesus Christ. My eager expectation and hope is that I will not be ashamed about anything, but that now as always, with all courage, Christ will be highly honored in my body, whether by life or by death. For me, to live is Christ and to die is gain. Now if I live on in the flesh, this means fruitful work for me; and I don't know which one I should choose. I am torn between the two. I long to depart and be with Christ—which is far better.* (Phil 1:12-14,19-23)

Many Romans were hearing the good news, and Christians were becoming bolder as a result of Paul's witness. He was a man consumed with Jesus Christ. Let's follow Paul's example. Wherever the Lord has you, make him known!

In verse 17 Paul calls together the local Jewish leaders. Even in Rome he sought to minister to the Jews. Two points about Paul's outreach efforts to the Jews in Rome stand out.

First, while the apostle's first encounter with the local Jews came at his request, the second happened because they requested to hear more. Perhaps part of their willingness to listen further can be linked to Paul's assuring them of his *innocence* (28:17-19). He had done nothing wrong to the Jewish people, and he had not violated their customs. Still, however, he was handed over to the Romans and was mistreated (cf. 21:33; Luke 9:44; 18:32; 24:7). Nevertheless, Paul clarified that he had no charge to make against the Jews. This suggests that he wanted the Roman Jews to know that he had no desire for vengeance. In spite of their ill treatment of him, he had no countercharges to bring against the Jewish population.

Once his own clean slate was established, Paul went on to mention "the hope of Israel" (v. 20). These words served as a teaser meant to gather interest about Paul's main message. By using Old Testament terminology familiar to them, Paul was setting up the Jewish leaders of Rome to hear his proclamation of the risen Christ (cf. Jer 14:8; 17:13).

The group of Jewish leaders responded to Paul's efforts in two ways. First, they claimed *ignorance* regarding Paul's trials (v. 21). Such lack of awareness may be owing to (1) the fact that Paul and the crew traveled early in the season and got to Rome before any Jews from Palestine could get there to tell tales about him, or more likely, (2) the Judean leaders had decided to back off, believing their case against the apostle had no chance in Rome, and thus they did not send a prosecutor.

The Jews' second response was an expression of *interest.* Curiously, they claimed to have no real understanding of Christianity though there was a vibrant church in Rome. This makes it likely that the Roman Jews were intentionally keeping their distance from Christians by the time Paul arrived. The edict of Claudius (in which Jews were expelled from Rome; cf. 18:2) had happened about ten years earlier, and the Jews had begun resettling in Rome about four years after their expulsion (Gangel, *Acts,* 466). Perhaps, then, because of a sense of insecurity, the Jews had been trying to avoid association with Christians up to this point.

Importantly, this first meeting with Paul set up the next meeting. The Jews wanted to hear more, so Paul made the most of his situation by welcoming them and exalting Jesus from the Scriptures.

Teach All People about King Jesus from the Scriptures
ACTS 28:23-31

As with his ministry in Pisidian Antioch, Paul's second meeting with the Jews drew a much larger crowd (28:23; cf. 13:44). Paul's expositional ministry in this meeting appears to have been focused on persuading the Jews about Christ's importance through the use of the Law of Moses and the Prophets. Nevertheless, as the larger passage indicates, Paul taught *all* people about the King and the kingdom as he had opportunity (vv. 30-31). This reminds us of the necessity of making disciples by teaching everyone about Jesus and his kingdom from the Scriptures.

From Dawn to Dusk (28:23)

Paul had some amazing preaching stamina! In Troas he preached all night (20:7,11). Here he preached all day. This meeting requested by the Jews wasn't over after a quick, three-minute gospel presentation. Instead, Paul took his time to explain the plan of God within the context of the Scriptures. He built on his hearers' existing background.

Explaining the gospel to unbelievers—especially those who lack any concept of the Christian worldview—may take considerable time. A friend who ministers in a diverse region of the States and I were talking about this issue recently. We agreed that much preevangelism has to happen today before most are ready to respond to a call for repentance. We as Christians have to provide a framework. We have to explain that God made a perfect world, that sin broke it, and that God—out of love—stepped into his creation on a rescue mission to save humans from our wicked choices. Millions today—even highly educated people—have no concept of basic Bible stories or the Christian principles of sin and salvation that we often take for granted. That means we must patiently teach.

From Cover to Cover (28:23)

Paul taught about Jesus in accordance with the Old Testament, showing Christ as the hero of the Scriptures. He magnified Jesus as the Messiah throughout his exposition, imitating the pattern set forth by Jesus on the Emmaus road (Luke 24:27,44-47). Likely influenced by this, Luke ends both his Gospel and Acts by highlighting the exposition of Scripture and the central figure in the Scriptures, Jesus. Here in Acts, Paul's main two subjects are the "kingdom of God" and "Jesus" (vv. 23,31); they summarized the heart of Paul's instruction.

We must continue the church's mission by continuing to expound the Scriptures and pointing people to the hero of the Scriptures!

The text doesn't tell us exactly what Paul said about the kingdom, but surely he described how Jesus was the long anticipated Ruler, the true and better David, whose kingdom was inaugurated at his first coming and will one day be consummated at his second. He may have also contrasted the unending reign of Jesus with the kingdom of Caesar. Indeed, there's much he could have said about the kingdom of heaven, including its inside-out nature (cf. Luke 11:39-41; Rom 14:17), its upside-down nature (cf. Matt 19:30; Luke 6:20-26; 14:11; Phil 2:1-11), and its fascinating already-not yet aspects (cf. Ps 110:1; Eph 1:13-14). The Jewish people definitely would have been interested in Paul's take on the subject, as the disciples' question in Acts 1:6 illustrated.

As King, Jesus now reigns in the hearts of all who will come to him. In this way he reigns in the midst of his enemies. Local churches are outposts of his kingdom. The King's people, each a part of those local churches, are called to display the values and virtues of the King, giving the world a foretaste of the (consummated) kingdom to come. As the King's people, we should "seek first the kingdom of God" (Matt 6:33), and we should invite the world to bow to the King now in order to participate in his coming kingdom later (cf. Luke 14:12-24). Paul cared about the kingdom because he cared about the King. And we will have no passion for the kingdom if we don't have a passion for its Ruler.

In teaching about the Lord Jesus, Paul would have set forth stories of his birth, life, death, resurrection, and ascension. He would have talked about the pouring out of the Spirit and about the anticipated return of the Messiah. To do that he would have pointed to various Old Testament texts.

Paul's method provides us an example of what it looks like to fulfill the Great Commission charge of making disciples of all nations through "teaching" (Matt 28:18-20). Patiently and faithfully, each Christian must teach the Word of Christ and the Christ of the Word. "We proclaim him," Paul said to the Colossians (1:28). So let's never stop opening up the Scriptures, explaining texts, and showing people—those within our homes, within our classrooms, and within our communities—how Christ fits within the larger redemptive story.

From Heart to Heart (28:23-24)

Key to understanding verses 23 and 24 is the fact that Paul was not giving a boring all-day lecture to those who gathered at his lodging. Rather, Paul was trying to "persuade" (*peitho*) or "convince" (ESV) the Jews of the truth about God's kingdom (v. 23). Some were "persuaded" (v. 24; cf. 17:4) by his arguments. This may or may not mean they were actually converted to Christianity, however. Perhaps some were simply convinced of Paul's innocence as they heard his teaching or were satisfied that Paul did indeed know how to make a coherent argument.

These possibilities serve to remind us that many people today are convinced of the truthfulness of the gospel but are not converted. Some wrongly equate mental assent that Jesus was who he claimed to be with placing saving faith in Christ. So after teaching the gospel to people, we must press on them the need to repent and embrace Christ in faith. They need to call on Jesus as Lord (Rom 10:9).

Whatever kind of "persuading" Paul did in his exposition, it divided the synagogue. Those who weren't convinced by what he said expressed the same kind of hard-heartedness that we have observed throughout Acts. Ajith Fernando says, "There isn't much new here. Luke underscores the tragedy of Jewish rejection of the gospel. What is new is Paul's use of a familiar text (Isa 6:9-10)" (*Acts,* 625).

As we expound the gospel to others, we're not merely trying to transfer information from our brains to theirs. Instead, we should evangelize from our hearts to the hearts of others, always seeking to persuade our hearers to bow the knee to King Jesus—the One who loves them and desires that they too become citizens of his kingdom (cf. 2 Cor 5:11).

From Jew to Gentile (28:25-28)

In verse 25 the Jews were "disagreeing among themselves," and they began to leave after Paul made one final statement based on Isaiah 6:9-10.

The point that caused the dispute began with an introductory comment in which Paul affirmed the inspiration of Isaiah, a section of Old Testament Scripture. Throughout the book of Acts, biblical citations are introduced with references to the Spirit (cf. 1:16; 4:25). Also, Paul distanced himself from the Jews by saying "your ancestors" rather than sticking to his initial approach of calling the Jews his "brothers" (v. 17). The point here is that Paul's faith in Christ has separated him from the Jews, who rejected the Messiah, as Isaiah "was right in saying."

Paul cited Isaiah, who highlighted *hearing, seeing,* and *the heart.* If the people who listened to Paul's message would actually act on what they saw and heard and understood in their hearts, then they would repent and be healed.

Hearing the word of God always has an effect on people, but the same sun that melts the ice also hardens the clay. Either people are melted and moved by Jesus when they hear the word, or they reject him and become increasingly hard-hearted toward him as a result. No one can listen to the gospel and remain neutral to it. That's why we must warn unbelievers that they must respond positively to God's word, or the Lord may give them what they want—eternal separation from him and from his grace.

Sadly, in this passage the Roman Jews heard the message about Jesus, but many refused to respond to it. The concept of "hearing" appears throughout these meetings with the Roman Jews (cf. 28:22,26-28). The last time Paul uses this verb in verse 28, he says that Gentiles will "listen" and respond appropriately to God's message of salvation.

Paul's words here remind us of Jesus's emphasis on the proper hearing of God's Word. In his parable of the Soils, he too quoted Isaiah 6 (cf. Matt 12:39-40; Mark 4:12; Luke 8:10). Isaiah 6:9-10, in fact, appears in various places in the New Testament (cf. John 12:39-40; Rom 11:8)—always in contexts of unbelief and hardness of heart.

In Romans 11 Paul discusses the Jews' failure to hear the gospel (11:8; citing Isa 29:10 and Deut 29:4)—a rejection that's something of a riddle. Paul suggests that the Jewish rejection may be temporary. During this temporary rejection, many Gentiles will believe, and in the end, in the mystery of God's purposes, there will a great turning of Jews to Christ. Here in Acts 28 Paul simply notes the tragedy of the Jewish rejection of Jesus. A message of salvation was foretold by Jewish prophets, fulfilled in a Jewish Messiah, preached by Jewish evangelists, rejected by the Jews, but embraced by the Gentiles (Polhill, *Acts*, 544).

Initially the conversion of Gentiles like Cornelius was the exception in Christianity, not the norm. At first the Jewish Christians wrestled with the inclusion of the Gentiles (Acts 15). But by the end of Acts, things have changed. Jewish converts are the exception, and Gentile converts are the norm. God's kingdom encompasses the nations. Jewish evangelism must continue, but Christianity primarily involves Gentiles who place faith in Jesus.

Verse 28 is the third time in Acts in which Paul turned to the Gentiles (cf. 13:46; 18:6), and Paul's ministry among them has been fruitful. So, is Paul at this point turning from the Jews to Gentiles in a final and definitive move (Polhill, *Acts*, 544)? Is Paul finished with the Jews? In one sense, no. "All" were welcome to hear the message, including Jews (28:30). John Stott notes, "The most natural explanation of this is that the 'all' who came to see Paul included both [Jews and Gentiles]" (*Message of Acts*, 400). And all along, some Jews had believed through his ministry, though not in great number (v. 24). This passage is a reminder that we too must continue evangelizing our Jewish neighbors. But in another sense we might say yes. Paul believed "official Judaism," the Jewish people as a whole, wouldn't embrace Jesus (Polhill, *Acts*, 545)—at least not at this point in redemptive history. Paul therefore turns his attention mainly to the Gentiles.

We must teach the nations about King Jesus from the Scriptures. To do this, we need the Spirit's help.

Ask God to Grant You Spirit-Empowered Boldness
ACTS 28:30-31

In verses 30-31 Luke concludes Acts suddenly. Here we learn that since the Romans weren't in a hurry to deal with Paul, he continued to receive all kinds of visitors throughout his house arrest (v. 30). It's easy to picture Paul in this house, teaching the Scriptures day after day, just as he taught in the lecture hall of Tyrannus a few years earlier (19:9).

During this time Paul wrote four important letters known as the Prison Epistles: Ephesians, Philippians, Colossians, and Philemon. Through studying these documents, we know of some of the people who visited him: Tychicus, Onesimus, and Epaphroditus. When these and others stopped by his rented home, Paul continued to share about the kingdom of God and about the things concerning the Lord Jesus Christ (v. 31). Paul communicated this message with Spirit-empowered "boldness."

Throughout the book of Acts, this Spirit-produced courage is highlighted as a character trait of faithful witnesses (cf. 4:29-31). Luke wrote earlier,

> *When they observed the* boldness *of Peter and John and realized that they were uneducated and untrained men, they were amazed and recognized that they had been with Jesus.* (4:13; emphasis added)

Paul, too, was known for speaking boldly—even in his writings. Let's ask God to grant us this same type of boldness in our evangelistic efforts (cf. Eph 6:19-20).

Maintain an Unshakeable Confidence in the Gospel
ACTS 28:31

Luke says that Paul continued to proclaim Jesus boldly and "without hindrance" (*akolutos*). Perhaps this is meant only to indicate that because the Romans didn't perceive Paul as being dangerous, they put no stumbling block in the way of his gospel proclamation. But it could also be that in using this word here, Luke was alluding to the unbound nature of the gospel; it triumphs over every worldly and spiritual barrier. Though Paul was chained, for instance, the Word of God wasn't bound (cf. 2 Tim 2:9)! Though he was hindered from traveling beyond a set area, it was not. Consider how Luke has been tracking the triumph of the gospel in Acts:

So the word of God spread, the disciples in Jerusalem increased greatly in number, and a large group of priests became obedient to the faith. (6:7)

So the church throughout all Judea, Galilee, and Samaria had peace and was strengthened. Living in the fear of the Lord and encouraged by the Holy Spirit, it increased in numbers. (9:31)

But the word of God flourished and multiplied. (12:24)

So the churches were strengthened in the faith and grew daily in numbers. (16:5)

In this way the word of the Lord flourished and prevailed. (19:20)

We may now add 28:31 to the list of summary statements expressing the triumph of the Word.

We should stop and marvel at the spectacular spread of Christianity. Since the start of Acts, the gospel has taken hold in Jerusalem, in cities all over the ancient world, and has finally made it to Rome. We often assume that Jerusalem was the center of action in the ancient world, but it wasn't. It was important to the Jews, and it was the center of the messianic hope, but the city itself was rather insignificant in many ways (Richards and O'Brien, *Misreading Scripture with Western Eyes*, 65). It was on the eastern fringe of the Roman Empire. Rome controlled the area, but the activities there didn't really occupy Roman interest (ibid.). Randolph Richards and Brandon O'Brien note the following about the humble beginnings and the explosive growth of the Christian faith:

> Pilate was more the main finance officer or tax collector than anything else. The events of Jesus's life, death and resurrection, so important for the Jews and Christians at the time, were marginal events in a nothing town on the edge of an empire with more important matters to consider. If we fail to recognize this, we can fail to recognize just how remarkable the rapid growth of the early church really was. For the first couple of centuries, Roman writers often referred to Christians as "Galileans," indicating how nominal and provincial they considered the early Jesus movement to be. (Ibid.)

Yet, at the end of Acts, we see the beginnings of the worldwide movement of a people who worship the risen King from Nazareth. The gospel's progress and tenacity are breathtaking!

But nearly two thousand years after Christ's resurrection, we who live so far away from Jerusalem and Rome can easily fall prey to our culture's general doubts about the power of the gospel. People seem disinterested in the Bible's message. Some mock the idea of a crucified man from Palestine dying for their sins and then returning to life in triumph. Do not let the skepticism of others take your mind off our mission. The world's scorn is nothing new.

Kent Hughes notes that visitors to Rome can see a square of plaster cut from the wall of the barracks in the Palace of the Caesars (*Acts*, 344). On this plaster is a sketch of a human figure with the head of a donkey who is nailed to a cross. At the foot of the cross is the sketch of a man kneeling before it. Clearly this ancient picture was intended to mock someone who had converted to Christianity—possibly a Roman soldier. The inscription reads, "Alexamenos worships his God" (ibid.).

Now as then the gospel sounds like foolishness to some, yet we who have heard and embraced the message of Scripture know it to be the power of God (cf. 1 Cor 1:18; 2 Cor 2:16). So let's not doubt the power of the gospel! Let's not try to domesticate the message. If we empty the cross of its supposed foolishness, we empty it of its power (cf. 1 Cor 1:27).

Pour Yourself Out for the King Until You See the King
ACTS 28:30-31; 2 TIMOTHY 4:6-8,17-18

From everything we read in these last chapters of Acts, from what we can piece together from Paul's letters (e.g., Phil 1:12-26), and from what we learn from church history (see Witherington III, *Acts of the Apostles*, 792), it seems that Paul was likely released around AD 62 or 63. When given his freedom, he resumed his traveling ministry. During this obscure period Paul went to various places, visited his churches, and wrote 1 Timothy and Titus before being rearrested. After this second arrest, and just prior to his martyrdom, he wrote 2 Timothy. Richard Longnecker offers a summary of Paul's final years:

> We may believe that after Paul's release from this [first]
> Roman imprisonment he continued his evangelistic work
> in the eastern portion of the empire (at least in lands
> surrounding the Aegean Sea)—perhaps even fulfilling his long
> cherished desire to visit Spain (Rom. 15:23-24; cf. 1 Clement
> 5). And since 2 Timothy 4:16-18 speaks of an approaching
> second trial and a tone of resignation, we may conclude that

Paul was rearrested about 67 and, according to tradition, beheaded at Rome by order of the Emperor Nero. (*Acts*, 572)

In 2 Timothy, Paul's last letter, he concluded with these moving words to his protégé Timothy:

> *I am already being poured out as a drink offering, and the time for my departure is close. I have fought the good fight, I have finished the race, I have kept the faith. There is reserved for me the crown of righteousness, which the Lord, the righteous Judge, will give me on that day, and not only to me, but to all those who have loved his appearing. . . .*
> *At my first defense, no one stood by me, but everyone deserted me. May it not be counted against them. But the Lord stood with me and strengthened me, so that I might fully preach the word and all the Gentiles might hear it. So I was rescued from the lion's mouth. The Lord will rescue me from every evil work and will bring me safely into his heavenly kingdom. To him be the glory forever and ever! Amen.*
> (2 Tim 4:6-8,16-18)

Indeed, the Lord delivered Paul safely to Rome, and in time he welcomed the war-torn apostle to his heavenly home.

Until we too see the King, let us follow Paul's model of pouring ourselves out in service to the kingdom. Keep fighting. Keep running the race. When you see Jesus Christ with your own eyes, you won't regret having served him faithfully until your dying breath. We as blood-bought Christians will be in the presence of the glorified Nazarene forever. We will be there with the saints from every tribe and tongue, including those, like Paul, who were slain for the sake of the Name. And there we will join a multitude of the redeemed in singing praises to the One who is worthy of all our adoration. The mission of Acts is to be continued until Jesus, the source of life, concludes it.

Reflect and Discuss

1. Describe your reaction to Luke's ending of Acts.
2. Read Philippians 1:12-26 in light of Acts 28. What can we learn from Paul's perspective on his imprisonment in Rome?
3. How did Paul make the most of his house arrest in Rome? What does his example teach about making the most of every ministry opportunity the Lord gives us?
4. What does the conversion of Onesimus teach (Phlm 8-16)?

5. What can we learn about disciple making from Acts 28:23-31?
6. Why do you think we are often tempted to doubt the power of the gospel? What does this passage teach about the ultimate triumph of the gospel?
7. Does Paul's vision of the heavenly kingdom in 2 Timothy 4:6-18 inspire you to greater faithfulness? Why or why not?
8. What might it look like for you to speak about Jesus with boldness? Take a moment to pray for boldness to share the good news of Jesus this week and ask God to help your listeners to respond in repentance and faith.
9. What are your top three takeaways from having read the book of Acts? What lessons have been most meaningful?
10. Pause to pray for faithful evangelists who are taking the gospel to unreached people groups as they continue this mission of making disciples among all nations. Ask the Lord to bless their ministries and to draw many people into his kingdom.

WORKS CITED

Adams, Mark. "Attitudes Essential to Evangelism." Sermon available online at http://www.pastorlife.com/members/sermon.asp?SERMON_ID=3586&fm=authorbio &authorid=3415. Accessed January 25, 2016.

"The Anti-Maricon Prologue to Luke." Translated by Roger Pearse. Article available online at http://www.tertullian.org/fathers/anti _marcionite_prologues.htm. Accessed January 25, 2016.

Aristides. *The Apology of Aristides.* http://www.earlychristianwritings .com/text/aristides-kay.html. Accessed January 4, 2017.

"Ask Amy: Reader Finds Faith Queries Offensive." https://www.washington post.com/lifestyle/style/ask-amy-reader-finds-faith-queries-offensive /2015/02/10/c0a50f4e-ad8f-11e4-9c91-e9d2f9fde644_story.html ?utm_term=.566e2d8223c6. Accessed January 4, 2017.

Azurdia, Art. "The Antioch Paradigm." Sermon available online at http:// trinityportland.com/sermons/sermon/2015-01-04/the-antioch -paradigm. Accessed January 25, 2016.

———. "The Conversion of Peter (Part 1)." Sermon available online at http://www.trinityportland.com/sermons/sermon/2014-12-07 /the-conversion-of-peter-part-1. Accessed January 25, 2016.

———. "Ensuring Evangelistic Expansion." Sermon available online at http://www.trinityportland.com/sermons/sermon/2014-08-03 /ensuring-evangelistic-expansion. Accessed January 25, 2016.

———. "The Pendulum of Gospel Ministry." Sermon available online at http://trinityportland.com/sermons/sermon/2015-01-11/the -pendulum-of-gospel-ministry. Accessed January 25, 2016.

———. "Progression by Intention (Part 2)." Sermon available online at http://trinityportland.com/sermons/sermon/2015-02-01 /progression-by-intention-part-2. Accessed January 25, 2016.

———. "Progression by Intention (Part 5)." Sermon available online at http://trinityportland.com/sermons/sermon/2015-02-22 /progression-by-intention-part5. Accessed January 25, 2016.

————. The Simplicity of Unity." Sermon available online at http://
trinityportland.com/sermons/sermon/2014-05-18/the-simplicity
-of-unity. Accessed January 25, 2016.

Bavinck, Herman. *Reformed Dogmatics*. Vol 2. Grand Rapids, MI: Baker,
2004.

Begg, Alistair. "About Twelve Almost Christians." Sermon available
online at https://www.truthforlife.org/resources/sermon/about
-12-almost-christians. Accessed January 25, 2016.

————. "He Plants His Footsteps in the Sea." Sermon available online
at https://www.truthforlife.org/resources/sermon/he-plants
-his-footsteps-in-the-sea. Accessed January 25, 2016.

————. "Persuasive Preaching." Sermon available online at https://
www.truthforlife.org/resources/sermon/persuasive-preaching
-part-1. Accessed January 25, 2016.

————. "Reaching the City." Sermon available online at https://www
.truthforlife.org/resources/sermon/reaching-a-city. Accessed January
25, 2016.

Bock, Darrell L. *Acts*. Baker Exegetical Commentary on the New
Testament. Grand Rapids, MI: Baker Academic, 2007.

Boice, James Montgomery. *Acts: An Expositional Commentary*. Grand
Rapids, MI: Baker Books, 1997.

Bonhoeffer, Dietrich. *Life Together*. New York: HarperCollins, 1954.

Bruce, F. F. *The Book of Acts*. Rev. ed. The New International Commentary
on the New Testament. Grand Rapids, MI: Eerdmans, 1988.

Calvin, John. "Christ the End of the Law." Chapter available online at http://
www.wts.edu/stayinformed/view.html?id=495. Accessed January 25,
2016.

Carson, D. A. "The Cross and Christian Ministry." Sermon available online
at https://www.monergism.com/topics/sermon-manuscripts-mp3s
-scripture/acts/audio-and-multimedia/chapter-acts/chapter-17.
Accessed January 25, 2016.

————. *For the Love of God*. Vol. 1. Wheaton, IL: Crossway, 2006.
Available online at https://blogs.thegospelcoalition.org/loveof
god/2013/01/10/genesis-11-matthew-10-ezra-10-acts-10/. Accessed
November 11, 2016.

————. "Lessons from Athens." Sermon available online at https://
www.monergism.com/search?keywords=Acts%2017&format
=All&page=1. Accessed January 25, 2016.

———. "Pentecost." Sermon available online at http://resources .thegospelcoalition.org/library/pentecost-en. Accessed January 25, 2016.

———. "Rejoice to Suffer for the Name." Sermon available online at http://s3.amazonaws.com/tgcaudio/carson/20090720_%20Acts _5.41_rejoice_to_suffer.mp3. Accessed Jan. 25, 2016.

Chandler, Matt. "Like a Wildfire." Sermon available online at http:// www.thevillagechurch.net/resources/sermons/detail/like-a -wildfire-denton. Accessed January 25, 2016.

———. "My Heart Is Full . . . I Am Thankful." Blog available online at http://www.thevillagechurch.net/the-village-blog/my-heart-is-fulli -am-thankful. Accessed November 15, 2016.

Driscoll, Mark. "Empowered by the Spirit to Fail." Sermon available online at http://markdriscoll.org/sermons/empowered-by-the -spirit-to-fail. Accessed January 25, 2016.

Etter, Josh. "The Leading and Quenching of the Spirit." Article available online at http://www.desiringgod.org/articles/the-leading -and-quenching-of-the-spirit. Accessed January 25, 206.

Eswine, Zack. *Spurgeon's Sorrows: Realistic Hope for Those Who Suffer with Depression*. Scotland, UK: Christian Focus, 2014.

Ferguson, Sinclair. "Acts 13:13-57." Sermon available online at http:// tapesfromscotland.org/Audio3/3602.mp3. Accessed January 25, 2016.

———. "No Little Disturbance." Sermon available online at https:// www.monergism.com/content/no-little-disturbance-acts-191-20. Accessed January 25, 2016.

Fernando, Ajith. *Acts*. The NIV Application Commentary. Grand Rapids, MI: Zondervan, 1998.

Gangel, Kenneth. *Acts*. Holman New Testament Commentary. Nashville, TN: B&H, 1998.

Goheen, Michael W., and Craig G. Bartholomew. *Living at the Crossroads*. Kindle edition. Grand Rapids, MI: Baker, 2008.

Green, Michael. *Evangelism in the Early Church*. Rev. ed. Grand Rapids, MI: Eerdmans, 2004.

———. *Thirty Years That Changed the World: The Book of Acts for Today*. Grand Rapids, MI: Eerdmans, 2004.

Hamilton, James. "How Often Should a Church Take the Lord's Supper?" Article available online at http://jimhamilton.info/2011/05/03 /how-often-should-a-church-take-the-lords-supper. Accessed January 25, 2016.

Hughes, R. Kent. *Acts: The Church Afire*. Preaching the Word. Wheaton, IL: Crossway, 1996.

——, and Bryan Chapell. *1 & 2 Timothy and Titus: To Guard the Deposit*. Preaching the Word. Wheaton, IL: Crossway, 2000.

Johnson, Dennis E. *Let's Study Acts*. Edinburgh, Scotland: Banner of Truth, 2003.

——. *The Message of Acts in the History of Redemption*. Phillipsburg, NJ: P&R, 1997.

Keller, Timothy. *Center Church: Doing Biblical, Gospel-Centered Ministry in Your City*. Grand Rapids, MI: Zondervan, 2012.

——. *Evangelism: Studies in the Book of Acts*. Leader's Guide. New York: Redeemer Presbyterian Church, 2005.

——. *Generous Justice: How God's Grace Makes Us Just*. New York: Dutton, 2010.

——. "Spiritual Friendship." Sermon available online at https://www.monergism.com/content/spiritual-friendship. Accessed January 25, 2016.

——. "A World of Idols." Sermon available online at http://www.gospelinlife.com/a-world-of-idols-6538. Accessed January 25, 2016.

Keller, Timothy, and J. Allen Thompson. *Church Planter Manual*. New York: Redeemer City to City, 2002.

Kuyper, Abraham. *Encyclopedia of Sacred Theology*. Translated by Hendrik. New York: Charles Scribner's Sons, 1898.

Lewis, C. S. *The Lion, the Witch, and the Wardrobe*. New York: Collier, 1950.

——. *Surprised by Joy*. San Diego, CA: Harcourt Brace, 1955.

Lloyd-Jones, Martyn. *Preaching and Preachers*. Fortieth Anniversary Edition. Grand Rapids, MI: Zondervan, 2011.

Longenecker, Richard. *Acts*. The Expositor's Bible Commentary. Vol 9. Grand Rapids, MI: Zondervan, 1981.

Longman, Tremper, III, and David E. Garland. *Luke–Acts*. The Expositor's Bible Commentary. Vol. 10. Grand Rapids, MI: Zondervan, 2007.

Marshall, I. Howard. *The Acts of the Apostles: An Introduction and Commentary*. Tyndale New Testament Commentaries. Leicester, England: IVP, 1980.

Mulvihill, Geoff. "Stephen Colbert Tells Princeton Graduates Not to Change the World." Article available online at http://www.huffingtonpost.com/2008/06/03/stephen-colbert-awarded-h_n_104843.html. Accessed January 25, 2016.

Neyrey, Jerome H., ed. *The Social World of Luke-Acts: Models for Interpretation*. Peabody, MA: Hendrickson, 1993.

Packer, J. I. "The Glory of God and the Reviving of Religion: A Study of God in the Mind of Jonathan Edwards." In *A God-Entranced Vision of All Things.* John Piper and Justin Taylor, eds. Wheaton, IL: Crossway, 2004.

———. *Rediscovering Holiness.* Ann Arbor, MI: Servant Publications, 1999.

Paton, James, ed. *The Story of John G. Paton.* Thirteenth ed. London: Hodder and Stoughten, 1894.

Peterson, David G. *The Acts of the Apostles.* The Pillar New Testament Commentary. D. A. Carson, gen. ed. Grand Rapids, MI: Eerdmans, 2009.

Piper, John. "Execution, Escape, and Eaten by Worms." Sermon available online at http://www.desiringgod.org/messages/execution -escape-and-eaten-by-worms. Accessed January 25, 2016.

———. "History Is God's Story." Sermon available online at http://www .desiringgod.org/messages/history-is-gods-story. Accessed January 25, 2016.

———. "Jesus' Name Made This Man Strong." Sermon available online at http://www.desiringgod.org/messages/jesus-name-made-this-man -strong. Accessed January 25, 2016.

———. *Let the Nations Be Glad.* Second Edition. Grand Rapids, MI: Baker, 2007.

———. "The Lofty Claim, the Last Command, and the Loving Comfort." Sermon available online at http://www.desiringgod.org/messages /the-lofty-claim-the-last-command-the-loving-comfort. Accessed January 25, 2016.

———. "Serving Widows, Preaching the Word, and Winning Priests." Sermon available online at http://www.desiringgod.org/messages /serving-widows-preaching-the-word-and-winning-priests. Accessed January 25, 2016.

———. "What God Has Cleansed Do Not Call Common." Sermon available online at http://www.desiringgod.org/messages/what-god -has-cleansed-do-not-call-common. Accessed January 25, 2016.

Platt, David. "A Mission Only the Church Can Stop." Sermon available online at http://www.radical.net/sermons/sermons/a-misson -only-the-church-can-stop. Accessed January 25, 2016.

Polhill, John B. *Acts.* The New American Commentary. Nashville, TN: B&H, 1992.

Richards, E. Randolph and Brandon J. O'Brien. *Misreading Scripture with Western Eyes.* Kindle Edition. Downers Grove, IL: IVP, 2012.

Rowe, C. Kavin. *World Upside Down: Reading Acts in the Graeco-Roman Age.* New York: Oxford University Press, 2010.

Schreiner, Thomas. "A God-Glorifying Ministry." Sermon available online at http://resources.thegospelcoalition.org/library/a-god -glorifying-ministry. Accessed January 25, 2016.

———. "God's Inscrutable Sovereignty." Sermon available online at http://resources.thegospelcoalition.org/library/god-s-inscrutable-sovereignty. Accessed January 25, 2016.

———. "Living as Disciples." Sermon available online at http://clifton baptist.org/sermons-and-audio/sermon/2007-02-11/living-as-disciples. Accessed January 25, 2016.

———. "Power of Lord Jesus." Sermon available online at http://resources.thegospelcoalition.org/library/power-of-lord-jesus. Accessed January 25, 2016.

Shaw, Joey. *All Authority.* Nashville, TN: B&H, 2016.

Sire, James W. *The Universe Next Door: A Basic Worldview Catalog.* Kindle edition. Downers Grove, IL: IVP, 2009.

Sproul, R. C. *Acts.* St. Andrew's Expositional Commentary. Wheaton, IL: Crossway, 2010.

Spurgeon, C. H. *Lectures to My Students: Complete and Unabridged.* Grand Rapids, MI: Zondervan, 1954.

———. "Paul Cheered in Prison by His Lord." Sermon available online at http://www.spurgeongems.org/vols55-57/chs3153.pdf. Accessed January 25, 2016.

———. "Songs of Deliverance." Sermon available online at http://www.romans45.org/spurgeon/sermons/0763.htm. Accessed January 25, 2016.

Stott, John R. W. *The Message of Acts: The Spirit, the Church and the World.* The Bible Speaks Today. Leicester, England: IVP, 1990.

Thomas, Derek W. H. *Acts.* Reformed Expository Commentary. Phillipsburg, NJ: P&R, 2011.

Timmis, Steve. "How to Plant a Church." Article available online at http://www.acts29.com/how-to-plant-a-church-five-principles-from-steve-timmis. Accessed January 25, 2016.

Tozer, A. W. *The Knowledge of the Holy: The Attributes of God: Their Meaning in the Christian Life.* New York: HarperCollins, 1961.

Van Neste, Ray. "The Lord's Supper in the Context of the Local Church." In *The Lord's Supper.* Nashville, TN: B&H, 2010.

Wilson, Sandy. "Counted Worthy." Sermon available online at http://resources.thegospelcoalition.org/library/counted-worthy. Accessed January 25, 2016.

Witherington, Ben, III. *The Acts of the Apostles: A Socio-Rhetorical Commentary.* Grand Rapids, MI: Eerdmans, 1998.

———. *Making a Meal of It.* Waco, TX: Baylor University Press, 2007.

SCRIPTURE INDEX